Immigrants in the Lands of Promise

Cornell Studies in Comparative History

George Fredrickson and Theda Skocpol, *editors*

Machines as the Measure of Men: Science, Technology, and Ideologies of Western Dominance, by Michael Adas

Immigrants in the Lands of Promise: Italians in Buenos Aires and New York City, 1870–1914, by Samuel L. Baily

Empires, by Michael W. Doyle

Immigrants in the Lands of Promise

Italians in Buenos Aires and New York City, 1870–1914

Samuel L. Baily

Cornell University Press

ITHACA AND LONDON

First published 1999 by Cornell University Press
First printing, Cornell Paperbacks, 2003

Printed in the United States of America

Library of Congress Cataloging-in-Publication Data

Baily, Samuel L.
    Immigrants in the lands of promise : Italians in Buenos Aires and New York City, 1870–1914 / by Samuel L. Baily.
        p.   cm.
    Includes bibliographical references and index.
    ISBN 0-8014-3562-5 (cloth : alk. paper)   ISBN: 0801488826
    1. Italy—Emigration and immigration—Case studies. 2. Italians—
Argentina—Buenos Aires—History. 3. Immigrants—Argentina—Buenos Aires—
History. 4. Buenos Aires (Argentina), Emigration and immigration—Case studies.
5. Italians—New York (State)—New York—History. 6. Immigrants—New York
(State)—New York—History. 7. New York (N.Y.)—Emigration and immigration—
Case studies. I. Title.
JV8131.B34   1999
305.85′108212′09034—DC21   98-12399

Cornell University Press strives to use environmentally responsible suppliers and materials to the fullest extent possible in the publishing of its books. Such materials include vegetable-based, low-VOC inks and acid-free papers that are recycled, totally chlorine-free, or partly composed of nonwood fibers.

Cloth printing   10   9   8   7   6   5   4   3   2   1
Paperback printing   10   9   8   7   6   5   4   3   2   1

To Jennifer, Sarah, and Benjamin
who have so greatly enriched my life

Contents

Illustrations

Tables

Preface

The inherent humanity and comparative nature of the migration process have compelled me to write this book. Quite by accident I stumbled onto the topic when asked to present a paper on it for an American Historical Association meeting in New York some time ago. Although I come from English ancestry, I soon became totally absorbed in the experience of Italian immigrants. Several things have influenced the way I have approached my subject. Living for two years in a small Mexican village many years ago first made me aware of a village-outward perspective on what happens in this world. Participating in the publication of the Sola family letters (Baily and Ramella, *One Family, Two Worlds*) reinforced my long-standing commitment to incorporating something of the perspective of the participants in my work.

Comparative history is not easy to do. For me it involved learning a new language, developing my computer skills, working in archives in five countries, and reading extensively in several distinct bodies of scholarly literature. The effort, however, has been worth it. My belief in the importance of comparative history has grown over the years. It is my hope that this book will encourage and help others to undertake such projects on their own.

Over the years of researching and writing, I have become indebted to many individuals and institutions. I found scholars, librarians, archivists, and Italian immigrants and their descendants in the United States, Canada, Brazil, Argentina, and Italy interested in what I was doing and anxious to help me do it. There are too many to acknowledge individually, but I want them all to know that I am grateful and recognize that I would not have been able to complete this project without the selfless giving of time and information by so many.

I want to note especially the help of Michael Adas, Donna Gabaccia, Mark Wasserman, and Virginia Yans-McLaughlin, who read the entire manuscript and gave me the benefit of their insightful comments. Others who have read parts of the manuscript, discussed their ideas on immigration with me, or assisted me in some other way include Rudolph Bell, Frank Dauster, William Douglass, Glen Kuecker, John Lenaghan, José Moya, Jane Orttung, Ingrid Scobie, Franc Sturino, Camilla Townsend, and Rudolph Vecoli. Sarah Buck did an exceptional job of assisting me long distance when I was in Italy and Spain in 1996 and 1997. The former and current directors of the Center for Migration Studies on Staten Island, Sylvano and Lydio Tomasi, have always encouraged and supported my research. The Cerruti family, the children and grandchildren of Ida Sola Cerruti, have been indispensable to me. I wish to thank them all, and especially Pat Sisti and Alice Petkus Mason for their help setting up interviews with Ida's children and arranging access to the various materials in the Cerruti archives. In addition, I wish to acknowledge the important contributions to my work of four very special people who are now deceased—Robert Harney, George Pozzetta, James Scobie, and Carl Solberg. Peter Agree, my editor at Cornell University Press, has been enthusiastic and encouraging in seeing this manuscript through to publication.

My Argentine colleague Fernando Devoto and I have, since 1985, debated the fine points of Italian migration in our homes and at various meetings in Argentina, Italy, the United States, and Spain. He kindly read the entire manuscript and gave me the benefit of his extensive knowledge of the subject. He, Luigi Favero, Alicia Bernasconi, Carina Silberstein, and the whole group associated with the Centro de Estudios Latinoamericanos in Buenos Aires have continually been most gracious and helpful to me. I also wish to thank Alberto Agnelli, Antonio Busich, Lorenzo Ferro, Ruben Granara, Eduardo Miguez, Mario Nascimbene, Patricio Randle, and Hilda Sabato for their assistance in Argentina. My thanks also to the staffs of the Unione e Benevolenza, the Archivo General de la Nación, and the Biblioteca Nacional for their patience and willingness to help me use their collections. I want to acknowledge a special intellectual debt to the distinguished scholars Gino Germani and José Luis Romero, who early on taught me so much about Argentine history and immigration.

In Italy and several other European countries as well, many individuals aided my work. Gianfausto Rosoli of the Centro Studi Emigrazione in Rome greatly facilitated my research trips to Italy, generously opened the resources of the Centro to me, and was always willing to share his vast knowledge of migration. Franco and Luciana Ramella, coeditors with me of the Sola family letters, shared their extraordinary understanding of all things related to Italian migration and especially their intense interest in real people in local settings. Aldo Sola, the custodian of the Sola family letters, generously gave the Ramellas and me access to these letters and to many other things in his library and archive. Antonio Arduino, director of the Biblioteca Comunale of Agnone, extended himself every time I visited Agnone and provided me with many essential documents. My thanks also to the employees of the town archives of Agnone, Piedimonte d'Alife, Sirolo-Numana, and Valdengo, whose diligence and cooperation helped me uncover some difficult-to-locate source material. And finally, I wish to thank Maria Baganha, Romolo Gandolfo, Dirk Hoerder, John MacDonald, and Nuria Tabanera, European colleagues who invariably stimulated my thinking and clarified some of my ideas on immigration.

I wish to acknowledge the generous financial support of the American Philosophical Society, the Fulbright Commission, the Social Science Research Council, and the Rutgers University Research Council, which made possible a number of research trips to Argentina and Italy and the writing of the manuscript. York University permitted me to spend a semester in Toronto working on the manuscript by making me the Mariano C. Elia Research Chair in Italian Studies for the spring of 1992.

I am also grateful to the following for permission to make use of materials and information in this book: the editors of *Estudios Migratorios Latinoamericanos* for use of the material in my article "Patrones de residencia de los italianos en Buenos Aires y Nueva York: 1880–1914," Rutgers University Press for the picture of Oreste and Corinna Sola, Stephanie Bowers for her District 15 data, Timothy Delpapa for his interviews and letters, and the Cerruti family for their interviews and letters and the picture of Ida Sola and her husband.

My friends Michael and Jane Adas, Frank and Helen Dauster, Stuart and Rita Faden, Lloyd and Nancy Gardner, Richard and Terry Hixson, John and Lydia Lenaghan, Ruth Ross, and Mark and Marlie Wasserman provided support and encouragement as well as intellectual stimulation and insight that was essential to completing the project.

It is hard to acknowledge adequately the many contributions of my wife, Joan, and to thank her properly for all she has done. She has willingly read and reread drafts of this manuscript, discussed and debated the contents with me, and consistently given me helpful insight into the problems at hand. Her patience, love, and continued support have made the completion of this work possible. I want to thank her as best I can for being the person she is.

Finally, I want to thank my three children—Jennifer, Sarah, and Benjamin—to whom I am dedicating this book, and Jennifer's husband, Mike Zona, and their wonderful children, Josie and Luke, for their love and encouragement.

Piscataway, N.J.   SAMUEL L. BAILY

Immigrants in the Lands of Promise

Wedding photograph of Ida Sola and Eugenio Cerruti, 1905

Formal, professionally taken photograph of Oreste Sola and his wife, Corinna, 1910

Prologue

At the turn of the nineteenth century, two cousins, Oreste and Ida Sola, left the small north Italian hill town of Valdengo, he for Buenos Aires and she for New York.[1] These two would live the rest of their lives many thousands of miles apart from each other and from their homes in Valdengo. Both Oreste and Ida had other relatives who migrated to Buenos Aires or New York. Some of the Solas moved permanently; others returned to Valdengo after stays of various lengths. But wherever the members of the family were, they remained in contact with one another through letters, visits, and the exchanges of information carried back and forth by friends and *paesani*.[2]

Valdengo had a long tradition of migration. It was one of nearly eighty small towns in the densely populated district of Biella located in the foothills of the Alps. Most residents were peasant farmers who cultivated grain, grapes, and other crops on rented land to supplement what they could produce on their own small farmsteads. Some, such as Ida's father, Giacomo, were artisans; he was a shoemaker in addition to being a part-time farmer. Young women like Ida often became servants in the households of the wealthy. Others, both men and women, worked in the textile mills of Biella.

Biella was an area of both emigration and immigration at the turn of the century. The rapidly growing textile mills increasingly attracted internal migrants. At the same time, many people participated in a seasonal migration to other places in Italy, to Switzerland, and to southern France. With the improvement in overseas transportation in the 1870s, a few began to travel to Argentina and shortly thereafter to the United States. Emigration from Valdengo was most frequently seen as a way to augment family income and, if possible, to purchase a little more land.

Like many other families in the area, the Solas had a long tradition of migration. Oreste and Ida's great-uncle Andrea had traveled to France and to various countries in Latin America and Africa during the three decades after 1850, spending six of these years in Buenos Aires (Figure 1). Luigi, Oreste's father, had wanted to join his uncle Andrea abroad, but when Andrea discouraged him from doing so, he decided to remain at home. Ida's father lived at various times in Europe, Africa, and the United States as well as in Valdengo. Other cousins spent time in France and Cuba.

Oreste's father, Luigi, had inherited a small farmstead, but it was insufficient to support the family. Although Luigi moved to Biella to become a factory worker in the textile mills, he still kept his small property in Valdengo. Many years later, he retired there. Through involvement in local labor organizations, Luigi was introduced to radical politics and became increasingly active in the Socialist Party. Oreste's mother, Margherita, also worked in the textile mills of Biella and there met her husband. The couple had three children—Oreste, a younger daughter, named Narcisa, and a younger son, Abele.

Luigi and Margherita wanted their two sons to have a better life than theirs, and they mobilized the resources of the entire family to achieve this end. Margherita, unlike most married women of her age, continued to work in the factory so her sons could pursue their education beyond grammar school. Narcisa left school at an early age to work in the textile factory for the same reason.

Oreste decided to migrate to Buenos Aires at age seventeen, shortly after he graduated from the Biella technical/professional school. His choice of destination was most likely determined by the fact that his godfather worked there as a contractor and at the time the city was known as a place of considerable opportunity in the construction business. Oreste departed from Genoa with several friends and arrived in Buenos Aires on August 5, 1901. As he explained in the first letter he wrote to his parents from Argentina, he went immediately to his godfather's house at Calle Rivadavia 1892: "I have been here since the 5th of this month; I am in the best of health as are my two companions. As soon as we got here, we went to the address of Godfather Zocco, who then introduced us to several people from Valdengo who have been in America for some years and all are doing well more or less."[3]

Ida's reasons for migrating were different from her cousin's. She apparently wanted to escape a difficult family situation and was not primarily motivated by aspirations to economic and social achievement. Ida's father, Giacomo, was a peasant farmer and a shoemaker who traveled abroad extensively during his lifetime. Giacomo and his first wife had three children: Ida and then two sons, Abele and Andrea. Ida's mother died shortly after having the children. Her father remarried, but Ida did not get along

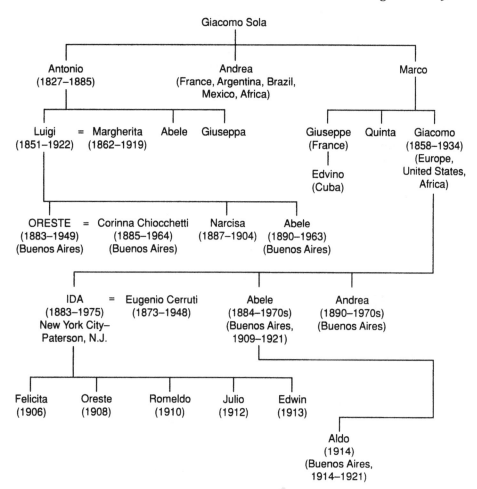

Figure 1. The Sola family tree—with travel destinations

well with her stepmother. Ida worked as a servant for several years and by the age of twenty-one had saved enough money to buy her own ticket to New York. She left Cherbourg on the *Germanie* in the company of two cousins, Isolina and Rinaldo Bonardi, and three other individuals from a nearby town. She arrived in New York on May 31, 1904, with thirteen dollars in her pocket.

Ida chose New York rather than Buenos Aires or some other destination apparently because of her family ties there. Thirty- four-year-old Rinaldo was returning to his wife in New York. Isolina, sixteen and unmarried, went to stay with her uncle, Ferdinando Bonardi, who lived at 161 W. 32nd Street in Manhattan. Ida accompanied her. The three other people traveling with them went directly to the well-known Biellese destination of nearby Paterson, New Jersey.[4]

After arriving in Argentina, Oreste initially considered joining his cousin Edvino in Cuba but decided instead to remain in Argentina. He spent a year and a half exploring opportunities in the Argentine interior and then returned to Buenos Aires. In March 1903 he obtained a job as a draftsman with a firm constructing the new Argentine congressional buildings. Four years later he acquired a second job taking care of the heating and ventilation of these buildings. He explained to his parents in a letter of May 3, 1907:

> As you see, after such great and tremendous efforts I have succeeded in becoming an employee of the government, in the service of the National Senate. I hold the position of the technical chief in the Congress. I constantly have to deal with deputies and senators. I am getting indigestion from politics, something that doesn't agree with me at all. I am, however, still holding the job I had before, so I am two employees, but they aren't ruining my life. In the government position I have the responsibility of taking care of the heating and ventilation of the Congress, as well as all the other piping installations, like gas, hot water, sewers, and cold water. In the job which I already held I do the computations for the work on the part of the firm which is constructing this very building.[5]

Oreste's financial success enabled him to start sending money home, to buy a piece of property in Buenos Aires, and to marry Corinna Chiocchetti, a young woman originally from a village near Valdengo. The newly married couple moved into a house just two blocks away from Oreste's godfather. In 1910 Oreste was awarded a contract to build a short stretch of railroad in the Argentine interior; he became an independent contractor.

The world Oreste entered in Buenos Aires was a remarkably familiar one that included relatives, friends, and others from the Biella area with whom he would associate. Oreste lived with his godfather for nearly five years until he married, and as he told his parents, "The life that he [the godfather] leads is also mine."[6] His social activities centered around fellow Biellesi, and he met his wife within this community. Cousin Abele, Ida's brother, arrived with his family in Buenos Aires in 1909 and stayed there for the next twelve years.[7] When Oreste became an independent contractor, he hired a friend as his chief assistant for the railroad project and employed nine Biellese masons. This world was so familiar that Oreste could walk down a street in the Puente Alsina section of Buenos Aires and be recognized as his father's son. "In this town," Oreste explained, "I have met several friends of yours, Dad, who remember you with affection and pleasure. Why, one recognized me right off as your son because I look so much like you. We had never seen each other before, but he stopped to ask me if I was Mr. Sola."[8]

Oreste's brother, Abele, traveled with friends to Buenos Aires in 1912. Oreste paid for the ticket, took Abele into his home, introduced him to members of the Biellese community, and helped him find a good job as an engineer with a large metallurgic firm. Benefiting from his brother's connections, Abele achieved rapid financial success and started sending money home within five months of his arrival in Buenos Aires. It had taken Oreste five years to be able to do this.

The two brothers shared the same social world of Biellese friends and relatives. In fact, since Abele was more gregarious than his brother, their community-based social life became more active. The letters home speak frequently of good friends such as the Sassos and the Pellas from Biella, and of the profound sorrow the Sola brothers felt when the Sassos returned home. They also describe numerous visits with cousin Abele (Ida's brother, who came to Buenos Aires in 1909 at age twenty-four), the arrival of cousin Andrea (Ida's other brother, who reached Buenos Aires in 1920 at age twenty-nine), and then of the return of cousin Abele and his family to Valdengo in 1921.

Though physically separated, the members of the family remained close and continued to support one another. The parents had mobilized all of the family resources to educate the two boys at the technical/professional school and to continue to facilitate their subsequent careers abroad. During Oreste's early years in Buenos Aires, Luigi and Margherita sent him clothes, food, cameras, and books. When the daughter Narcisa died of cancer in 1904, all the members of the family shared the grief and consoled one another. Later on, when Oreste needed money to buy equipment for the railroad project, Luigi helped him obtain a loan from a friend in Biella and personally guaranteed the loan with his farmstead. The boys also assumed the responsibility of supporting their parents after their retirement. Oreste (beginning in 1906) and Abele (beginning in 1912) regularly sent enough money home for their parents to live comfortably. They were especially solicitous during Margherita's long bout with bone cancer and when she died in 1919.

When Ida arrived in New York with her cousins in May 1904, she initially lived with her uncle and worked at a restaurant owned by a woman from the Biella area. She quickly became acquainted with the Biellese network in New York and New Jersey and soon met her future husband, Eugenio Cerruti, at the house of a friend in Hackensack, New Jersey. Eugenio was a weaver from a town near Valdengo who had served in the Italian army in Ethiopia and had worked for a time in France before coming to the United States in 1903. The two were married on April 22, 1905, a little less than a year after Ida's arrival.

Ida and Eugenio lived the rest of their lives in nearby Paterson, New Jersey, and a neighboring town. Ida had five children between 1906 and 1913 and devoted most of her time to raising them. As the children got older, she took in washing from her neighbors, but she never worked outside her home. Eugenio was employed in the Paterson textile mills until 1913 when, as a result of his participation in the strike of that year, he was dismissed. He then worked at a number of jobs for various periods of time—at the Waldorf Astoria Hotel in New York City in some capacity, as a field hand on a farm in nearby Clifton, as a manager of a small hotel, and finally he returned to the Paterson mills. He also raised chickens and vegetables, but only for family consumption. However he earned his money, Eugenio was financially successful enough to buy a small house in Paterson in 1912, the lot next door sometime later, and a Model T Ford in 1927. A year later he sold the original house and bought another in nearby Haledon. All the children had some schooling, but worked from an early age to contribute to the support of the family.

Ida's story shows that in New York and Paterson, the Biellese network operated as it did in Buenos Aires. She migrated with relatives and paesani. She lived with an uncle in New York and worked at a restaurant owned by a Biellese family. She met her husband at the home of Biellese friends. Her father, Giacomo, made several trips to New York, and on one of them brought wooden clogs he had made for Ida's children. The family frequently visited friends of Eugenio in Hoboken. And in 1928, they moved to Haledon, where many Biellesi lived.

Unlike Oreste, Ida, as a woman, was not expected to support her father, Giacomo, in retirement and did not do so. Nor did her brother Andrea. Andrea was upset when their father left Valdengo for New York in 1913 without saying goodby to his family.[9] Andrea served in the Italian army during World War I and then in 1920 migrated to Buenos Aires. He never wrote to his father after that. Ida's other brother, Abele, who lived in Buenos Aires from 1909 to 1921 and then returned to Valdengo, was the one to assist their father when needed, but in fact Giacomo managed for the most part very well on his own.

Ida, nevertheless, served as the principal contact for the family. Everyone wrote to her even when they refused to communicate with one another. Brother Andrea did not write either to his father, Giacomo, or to his brother, Abele. The two brothers broke off relations in 1921 over the disposition of the dairy business Abele had started in Buenos Aires a number of years before. But all three men—Giacomo, Abele, and Andrea—continued to write to Ida and at times asked her to intervene on their behalf with one of the others.

Neither Oreste nor Ida returned to Valdengo except for brief visits and then only after their parents had died. Yet their letters and actions suggested a good deal of ambivalence about their intentions. Oreste indicated much uncertainty on the subject of his return to Valdengo, either to visit or to stay. When he left for Buenos Aires in 1901, he clearly expected to return and wrote home a number of times about the possibility. A half dozen years later, however, when he bought property in Buenos Aires, he talked about building a house on it and settling there. Yet, probably to reassure his parents, he explained that buying property in Buenos Aires was a good investment and therefore not necessarily an indication of his intention to remain permanently abroad. Even after his parents' deaths, he never sold the family house in Valdengo. And he never became an Argentine citizen.

Luigi and Margherita assumed that Oreste would return and frequently urged him to do so. After Oreste married, his parents urged Oreste to bring his bride home so that they could meet her. They also wrote about how they had fixed up the house in Valdengo and used some of the money the boys had sent home to add to the family farmstead in anticipation of the return. Early in 1919 Margherita got worse from her bone cancer and Luigi desperately pleaded with his sons to come home. The parents had not seen Oreste for eighteen years and Abele for more than six. They had never met Corinna. In a brief letter dated February 23, 1919, Luigi told his sons:

> I don't know if your dear mother will still be alive when you get this letter. For several weeks she has gotten painfully worse. She hasn't gotten out of bed for the past fifteen days. She suffers terribly; only morphine in large doses relieves the pain a bit. Consider that this doesn't cure her; it kills her sooner. And yet what's to be done? Either let her die in despair from the pain or make her die with pain killers. It is tragic.

Luigi closed the letter by imploring his sons to return "just to be able to embrace you at least one more time before dying since, if fate takes your dear mother, I won't be around much longer." [10]

Nevertheless, there was always some reason why Oreste could not return. At first he was concerned with his career. Then the war increased his fear of being drafted and made travel impossible. Yet even after the war, when the Italian government declared an amnesty for all young men who had been subject to the draft, Oreste did not return. Perhaps the cost of the trip discouraged him, or possibly his constant concern with work. When Oreste finally did make the trip home, it was after both his parents had died. He subsequently made only one or two brief trips to Italy.

Oreste died in Buenos Aires in 1949. His body was cremated, the ashes carried to Valdengo by a returning immigrant, and he was buried in the family plot alongside his father, mother, and younger sister. Oreste's brother, Abele, died in 1963, and Oreste's wife a year later. Their ashes were also transferred to the cemetery in Valdengo. There is a bit of irony in the fact that in death the entire family of Oreste Sola was finally reunited.

It is unclear if Ida left Valdengo with the intent of returning. Her husband, Eugenio, did not write to his relatives; he also made it clear to his children that he never wanted to see Italy again. Eugenio became a U.S. citizen on April 20, 1920, and Ida did likewise during the early 1940s, in part because one of her sons was missing in action in World War II. Ida maintained continual contact with her family in Buenos Aires and Valdengo, however, and thought about the possibility of returning after the death of her husband in 1948. Her brother Abele encouraged her to do so. At the end of 1951, Ida's brother Abele wrote to his sister and explained that their cousin Abele (Oreste's brother) had been in Valdengo for several months, was about to return to Buenos Aires, and would try to persuade Andrea to visit Italy.[11]

Ida did return to Valdengo in the summer of 1954 for a reunion with her two brothers. It was her only visit home and it tempted her to stay. As Ida wrote from Haledon a dozen years later, "If I had been free I would not have come back here, I was going to settle there for the rest of my life. Now, however, I can't make the change, I'm tied down here, I must stay here."[12]

When Ida died in 1975 she was buried in the Paterson cemetery next to her husband. Her five children and many grandchildren have lived their lives in the United States. Only one of them has ever visited the ancestral home, and the correspondence across the Atlantic, once so frequent, has diminished to practically nothing.

Introduction

The Sola family history provides a road map to guide my inquiry into
the experiences of the Italians who migrated to Buenos Aires and New
York City at the turn of the past century. Although this story — or the story
of any one family — cannot encompass the entire range of experiences of
all migrants, it illustrates many of the most important features of the Italian migration process and it does so from the subjective perspective of
those who actually participated in it. Through the personal histories of
Oreste, Ida, and the other family members, we see that migrants went to
multiple destinations in different countries, and that family and village-
based networks were essential to the successful negotiation of each phase
of the process. More specifically, the experiences of the Solas help us understand who migrated and why, how they chose their destinations, and
with whom they made the trip abroad. In addition, these histories give us
some insight into how, once they arrived at their destinations, the family
members found jobs and places to live, created a social life, and sought to
improve their situations. And finally, the Sola history documents the importance of the continuing, though evolving, ties between family and community members in Italy and abroad.

Oreste and Ida were among millions of Italians who migrated to the
United States and Argentina between 1870 and 1914. More than half ultimately settled in destinations abroad. Others returned home. Still others
went back and forth a number of times. A few moved from one overseas
destination to another. By the beginning of World War I, however, approximately a million Italians resided in Argentina and a million and a half
in the United States. In both countries, the Italians concentrated overwhelmingly in the urban areas, and especially in the rapidly growing port
cities of Buenos Aires and New York. In 1914, 312,000 Italians lived in
Buenos Aires, and 370,000 in New York. These numbers represented one-

third of all Italians living in Argentina and one-quarter of those in the United States.

What happened to Oreste, Ida, and the many other Italians who migrated to Buenos Aires and New York City between 1870 and 1914 is the central focus of this book. How did these immigrants adjust to their new situations abroad? As they looked for jobs and housing, attempted to make money, and decided how and where to spend it, in what ways did they interact with one another, with their families and friends in Italy, and with the members of the receiving societies? Where did they find the help they needed to achieve the objectives for which they had originally migrated? What strategies did they develop and adopt to realize their goals? What were the similarities and differences in the experiences of the Italians in the two cities, and how do we explain these respective patterns of adjustment?

The Reconceptualization of Migration

Although U.S. scholars have written extensively about migration to the United States for many years, in recent decades they have significantly reconceptualized their understanding of the migration process.[1] As a result, they have come to view migration in a manner that more closely conforms to the reality of the Solas' experiences. During the immediate post–World War II period, U.S. immigration historians viewed their subject through the lens of an assimilationist model and focused their studies only on the United States.[2] These scholars saw uprooted and socially disorganized immigrants who were shunted from place to place by the impersonal push and pull of demographic and economic conditions. Once migrants arrived in the United States, according to these historians, they inevitably progressed toward complete assimilation in the dominant host culture. Success depended on personal attributes that fostered individual achievement. Structural influences were given limited attention or completely ignored.

Subsequent immigration historians, confronted with the ethnic resiliency and pluralism of the 1960s, 1970s, and 1980s, have substituted a pluralist model for the classic assimilationist model, and have enlarged the spatial scope of their work to include places of origin and, to a lesser extent, alternate destinations.[3] These immigration historians see a more complex, dynamic, and open-ended process that began in the village of origin and continued outward with migration, incorporation into the host society, and sociocultural adjustment. They no longer assume a single outcome such as assimilation, the termination of the process after any given period of time, or the inevitability or irreversibility of specific patterns of interaction. Economic, social, and political structures—as well as the cultures of the villages of origin—become an essential part of the explanation of what happened to individuals abroad. The sending and receiving communities are conceptually linked in a framework of analysis that enables these scholars to explore the simultaneous influence of cultural persistence and change.

Those writing about Argentine immigration have also reconceptualized the way they view their subject.[4] In the post–World War II decades, scholars such as Gino Germani and José Luis Romero treated immigration as part of the larger themes of national development and modernization. Most significantly, they viewed immigration in terms of an assimilationist model not unlike the melting-pot paradigm then current in the United States. They emphasized what happened to the immigrants after they arrived in Argentina, the inevitability of assimilation, and the "fusion" of the various native and foreign elements into a new people of European stock.[5]

Since the late 1970s, and especially since 1983—when a civilian government replaced the ruling military regime—a number of researchers have argued that although there are no hyphenated citizens in Argentina as there are in the United States, some forms of ethnic identity were maintained more intensely and longer than Germani and Romero had indicated. This led them to question the adequacy of the assimilationist model and to reconceptualize the process of immigration along the lines of a more pluralist model. They saw an Argentine form of pluralism, not a pluralism identical to that of the United States.[6]

The new pluralist syntheses in both countries reflect the reality of migration as Oreste and Ida experienced it more closely than the older assimilationist models do. The Sola family story recounts the migration of men and women of different ages, educational achievement, occupation, class, and marital status. Regardless of their initial intentions, some remained abroad permanently, others returned home, and still others went back and forth. Those who remained abroad for any length of time selectively drew on what was useful from their past to help adjust to the new situations. Although all sought economic gain and undoubtedly defined success primarily in economic terms, they used the money they made in different ways and in different places. Furthermore, the family members had different and constantly evolving attitudes toward one another, their fellow paesani, and the members of the host societies. The terms *assimilated* or *unassimilated* inadequately describe the complexity of this experience.

The diversity of the Sola family migration suggests an issue that has increasingly interested recent migration historians—the relationship of ethnicity to class and gender.[7] Men and women, peasants, artisans, and professionals were among the Sola family members who went abroad, and each of them experienced the migration process somewhat differently. Most migrants were from the working class, and their thoughts and actions reflected various combinations of their class positions and their ethnicity. Many were women, whose roles in Italy differed from those of men. Migration frequently altered these traditional roles and the relationships between women and men. We need to be sensitive to the ways in which migration can be understood as class, gender, or ethnic behavior, and how the simultaneous interaction of all three influenced the actions of specific individuals and groups.

Those individuals portrayed in the Sola family history, whatever their class or gender, were active participants in the migration process who made meaningful decisions about their lives. Migration itself was a choice available to those living in the Italian villages, but not the only one. Most people stayed at home. Oreste and Abele, for example, could have remained in Valdengo and worked in the textile factory with their father, mother, and sister. Or, with their education, the two brothers might well have become engineers or contractors.[8] However, they chose instead to migrate.

Individuals were significant social actors, but they played on a structurally defined stage. The decisions they made were circumscribed by specific contexts of time and space, and these contexts were structured by economic, political, and social conditions. They had little if any control over such structural factors in Buenos Aires and New York as the availability of jobs and housing, the pace of migration, the presence or absence of other immigrant groups, the absolute or relative number of Italians in the population, or the levels of wages, prices, or unemployment.

Yet they could and did respond to these structures in various ways. For example, it was within their power to decide when and where to migrate, where to live and work, whether or not to take a second job, how to spend their money, with whom to associate, and in which—if any—immigrant or host society institutions to participate. The immigrants confronted a structural reality they could not easily change, but they were not helpless pawns whose fates were solely determined by larger impersonal forces such as the international labor market. Individuals and groups "creatively coped" with their situations. As Ewa Morawska explains, "While the structural environment delineates the general boundaries of the possible and impossible within which people live, it is at the local level of their immediate surroundings that they make their decisions, define purposes, and undertake actions."[9]

The Sola family history also illustrates a closely related point—the importance of what some scholars have recently referred to as the *collective strategies* immigrants used to facilitate their migration and adjustment.[10] Individual migrants acted as members of family, kinship, and community networks, ethnic institutions, and host society organizations—and they were influenced by these local group structures as they moved through the various stages of the migration process. Both Oreste and Ida were part of family, kin, and Biellese-based social networks. Although the cousins apparently did not participate in formal ethnic or host society institutions as most other immigrants did, all of Ida's children attended school and some of them joined labor unions, a church, and the navy.

The most important of the collective strategies was the informal personal networks the immigrants used to assist them as they negotiated the various phases of the migration process. Originally scholars referred to this strategy as *chain migration*.[11] The metaphor is certainly convenient and suggestive, but it is not entirely accurate. I prefer the term *network* because it more effectively describes the complex relationships involved. *Chain* implies a sequential linear relationship between individuals, but the ties among these individuals were most frequently multidimensional. Whatever word we use, it is essential to conceptualize the personal relationships among individual immigrants in terms of multidimensional clusters.[12]

The general features of network migration are fairly clear and widely acknowledged. Like the Solas, most migrants were part of informal personal networks, based in both the sending and the receiving communities, which assisted them during the migration process. Social ties bound "migrants and non-migrants within a complex web of complementary social roles and interpersonal relationships that are maintained by an informal set of mutual expectations and prescribed behaviors."[13] Thus migrant networks developed out of existing networks in the communities of origin, which were extended gradually and often in stages to accommodate the new circumstances. Once they were established, the migrant networks became important social structures in their own right, significantly influencing the lives of the migrants. The networks evolved further as migrants continued to negotiate "new relationships both within and across networks."[14] Ida, for example, became the focal point for family communication after she migrated, though she had not played that role when she was in Valdengo.

Immigrant networks developed because they performed important functions. They helped individuals do specific things. Potential migrants needed to know where it was most advantageous for them to go, how to get there, how to find a job and housing, and if there was a community of familiar paesani with whom they might interact socially. Where networks were in place, they both facilitated migration and influenced the decisions the migrants made. Established networks at the point of origin, linked to specific destinations abroad, created important parameters within which most migrants operated.[15]

And finally, the Sola family history illustrates the global spatial dimension of Italian migration that has become increasingly important to some immigration scholars. Although Oreste and Ida migrated to cities and towns in Argentina and the United States, other members of the family went to various places in North Africa, France, Brazil, and Cuba as well. And Oreste talked about joining his cousin Edvino in Cuba or his friend Berretta in Peru. Viewed from the perspective of Valdengo, multiple potential migration destinations spread out over four continents, and people there understood migration in multidimensional and global rather than unilateral, national terms.

A few historians and scholars in other disciplines have perceived what the Solas understood and have explicitly conceptualized migration as a global phenomenon.[16] Although these authors differ to some extent, they all view nineteenth- and twentieth-century migrations within broad economic systems such as the Atlantic economy or world capitalism. Their underlying concern is to situate their subjects of study in the appropriate explanatory context, which they believe to be an extended regional or global economy. Dirk Hoerder, for example, views European migration within the context of the Atlantic economy. His interest is in studying the development of international labor markets linking "peasant cultures and societies within a worldwide capitalist market system."[17] One of the additional benefits, as John Gould points out, is that the global perspective provides an important corrective to the assumption of exceptionalism on the part of scholars from a specific receiving society. This, he explains, is most important for U.S. historians, who have "too often analyzed the issues as though the United States were the only country of immigration, as though its links with each sending country could be considered separately and in isolation."[18]

The vision that emerges from the Sola family history—and from much of the recent scholarly literature in the United States and Argentina—is that of migrants as historical actors of varying class, gender, and ethnic identities with meaningful though structurally circumscribed parts in a global drama, of individuals embedded in social networks that linked them to one another, and of a complex and dynamic process with multiple outcomes. This vision is one that includes hardship, frustration, disappointment, and suffering—but not, for the most part, social disorganization or alienation.

Comparing Italians in Two Cities: Methodological Issues

"Migration history by its very nature," Rudolph Vecoli recently observed, "demands a transnational perspective."[19] The Sola family history demonstrates the multinational scope of migration and therefore the logic of using the comparative method to study it. Like Valdengo, thousands of villages throughout Italy saw different individuals migrate to

many places abroad. Although the numbers varied considerably from village to village and over time, the basic pattern was one of migration to
multiple destinations.

To understand the complex global reality of the migration process, we
need to compare the experiences of the migrants in their various destinations. Comparison enhances our understanding of migration in several
ways. As is true of all comparisons, multinational comparison of immigrants helps us ask new questions, identify significant research problems,
and formulate generalizations and causal explanations that we could not
as confidently make on the basis of one case alone. It is a method for test-
ing conclusions otherwise based on a single example. Comparison enables
immigration historians to see what is unique to a specific situation and
what is general to the migration process. With the use of multinational
comparison we have a way to determine if the United States or any other
country was unique in its ability to attract and assimilate immigrants, if a
particular ethnic group always integrated into the economy in the same
way, or if the number of immigrants was large in a relative sense.

Although the benefits of the comparative method seem obvious and
many of the best historians praise comparison, few use it explicitly in their
writings.[20] This hesitancy to use comparison arises from a perceived
conflict between historical and comparative methods. Ideally, historical
method is inductive. Historians—especially mindful of the particularity,
complexity, and ambiguities in their subjects—move cautiously from primary data to arrive at conclusions and generalizations. They are concerned
primarily with maintaining the empirical integrity of what they study. To
many, comparative methodology suggests a deductive approach involving the imposition of already established categories on the data. For most
historians, as Raymond Grew points out, "this is not a comfortable way to
work."[21]

Comparative method can, however, be inductively based and therefore of great value to historians. What is essential is that those who write
comparative studies of two or more cases of a historical process (such
as migration) use the same techniques of gathering and analyzing evidence that they would use to study one case. They must in effect write two
or more historical monographs, depending on the number of cases they
choose to investigate, and combine the results in a single integrated work.
This will involve use of primary sources, immersion in the details of the
cases, and attention to the difference among cases and the larger contextual factors that gave rise to them. In addition, it may necessitate learning
a number of languages and examining archival evidence in several different countries. But this, I believe, is the best way to construct meaningful
historical comparisons.[22]

As with the historical field in general, some historians have long recognized the importance of employing comparison in the study of migration—but, until recently, few have actually done it.[23] Beginning in 1975 with Josef Barton's seminal work on Italians, Rumanians, and Slovaks in Cleveland, however, a growing number of scholars have used comparison to analyze Italian and other migrations.[24]

The comparative migration literature provides an important foundation for this book. The spatial and temporal focus has overwhelmingly been on urban communities during the late nineteenth and twentieth centuries. These limits of space and time are significant because they have better enabled the authors to explore the interaction of individuals and the groups in which they participated.

The specific subjects of comparison have varied, but most of these works can be categorized into four groups. The majority of authors, including Barton, compared several immigrant groups in the same city.[25] In these studies the receiving city was the most important constant. The differences in the societies of origin for the most part explained the subsequent differences in the experiences of each group. Other scholars compared the same group in its place of origin and destination.[26] Works using this approach focused on what changed and what remained the same for those who moved to a new location. Still other authors compared the same immigrants in different cities of the same country.[27] And finally a few compared the same immigrants in cities in different receiving countries.[28] A major constant in both these multidestination comparisons was the immigrant group. The primary though not exclusive explanation of differences was the nature of the receiving societies.[29]

Although these works provide guidance regarding the unit of observation, the level of analysis, and the approaches to comparison, rarely is comparison used in a methodologically explicit and systematic manner. Few define the types of variables they use or refer to the existing theoretical literature on comparison.

My purpose in this book is to expand our understanding of migration through the use of the comparative method. Specifically, I seek to accomplish four things. First, to describe the experiences of the Italians who went to Buenos Aires and New York City at the turn of the past century, and their adjustment to the respective situations they encountered. Second, to compare systematically the situations and explain the similarities and differences in outcomes. Third, to identify the relevant categories of variables that immigration scholars need to consider when making multinational comparisons. And fourth, to develop explanatory propositions or hypotheses based on my detailed analysis of Buenos Aires and New York that might also be useful in understanding and explaining Italian adjustment in other destinations.

In this book I draw selectively from the comparative migration literature and the theoretical formulations of a number of scholars.[30] Along with the large majority of migration historians, I have chosen to focus on the community level so as to be able to evaluate both the actions of individuals and the interaction between the immigrant group and the society they encountered. Nevertheless, I situate these communities within the larger contexts of the nation-state and the Atlantic economy. Unlike the work of most immigration historians, however, my comparisons are explicit and systematic. The type of comparison I make fits within the approach of those who study the same immigrant group in different destinations abroad. I seek to illustrate the uniqueness (and similarities) of my cases and I also seek causal explanations by linking dependent and independent variables. This is not a multi-society study based primarily on secondary sources in the tradition of the "grand historical sociology" practiced by Barrington Moore, Immanuel Wallerstein, and Theda Skocpol, among others.[31] Instead, it is a much more narrowly focused comparison of Italians in two communities abroad based on my in-depth analysis of the primary sources. It is, in sum, two monographs integrated into one work.

What I am trying to explain—the dependent variable—is the nature and extent of the adjustment of the Italians in Buenos Aires and New York from 1870 to 1914. I chose these two cities to study because they contained by far the largest communities of Italians living abroad anywhere in the world. I am controlling for ethnic group (Italians), absolute size of the immigrant community within the receiving cities (300,000+ in 1914), and time (1870–1914).

I examine a large number of independent variables to explain the respective patterns of adjustment, but before I discuss them I need to elaborate more fully what I mean by the term. *Adjustment* refers to a phase of the migration process that began when the migrants arrived at a destination abroad and continued for an indeterminate time depending on the individuals, groups, and circumstances involved. All immigrants, whether permanent or temporary, confronted economic, social, political, and cultural structures in their new environments over which they had little if any influence or control. However, they could and did respond to these structural factors in a variety of ways. This "creative coping" within a particular set of structures is what I mean by adjustment.[32]

To survive and make money, all migrants needed to find a job, a place to live, and people with whom to socialize, but they had some choices as to how they would do these things. They could, for example, take a second job to increase their earnings, or they could minimize their expenses on housing and clothing to save more money. Frequently, they participated in one or more social networks to facilitate this adjustment. Those who remained for longer periods or permanently also needed immigrant and host society organizations and institutions to articulate and defend their interests. The collective effort of the individual Italians, as they adjusted to the structurally defined contexts they encountered, created patterns that can be measured and compared. We can gauge the relative speed, effectiveness, and completeness of adjustment by comparing the outcomes of their collective efforts to obtain jobs and housing, to make a new social life, to fight for better working and living conditions, to increase economic resources, and to develop strategies to facilitate the achievement of these things.

Any such comparison raises the problem of value judgments. If the Italians in one location adjusted more rapidly, completely, and effectively than those in another, all too often the implicit assumption is that one group was somehow better or more successful than the other. But limited adjustment was sufficient for some immigrants to achieve their goals, whereas others could not fulfill their objectives without adjusting more completely. Almost all the Italians who went to Buenos Aires and New York did so primarily to earn more money than they had been able to earn in Italy, but they spent this money in different ways. For those who remained abroad permanently, or at least for a long period of time, increased financial resources enabled them to live a better life where they were and also to send some money home to fulfill familial obligations.[33] In contrast, for those who planned to return home and stayed abroad only a brief time, increased earnings enabled them to save money, to return in a shorter time, and subsequently to live a better life at home.

Whether permanent or temporary, all immigrants needed to adjust to some extent. But if their stay was temporary, they might well accept poorer housing, feel less need to develop a social life, and not participate as fully or at all in organizations of assistance and self-protection. Although more permanent immigrants were of necessity likely to adjust more completely than temporary immigrants, their level of adjustment did not make them better or by definition more successful. I do not intend any such value judgment when comparing the patterns of Italian adjustment in the two cities.

To explain the respective patterns in New York and Buenos Aires, I use an inductively based analytical framework of immigrant adjustment in an urban setting. This framework structures the explanatory variables in three interrelated clusters: those relating to what the immigrants brought with them, those relating to what they found when they arrived, and those relating to the subsequent structural changes and to the interaction of the immigrants and the host environment over time. Table 1 presents examples of the specific variables in each cluster as well as some of the indicators of the nature and degree of adjustment.

Table 1. Examples of variables used to evaluate and explain patterns of immigrant adjustment in Buenos Aires and New York City

What they brought with them	What they found abroad	Subsequent structural changes and interaction
Reasons to migrate:	Economic conditions:	Structures:
Push-pull factors	Labor market	Pace of Italian migration
Expectations of	Housing market	Absolute and relative
permanency	Cost of living	number of Italians
		Concentration of Italians
Social and economic resources:	Social conditions:	Strategies:
Education	Class structure	Short versus long term
Occupational skills	Italian community	
Organizational skills	Other immigrants	
Money	Institutions	
Social networks		
Social and cultural traditions:	Culture:	Interaction:
Campanilismo	Religion	All variables
Family	Family	
Religion	Attitude toward Italians	
Worldview		
	Political system:	
	Closed versus open	
	Indicators of outcome:	
	Economic surplus (how much; how and where spent) Mobility (occupational; residential) Intermarriage Institutional participation (host society versus ethnic; formal versus informal)	

The argument I develop in this book is that because the Italians who went to Buenos Aires and New York brought different combinations of things with them and "creatively coped" within different structural contexts, their patterns of adjustment also differed. Part I presents the stages upon which this drama played. Chapter 1 discusses the causes of migration, the characteristics of the Italians who migrated, and the reasons some chose the migration option while most remained at home. Chapter 2 describes the Italian diaspora to all of its multiple destinati ns, the return migration, and the subsequent moves abroad and between destinations. I also analyze the pace and size of the migration to Buenos Aires and New York and the social, economic, and cultural resources the immigrants brought with them. In Chapter 3, I explore the nature of the receiving societies, especially their economic, social, cultural, and political characteristics, and the host society perceptions of Italians. In addition, I examine whether or not these societies were hospitable or hostile to the immigrants, and how much competition there was from natives and other immigrant groups.

Part II examines the adjustment process. Chapters 4 and 5 focus on the critical issues of economic success and residential mobility. I evaluate whether or not the Italians were able to earn a surplus, how they spent their surplus, and the strategies they used to achieve their goals. I also examine what kind of occupational and residential mobility they experienced and the meaning of this mobility. In Chapters 6 through 8, I investigate the most important informal and formal institutions in which the immigrants participated—family, household, neighborhood, immigrant organizations, and host society institutions. The nature of immigrant participation in these institutions is crucial to understanding how they adjusted.

In the concluding chapter, I compare the overall adjustment of Italians in Buenos Aires and New York, set forth similarities and differences in the patterns, and explain why they differed. What becomes clear is that the immigrants' "creative coping" with the structures and cultures they encountered resulted in differing outcomes. Although most migrants arrived in either city with the intention of returning to Italy, a significantly larger proportion pursued a long-term strategy and chose to stay in Buenos Aires, with its larger population of Italians, more hospitable economic and social climate, and vital ethnic community. For Italians in New York City, competition with other immigrant groups, a relatively limited immigrant community, and a less congenial economic and social climate meant that many adopted a short-term strategy of underconsumption, saving, and return.

To explore the wider applicability of the variables and the explanatory propositions that have emerged from the analysis of Buenos Aires and New York, I briefly examine the adjustment of Italians in San Francisco, Toronto, and São Paulo. On the basis of these five cases, I propose a continuum of Italian immigrant adjustment in New World urban centers.

Buenos Aires, I hypothesize, represents the polar case of rapid, effective, and relatively complete adjustment. New York represents the polar opposite case. The other three cases fall at different points in between. San Francisco would be closer to the Buenos Aires pattern. Toronto would be closer to that of New York. And São Paulo would be somewhere in between.

Ultimately, my hope in writing this book is that the comparative method, with the variables and theoretical propositions I have identified as important for understanding the experiences of the Italians in Buenos Aires and New York, will also prove useful for the analysis of immigrants in urban settings throughout the world.

Part I

The Italian Diaspora and the Old and New World Contexts of Migration

The hundreds of thousands of Italians who went to Buenos Aires and New York City during the years surrounding the turn of the past century were part of a much larger migration of Europeans within the Atlantic economies. Between 1821 and 1915 perhaps as many as fifty million individuals left the continent for non-European destinations.[1] This mass overseas migration began in northern and western Europe during the first half of the century, and gradually, in what J. D. Gould describes as a process of "diffusion," spread thereafter to the east and the south.[2] Additional millions migrated to destinations within Europe and also internally to different locations within their respective countries. Many of those who left eventually returned home. Migration of all types was a common phenomenon in nineteenth- and early twentieth-century Europe.

Italian intercontinental mass migration began in the decades following the final unification of the country in 1870, and has continued ever since. This century-long movement was global; individuals migrated to multiple destinations on at least five continents. The pace of migration and the destinations of choice changed many times. In an imperfectly documented process that involved the movement of individuals back and forth from Italy to various locations abroad an unknown number of times, approximately twenty-six million Italians left home and more than half of them returned.

As Table 2 shows, the general contours of this emigration and return migration are clear. Mass migration began during the last twenty-five years of the nineteenth century (1876–1900) with Europe and South America the main destinations. Emigration increased dramatically and reached a peak in the early years of the twentieth century (1901–1915). The annual average of migrants during the years before World War I more than doubled that of the preceding period. Major destinations also changed; smaller

Table 2. The general contours of the Italian diaspora, 1876–1976

Dates	Total emigration (in millions)	Annual average	Destinations				Return
			Europe (%)	South America (%)	North America (%)	Others[a] (%)	
1876–1900	5.3	212,000	48.5	35.0	15.0	1.5	—
1901–1915	8.8	587,000	41.0	17.0	40.0	2.0	50[b]
1916–1942	4.4	163,000	51.5	19.0	25.0	4.5	52
1946–1976	7.4	239,000	68.5	12.5	12.5	6.5	58

[a] Includes the small emigration to Australia, Africa, and Asia.

[b] Official Italian statistics on return migration were not kept before 1905, and between 1905 and 1915 did not include Europe. This figure therefore represents return migration from overseas only between 1905 and 1915. A useful discussion of the data on return migration is J. D. Gould, "European Inter-Continental Emigration, 1815–1914," *Journal of European Economic History*, 9, 1 (Spring 1980), pp. 41–112.

Sources: Gianfausto Rosoli, ed., *Un secolo de emigrazione italiana, 1876–1976* (Rome, 1978), pp. 22, 26, 28, 34, 35, and 39; Commissariato Generale dell'Emigrazione, *Annuario statistico della emigrazione italiana dal 1876 al 1925* (Rome, 1926), p. 8. Hereafter cited as *Annuario statistico*.

percentages of Italians went to Europe and South America while a substantially larger percent went to North America. From the beginning of World War I through the Depression years and World War II, the numbers declined significantly. After 1946, migration resumed at levels similar to those during the pre-1900 period. In this post–World War II period, migrants went primarily to the other European countries and to Canada.

Italian mass migration to the Americas can best be understood within the context of capitalist development. As capitalism expanded during the second half of the nineteenth century, it brought about new exchanges of technology, capital, and labor within the Atlantic economies. Migration was one response of Italians adapting to the new capitalist order. Local and regional migration became increasingly international. Italy became part of the periphery supplying labor to the industrial core areas of northern Europe, to the commercialized agricultural areas of South America, and, by the turn of the century, to the industrial core area of the United States.

Because the movement of Italians to and from Buenos Aires and New York City was part of a larger Atlantic migration system, it linked individuals and families in the villages of origin with those in these two destinations abroad and often with others as well. Both the sending and the receiving contexts were integral parts of the migration process, and as such influenced the decisions to emigrate, to remain, to remigrate, or to return home.

Italy and the Causes of Emigration

Although some Italians emigrated before 1876 and after 1915, considerably more left their country during the four decades preceding World War I than at any other time during the history of the peninsula. Fourteen million individuals went abroad during this forty-year period.[1] They chose to do so for many reasons that depended on who they were, when and where they lived, their circumstances at home, their opportunities abroad, and how they were linked to the larger world around them.

In this chapter I explore the reasons that relate to the situation in Italy during the period of mass emigration. First I develop a statistical overview to establish from where within Italy the emigrants came and who they were. Then I discuss the general causes that prompted individual Italians to leave their country. And finally I examine in depth one village of heavy migration in an effort to understand how individuals living at the local level interpreted and responded to the general causes and in some cases made the decision to emigrate.

Where the Emigrants Came From and Who They Were

Italian emigration was a selective process. Most Italians did not go abroad. Those who chose to leave left from many parts of the country, in varying numbers, and at different times. They came from some regions and provinces and not others. Within these regions and provinces, they came from certain villages. And even within most villages, the migrants represented only a small minority of the population.

The exodus of Italians was not evenly distributed over the forty-year period, as is shown by the countrywide annual averages grouped in five-year periods (Table 3). At the beginning (1876–1880), the annual average was 109,000; it increased steadily until it peaked at 651,000 during the 1906–1910 period. Most strikingly, nearly two-thirds of the emigrants (62.5 percent) left in the fifteen years between 1901 and 1915 alone.

Although some came from almost every part of Italy, certain broad areas and regions contributed significantly more emigrants than others. The overwhelming majority were concentrated in two of the three broad areas of the country; half were from the North and approximately two-fifths (39 percent) from the South. The Center accounted for only 11 percent (Table 3; Map 1). Emigration from the North began the earliest; two out of every three emigrants before 1900 left from this area. However, during the first decade of the twentieth century—the period of greatest overall emigration from Italy—departures from the South exceeded by a small amount those from the North.

A little less than half of the migrants went to France, Switzerland, Germany, and other European countries, and a little more than half went overseas, primarily to the United States, Argentina, and Brazil. Of those who left the North, however, over 70 percent went to the nearby European countries; in contrast, nearly 90 percent of the emigrants from the South went overseas.

A distinct pattern emerges from these data on the three broad regions of Italy. On the one hand, there was a continuously large emigration (annual average of over a hundred thousand) from the north of Italy directed primarily, though not exclusively, toward Europe. On the other hand, there was a later (after 1896) and more concentrated (1901–1915) mass migration from the south directed nearly entirely overseas to the Americas.

Within these three large areas, there was considerable variation in the origins and timing of migration. At the beginning of World War I there were sixteen regions, seventy-three provinces, and nine thousand towns and villages in Italy.[2] If we were to chart the rates of emigration for each of these many subdivisions, we could produce a much more refined definition of high emigration areas. This, however, is not feasible nor essential for my study. Let it suffice here to reiterate that although all parts of the country contributed some emigrants, these emigrants came predominantly from a limited number of areas, regions, provinces, and villages.[3]

Migration was also a selective process in terms of who the emigrants were. It is true that in the aggregate most of those who decided to migrate were young males from the lower socioeconomic ranks of society. Yet, as John Briggs has emphasized, this does not mean that they were a homogeneous group.[4] The most typical emigrant was a male between sixteen and forty-five years of age. Nearly 90 percent were sixteen years of age or older and this percentage remained essentially consistent between 1876 and 1915 (Table 4). Similarly, the ratio of male to female emigrants

Table 3. Italian emigration, 1876–1915 (annual averages)

Years	Italy			Northern Italy			Central Italy			Southern Italy		
	N	E (%)	A (%)[a]	N	E (%)	A (%)	N	E (%)	A (%)	N	E (%)	A (%)
1876–1880	109,000	73	24	87,200[b]	82	18	7,600	79	15	14,000	20	71
1881–1885	154,100	59	38	106,300	73	26	11,300	69	28	36,500	12	77
1886–1890	221,700	39	59	142,600	53	46	14,700	49	48	64,400	7	90
1891–1895	256,500	41	57	164,000	58	42	15,200	34	64	77,300	8	89
1896–1900	310,400	47	52	170,700	75	25	28,200	36	61	111,500	6	91
1901–1905	554,000	42	55	231,300	78	21	64,400	48	50	258,300	9	88
1906–1910	651,300	38	60	259,200	72	27	87,100	48	51	304,900	6	92
1911–1915	548,600	43	55	243,900	75	24	76,100	50	49	228,600	7	91
Total	14,028,000	44	54	7,029,000	71	28	1,522,000	49	49	5,477,000	7	90
Percentage	(100)			(50)			(11)			(39)		

[a] (%E) = the percentage to Europe. (%A) = the percentage to America. These figures have been rounded off to the nearest percent. They do not add up to 100 percent because between 2 and 3 percent went to other than European and American destinations.
[b] The figures in boldface are the largest for the period.
Source: *Annuario statistico*, pp. 8–11.

Map 1. Regions and areas of heaviest emigration, 1876–1915

was consistently high (between 355 and 567 men per 100 women). There was nevertheless a significant range of ages within the sixteen- to forty-five-year-old category, and for the last three decades of the period (1886–1915), there were between 22 percent and 28 percent women among the emigrants.[5]

The most common method to measure socioeconomic status is by occu-

Table 4. Italian emigration, 1876–1915 (age and sex)

Years	Age (16+) (%)	Masculinity index (men/100 women)
1876–1885	89.5	567
1886–1895	85.0	355
1896–1905	88.7	456
1906–1915	89.3	426

Sources: *Annuario statistico*, p. 167; Rosoli, ed., *Un secolo de emigrazione italiana*, pp. 375–376.

pation, but because of the way the government recorded employment, the data on occupations are difficult to evaluate.[6] When they emigrated, all individuals were classified in one of fifteen broad and poorly defined categories, which frequently masked internal distinctions of skills and remuneration.[7] This is especially true of some of the largest categories such as "Rural Work" and "Industrial and Artisanal Work." The other large categories, "Day Labor" and "Domestic Work," are less problematic.

At the categorical level, nevertheless, these data are indicative of some general occupational trends. More than 90 percent of the male emigrants held occupations throughout the period in rural work, industrial and artisanal work, and day labor (Table 5). Between 1880 and 1904, the large majority (approximately 80 percent) of the women who indicated that they worked also held jobs in the same three occupational groupings, and an additional 5 percent were employed in domestic work.[8]

During the thirty-five years from 1880 to 1914, however, there were significant changes in the percentages employed in all of these categories. At the beginning of the period (1880–1884), nearly half of the men (46 percent) were engaged in rural work, a quarter (26 percent) in day labor, and slightly less than a quarter (23 percent) in industrial and artisanal work. At the same time, 60 percent of the women who listed jobs were rural workers, 17 percent day laborers, 10 percent industrial workers and artisans, and 5 percent domestic workers. Subsequently, there was a significant decline among both men and women in the percentages employed in rural work and a corresponding increase in those involved in industrial and artisanal jobs. Simultaneously, the number of men who worked as day laborers gradually increased, while that of women fluctuated but ultimately dropped below the 1880–1884 levels. Table 5 also indicates that domestic service became significantly more important for women during the 1910–1914 period.

The gradual shift from agricultural to nonagricultural employment categories among the emigrants is an important indicator of the increasing

Table 5. Italian emigration, 1880–1914 (occupations by sex)

Occupations	1880–1884 M (%)	1880–1884 W (%)	1890–1894 M (%)	1890–1894 W (%)	1900–1904 M (%)	1900–1904 W (%)	1910–1914 M (%)	1910–1914 W (%)
Rural work[a]	45	55	44	59	40	45	32	24
Industrial and artisanal work[a]	23	10	24	9	23	13	27	17
Day labor[a]	26	17	26	15	30	20	32	14
Domestic service[a]	<1	5	<1	5	<1	6	<1	12
Others[a]	5	13	6	12	6	16	7	33[b]
Total	100	100	101	100	100	100	99	100
N of men	(584,600)		(838,600)		(1,828,000)		(2,421,800)	
N of women	(83,000)		(191,800)		(332,200)		(482,100)	

[a]The occupational groupings include the following: *Rural work*—agriculturalists, herders, gardeners, woodcutters, and so on; *Industrial and artisanal work*—masons, bricklayers, stonecutters, kiln workers, miners, metal and glass workers, textile workers, carpenters, tailors, shoemakers, etc.; *Day labor*—unskilled digging and road workers (*braccianti, giornalieri*), and so on; *Domestic service*—servants, butlers, nurses; *Others*—commerce, food and lodging, transport, professions, arts, miscellaneous, housewives and without occupation, and unknown.

[b]This figure includes 25 percent housewives and those without professions, groups that were not recorded as separate categories during the previous periods.

Sources: This table is based on a reworking of data in *Annuario statistico*, pp. 241–242. For the equivalent regional data see pp. 245–274.

proletarianization of rural Italians during this period. It should not, however, obscure the range of occupational diversity within these categories or the fact that a considerable number of emigrants were simultaneously active in more than one category.[9] Existing Italian data do not permit us to gauge the precise changes within categories. Nevertheless, the major occupational groupings included a wide range of jobs that required different levels of skill and earned different levels of remuneration. Rural work included agriculturalists, herders, gardeners, and woodcutters. Industrial and artisanal work signified masons, bricklayers, stonecutters, miners, metal and glass workers, textile workers, carpenters, tailors, and shoemakers. And frequently an individual was both an agriculturalist and an artisan, as was the case with Ida Sola's father, Giacomo. In sum, even though there remained some overlapping of categories, the emigrants were for the most part from the lower socioeconomic strata of society and predominantly and increasingly from the nonagricultural sectors.

Although at the broadest level we can describe the so-called typical emigrant as a young male who at the time of departure was employed as an agricultural or nonagricultural worker in the lower portion of the occupational hierarchy, there was considerable diversity among those who chose to leave the country. Emigrants ranged in age between sixteen and forty-five and a few were older and younger. There were always some women among the men. And there was a variety of occupations within the broader categories. To understand the complex reality of the migration process, we need to keep in mind the age, gender, and occupational diversity of the emigrants as well as the commonalities with which they are frequently described.

The Causes of Italian Emigration

Because Italian migration of the pre–World War I era was a village- and family-outward process that linked the places of origin with the multiple destinations within Italy and abroad, the exploration of causation must ultimately focus on the villages.[10] It was individuals and families in the nine thousand Italian villages, such as Valdengo, Agnone, Sirolo-Numana, Piedimonte d'Alife, and others, who decided whether or not to emigrate, where to go, how long to stay, and whether or not to return and perhaps to emigrate again. They were confronted with larger economic, political, and social forces over which they had no control, but, as Rudolph Bell correctly emphasizes, the "total impact of such factors left rural Italians with meaningful decisions to be made."[11]

Emigration was but one of several possible responses to the larger forces that differentially intruded on the lives of rural Italians and disrupted the stability of the local communities. Of the majority who remained at home, some organized to protest the changing circumstances in which they lived, while others accepted the new conditions. These individuals and their families calculated the advantages and disadvantages of each option and made their decisions accordingly. My concern is to explain the self-selection process of those within the larger Italian population who decided to emigrate overseas to the Americas.

Interrelated forces operating simultaneously at several levels influenced the decision to emigrate: general changes in Italian society, specific changes in local communities, and personal issues specific to particular individuals. The societal-level issues can be further divided into those that enabled or made it easier for the individual to leave and those that directly increased the pressure on the ability of rural Italians to survive.

Developments in Italian railroad and shipping transportation during the second half of the nineteenth century increased the possibilities for all those who wanted to emigrate. The construction of a national railroad system connected the various parts of the country to each other, thus enabling people to move more easily as well as enhancing the exchange of information. In 1861, Italy had 1,623 kilometers of railroads concentrated for the most part in the North. Thirty-five years later, the system had expanded tenfold to 16,053 kilometers, covering the entire country. The completion of a railroad-ferry connection between Sicily and the mainland in 1881 furthered the integration of the island into the nation.[12]

Changes within the shipping industry improved the overseas portion of the journey. Technological innovations between 1850 and 1900 significantly changed the nature of the ocean voyage in ways that facilitated migration. Steamships gradually replaced sailing vessels. Metal hulls replaced wooden ones. New and more powerful engines replaced lesser ones. Ships became larger and faster, and their schedules more consistent.[13]

Although the ocean voyage was never easy, these innovations made the trip better in a number of ways. Most of the improvements had to do with the duration and predictability of the voyage. The trip from Naples to New York in a sailing ship could take anywhere from five weeks to two months and that to Buenos Aires even longer. Steamships at the turn of the past century traveled the distance to New York in ten to twelve days and to Buenos Aires in eighteen to twenty days. Fares came down somewhat, but the much shorter duration of the trip represented a major additional savings in terms of fewer work days lost. Larger ships had more public space and relatively better health and sanitary conditions. Yet in the end, it was probably the shorter duration of the trip that made it significantly more bearable.

In addition, Italian emigration legislation was essentially nonrestrictive during the half century preceding World War I; thus individuals enjoyed unprecedented legal freedom to emigrate. Although Italian leaders actively debated the pros and cons of emigration for the economic development of the country, they placed few legal restrictions on those who wanted to go abroad. The first major piece of legislation, the Emigration Law of 1888, was based on the belief that emigration was essentially a private matter; the role of the state was to intervene only to eliminate the most egregious abuses in the process. The law focused on the regulation of agents and contracts and on security and health aboard ship, but it made no provisions for a state agency to oversee emigration.[14]

After years of additional debate fueled by the competition between the shipping companies of Naples and Genoa, the Parliament passed the Emigration Law of 1901. This law also reflected the notion that emigration was essentially a private matter largely beyond state control, but it did provide for increased state oversight of the process. The 1901 law abolished emigration agents and thus increased the responsibility of the shipping companies in the emigration process. It also provided the legal basis for state intervention in certain circumstances to protect the emigrants; for example, the Prinetti Decree of 1902 prohibited subsidized emigration to

Brazil, and the Italian government suspended emigration to Argentina for thirteen months in 1911 and 1912. Finally, the law created the *Commissariato Generale dell'Emigrazione* (the General Commission of Emigration) to carry out the new policies. The emigration commission had modest powers, however, and—more important—limited resources. It did, nevertheless, provide better information to emigrants and collect better data on emigration.[15]

In addition to these enabling developments, there were other societal-level changes that increased the pressures on rural Italians to survive and make a living. Rapid population growth during the nineteenth century was one of these. Although the birth rate remained essentially constant between 1861 and 1891 and declined thereafter, the death rate declined more rapidly. As a result, the absolute population increased by nearly 40 percent between 1861 and 1911 (25 million to 34.7 million), even though millions left the country permanently for destinations abroad.[16]

The crucial issue about population was not growth per se. Rather, it was the ability of the economy to absorb the larger population and to enable rural Italians to sustain their standard of living. The Italian economy during the second half of the nineteenth century did not grow rapidly enough to support the increased population. Moreover, the spread of commercial agriculture and the gradual development of industry altered the rural economy and limited employment opportunities.

In the second half of the nineteenth century, the Italian economy relied primarily on agricultural production. Although the country achieved substantial industrialization in parts of the North by the turn of the century, the absolute number of the active population employed in agricultural pursuits did not decline until World War I. Industry did not contribute as much as agriculture to the national income until the 1930s.[17] In large part, the inhabitants—and especially the rural inhabitants—of Italy depended on agriculture for their livelihood throughout the period of mass emigration.

A number of problems confronted the rural populations during this period. Agricultural productivity was generally low, although it varied from area to area. Much of the country lacked good farmland; less than half of Italy's land was arable and much of this was in marginally productive hilly and mountainous areas. Uneven and frequently inadequate rainfall, deforestation and erosion, and disease made matters more difficult.[18]

Land tenure patterns and government policies created additional problems. Land was of critical importance to rural Italians because it was essential for their survival. Continued access to land on reasonably favorable terms meant financial security. Ownership of land represented security and status. In areas where land was more widely distributed, the goal was ownership. In those areas where ownership was concentrated in the hands of a few—and land was therefore not available—the more immediate goal was better share farming and labor contracts and improved working conditions.

During the nineteenth century, a considerable amount of land changed hands. The commercialization and redistribution of land began as a result of the abolition of feudalism and the expropriation of church properties at the beginning of the nineteenth century. After 1861, additional church property, state lands, and communal holdings were put up for sale. Between 1861 and 1899 some three hundred thousand parcels of land changed hands. The relative size of this number is clearer when we consider that in 1881, Italy had approximately five hundred thousand to six hundred thousand landowners.[19]

The process of redistribution, however, involved both the subdivision and recombination of land. Much of the land was initially sold in small plots. In some areas, land became more widely distributed, but most peasant holdings were too small to sustain efficient agricultural production or to support a family. In other areas, land increasingly ended up in the hands of the propertied elites. Small owner-cultivators borrowed the money to buy this land. When they had a poor harvest or agricultural prices declined, they were frequently forced to sell their property to pay the mortgage and taxes. Those with the resources to profit from this situation were the larger landowners, land speculators, and in some cases, returned emigrants.[20]

Especially during the last quarter of the century, there were many forfeitures of small holdings. The influx of cheap American and Russian grain in the 1870s and 1880s and the 1888–1898 tariff war with France—Italy's main customer for agricultural exports—resulted in a substantial decline in agricultural prices and exports. At the same time national and local taxes remained high.[21] Rural Italians found it increasingly difficult to make ends meet. As a result, between 1881 and 1901 the number owning land, particularly among those living in the South, decreased substantially.[22]

A number of scholars have postulated a relationship between the land tenure systems that emerged from this century-long redistribution and recombination process on the one hand and the respective rates of emigration on the other.[23] Although these authors emphasize different aspects of rural community life and do not agree completely on all points, their studies provide the basis for several important generalizations regarding the relationship between the rural economy and emigration. First, changes and developments at the societal level increasingly restricted the possibilities for most rural Italians to make a living and also made it easier for those who wanted to emigrate overseas to do so. Second, emigration was only one of several options (protest, accepting the status quo) available to rural Italians, who during the four decades preceding World War I were confronted with increasingly restricted opportunities. Third, emigration was heaviest in areas characterized by relatively widespread distribution of land, family-based agriculture, subtle gradations in socioeconomic status, and competition among peasants. Fourth, the agricultural and nonagricultural economies were closely linked and thus the decline in cottage and artisanal industry frequently had a negative impact on the opportunities available to peasant households. Fifth, market relations and capitalist enterprise also affected the opportunities available to rural Italians. And sixth, although we can characterize areas of high emigration, we must not assume that such characteristics exclusively defined areas of emigration as opposed to those of protest.

The Village-Outward Perspective and the Causes of Emigration

The village-outward perspective shifts the focus of enquiry from the societal to the local level, where the decisions to emigrate were made.[24] Such a focus enables us to probe the impact of the national and global changes that led individuals to emigrate, to introduce local structural and personal reasons for emigrating, as well as to explain the variations in emigration patterns. Although no single location can be fully representative of all nine thousand Italian villages and towns at the turn of the past century, any effort to develop general explanations of emigration must be informed by specific cases.[25] My firsthand knowledge of Oreste's and Ida's hometown of Valdengo and the surrounding Biella areas plus my knowledge of other towns such as Agnone, Sirolo-Numana, and Piedimonte d'Alife has significantly informed this book. Here I will examine the causes of high emigration from the southern Italian town of Agnone in Isernia (formerly Campobasso) and place its experience in the context of a number of towns studied in depth by other scholars.

Agnone is an especially illuminating case study for our purposes. In 1861, there were 10,637 inhabitants in the town, and during the subsequent half century, at least 7,000 left home. The vast majority of these emigrants went to Argentina and the United States, many of them settling in Buenos Aires and New York City. And finally, the history of the town and its migration abroad are exceptionally well documented.[26]

A number of physical and climatic conditions have defined the context in which Agnone's inhabitants lived.[27] At the time of mass emigration, it was a relatively large and isolated community of more than ten thousand people living on 9,630 hectares of land located in the mountains of the Alto

Molise. The closest community of any size was Isernia, connected to it by forty-three miles of treacherous winding roads. Uneven topography, high altitude, and harsh climate have always made life in Agnone difficult. Altitude ranges from 1,300 to 4,800 feet; the urban center, which houses much of the population, is located at 2,300 feet. Winters are cold and snowy. Summers are cool.

Agnone's size and physical isolation enabled it to develop as a regional economic, administrative, and cultural center that exerted influence over the numerous small towns within its large hinterland, and at the same time to resist the influence of the distant larger cities such as Naples, Caserta, Chieti, Campobasso, and Isernia. The economy was based on agriculture and artisanal industry. Most inhabitants were active in various types of agriculture. In the lower areas of town, farmers grew wheat, olives, and grapes. At the higher altitudes, potatoes, animal grazing, and forestry replaced these crops. A sizeable minority of the population, however, were artisans. In the twelfth century, Venetian traders introduced metal working to the town. Subsequently, Agnonese goldsmiths, coppersmiths, silversmiths, and ironsmiths traveled to towns as far as 125 miles away to sell their wares. Goods of all sorts were traded at the town's weekly fair, where, for the day, residents and outsiders alike were exempted from paying municipal taxes.

During the second half of the eighteenth and the first part of the nineteenth centuries, a new class of *galantuomini* (merchants, professionals, and a few of the more successful artisans) emerged in Agnone to replace the feudal *baroni* and the church as the dominant force in society. The emerging liberal elite supported the development of a new economic order based on increasing land speculation, commercialized agriculture, and free enterprise. The liberals controlled the town from 1806 to 1815 and exerted considerable influence there, even during the period of the Bourbon restoration from 1815 to 1860. Garibaldi's triumph in 1860, and the final unification of Italy and the establishment of a national economy in 1870, allowed the new elite (the galantuomini) to consolidate their control of the town. It was under their control that mass emigration from the town took place.

During the early months of 1885, *L'Aquilonia*, Agnone's recently established newspaper, noted that many inhabitants, including whole families, were leaving for the Americas. On January 1, it reported that seventy-five had left the preceding Sunday and that thirty-eight more planned to leave soon. On February 1, it recounted that twenty-nine were sailing from Genoa that day. On April 16, eighty people were reported to have left Agnone in the last four days alone. Three years later, however, the paper decried the large numbers who were emigrating and urged the government to help the town's inhabitants remain at home.[28]

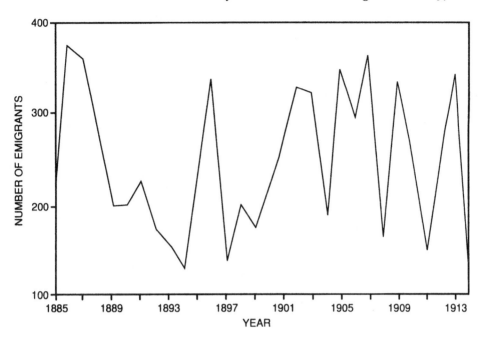

Figure 2. Passports issued by Commune of Agnone, 1885–1914 (total)

What the town's first newspaper had observed was indeed a mass exodus of citizens to Buenos Aires and New York. In the four-year period from 1885 to 1888, 1,245 passports were issued by the commune of Agnone. Perhaps as many as 1,456 people, or 14 percent of the population, actually left the town.[29] Overseas emigration from Agnone had begun several decades earlier. Douglass claims that the first Agnonesi may have left for Buenos Aires as early as 1858. Carlomagno argues that the first overseas emigrants left the town in 1870 and that several thousand went to Buenos Aires during the subsequent decade and a half.[30] Population data indicate that at least several hundred left during the 1860s, 1,300 left during the 1870s, and 1,650 left during the 1880s.

By 1885, the year for which the first passport data is available, emigration had become massive, and similarly high levels continued up to World War I, as shown in Figure 2.[31] During each of the three subsequent decades following 1885, an average of 2,451 passports were issued, with the number increasing slightly over time. My estimate of those who actually left is 2,729 between 1885 and 1894, 2,491 between 1895 and 1904, and 2,105 between 1905 and 1914.[32] However calculated, the number was consistently high (2,100+) and of massive proportions (about 20 percent of the population each decade). Furthermore, as Figure 3 shows, the over-

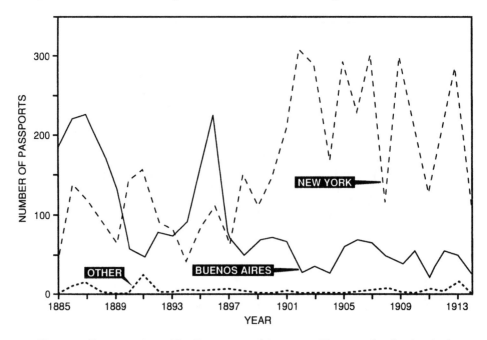

Figure 3. Passports issued by Commune of Agnone, 1885–1914 (by destination)

whelming number of Agnonese emigrants went at first to Buenos Aires and New York City, although a considerable number subsequently moved to other cities in Argentina and the United States.

The annual variations in the numbers leaving the town indicate how quickly overall emigration responded to changing conditions. From 1885 to 1914, more than 300 passports were issued by the Commune of Agnone during nine widely dispersed years, and in three exceptional years (1886, 1887, and 1907), there were more than 360. Intermingled with these years of high volume were eight widely dispersed smaller-volume years in which fewer than 200 passports were issued. In the three lowest years (1892, 1897, and 1904), fewer than 140 people acquired passports. Clearly the reasons to emigrate were greater in some years and less pressing in others.

The passport records also provide important information about who the emigrants were. Between 1886 and 1908 approximately two-thirds were peasants and one-third were artisans and small businessmen.[33] A tiny fraction were professionals or domestic servants. The emigrants were also predominantly young adult males and increasingly so in the first decade of the new century. In 1889, 1899, and 1908, between 60 percent and 71 percent were adults in the twenty-one to forty-year-old range. Thus the emigrants with occupations were predominantly young male peasants, but a sizeable minority had nonagricultural occupations.[34] The women were for the most part seamstresses and weavers, peasants, and domestic servants. And over time, those who emigrated were older.

A number of general causes contributed to Agnone's high emigration. At the national level, the lessening of government restrictions on emigration after 1860, the development of an Italian railroad system, and the increasing use of steamships in the Mediterranean and the Atlantic made it much easier for the Agnonesi to go to Buenos Aires and New York. Although these developments influenced all Italian rural communities, the impact was not uniform. In the case of Agnone, the railroad greatly facilitated travel to the port of Genoa—the port from which virtually all Agnonesi sailed for the Americas. Until 1897, the most difficult part of the journey remained the forty-three miles over nearly impassable mountain roads to the railroad station in Isernia. In 1897, the distance to the nearest railroad station was reduced to thirteen miles when the Isernia–Sulmona rail link was completed with a station in nearby Carovilli. A direct railroad link to Agnone, however, was not opened until 1915, after more than thirty years of mass emigration. Emigration in this case was not deterred by the difficult nature of local transportation.[35]

The relationship of Agnone to the outside world was complex. On the one hand, Agnone was physically isolated and the social space of the town's inhabitants, as measured by marriage patterns, was confined.[36] Based on a sampling from four decades, the overwhelming majority of marriages in Agnone involved partners who were born and resided in town. In 1876, 1886, and 1896, 93 percent to 95 percent of the grooms and 97 percent to 99 percent of the brides had been born in Agnone, and 99 percent of the grooms and 100 percent of the brides were residents. As late as 1906, only a slightly lower number of Agnone marriage partners had been born and resided in town.[37]

On the other hand, some of Agnone's residents had long- standing contacts with the outside world. A number of townspeople had regularly moved in and out of the community—members of the social elite, artisans selling their goods (coppersmiths, goldsmiths) or their skills (bellmakers, stonemasons, carpenters), and shepherds who annually took their flocks to the plains of Apulia. Most were temporary sojourners, but a few who left decided to remain in these distant locations. The town had a limited but significant tradition of migration.[38] Thus, although Agnone was physically isolated and its social space as measured by marriages limited, it also had established contacts with the outside world that could, under certain circumstances, facilitate mass emigration.

Table 6. Agnone population data

Year	Population Resident	Population Present	Net population change[a] Annual average
1753	4,823		
1790	7,500		
1837	9,700		
1861	10,637	10,230	
			−31.3
1871	11,615	11,073	
			−131.2
1881	10,832	10,687	
			−164.9
1901	10,189	9,793	
			−162.7
1911	10,106	9,134	
			−68.4
1921	10,142	9,122	

Net change over whole period: −7,244

[a]Net population change, which is the basis of our conservative estimates of emigration, is calculated by adding the surplus of births over deaths to the population at the beginning of the period between two censuses and subtracting the total from the population at the end of the period. Multiple exits and reentries are not reflected in these figures. Present population is used as the base of all calculations.

Source: Population figures are taken from Istituto Centrale di Statistica, *Popolazione residente e presente dei comuni, censimenti dal 1861 al 1971* (Rome, 1977), and from Antonio Arduino, "Schemi particolari di demografia (dal 1532 al 1977) del Comune di Agnone nel Molise," an unpublished chart on the demographic history of Agnone. Professor Arduino, who is director of the Biblioteca Comunale of Agnone, very kindly gave me a copy of the "Schemi." His figures on population differ somewhat from official census figures, especially the 1901 and 1921 figures.

A more direct cause of mass emigration was the preceding century of rapid population growth, which had enormously increased the pressure on the resources of the town's inhabitants. Between 1753 and 1837, the population doubled (from 4,823 to 9,700), and it grew an additional 20 percent between 1837 and 1871 (Table 6). The 1871 population of 11,615 was the maximum for the town throughout its history. The number of inhabitants gradually declined thereafter to its current size of approximately 6,000 people.

Agnone's economy did not grow sufficiently to be able to support its burgeoning population. This imbalance resulted in a long cycle of decline in the standard of living for peasants, day laborers, artisans, and small businessmen. In 1753, most of the 4,823 inhabitants made their living entirely or in part by farming and herding animals. Some were also involved in the production of handcrafted metal goods and animal by-products and in small businesses. Many of these artisans also served as itinerant merchants who sold their goods in nearby and more distant towns. Although Agnone was a feudal town with fourteen private estates, almost all individuals had access to land. Eighty-nine percent of the peasant and manual labor households and 79 percent of the artisan households owned at least one small plot of land, and 98 percent of all households leased a portion of the town commons. To support the population in this early period, the town needed to devote only 10 percent of the total land area to the cultivation of wheat.[39]

A century later (1845), the economy had changed significantly. The commercialization and redistribution of land and the traditions of partible inheritance and dowering had led to the parcelization of landholdings, but not to more widely distributed land ownership. Although 12.5 percent of the population owned some land in 1814, by 1845 the number had declined to 6 percent. To meet the needs of a growing population, the landowners intensified and extended the cultivation of grain into pastures and marginal lands. Forty-one percent of the land was used for grain, an increase of more than four times over what it had been in 1753. The yield per hectare declined, as did the number of livestock.[40] Thus rapid population growth and the development of a land market resulted in an economy dominated by a new entrepreneurial class (the galantuomini), the simultaneous concentration and fragmentation of landownership, the extension of grain cultivation at the expense of more traditional agricultural crops and activities, and severe dislocations and losses to the peasants and artisans.

The policies of the post-unification national and local governments exacerbated these developments; they added to the pressures on the local economy and on the ability of the peasants and artisans to make ends meet. The creation of a national economy and the initial loss of tariff protection led to the influx of more efficiently produced grain and goods with which the humbler Agnonesi could not successfully compete. The national government also increased taxes to pay for its new development programs. And the galantuomini, who by this time dominated the local government and owned most of the land, shifted the tax base from the land to the consumer.[41]

The pressure of population on the town's resource base can be gauged if we look at the number of inhabitants per square kilometer of land. Bell estimates that the population density ceilings for rural nineteenth-century Italy were approximately 50 people per square kilometer of pastoral land and 100 persons per square kilometer of intensely cultivated land.[42] In 1871, at the beginning of mass emigration, Agnone had 120.6 persons per square kilometer of land. If we subtract the urban or barren and the forest areas from the total, the population density per square kilometer increases to 158.7.[43] Even though a considerable minority of Agnonesi were artisans and merchants, many of them depended to various degrees on agricultural production. Thus the pressure of population on land resources was very great indeed.

Nature also seemed to conspire against the peasants and artisans of Agnone. The town was periodically confronted with serious outbreaks of disease: epidemics in 1873–1874 and 1896–1897; cholera in 1884–1885 and 1892–1893; smallpox in 1888–1889. In addition, there were bad harvests and famines in 1875, 1880–1881, and 1896.[44] Disease and famine clearly help explain the exceptionally high numbers of emigrants in the mid-1870s, 1886–1887, and 1896.

Agnone's inhabitants responded to these circumstances in several ways. Most apparently accepted their deteriorating situations fatalistically. Under certain circumstances, however, some protested. Until the twentieth century, Agnone's social hierarchy was rigid and mobility very limited. The galantuomini were at the top followed by the clergy and professionals, the larger merchants, the artisans, and the peasants. The peasants were by far the largest group and the social distance between them and everybody else was substantial. The artisans were further divided according to the prestige of specific occupations; goldsmiths and silversmiths were at the top of this sub-hierarchy, followed by coppersmiths and shoemakers. Stonemasons were at the bottom and were perceived socially as being just above peasants and day laborers. The distinctions between social groups eased somewhat during the early years of the twentieth century as returning emigrants bought land and became active in local politics, but the elite's firm control over land and politics during the second half of the nineteenth century exacerbated class tensions.[45]

These class-based tensions erupted into protest and conflict in the 1860s. On April 30, 1860, a crowd of two thousand provoked by a sudden shortage of bread attacked such visible local symbols of power as the residences of the municipal registrar, a former mayor, and the caretaker of the municipal pawn shop as well as the Convent of Santa Chiara. A few days later, the provincial police arrived in sufficient numbers to put down the uprising. A similar uprising took place six months later, and in subsequent years, brigands frequently operated in the area.[46] However, these open forms of protest ceased for the most part during the rest of the century and only resurfaced in the early twentieth century in the form of working class organizations.[47] With the failure of these protests, when the opportunity arose, a considerable number chose to migrate overseas.

Personal considerations and circumstances also entered into the decision to emigrate, although the data to document this are limited and often fragmentary. Certainly in Agnone, as in other towns of heavy emigration, young males from the working classes were more likely to leave than others. Frequently within a family some would go and others would stay to take care of parents or children. Some left because for various reasons they did not fit in the family or the village—the young woman who (like Ida Sola) did not get along with her stepmother, the illegitimate child, the prostitute, or any other individual whose life was constrained by family or village society. For example, we know that between 4 percent and 5 percent of those who left Agnone were of illegitimate birth.[48]

Yet no matter how much an individual wanted or felt compelled to emigrate, no one could leave without the resources of various kinds that the endeavor required. It cost money to pay for the passage. In addition, the emigrant needed information on where to go and how to get there, assistance in finding a job and a place to live in the potential destination, and further guidance on how to survive and save. It was thus not the very poorest individuals who emigrated but those who had access to some cash and to social networks that could provide the necessary information and support.[49]

Well-established family and kinship networks existed in Agnone. The nature of the Agnonese family assured this. The ideal form was the patrilineal joint family, which over the life course of the family members was obtained in over half of the cases. The individual family members were bound together through mutual obligations and responsibilities that varied as they passed through the life course. These extended family networks facilitated Agnonese emigration by providing a broader base than the nuclear family for raising the passage money and, in combination with the paesani networks, the support system necessary for some members to go abroad. As the number of emigrants abroad increased, they frequently sent money and prepaid tickets back to family members.[50]

Local agents provided part of this support for some emigrants. Apparently the initial emigrants were financed by the family. Beginning in the 1880s, however, a small number (approximately 2 percent) began to use the services of agents. This number increased to 5 percent in the early 1890s and jumped dramatically to two-thirds during the second half of the decade. Then, in the early twentieth century, the number who listed an agent on their passport declined to about one-quarter, and after World War I it dropped to almost nothing.[51]

Evidence I have gathered on a number of specific Agnonesi families, while limited to a few cases, is nonetheless suggestive of which family members emigrated and why they did so. Felice (1842–1916) and Maria Antonia Del Papa (1853–1925) had four children: Maria Domenica (1887–1967), Pietro (1880–1954), Giuseppe (1884–?), and Maria Annunziata (1889–1955). The family had access to a fairly large (though of unknown size) parcel of land on which they raised sheep, hogs, and chickens, and grew grapes, wheat, and tomatoes, as well as hay for the animals. It is not clear how much of this land they owned and how much they worked for others, but, since Felice passed some land to one of his children at his death in 1916, it is obvious that they owned some of it. The oldest daughter, Maria Domenica, received none of the land. The two sons, Pietro and Giuseppe, apparently went to Argentina several times at the turn of the century as seasonal laborers to harvest the wheat crop there. Giuseppe eventually settled in Argentina and the family lost contact with him. In 1904, shortly after he married, Pietro emigrated to the United States, where his wife joined him a few years later. The youngest daughter, Maria Annunziata, remained in Agnone, obtained ownership of all the family land, and left the land to her five sons when she died in 1955.[52]

This information suggests a number of things. The family supported itself through a variety of agricultural activities (animal husbandry, crop cultivation) on land it owned, leased, or share-farmed in some combination. However, the growing family could not, by the turn of the past century, continue to support itself and thus the two sons emigrated. Since the youngest daughter eventually obtained ownership of all the family land, it is likely that the two sons received their share of the family enterprise in the form of resources to emigrate and get started abroad. The oldest daughter, who received no land, probably was compensated in some other form to provide her with a dowry. Thus each of the four children got something, but in different forms, and two of them had to emigrate to enable the family to survive.[53]

The story of the Santorelli family differs in important ways from that of the Del Papas. The eight Santorelli brothers worked as share croppers in Agnone and owned only their homestead. Obviously the family found it increasingly difficult to make ends meet in Agnone and five of them decided to emigrate. Four brothers went to the United States and one to Argentina. It is not clear how they financed the journey and settlement, but the known facts suggest the possibility that even without land they were collectively able to obtain the necessary resources for five of the brothers to emigrate. Or perhaps agents underwrote the initial costs of emigration, since by that time a considerable number of emigrants were using agents.[54]

As these brief family histories indicate, in Agnone as elsewhere it was at the family and individual level that the impact of larger structural forces, local conditions, and personal circumstances were evaluated, and it was at this level that the decision to emigrate was made. Large numbers did decide to emigrate; during each of the four decades preceding World War I, approximately 20 percent of Agnone's inhabitants left for destinations overseas.

❦

The Agnone experience enables us to understand more precisely how the general causes of Italian emigration actually had an impact on the individuals living in the thousands of local communes and made some of them decide to leave. If we include the longer period from the mid-eighteenth to the end of the nineteenth century rather than focusing only on the years immediately surrounding the beginning of mass migration in the 1870s, the Agnone experience fits fairly closely with the description of villages and local areas of high emigration set forth earlier.

During the century and a half preceding mass emigration, Agnone clearly had family-based agriculture, relatively broad distribution of property, a land market, competition among peasants, and some gradations of income and social status. However, the specific configuration of these characteristics changed over time, and by the beginning of mass emigration only some of them were still present. In 1871, land was concentrated in the hands of the galantuomini, with only a limited amount divided into very small plots for family-based farming. Some land was still bought and sold, but the peasants did not have the funds to participate in this market. Subtle gradations of income and status had essentially disappeared.

Although in 1871, land may not have been available to the overwhelming majority of Agnone's peasants and artisans, it had been in the past and therefore could be again in the future. The land market never completely disappeared; land ownership remained an important goal. With land would come security and new status. Emigration was a way to raise the cash to buy it.

By 1900, after several decades of emigration, the situation had begun to change again. Returning emigrants bought land and became involved in politics. These changes in turn initiated a gradual process in which the land market became more active, land became more widely distributed, and peasants competed with each other for land. Artisans and peasants also began to form working-class organizations. All this led to some new gradations of income and social status and to continued high levels of emigration from the town.

Thus Agnone's particular configuration of causes, if considered within the longer historical context of the town's development, fits for the most part within the general patterns of emigration causation. Although the characteristics of high emigration areas and the causes of emigration set forth here are valid as generalizations, each village will inevitably differ to some extent from the norm. The aggregate data provide an overall view of the causes of emigration, but only the individual cases will allow us to understand the variations in the process and the actual circumstances that led to the decision to emigrate.

2

The Italian Migrations to
Buenos Aires and New York City

The largest number of Italians migrating during the four decades preceding World War I went to the United States and Argentina. Of the fourteen million Italians who emigrated between 1876 and 1915, 29 percent of the total went to the United States and 15 percent to Argentina. By the beginning of World War I, the Italian colonies in New York City and Buenos Aires were by far the largest single concentrations of Italians anywhere in the world outside Italy.[1] Thus these particular cases are of special interest to those who seek to understand the Italian migration process at the turn of the century.

A description and comparison of these movements helps put in place some of the most frequently overlooked aspects of the structurally defined stage upon which individuals acted out the drama of migration. After examining the actual move and how it was organized and carried out from the villages of origin to the destinations abroad, I focus on some of the important structural factors that affected the experiences of Italians in Buenos Aires and New York. I review the numbers involved, the pace and concentration of the migrations, the date by which the communities obtained a "critical mass," and the patterns of return. Finally I set forth the demographic and occupational characteristics of the migrants. Together these features define two somewhat structurally distinct movements whose specific dimensions contributed in important ways to the different outcomes of migration to the two cities.

The Move

Although, as we shall see, the migrations to Buenos Aires and New York differed in many respects, the actual process of moving from the various

Italian villages to the two New World cities was very similar. Those who decided to make the trip abroad faced a common set of problems, and they responded to these challenges in comparable ways. The migrants, many of whom were illiterate and had little direct knowledge of the world beyond the village, now had to confront the rules and regulations of governments, the dictates of transportation companies, and the multiple schemes of hustlers seeking to take advantage of them at every step of the way. A successful move always demanded careful preparation, planning, and organization.

Whether they were going to Buenos Aires or New York, the migrants turned primarily to two sources to help them negotiate the move—the informal personal networks of family, kin, and paesani (on which Ida and Oreste Sola relied) and the local agents. The networks and local agents were used because the migrant personally knew those involved and therefore could evaluate their trustworthiness. As Franc Sturino explains, the degree of trust was based on the closeness of blood ties between the two parties and the reputation of other members of the local community. Immediate family were the most trustworthy, followed in descending order by kin, peasants from the same village, and local middle-class intermediaries. The migrant resorted to outsiders for help only when assistance from local sources was unavailable.[2]

Informal personal networks were most important because they provided assistance based on reciprocity among individuals who knew and trusted each other. There were no formal payments for this assistance. Rather it was understood by all that those who received help would return the favor in some form at a later date.

Through these networks the migrant could obtain financial resources, reliable information and advice, assistance before and during the journey, and help finding a place to live and a job at the destination. Close family members were most likely to give financial support; Luigi Sola, for example, paid the fare for his son Oreste to go to Buenos Aires, and Oreste in turn paid the passage for his brother, Abele, to migrate. The two sons both sent money home to support their parents. Ida Sola paid her own fare but nevertheless relied on her cousins to help her make the voyage and her uncle for a place to stay and a job when she first arrived in New York City.

More distant relatives and paesani generally contributed other than financial assistance. Letters from abroad and especially the advice of returned immigrants provided valuable information on every phase of the experience for those contemplating the trip. Veterans who had made the journey before regularly served as guides for the first-timers. Those members of the network living in Buenos Aires and New York frequently helped the new arrivals settle in these cities. Oreste's godfather helped him

adjust to life in Buenos Aires, and Oreste in turn helped subsequent Biellese migrants.[3]

There can be no doubt about the importance of the informal personal
networks to those who made the journey abroad.[4] Once they were established, the networks were an essential source of assistance for the migrants crossing the ocean. The U.S. Immigration Commission reported that
in 1908 and 1909, 98.7 percent of southern Italians and 92.6 percent of
northern Italians who entered the United States joined friends or relatives.[5] Even if the percentages were somewhat smaller in earlier years, the
magnitude of these figures leaves no doubt as to the importance of the informal networks.

In the times and places where informal personal networks were not
sufficiently developed to provide the necessary assistance, those who
wanted to migrate frequently turned to local agents for help. The term
agent covers a variety of individuals who rendered services of various
sorts to migrants for a fee. Included under this rubric were representatives
of steamship companies and foreign governments, labor contractors in
Italy and abroad, and members of the local village petit bourgeoisie. All
of them profited from what Robert Harney has called the "commerce of
migration."[6]

Shipping companies and their agents were important at various times
and in some places. For example, they proved especially important in di-
recting early Italian migration to the Rio de la Plata. Ligurian sailors had
by the mid-nineteenth century established a major presence in Argentine
coastal and river shipping and had created a small colony in the Boca district of Buenos Aires. Subsequently, the Sardinian government and then
the government of a united Italy encouraged Ligurian shipowners to
develop regular routes to Buenos Aires. By the beginning of mass migration, emigrants—often recruited by Ligurian shipowners—followed the
clearly established commercial and personal paths to Buenos Aires. Some
in Italy even thought that Argentina offered the country a chance to create
an informal colony, a "Greater Italy" abroad of Italian emigrants.[7]

But the most important of these agents for those planning and making the trip abroad were local businessmen and professionals who sold
railroad and steamship tickets, wrote letters, lent money, helped obtain
official documents, and did whatever else was necessary to make the voyage possible. They were the direct representatives of the railroads, steamship companies, and labor contractors who were anxious to stimulate emigration. The local intermediaries were most often of a higher social status
than the migrants, but they were part of the community and therefore subject to its customs. These individuals were known and had reputations
regarding their business dealings and thus were considered more trustworthy than outsiders.[8]

In Agnone, for example, there were a number of such local agents, members of the local business class, who were especially active in the "commerce of migration" at the turn of the century. Before 1895, most of the Agnonesi apparently relied on the informal networks of kin and paesani to migrate to Buenos Aires and New York.[9] They generally joined husbands, brothers, and cousins already abroad. Those who had made the trip before served as informal guides and as custodians for young people traveling without their families.[10]

Beginning in the late 1890s, however, more and more migrants used paid agents to arrange the trip. Approximately two-thirds of those who left Agnone between 1897 and 1900 listed an agent on their passport. During the first decade of the new century, this number fluctuated from year to year, but overall declined to about one-third.

The Marinelli family established and ran one of the most respected and successful of these agencies.[11] Allessandro Marinelli was a businessman in Agnone who became involved in helping migrants obtain passports, selling tickets, and organizing groups to make the trip. In 1876, his oldest son, fifteen-year-old Francesco Paulo, migrated to Buenos Aires and was subsequently joined by his brothers Enrico and Vincenzo. Francesco held several different jobs before settling in the Barrio del Carmen in downtown Buenos Aires (shown in Map 10), where many Agnonesi lived and worked, and he opened a business to import Italian foods. He and his brothers gradually expanded the business to include travel services. In 1890, they formally established the Marinelli Agency. Ten years later, Enrico returned to Agnone to take over from their father. The Marinelli Agency, with offices in Agnone and Buenos Aires and business contacts in New York, served many important functions for Agnonese migrants.[12]

The exact combination of help provided by personal networks and paid agents varied according to time, place, and the nature of the agency. In addition, the services of the two sources of help often overlapped. If the migrants could obtain the information and assistance they needed through family and relatives, they would. If not they turned to paesani. Only if there was no other local alternative would they deal directly with outside agents. As time passed, and the informal networks became better established abroad, the migrants were generally able to rely on their families, kin, and paesani to make the trip. However, these networks could become overwhelmed by large numbers—as was the case of the Agnonese networks at the turn of the century, and immigrants would then resort to agents.

With the support of informal networks and paid agents, the migrants organized and carried out the journey. This involved several steps: the preparations in the village before leaving, the trip from the village to the port, the voyage across the ocean, and the arrival in Buenos Aires or New York.[13] The undertaking held great promise, but there were many difficulties to be overcome and each phase demanded careful planning.

The prospective migrant had to do many things in the village before leaving. He needed a passport—for which he required a birth certificate, clearance from the local police, and clarification of his military obligations. The ticket was easy to buy from local agents, but the migrant had to arrange for the cash or a loan to purchase it. In addition, he had to settle his affairs, decide what to take, and organize or join a group with which to travel.

The exact cost of the steerage or third class fare is difficult to determine because it varied considerably according to type and owner of ship, competition, time of year, and whether or not it was an outbound or return trip. Italian government data on steamship fares from 1902 to 1910 do, however, permit us to make some general statements.[14] Although the distance from Genoa or Naples to Buenos Aires was twice as long as to New York, the cost of the trip to Buenos Aires was only slightly higher. Seasonal variation was minor as well. Return passage was cheaper than the outbound trip. And prepaid passages—those paid for in the receiving country—were, with one or two exceptions, somewhat more expensive than those purchased in Italy. Initially it was cheaper to travel from Palermo or Messina than from Genoa or Naples to New York and more expensive to do so to Buenos Aires, but the difference in price from the various Italian ports evened out over the decade. Thus, it would seem, the cost of passage was of marginal significance in the choice between these two destinations.[15]

The organization of a group with which to travel was of the utmost importance. These groups were generally made up of a half dozen or so individuals and often included a veteran who had made the voyage at least once before and therefore could help the novices avoid the pitfalls that awaited them during the trip.[16] Passport records from Agnone and New York ships' manifests indicate in some cases the composition of such groups. Similarly, Agnone newspapers frequently mentioned the names and relationships of individuals planning to travel together to New York or Buenos Aires. These latter groups were larger than a half dozen individuals and obviously included a number of smaller subgroups.

What is most important about the newspaper accounts is that they suggest the planning and preparation involved in migration. A typical account would note that in two weeks sixty-six individuals will be leaving on the *Umberto I* from Genoa for Buenos Aires and will include nineteen men, sixteen women, a man and wife, eight women with children, and two men with children. Long before they were to leave, people knew exactly when they would go and from which port, how they would get from Agnone to Genoa, and the subgroup of a half dozen or so whose members would travel together and rely on each other.[17]

The actual journey from village to destination abroad was the next phase of the trip. The migrants first had to travel from their village to the Italian port of departure. This involved walking or riding to the nearest train station and then taking the train to the port. Once in Genoa, Naples, or Palermo, the migrants had to have their baggage inspected, to be fumigated and vaccinated, to undergo a medical examination, and to go through a final passport check. What made this especially trying was that they were constantly confronted by peddlers, hustlers, and runners from hotels, all of whom sought to take advantage of them. One official guide for Italians going to Argentina urged the migrants to deal only with officials and warned: "Do not trust anyone else who shows interest in you."[18]

The ocean voyage on a steamship took between eighteen and twenty-three days to Buenos Aires and between ten and fourteen days to New York. Steerage and third class conditions varied according to the age, size, and ownership of the particular boat, but at best they were not very good. Crowding, lack of privacy, seasickness, limited washing facilities, poor food, hustlers, and in some cases corrupt officials all contributed to the difficulties. As one of the on-board investigators for the Immigration Commission commented: "When to this very limited space and much filth and stench is added inadequate means of ventilation, the result is almost unendurable. Its harmful effects on health and morals scarcely need be indicated." Another summed up: "The atmosphere was one of general lawlessness and total disrespect for women. . . . During these twelve days in steerage I lived in disorder and in surroundings that offended every sense. . . . The vile language of the men, the screams of the women defending themselves, the crying of children. . . . Everything was dirty, sticky, and disagreeable to touch."[19] And the official guide for Buenos Aires explained that steerage passengers would face essentially identical conditions traveling there. There would be little activity, many people, promiscuous contact, intense heat, lack of drinkable water, dormitories that smelled of urine and vomit, and professional gamblers ready to take money from anyone.[20]

As new, larger, and faster boats were introduced into the Atlantic migration trade, conditions improved somewhat. The descriptions in the preceding paragraph refer to the Old Steerage. The New Steerage was less crowded, but the air was still bad. There was also, for the most part, more space, more privacy, better food, and better treatment.[21] Yet there were very few boats that provided New Steerage. Most migrants therefore had no choice but to endure very difficult conditions. Increased speed—and the resulting shorter duration—was perhaps the most important thing to make the trip more bearable.

Although the veteran members who were part of most groups played an important role helping the first-timers manage all phases of the trip, they were especially useful preparing the others for landing in New York or Buenos Aires. People knew that when they arrived at their destination, they would have to undergo health, customs, and immigration inspections. This meant that they would be examined by doctors and queried by government officials to determine if there was reason to detain them or send them back home. Any number of things could result in such an unthinkable fate—signs of a contagious disease or mental illness, evidence of being a political radical, the possibility that one might become a public charge, and in New York, any indication that one was traveling under a labor contract.[22] Furthermore, although there would be some interpreters available, for many immigrants much of this encounter would be conducted in a foreign language. To prepare for this moment and the anxiety it generated, the new immigrants sought the advice and schooling of the veterans on how to act, what to say, and most important, what not to say.[23]

Despite the uncertainty and tension associated with landing, the overwhelming majority of immigrants to both cities managed to get through the process—and to do so quickly. In New York, 80 percent of the immigrants passed through Ellis Island within five hours and only 2 percent were denied entry. There are no such precise data on Buenos Aires. Nevertheless, all observers indicate that those who entered Argentina were processed quickly and very few were rejected.[24] Thus, of the hundreds of thousands of Italian emigrants who attempted to migrate to Buenos Aires and New York, almost all were able to overcome the difficulties inherent in making the trip and to achieve their first goal of landing in the New World.

How Many Came and When? A Statistical Overview

Although the two migrations were very similar with respect to how individuals actually made the move, they differed significantly in other respects. Italians went to and returned from Buenos Aires and New York in different numbers, at different times, and at different rates. Furthermore, as we shall see in the next section, they came with different backgrounds, skills, experiences, and expectations. Part of the explanation of why the patterns of Italian adjustment differed in the two cities lies in these distinctions.

Very large numbers of Italians migrated to both Argentina and the United States between 1861 and 1914; a little more than two million went

Table 7. Italian immigration to Argentina and the United States, 1861–1920 (by decade)

	To Argentina			To United States		
Period	Total	Italian	%	Total	Italian	%
1861–1870	159,570	113,554	71	2,314,824	11,725	<1
1871–1880	260,885	152,061	58	2,812,191	55,759	2
1881–1890	841,122	493,885	59	5,246,613	307,309	6
1891–1900	648,326	425,693	57	3,687,564	651,893	18
1901–1910	1,764,103	796,190	45	8,795,386	2,135,877	24
1911–1920	1,204,919	347,388	29	5,735,811	1,109,484	19
Total Italians 1861–1914		2,270,525	47		4,051,859	14
Total Italians 1900–1914 as percentage of total Italians 1861–1914			50			77

Sources: República Argentina, Dirección de Inmigración, *Resumen estadística del movimiento migratorio en la República Argentina, 1857–1924* (Buenos Aires, 1925), pp. 4–5. Hereafter cited as Argentina, *Resumen.* U.S. Department of Commerce, Bureau of the Census, *Historical Statistics of the United States: Colonial Times to 1970* (Washington, D.C., 1975), pp. 105–106. Hereafter cited as U.S. *Historical Statistics 1970.*

to Argentina and four million to the United States (Table 7).[25] Before 1890, the large majority chose Argentina as their destination, but after that year, and especially after 1900, the overwhelming number made their way to the United States.

Table 7 shows that although twice as many Italians went to the United States as to Argentina, in the latter case they made up a much larger percentage of total immigration. Before 1900, Italians represented approximately 60 percent of all immigrants to Argentina, and just under half (47 percent) of the total for the entire period (1861–1915). In the United States, on the other hand, Italians represented an average of only 14 percent of total immigration.

The pace of these migrations differed considerably as well. The flow of Italians to Argentina was more evenly spread out over the period. Italian immigration to Argentina had begun earlier and had reached a substantial level at an earlier date than in the United States. As Table 7 illustrates, more than a hundred thousand Italians arrived in Argentina during the 1860s and again during the 1870s. Massive migration began in the 1880s and continued up to World War I. In contrast, few Italians went to the United States before the 1880s. Massive migration began in the 1890s, a decade later than in Argentina, and continued up to World War I.

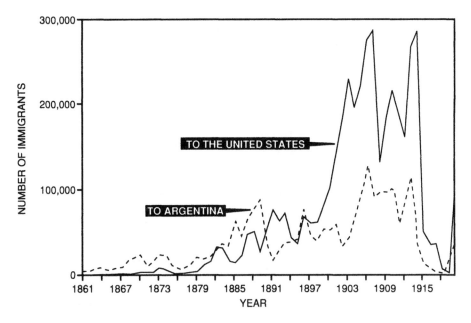

Figure 4. Italian immigration to Argentina and the United States, 1861–1920

Most important, more than three-quarters of all Italians who arrived in the United States during this fifty-five-year period did so during the fifteen years from 1900 through 1914. In Argentina, only half the Italians arrived during the same period. The large number of Italians who came to the United States in such a short period strained the ability of existing immigrant and host society institutions to absorb them effectively. In Argentina, on the other hand, the more gradual pace of migration made it easier for both immigrant and host society institutions to help the Italians adjust.[26]

When we shift from decade to yearly data, we can better see the significant fluctuations in the flow to both countries and the often rapid yearly changes in choice of destinations (Figure 4). These fluctuations were caused by a number of factors at work in both the sending and receiving countries. In Argentina, the number of Italian immigrants increased during the 1860s, reaching a peak of 23,000 in 1870. The next year a severe yellow fever epidemic struck the country and the number of immigrants dropped to 8,170. Immigration grew to nearly 27,000 in 1873 but dropped off dramatically with the depression of 1875–1877. The economic recovery of the late 1870s continued throughout the 1880s and Italian immigration rose fairly steadily to reach a new peak of 88,647 by 1889.

The years 1890 and 1891 were important in the history of Argentine immigration. The country was engulfed in a major depression caused by overspeculation during the preceding decade. Immigrants responded accordingly; for the first time more Italians left Argentina than arrived. In addition, 1890 was the first year during which there were more Italians going to both the United States and Brazil than to Argentina. Italian immigration resumed with the Argentine economic recovery of the mid-1890s, and from then until 1914 expanded dramatically. Only in 1911 was there a net outflow of Italians, caused by the Italian government's temporary suspension of emigration to Argentina.[27]

The annual figures for the United States show similar dramatic fluctuations. Italian immigration reached an initial peak of 8,757 in 1873 and declined sharply during the next few years, during which the country experienced a recession. New highs were reached in 1882–1883, 1887–1888, 1891–1993, 1903, and 1906–1907, each one followed by a significant decline related to downturns in the economy. Only in 1908, however, was there a net outflow of Italians from the United States.

The annual figures also permit us to see more clearly the changes in choice of destination. Most Italians went to Argentina before 1890 and to the United States afterward. But the yearly figures show that Argentina had recovered sufficiently by 1895 and 1896 to once more take the lead in attracting Italian immigrants. This, however, was only a temporary situation. As soon as the United States recovered from its depression of 1893–1897, it moved into a fifteen-year period of growth that attracted more than a hundred thousand Italians a year—approximately three times as many Italians as went to Argentina.[28] Yet even during this period, in which the United States received by far the largest overall number of Italians, there is evidence of fluctuation regarding choice of destination. In 1904, 1908, and 1912, net immigration of Italians was greater in Argentina.

The passport data from Agnone show more precisely the often dramatic shifts in choice of destination at the village level (Figure 2). There were major yearly fluctuations in the respective movements of Agnonesi to the ports of Buenos Aires and New York. Between 1885 and 1889—a period of considerable economic expansion in Argentina—the majority of emigrants went to Buenos Aires. But with the four-year Argentine economic crisis that began in 1890, there was a shift of destination to New York. The abruptness of this shift is demonstrated by the fact that in 1889, more than two-thirds (70 percent) of the 200 passports were issued for Buenos Aires and a little fewer than one-third (30 percent) for New York. The next year, however, the figures were reversed; fewer than one-third (27 percent) of the 201 passports listed Buenos Aires as the destination and more than two-thirds (72 percent) put down New York. Then, with the economic downturn of the U.S. economy during the mid-1890s, there was a shift of emigration back to Buenos Aires. Subsequently, from 1898 to 1914, at least two-thirds of the Agnonesi went to New York, indicating the consistent relative strength of the U.S. labor market compared to that of Argentina during this period.

These data demonstrate that potential emigrants in Agnone and other villages had rapid access to accurate information about the changing conditions in potential alternative destinations abroad, and suggest that they often made their decisions based on this information. Although ties to existing social networks also affected the decision to emigrate in important ways, knowledge of the changing opportunities in various destinations was perhaps even more influential. Thus, if at any given time conditions were better in Buenos Aires, that is where most went. If, on the other hand, they were better in New York, the majority went there. If conditions were not particularly good in either destination, many stayed home to wait for another year.

In both countries, the Italians concentrated primarily in cities and in a few geographical areas, a fact that gave them the potential strength of numbers as they confronted the host societies and a base from which to build institutions. Ninety percent settled in U.S. cities and 70 percent in Argentine cities. Furthermore, in the United States more than three-quarters lived in a core area of seven adjacent states stretching from Massachusetts through Connecticut, New York, New Jersey, Pennsylvania, Ohio, and Illinois, while in Argentina more than nine out of ten lived in a core area including the city of Buenos Aires and the adjacent provinces of Buenos Aires, Santa Fe, Entre Rios, and Cordoba (Tables 8 and 9).

Most striking was the concentration of Italians in the leading ports and economic centers of Buenos Aires and New York City. Approximately one of every four Italians in the United States lived in New York City, compared to one of every three in Argentina who resided in Buenos Aires. Tables 8 and 9 indicate that although by the early years of the twentieth century the absolute number of Italians in both cities was essentially the same, these numbers represented significant differences in proportional terms. Both cities included high percentages of foreigners (approximately 40 percent in New York and 50 percent in Buenos Aires), but the percentage of Italians in the Buenos Aires population was much greater throughout (20 percent or more) than it was in New York (7 percent or less).

Not only were the Italians in Argentina more concentrated in Buenos Aires and the percentage of Italians in the Buenos Aires population much greater than that in New York, but the date at which the Buenos Aires Italian community attained a critical mass was considerably earlier. The absolute size of the group was important because a certain minimal size—a *critical mass* of roughly ten thousand individuals—was necessary for the establishment and effective development of a range of formal immigrant

Table 8. Italians as part of New York City population, 1860–1920

Year	Total population	Foreign born (%)	Italian born (Number) (%)	Italians NYC U.S.[a] (%)	Italians Core U.S.[b] (%)
1860	813,669	47	1,464 (0.1)	13	
1870	942,292	44	2,794 (0.3)	16	
1880	1,206,999	40	12,223 (1.0)	28	
1890	1,515,301	42	39,951 (2.6)	22	
1900[c]	3,437,202	37	145,433 (4.2)	30	77
1910	4,766,833	41	340,765 (7.1)	25	77
1920	5,620,048	36	390,832 (7.0)	24	79

[a] New York City Italians as a percentage of all U.S. Italians.
[b] Italians in the core area as a percentage of all U.S. Italians. The core area referred to here includes the states of Massachusetts, Connecticut, New York, New Jersey, Pennsylvania, Ohio, and Illinois.
[c] In 1898, New York City—which until that time had comprised only Manhattan and part of the Bronx—incorporated its neighboring counties to assume its current boundaries: Manhattan, Brooklyn (King's County), Queens (Queen's County), Richmond (Staten Island), and the Bronx. Thus, the pre- and post-1900 figures refer to different geographical boundaries of the city.
Sources: U.S. Department of Commerce, Bureau of the Census, Thirteenth Census of the United States Taken in the Year 1910 (Washington, D.C., 1913), vol. 1, p. 804. Hereafter cited as U.S. Census 1910. U.S. Department of Commerce, Bureau of the Census, Fourteenth Census of the United States Taken in the Year 1920 (Washington, D.C., 1922), vol. 2, pp. 698, 928. Hereafter cited as U.S. Census 1920.

institutions.[29] The earlier attainment of this critical mass thus made it possible for an immigrant group to create substantial community organizations at an earlier date.

The Buenos Aires Italian community had reached ten thousand individuals by the mid-1850s, whereas in New York the community did not attain this size until a quarter of a century later—in the late 1870s (as shown in Tables 8 and 9). By 1869, the Buenos Aires community was forty-four thousand strong—and again twenty-five years passed before the New York community was that large. Only after the early 1890s did the difference in absolute size between the two communities gradually diminish. They were approximately equal at about 230,000 to 240,000 by 1904 or 1905, and subsequently the New York community grew more rapidly than that in Buenos Aires. Thus the formal immigrant institution-building process was able to begin considerably earlier in Buenos Aires.

The figures on return migration complete the statistical overview (Table 10). They are important because they can reflect different strategies (short-versus long-term) and goals (settle in the new location versus return home) among the migrants to different destinations at different times. Although

Table 9. Italians as part of Buenos Aires population, 1855–1936

Year	Total population	Foreign born (%)	Italian born (Number)	(%)	Italians BA Argentine[a] (%)	Italians Core Argentine[b] (%)
1855	91,395	42	10,279	(11)		
1869	177,787	52	44,000	(25)		
1887	433,375	53	138,000	(32)		
1895	663,854	52	182,000	(27)	37	96
1904	950,891	45	228,000	(24)		
1909	1,231,698	46	277,000	(23)		
1914	1,576,597	50	312,000	(20)	34	93
1936	2,415,142	36	299,000	(12)		

[a]Buenos Aires Italians as a percentage of Argentine Italians.
[b]Core Italians as a percentage of Argentine Italians. The core area referred to here includes the city of Buenos Aires and the central provinces of Buenos Aires, Santa Fe, Entre Rios, and Cordoba.
Sources: República Argentina, Segundo censo de la República Argentina, mayo 10 de 1895 (Buenos Aires, 1898), 3 vols., 2, p. 163. Hereafter cited as Argentina, Censo 1895. República Argentina, Tercer censo nacional. Levantado el 1 de junio de 1914 (Buenos Aires, 1916–1919), 10 vols., 2, pp. 148, 219, 237, 248, 278, 395–396. Hereafter cited as Argentina, Censo 1914.

Table 10. Italian return migration from Argentina and the United States, 1861–1910

Year	Argentina (%)	United States (%)
1861–1870		56.3
1871–1880	75.5	
1881–1890	26.0	43.4[a]
1891–1900	52.7	47.6[a]
1901–1910	43.3	52.6[a]

[a]These are estimates of M. Livi-Bacci.
Sources: Argentina, Resumen, p. 8; Massimo Livi-Bacci, L'Immigrazione e l'assimilazione degli Italiani negli Stati Uniti (Milan, 1961), pp. 7–8, 34–35; U.S. Historical Statistics 1970, pp. 105–106; Robert F. Foerster, The Italian Emigration of Our Times (New York, 1919), chap. 2 (especially p. 30); and Istituto Centrale di Statistica, Sommario di statistiche storiche italiane, 1861–1955 (Rome, 1958), p. 67.

approximately half the Italians returned home from both countries, slightly more did so from the United States than from Argentina.[30] During the 1860s and 1870s, before mass immigration, the return rate from Argentina was high, 56.3 percent and 75.5 percent respectively. Unfortunately, we have no data on the United States to compare this with, but there were fewer Italians to begin with in the United States. During the 1880s, the beginning of mass Italian migration to Argentina, the return rate was only 26 percent. The percentage rose to 52.7 for the next decade (the 1890s) and from 1901 to 1910 dropped back to a relatively low 43.2.

Hard data for return migration from the United States do not exist before 1908, but the Italian demographer Massimo Livi-Bacci has carefully developed estimates that enable us to make the comparison. The return rate of Italians was considerably higher from the United States than it was from Argentina during the 1880s, somewhat lower during the 1890s, and higher during the critical decade and a half of the most massive migration before World War I. For the period 1881–1910, Livi-Bacci estimates that 50.6 percent of the Italians who entered the United States returned home, compared to official Argentine data showing that 41.6 percent of the Italians there returned.[31] Taking the period as a whole (1861 to 1913), the return rate from the United States was approximately 5 percentage points higher than it was from Argentina (52 percent compared to 47 percent).

Although there is no specific data on Italian return migration from the cities of New York or Buenos Aires, there is evidence to suggest that the difference in these rates at the national level was somewhat greater with regard to the two cities. The *golondrinas*—the Italians who like swallows went every year to Argentina to harvest the crops—numbered at least twenty thousand annually during the decade or so prior to World War I. Because the golondrinas went to rural destinations and not to Buenos Aires, we can reduce somewhat the percentage of Italians who repatriated from the capital city. The same cannot be done for New York City Italians. As many temporary migrants went to New York as to other parts of the United States. Thus I think it is reasonable to estimate that approximately half the Italians in New York returned home whereas perhaps only 40 percent of those in Buenos Aires did so.[32]

This statistical overview sets forth some of the significant differences in the migration of Italians to Buenos Aires and New York in the decades preceding World War I. Although during the first half of the period most went to Argentina and later most went to the United States, there was considerable fluctuation in numbers and choice of destination between the two at all times. Of greatest importance, the flow to Buenos Aires was more evenly distributed throughout the period, the relative concentration was much greater, the Italian community reached a critical mass a quarter of a century earlier, and fewer individuals returned home.

Who Came? The Demographic and
Occupational Profiles of the Migrants

The Italians who went to Buenos Aires and New York can be character-ized by a number of attributes, experiences, and expectations that further delineate the differences between these two migrations. Among the factors for which we have some data are origins in Italy, sex, age, literacy, occupa-tional and organizational skills, and expectations regarding the perma-nency of the move. Taken together they illustrate that, as a group, the Ital-ians who went to Buenos Aires were not the same as those who went to New York.

The Italians who went to Argentina and the United States came from practically all parts of Italy, but in different proportions. The resulting pat-terns of origin were therefore quite distinct. Italians in Argentina were much more likely to have come from the North of Italy than those in the United States, especially in the pre-1900 decades. Throughout the whole period, 42 percent of those who went to Argentina were from the North, 46 percent from the South, and 12 percent from the Center. In contrast, 80 percent of those who went to the United States were southerners.[33]

Within these broad areas, there were additional differences in the re-spective migrations (Table 11). In Argentina, over half (51.6 percent) came from Piedmont, Lombardy, Calabria, and Sicily, and four other regions (Marche, Campania, Veneto, and Abruzzi/Molise) each contributed at least 5 percent of the total. On the other hand, just three southern regions (Sicily, Campania, Abruzzi/Molise) accounted for 58 percent of the mi-gration to the United States, and only two other regions, both from the South, produced more than 5 percent of the total. The origins of the mi-grants to the United States were considerably more concentrated not only in the South but also within fewer regional areas of Italy.

For the Italian populations in both countries, origins shifted over time. Between 1876 and 1885, the Piedmont and Lombardy were by far the most important sources of migration to Argentina. Four decades later, however, Sicily and Calabria along with the Piedmont were the leading regions of origin. For the United States, Campania and Abruzzi/Molise consistently provided at least one-third of the migrants, whereas Sicily tripled the percentage of migrants it contributed from the first to the last decade of the period. In both cases, one or two regions consistently provided large

Table 11. Italian emigration to Argentina and the United States, 1876–1915: Leading regions of origin by decade (regions with 5 percent or more of total emigration)

	Argentina				
Regions	Total for period (%)	1876–1885 (%)	1886–1895 (%)	1896–1905 (%)	1906–1915 (%)
Piedmont	16.9	21.1	22.3	16.5	15.3
Calabria	13.2	7.3	10.9	15.3	12.9
Sicily	11.1	.2	.0	7.4	19.5
Lombardy	10.4	19.8	14.9	.5	8.7
Marche	8.2	3.0	4.0	11.2	9.4
Campania	7.5	4.9	10.0	10.9	5.1
Veneto	7.2	10.3	11.4	3.6	3.9
Abruzzi/Molise	6.4	.4	5.3	8.5	.6
N of emigrants	(2,192,000)	(188,800)	(415,600)	(490,800)	(718,700)

	United States[a]				
Regions	Total for period (%)	1876–1885 (%)	1886–1895 (%)	1896–1905 (%)	1906–1915 (%)
Sicily	23.4	7.7	16.6	23.2	23.8
Campania	21.8	32.0	28.8	26.3	19.0
Abruzzi/Molise	13.0	12.2	14.7	14.1	12.3
Calabria	10.5	7.9	11.8	11.1	10.2
Puglia	5.8	.8	1.7	4.0	6.6
N of emigrants	(5,077,000)	(89,200)	(384,600)	(1,329,300)	(2,502,400)

[a] These figures include emigration to Canada as well as the United States, but Canadian emigration was less than 3.5 percent of the totals.

Source: Annuario statistico, pp. 149–150. This table is based on Italian figures because they indicate region of origin within Italy. Argentine figures on Italian immigration for the period are 13 percent higher than the Italian figures; U.S. figures are 8 percent lower.

numbers of migrants, while the contribution of several other regions varied substantially over time.

Data on sex, age, and literacy provide additional indicators of the distinctiveness of the group of migrants to Argentina and Buenos Aires on the one hand, and to the United States and New York on the other (Tables 12 and 13). The Italian migration to both countries and both cities was primarily male, between fourteen and fifty years of age, and more than 50 percent literate. Yet the differences between the Italians in the two

Table 12. Age of Italian-born residents of Buenos Aires, the United States, and New York City

Year	Buenos Aires		
	Age 1–15 (%)	Age 16–50 (%)	Age 51+ (%)
1869	14	79	7
1895	11	77	12
1914	7	72	21

Year	United States		
	Age 1–13 (%)	Age 14–44 (%)	Age 45+ (%)
1881–90	15	69	16
1891–00	17	71	12
1901–10	11	84	5
1911–20	14	77	9

	New York City		
1920	6	70	24

Sources: (Buenos Aires) Argentina, Censo 1895, 2, pp. 28–29; Argentina, Censo 1914, 3, pp. 12–13. (United States and New York) U.S. Immigration Commission, Reports, 2, pp. 88–91; Niles Carpenter, Immigrants and Their Children (New York, 1969), pp. 414–417; Ira Rosenwaike, Population History of New York City (Syracuse, N.Y., 1972), p. 195; Livi-Bacci, L'immigrazione e l'assimilazione degli Italiani negli Stati Uniti, pp. 14–15.

cities, though not in all cases very great, are important for an understanding of their subsequent adjustment. The masculinity indexes for the two countries were considerably skewed, but less so in Argentina than in the United States; in the former there was approximately one Italian woman for every two Italian men, whereas in the latter, there was one Italian woman for every three Italian men.

While the country figures show many more men than women, in the two cities the balance was more nearly equal. Between the mid-1890s and World War I, there were approximately one and a half Italian men for every Italian woman in Buenos Aires compared to one and a third Italian men for every Italian woman in New York.[34]

These data alone, however, do not provide an accurate picture. The Buenos Aires Italian community had reached a critical mass a quarter of a century before that of New York. As a result, a sizeable second generation born of Italian parents emerged at an earlier date.[35] The combination of the Italian-born and second-generation Italians undoubtedly made the

Table 13. Sex ratio of Italian-born residents of Buenos Aires, New York City, Argentina, and the United States (number of males/100 females)

Year	Buenos Aires	Year	New York City
1887	195		
1895	159	1900	134[a]
1904	148	1905	117[a]
1914	160	1920	121

	Argentina		United States
1880–84	218	1880–90	376
1890–94	187	1891–00	335
1900–04	292	1901–10	335
1910–14	292	1911–20	223

[a]Sample data.

Sources: (Buenos Aires and Argentina) Buenos Aires, *Censo 1887*, 2, p. 36; Argentina, *Censo 1895*, 1, p. 643, and 2, pp. 6, 14; Buenos Aires, *Censo 1904*, pp. 23–25; Argentina, *Censo 1914*, 2, pp. 3–21, 397; Maria Cristina Cacopardo and José Luis Moreno, "Características regionales, demográficas y ocupacionales de la inmigración italiana a la Argentina (1880–1930)," in Fernando Devoto and Gianfausto Rosoli, eds., *La inmigración italiana en la Argentina* (Buenos Aires, 1985), p. 72. (New York and United States) Baily sample of Elizabeth Street, 1900; Gutman sample of Greenwich Village, 1905; U.S. *Census 1920*, 2, p. 548; Massimo Livi-Bacci, *L'immigrazione e l'assimilazione degli Italiana negli Stati Uniti* (Milan, 1961), pp. 14–15; U.S. Immigration Commission, *Reports*, 3, pp. 47, 84, 88ff.

sex ratios closer to parity in Buenos Aires than in New York. Thus, at the turn of the century, the masculinity index of Italians and those of Italian descent in both cities was closer to balanced than it had been earlier, but more nearly so in Buenos Aires.

Because there are no data that provide the age of Italians in New York City before 1920, we will with caution rely primarily on the figures on the age of Italians in the United States to compare with those on Buenos Aires (Table 12). Clearly the large majority of Italians in both situations was of working age (fourteen to fifty). What differs are the percentages of younger and older people in each population. The data on the Italian community of Buenos Aires show that between 1894 and 1914, there was a very slight decline in the sixteen- to fifty-year-old population, a significant decline in the population under sixteen, and a substantial increase in those over fifty. Together with the sex ratio, this reflects the longer duration and permanence of the community in Buenos Aires, the growth of a substantial second generation of children born of Italian parents, and the aging of the Italian-born population.

The U.S. data show a significant increase in the working-age population (fourteen to forty-four years) between 1880 and 1910, a decline in the young population (under fourteen years), and a major decline in the older population (over forty-four years). However, this pattern began to reverse itself during the second decade of the century. The New York City data for 1920 indicate that by that year the percentage of the working-age population was indeed declining, and that the percentage of the older population had increased dramatically to one out of every four Italians.

There is no way without additional data to know the exact age structure of the Italian population in New York City at an earlier date, but it is possible on the basis of the data in Table 12 to draw several reasonable conclusions. First, because of the large immigration to the city, there was most certainly an increase in the working-age Italian population of New York City and a decline in the over-forty-five population during the decades preceding World War I. This suggests the return to Italy of many in the older population cohort and their replacement by other generations of working-age individuals. Before World War I, the Italian-born population in New York was younger and less permanent than its counterpart in Buenos Aires. Second, this trend was reversed by 1920. As of that year we know that the Italian working-age population of New York City had diminished to 70 percent while the older population had increased to 24 percent.[36] This reflects the decision on the part of the older population to remain in New York during World War I and its aftermath. Clearly the Buenos Aires Italian migration was more permanent at an earlier date than that of New York.

A similar problem of data exists with regard to literacy; we have limited United States and New York City information to compare with the census figures in Buenos Aires. But here too what we have suggests an important difference between the migrations to the two cities. As early as 1887, nearly two-thirds of Italian males in Buenos Aires were literate, and over the next twenty-seven years, this figure increased to 70 percent. Italian women were consistently less literate than Italian men, and the difference between them increased slightly during the period.[37]

The U.S. Immigration Commission found that 53 percent of all Italians aged fourteen and older who arrived in the United States between 1899 and 1910 were literate. The commission data on several sample blocks in New York City show that 56.4 percent of southern Italian male heads of households and 32.8 percent of the female heads of households were literate. These data suggest that Italians in Buenos Aires and especially Italian males were somewhat more literate than those in New York City. In the years preceding World War I, 65 percent of the Buenos Aires Italians were literate compared to no more than 55 percent of those in New York.[38]

In terms of occupations, most of those in the active population were agricultural workers or unskilled laborers (Table 14). Seventy-five percent

Table 14. Occupations of Italian emigrants to the United States and Argentina (active population)

Occupations	United States 1899–1910 (%)	Argentina[a] 1876–1895 (%)	Argentina[a] 1896–1914 (%)	Argentina[a] 1876–1914 (%)
Agriculture	31.8	80.0	52.7	62.8
Day labor	43.4	10.9	18.9	15.9
Artisans	15.6	4.1	14.5	10.7
Commerce	—[b]	1.0	3.3	2.5
Professional	.5	1.2	1.1	1.2
Others	8.7	2.8	9.5	6.9
Total	100	100	100	100
N =	(1,768,590)	(660,780)	(137,870)	(1,798,650)

[a]These Argentine figures include all Italian emigrants twelve years of age or older. Since the United States figures include all Italian emigrants, the comparison can only be approximate.
[b]Those who came to the United States with commercial occupations are included under "Others."
Sources: U.S. Immigration Commission, *Reports*, 3, pp. 95–96, 131–135; Fernando Devoto, "Participación y conflictos en las sociedades italianas de socorros mutuos," in Devoto and Rosoli, *La inmigración italiana*, p. 147; República Argentina, Ministerio del Interior, Comisión General de Inmigración, *Memoria 1878*; República Argentina, Ministerio de Agricultura, Dirección General de Inmigración, *Memorias de 1897, 1909, 1913, 1914–1915*. See also Chapter 4, and Maria Cristina Cacopardo and José Luis Moreno, "Características regionales, demográficas y ocupacionales de la inmigración italiana a la Argentina (1880–1930)," in Fernando Devoto and Gianfausto Rosoli, eds., *La inmigración italiana en la Argentina* (Buenos Aires, 1985), p. 75.

of those who went to the United States between 1899 and 1910 and 63 percent of those who went to Argentina between 1876 and 1914 were in these categories (farmers or day laborers). Just under 16 percent of those who went to the United States and 11 percent of those who went to Argentina were artisans or skilled workers.

Sample data on New York and Buenos Aires Italians at the turn of the past century, however, indicate a different occupational structure.[39] According to these data, higher proportions of skilled and white-collar workers were in Buenos Aires (69 percent versus 42 percent), and a significantly larger percentage of unskilled laborers were in New York (42 percent versus 16 percent). In addition, because of the particular historical development of Italy, a greater number of those from the economically more developed North were skilled and literate than were those from the South. The northerners also had more experience with organizations such as labor unions and mutual aid societies.[40] Because Argentina and especially Buenos Aires received more Italians from the North, the resulting Italian population was somewhat more skilled and literate. The two cities attracted different occupational groups; the active Italian population of Buenos Aires included more skilled blue-collar workers and more white-collar workers than the active Italian population of New York did.[41]

The attitudes regarding expectations of permanency among the members of the two migrations are also important to an understanding of the subsequent patterns of adjustment, but the issue is especially difficult to document. The problem is that there is no direct evidence that enables us to know for certain the intentions of most emigrants as they left their villages in Italy. Letters such as those of the Sola family and interviews when possible provide some indication of intentions for a few. But we have such evidence for almost none of the migrants who went to Buenos Aires and New York at the turn of the past century.

What we do have is evidence on behavior, which at least for some is an indication of intentions. My analysis of this evidence leads me to argue that the Italians who went to Buenos Aires had greater expectations of settling there permanently than had those who went to New York. First of all, a greater percentage of the Italians who went to Buenos Aires before World War I did in fact settle there permanently. In addition, the sex and age composition of the Buenos Aires Italian population indicates greater permanency: there were more women and families, more older people, and more first- and second-generation children. And finally, as we will discuss at length in Chapter 4, most Italians in Buenos Aires adopted a long-term strategy of investing more of their savings there rather than sending them back home to Italy as those in New York tended to do.

❧

The data set forth in this chapter describe many of the important characteristics and attributes that defined the Italian migrations to Buenos Aires and New York City during the half century preceding World War I. What becomes clear is that although large numbers of Italians went to both countries and cities, as groups they differed in some important ways. The migration to Buenos Aires was more evenly distributed over the fifty years. The Italian community in Buenos Aires was more concentrated and obtained a critical mass at a much earlier date. Its members, who came to a much greater extent from the North of Italy, had higher occupational skills and literacy rates, and more experience with economic, social, and political organizations. And to the extent that we are able to determine, they had greater expectations of remaining permanently abroad when they left Italy. What is certain is that their return rate was somewhat lower than that of those from New York.

One must be careful not to overstate the case. Some of the differences were not very great and the evidence to document them is not always complete. But taken together, these characteristics describe two somewhat distinct Italian migrations to Buenos Aires and New York City. The comparison of the individual characteristics of the Italians who went to Buenos Aires and the structural characteristics of the Buenos Aires Italian migration with those of the New York migration bring into focus differences that are important for understanding the patterns of adjustment I will discuss in subsequent chapters.

The result of these two great migrations was that the emigrants had at last arrived in the New World and in the process had become Italian immigrants in Argentina and the United States. Now they were ready to find out firsthand what these two cities and societies were like.

3

What the Immigrants Found

Buenos Aires and New York City were the lands of promise for the Italian immigrants who had just arrived. In his first letter home to his parents, Oreste Sola articulated this feeling. "This city is very beautiful," he wrote. "There is an enormous amount of luxury. . . . There are some buildings beautiful beyond words . . . with ornamentation the equal of which you won't find in all of Turin. . . . The piazza Victoria (Plaza de Mayo) is also beautiful, where all around on two sides there are only banks. On another side is the government building where the president of the Argentine Republic resides. . . . There is also the railway station of the south, which is something colossal. With workshops, offices, and the station itself it will cover one million square meters. Now they are at work on a government building for Congress."[1]

The receiving societies provided the opportunities that attracted the Italians, and they also further defined the structural parameters within which the migrants would subsequently seek to make a better life. A number of attributes of these societies—the economies, the social structures, the political systems, the cultures, the Italian communities at the beginning of mass migration, and the perceptions of Italians—affected in varying degrees why Italian migrants chose Buenos Aires or New York as their destination and what happened to them after they arrived. On the one hand, these characteristics created the opportunities and possibilities available to the immigrants. On the other hand, they constituted limitations and boundaries. What the Italians encountered in these two societies provides an important part of the explanation of how they adjusted in their respective New World contexts.

This chapter begins with a introductory overview of the most salient features of the receiving societies, many of which will be discussed at greater length in subsequent chapters. The rest of the chapter explores in some detail the evolution of the important host society perceptions of the Italian immigrants as reflected primarily in government policy and legislation, first in Argentina and then in the United States.

Setting the Stage: The Nature of the Host Societies

Of the various characteristics that defined the nature of the host societies, none was more important than the economy. The economy generated the jobs and opportunities available to the immigrants and thus became the major determining factor for their chances of achieving their goals. Although the economies of both Buenos Aires and New York grew rapidly during this period, they were unlike in important respects and offered different opportunities to the newcomers.

Both Argentina and the United States in the second half of the nineteenth century were large and underpopulated countries with an abundance of fertile land and other natural resources.[2] Their economies grew in response to increased internal and foreign demands. Local labor was insufficient and immigration therefore became an essential part of continued economic growth.

By almost any measure the growth of these countries during this period was exceptional (Table 15). Between 1870 and World War I, the United States doubled its population and acres under cultivation, tripled its imports, quadrupled its exports, and quintupled its railroad mileage and foreign investments. Argentina, starting from a much smaller base in all categories, grew even more dramatically. It quadrupled its population and foreign investment, and increased its exports 17 times, its acres under cultivation 43 times, its railroad mileage 45 times, and its imports a remarkable 72 times!

These economies, however, differed. Argentine economic growth throughout was based primarily on the export of rural, land-intensive production destined for the expanding markets in the United Kingdom and other European countries. At first, the main exports were wool and hides. As time passed, frozen beef and wheat, corn, and linseed became increasingly important. By 1910 Argentina was one of the leading world exporters of these commodities. Manufacturing, except that related primarily to the processing of agrarian and livestock products, was a relatively minor part of the economy. Furthermore, the little industry that did not process agricultural and livestock products was dependent on imported raw materials and machinery. Finally, service emerged as the dominant sector of the economy, representing more than half the total gross domestic product (GDP) in 1910.[3]

Table 15. Indicators of Argentine and U.S. economic growth, 1870–1910

Indicator[a]	Argentina		United States	
Square miles (1910)	1,139,000		3,628,000	
Population (in millions)	1869	1.8	1870	39.9
	1895	4.0	1890	63.1
	1914	8.0	1910	92.4
Population/square mile (1910)	6.14		25.75	
Railroad miles	1871	460	1870	52,922
	1896	9,000	1890	167,191
	1915	21,000	1910	249,992
Acres under cultivation	1872	1.4	1870	189
(in millions)	1890	7.4	1890	248
	1914	60.1	1910	347
Exports[b] (Argentina = gold pesos in millions	1871	30	1870	451
U.S. = dollars in millions)	1890	101	1890	910
	1913	519	1910	1,919
Imports[b] (Argentina = gold pesos in millions	1870	49	1870	860
U.S. = dollars in millions)	1890	142	1890	1,109
	1910	3,520	1910	2,114
Foreign Investment	1892	0.8	1869	1.5
(U.S. dollars in millions)	1900	1.1	1897	3.4
	1913	3.1	1914	7.2

[a]Many of the economic data for this period are tentative and sources frequently differ. The figures in this table are presented to indicate the general magnitude of growth in the two countries and to facilitate a comparison between them.

[b]During much of this period the gold dollar was approximately equivalent to the gold peso, and there were five gold pesos per pound sterling.

Sources: Roberto Cortés Conde, "Problema del crecimiento industrial (1870–1914)," in Torcuato Di Tella et al., Argentina, sociedad de masas (Buenos Aires, 1966); Roberto Cortés Conde, "El 'boom' argentino: una oportunidad desperdiciada?" in Torcuato Di Tella et al., Los fragmentos del poder (Buenos Aires, 1969); Roberto Cortés Conde, The First Stages of Modernization in Spanish America (New York, 1974), chap. 6; U.S. Department of Commerce and Labor, Bureau of Statistics, Statistical Abstract of the United States, 1911 (Washington, D.C., 1912); U.S. Department of Commerce, Bureau of the Census, Historical Statistics of the United States: Colonial Times to 1957 (Washington, D.C., 1960); U.S. Historical Statistics 1970.

Agricultural products were and continued to be an important part of the U.S. economy, but from the beginning of the period the industrial and manufacturing sector was much larger and diversified than its counterpart in Argentina. Moreover, manufacturing increased dramatically thereafter. In 1860, much manufacturing was done by small-scale local industry, and in this period the agricultural sector produced greater income. By 1900, however, the United States was primarily a manufacturing nation, and had become one of the leading industrial nations in the world. In 1914, U.S. industrial production was more than twice that of the United Kingdom.

Although the dramatic growth in both economies attracted large numbers of immigrants, the economic opportunities available in the two countries were different. These differences were especially true in the commercial, financial, and manufacturing centers of Buenos Aires and New York City, as I discuss in some detail in the following chapter. The point to be emphasized here is that the primary unfulfilled needs for labor in the mature industrial urban economy of the United States were for semiskilled factory workers (such as Ida Sola's husband, Eugenio, who worked in the textile mills) and unskilled day laborers who would do the hard physical work no one else wanted to do. The artisans of a half century before were rapidly being replaced by machines; there was little unfulfilled demand in white-collar occupations.[4] The Argentine economy, driven overwhelmingly by agricultural exports, was not at the same level of development as that of the United States. There was a need for unskilled and semiskilled labor, but there was also a significant demand for skilled artisans, white-collar workers, and even some professionals. The special nature of Argentine manufacturing industries prior to World War I helps explain this. One sector of industry was made up of a few large-scale establishments—meat-packing plants, tanneries, sugar refineries, and textile mills—that used the most modern equipment and technology and large numbers of employees to produce goods for export. The other sector of industry consisted of construction and of hundreds of small workshops run with more traditional equipment and technology and a handful of employees. The latter sector's purpose was to satisfy the local demand for housing and new public buildings and for consumer goods such as shoes, bread, bricks, glass, and furniture.[5]

The highly developed agricultural, manufacturing, and financial economy of the United States and the less developed and primarily agricultural economy of Argentina (with its small manufacturing sector and large service sector) were an important part of the context that the Italians entered when they came to New York City and Buenos Aires at the turn of the century. The needs and the opportunities for labor were substantially different, and thus frequently attracted immigrants with different skills and training.

Although the economies were most important, other characteristics of the host societies affected the experiences of the Italian immigrants as well. The social structures reflected to a considerable extent the differences in the economies. In 1870, the social structures of the United States—and especially those of the large urban areas of the Northeast such as New York City—approximated a three-class model (upper, middle, and lower) with various subdivisions within these broader categories. The distinctions among them were based on a combination of occupation, wealth, education, ancestry, and self-perception.[6]

In Argentina, on the other hand, there were only two broad social groups, the small elite (the *gente decente*) constituting less than 5 percent of the population, and the non-elites (the *gente de pueblo*), the remaining 95 percent. Here the distinctions between the two groups were based primarily on ancestry and family, but clearly occupation, education, wealth, and self-perception reflected family status and ancestry. There were subdivisions within these broad categories just as there were in the United States, especially within the large non-elite category.[7]

The major difference between the two social structures was that Argentina had no middle class to speak of at the time. Those groups—small retailers and manufacturers, clerical workers, salespeople, and corporate and governmental bureaucrats—which in a more developed economy would constitute a middle class were not numerous, economically influential, or self-conscious enough to be a significant social presence in their own right. The dramatic growth of the Argentine economy and population in the decades after 1870 rapidly expanded the size and influence of these "middle sectors," especially in Buenos Aires and other urban areas.[8] Gino Germani found that by 1895 approximately one-third of the population of Buenos Aires and a quarter of the population of Argentina was among the "middle layers."[9] James Scobie also acknowledged the enormous growth of these "middle groups" of owners of commercial and manufacturing establishments and of other white-collar occupations, although he placed them within the non-elite *gente de pueblo* rather than defining them as a separate social category.[10]

The point is that all agree the immigrants created these middle groups as well as the urban proletariat of Buenos Aires. The elites focused on politics, law, and running their *estancias* (ranches), leaving commerce and manufacturing to the immigrants. The native lower classes were neither numerous enough nor sufficiently well educated nor in command of adequate resources to provide much competition to either the emerging immigrant middle sectors or proletariat of Buenos Aires. The growth of the economy created enormous opportunities for the Italian and other immigrants in commerce and industry, and the newcomers took advantage of the situation. Immigrants completely dominated commerce and industry at the turn of the century, as both owners and workers.[11]

In New York, the middle class, which already clearly existed in 1870, evolved during the following decades in response to the maturing industrial and commercial economy. In addition to the small retailers and producers of the earlier period, the middle class increasingly included corporate and governmental bureaucrats, engineers, accountants, public relations personnel, and salespeople, among others. David Hammack shows that in both 1890 and 1900, the middle and lower white-collar class in New York constituted nearly 30 percent of the active population.[12]

What is significant in comparison with Buenos Aires is that in New York native whites and older immigrants from northern Europe dominated these occupations and this class. When the Italians arrived at the turn of the century, most of these jobs were already taken. As a result, the Italians who went to Buenos Aires had greater economic and social opportunities than those in New York.[13]

The two political systems also differed significantly. In the United States the vote was an important potential resource for all adult men. For Italian immigrants entering New York, it was at least possible, if at first not very likely, to participate in electoral politics, whereas in Argentina this was for the most part not the case.

In the decades before World War I, middle- and lower-class New Yorkers were able to influence political decisions through the vote, petitions, demonstrations and strikes, and political organizations such as Tammany Hall. During the last quarter of the nineteenth century, Tammany Hall developed into a broadly based and effective political organization led by professional politicians who sought the votes of naturalized immigrants as well as native Americans. To compete with Tammany Hall and the Democratic Party, the Republicans also sought the votes of immigrants. In a system such as this, the Italians, like each new group before them, learned to work with the Irish and other immigrant groups and with long-established Americans in order to gain influence and power.[14]

The Argentine political system, from the fall of dictator Juan Manuel de Rosas in 1852 to the passage of an effective electoral reform law in 1912, was based on very limited participation of the adult male population. It consisted of a number of powerful groups, generally though not exclusively aligned in political parties and supported by their respective newspapers, competing within a restricted arena to influence the decisions of the national, provincial, and city governments. There were no urban political machines like Tammany Hall that could serve as the basis for mass political parties and as instruments of political control. Elections were a mechanism to provide the peaceful rotation of offices among the members of the recognized competing political groups, not a way for all adult male citizens to express their views and influence governmental actions. If challenged by the popular sectors, the political elites resorted to fraud—and, when deemed necessary, force—to maintain control and achieve their goals. Immigrant groups did find nonelectoral ways to exert some influence within the political system, but direct electoral participation was for the most part impossible. It is therefore not surprising that less than 2 percent of the foreigners became naturalized citizens and thus eligible to seek the opportunity to vote.[15]

In addition, there were some similarities as well as differences in the two host cultural environments. The overwhelming majority of Italian migrants originally came from rural areas and therefore both in New York City and Buenos Aires they had to adjust to new urban cultures. Although in both places they faced the common challenge of living in large cities, they nevertheless confronted distinct national cultures.

In Argentina, the Italians encountered a variant of a Latin culture not too dissimilar from their own. Catholicism was the religion of most Argentines. The Spanish language was more similar to most Italian dialects than English was. And many traditional Argentine values and customs, such as those relating to the family and the relationship of nuclear and extended family members to each other, were familiar to the Italian immigrants.[16]

The Italians in New York confronted significantly greater cultural differences than their counterparts in Buenos Aires. The English language was difficult to learn. Protestantism was the major religion, and even the growing Catholic Church was dominated by Irish hostile to the way the Italians practiced the religion. As a result, the Italians had problems with the language, were subjected to religious prejudice, and had greater difficulty understanding the values of the host society.[17] Clearly the cultural encounter of the Italian immigrants was more traumatic in New York than in Buenos Aires.

Furthermore, there were important differences between the Italian communities in the two cities. At the beginning of the mass phase of migration, Italians had a significantly stronger numerical position in Buenos Aires than in New York; in 1887 they represented 32 percent of the Buenos Aires population whereas in 1890 they made up only 2.6 percent of New York City's inhabitants. In addition, Italians in Buenos Aires were one of just two immigrant groups (Italians and Spaniards) that combined accounted for approximately 80 percent of total migration to the country. In New York, Italians were but one of five groups—Russians, Germans, Irish, Austrians, and Italians—that made up a similar percentage of all foreign-born residents. And finally, the Italian community in Buenos Aires at the beginning of mass migration had vastly larger and wealthier institutions than that of New York.[18]

Argentine Policies and Attitudes

In addition to the economy, the social and political structures, the culture, and the existing Italian communities, Italian immigrants had to contend with the crucial factor of host society perceptions and attitudes. The host societies' attitudes toward Italians affected adjustment in a variety of ways. Where there were widespread nativism and negative attitudes, they led to both formal and informal discrimination that limited the opportunities of the immigrants. Where attitudes were predominantly positive, the immigrants were better able to take advantage of the possibilities that existed in the new environment and therefore to adjust more easily.

As important as host society attitudes were, it is difficult to describe and measure them accurately. The views and feelings of the various members and groups of the host societies frequently differed and sometimes contradicted each other. Ideas also changed over time both in substance and the intensity with which they were felt and expressed. And in this pre-opinion-poll period it is hard to measure what people thought.

In this analysis I use government policy and efforts to encourage or restrict immigration as a major indicator of host society attitudes. In addition, I examine the opinions of some political thinkers, social commentators, writers, and newspaper and magazine editors. Together they give me a reasonable basis from which to delineate the evolving contours of host society attitudes toward the Italians.

Although a broad and enduring consensus on the necessity of attracting large numbers of immigrants to Argentina emerged among the elites during the nineteenth century, there was considerable debate both over the methods and specific objectives of population policies and over the impact of immigration on the country.[19] This consensus did sustain the largest immigration in proportion to its base population of any country in the world, but this must not obscure the fact that there were those who had reservations about how the immigrants were integrating into Argentine society. Some nativist sentiment gradually developed as the numbers of immigrants increased. When it did, it was frequently directed toward the Italians, who constituted by far the largest single group of immigrants. Nevertheless, the consensus that the country needed immigrants remained sufficiently intact so that the government did not restrict immigration in any significant way until the 1930s.

The elites who ruled Argentina during the second half of the nineteenth century generally viewed immigration as an essential element in the construction of a modern and "civilized" country. Because some of these leaders believed that the Spanish colonial heritage and the native population of the interior—symbolized by the *gauchos* (cowboys) and the *caudillos* (personalistic leaders)—were causes of the country's backward condition, they looked to the "civilized" nations of northern Europe and to the United States as their models of development and the best source of immigrants. Material progress, education, and immigration constituted the core of their program. European immigrants were crucial for two reasons. First, the immigrants would provide the necessary labor, skills, and knowledge to initiate and sustain economic development. And second, some among the elites thought the immigrants, intermarrying with the natives, would in time create a more progressive population.[20]

The pro-immigration philosophy was embodied in the Constitution of

1853, the document that guided the country's development in subsequent years. Article 25 opened the country to all persons who would contribute to the betterment of society. "The Federal Government," it stated unambiguously, "shall promote European immigration. It shall have no power to restrict, to limit, or to burden with taxes or charges of any kind the entrance into the Republic of any foreigner coming to it to cultivate its soil, to improve its industries, and to introduce and teach the sciences and arts." Furthermore, Article 20 gave foreigners the same civil rights as Argentine citizens. Foreigners, it proclaimed, "may engage in industry, commerce, and professions; possess, buy and sell real estate; navigate the rivers and coasts; exercise their religion freely; and bequeath and marry according to law. They are not obliged to acquire citizenship, nor to pay extraordinary or forced taxes. They may obtain nationalization after two years of continuous residence in the Confederation; but the authorities may shorten this period as a favor to the petitioner who alleges and proves his services to the Republic."[21]

Gradually, and often through trial and error, the government formulated specific policies toward immigrants.[22] It appointed the first Argentine immigration agent in Europe in 1864 and by 1871 there were seventeen agents, three of whom were in southern Europe. In addition, the government experimented with a policy of providing immigrants free room and board, placement assistance, and free railroad tickets to destinations in the interior. And finally, it sought, though unsuccessfully, to pass legislation to make land available for the immigrants to buy.[23]

The Law of Immigration and Colonization (1876) was designed to systematize and consolidate previous legislation and to further the efforts to enlist European immigrants in the exploitation of Argentina's vast uncultivated areas.[24] In addition, it provided for the appointment of more immigration agents, the continuation of the employment office, five days of free food and lodging in Buenos Aires and similar support in the provincial capitals, and free transportation to the destination within Argentina. In what its authors thought would be the Argentine equivalent of the U.S. Homestead Act, the law also established a central Office of Lands and Colonies and provided for a uniform system of surveying the national territories, dividing this land into small units, and colonizing it. Finally, the 1876 law created a National Department of Immigration as well as Provincial Immigration Commissions. It provided for a bureaucracy with the capacity to coordinate and oversee recruiting and placement efforts, to study the impact of population policy, and to recommend legislation.

Immigration increased dramatically in the 1880s as a result of the conquest of the desert and the economic boom of the decade, but the Law of Immigration and Colonization failed in its primary goals of attracting a significant number of northern Europeans or of settling large numbers in the underpopulated rural areas. More than half of the immigrants who arrived in Argentina during the last quarter of the nineteenth century were Italians, and nearly half of the total settled in the cities.[25]

Although the Argentine elites had sought to attract large numbers of northern Europeans, most within this group also viewed northern Italians in positive terms. This was so for a number of reasons. The Italians were part of the larger immigration deemed essential to transform the country; they contributed significantly to the development of Argentina as able farmers, skillful artisans, and industrious workers, and as much-needed businessmen and professionals. In addition, there was an ideological affinity between the local Italian elites and some within the Argentine ruling elites; both sought to construct new nations on similar liberal, anticlerical principles. Giuseppe Garibaldi and other Italians, for example, had fought in the Rio de la Plata against the caudillos of the interior. The tiny Argentine elite may have looked down on Italian immigrants as their social inferiors, but they still saw them as superior to the rest of the native population. In this sense the Italians were perceived as bearers of civilization.[26]

As immigration reached mass proportions in the late 1870s and the 1880s, some Argentines began to voice concerns about the impact of immigration on the country. The Italians as the largest immigrant group were often the specific object of these nativist sentiments. José Hernández and Eduardo Gutiérrez sympathetically portrayed the struggle of the vanishing Argentine gaucho against the advance of modern civilization and the influx of immigrants. Eugenio Cambaceres more stridently and directly attacked what he saw as the detrimental influence of the Italians on the Argentine elites.[27]

Domingo F. Sarmiento, president of Argentina from 1868 through 1874 and formerly one of the strongest proponents of immigration, had major concerns regarding the integration of the immigrants and especially of the Italians. He was increasingly troubled by those groups that remained apart from Argentine society and by the institutions he believed to be obstacles to integration. The main object of his attack was the schools of the large and wealthy Italian mutual aid societies, but he also criticized the Italian government for extending citizenship to children born in Argentina of Italian parents and the Italian-language press for promoting loyalty to Italy rather than Argentina.[28] Buenos Aires "is a city without citizens," he warned shortly before his death in 1888. "The most industrious and progressive of its 400,000 inhabitants are strangers. . . . Growing and expanding, we shall build, if we have not already built, a Tower of Babel in America."[29]

Some within the Department of Immigration also expressed concern about foreigners who did not become naturalized citizens nor integrate into Argentine society. In 1881 the Commissioner of Immigration noted that while Argentina granted all the benefits of citizenship to non-natural-ized resident foreigners, the United States demanded formal citizenship in return for such benefits. Argentina, he believed, should follow an immi-gration policy similar to that of the United States. Specifically, Argentina should perfect a system to attract northern Europeans, to avoid homoge-neous concentrations of any one group, and to encourage integration.[30]

The critical issue was how to implement these ideas. Some favored var-ious types of direct government sponsorship, government subsidies, or government contracting with private agents. After several years of debate, in 1887 the legislature adopted its first subsidized passage law (*Ley de Pasajes Subsidiarios*). The Commissioner of Immigration noted that even though the Italians had made important contributions to the development and progress of the country, "other nationalities of the Old World . . . would also contribute in an important way to our progress as has been demonstrated by experience." The subsidized passage law, he argued, would allow the country to attract other nationalities.[31]

From 1888 to 1890 Argentina experimented with subsidized immigra-tion. During this three-year period, 426,830 immigrants entered the coun-try from overseas, of whom 134,000 (31 percent) came on state-subsidized passages. The subsidies increased the total number of immigrants, but were only marginally successful in attracting northern Europeans. Al-though 15 percent of the subsidized immigrants were northern Europeans (Belgian, English, Dutch, German) and less than 5 percent Italian, 45 per-cent were Spanish and 34 percent French. And of the total number of im-migrants (subsidized and spontaneous combined) who entered Argentina from overseas during these three years, nearly half (48 percent) were Ital-ian and a quarter (26 percent) were Spanish.

In addition, the quality of the subsidized immigrants was widely deemed to be poor. As Juan Alsina, who would become Commissioner of Immigration in 1889, summed up, the subsidized immigrants came "with-out preparation, without resources of their own, without will or determi-nation . . . they have not been able to serve the progress of the Republic, they have not been able to develop by themselves, due to lack of qualifi-cations. Two-thirds of the subsidized immigrants have not been good."[32]

Alsina, who served as Commissioner of Immigration from 1889 to 1898 and as Director of Immigration from 1898 to 1912, opposed subsidized im-migration. Instead, he strongly supported spontaneous immigration and argued that natural attractions—political stability, economic opportunity, existing ties of family and friends—would increase immigration of the right sort and be most beneficial to the country.[33]

Argentina's natural attractions did, as Alsina predicted, produce ex-ceptionally large numbers of immigrants—mostly southern Italians and Spaniards—in the two decades preceding World War I. This success, how-

ever, brought with it some unanticipated and, for the elites, unwanted results. As was the case in the 1880s, too many of the immigrants were attracted to Buenos Aires and other cities and not enough to the underpopulated rural areas. Furthermore, the urban immigrants initiated efforts to
bring about social change. Middle-class immigrants sought greater participation in political and economic decision making as well as greater social
recognition. In addition, the immigrant workers began to organize to defend their interests.[34]

The problem for the elites was to devise strategies to contain these
challenges without undermining economic growth and prosperity. They
resorted to a combination of formal and informal mechanisms to achieve
their objectives: electoral fraud, physical force and repression when necessary, mockery, and social discrimination, among others. "Without re-
nouncing its progressive ideals," José Luis Romero explained, "the oli-
garchy attempted to evade the process of social reform at work in the
country. Henceforth, the intent of the elite was to draw a line between politics and economics, emphasizing reform in the latter field while restrain-
ing any attempt to change the former."[35]

The pragmatic elite's major concern was the growing social conflict in
the cities. Along with immigration and rapid urbanization came congestion, slums, crime, alcoholism, prostitution, and disease. The working
class, influenced by the doctrines of anarchism, syndicalism, and social-
ism, began to organize and to demand better living and working conditions. A series of strikes erupted during the 1890s and many more during
the first decade of the twentieth century.

The response of the elites was to claim that working-class protest was
the result of foreign agitators who were unnecessarily disturbing the peace
and the orderly development of Argentina. Nativism and nationalism
proved useful in justifying anti-labor legislation and activity. In 1902, the
government passed the first legislation restricting immigration since
the Constitution of 1853 had made the pro-immigration policy the law of
the land. The Law of Residence authorized the chief executive to deny entry to foreigners condemned by foreign criminal courts and to deport
foreigners whose conduct "compromised the national security or dis-
turbed the public order." A similar law, the 1910 Law of Social Defense,
singled out the anarchists as foreign social agitators and prohibited them
from entering the country, holding public meetings, or expounding their
doctrines.[36]

Although these laws did restrict some immigration, the emphasis was
on selectivity, not restriction. Only a few hundred anarchists or labor leaders were actually deported under these laws, and even fewer were denied
admittance to the country. The laws targeted leaders of social protest who
were immigrants rather than targeting immigration per se. Indeed, immi-

grant employers also attacked the working-class leaders of social protest. The government used anti-immigrant sentiments to justify repression of the workers, but this was not meant to stop immigration or restrict it in any but a most specifically limited way.[37]

Along with the government's attacks on social protest and foreign working-class leaders, some among the elites sought more effective ways to integrate immigrants into Argentine society.[38] Many believed that the public schools provided the best means to incorporate the immigrants. In 1908, the nativist José Maria Ramos Mejia became president of the National Council of Education and from this position greatly strengthened "nationalistic education." In a manner reminiscent of Sarmiento some thirty years before, the council under Ramos Mejia's leadership attacked the private schools of the Italians and other nationalities and the widespread use of foreign teachers in the public schools. More positively, the council sought to emphasize the teaching of Argentine history, geography, and civics in both public and private schools, and to do so in such a way as to stimulate the students' loyalty to Argentina.[39]

Perhaps most important, the main thrust of the educational reforms was to incorporate the immigrants, not to restrict them. As Halperin-Donghi has observed, new ideas regarding the integration of the immigrant replaced those of the preceding generation; the Argentine nation would be constructed by including its Hispanic gaucho tradition, not by rejecting it. The immigrants would no longer replace the native Argentines. Rather they would join with the Argentines in an emerging new society.[40]

I need to address one final question in this analysis of attitudes: Did working-class Argentines view Italians in the same terms as did the elites? One of the difficulties in approaching the question is that foreigners constituted such a large percentage of the urban working-class population that it is hard to distinguish the thoughts of natives from those of the immigrants. Throughout this period, 80 percent of the active population of Buenos Aires was foreign born or children of the foreign born. The immigrants were not anti-immigration. Nativism did not develop among this group.

There were some manifestations of nativism among the popular sectors in the rural areas of the country, but they were sporadic and isolated incidents, not part of a systematic and organized pattern of hostility to the immigrants.[41] There were of course some native working-class Argentines in Buenos Aires and the other cities of the country, even if they were a small minority. They obviously competed with the generally more skilled immigrant workers for jobs, especially during periods of high unemployment. It is thus reasonable to assume that there were some feelings of hostility toward immigrants among members of the small native urban working class.[42]

While there is little direct evidence to document the extent and intensity of nativism among the native urban working class, some of the themes and characters presented in the popular theater of Buenos Aires indicate such anti-immigrant sentiment did exist among this group. Many presentations dealt with the immigrant-native and especially Italian-native encounter in various circumstances.[43]

One of the most significant illustrations of this encounter was the emergence and sustained popularity of the Cocoliche character. Cocoliche, an improvised creation first presented in the circus ring during the mid-1880s, was a partially socialized "Italian gaucho" who spoke broken Spanish and did not know how to dress or act his new role properly. The Cocoliche character and his mixed Italian-Spanish speech immediately became popular. Subsequently the term *Cocoliche* was widely used to refer to any personification of a comic Italian character and to designate bad taste in general.[44]

Watching and laughing at the Cocoliche character was a way for Argentines to mock the foreignness of the Italians and to affirm native traditions. But, as Cara-Walker convincingly argues, Cocoliche was also a means by which non-elite Argentines and immigrants could "negotiate their differences through ritual and symbolic confrontations onstage, in carnival activities, in print, and ultimately in everyday life."[45] As with the patriotic education of the elites, the popular nativism expressed by the Cocoliche phenomenon was inclusive of the immigrant.

In evaluating the significance of this popular nativism we must keep several things in mind. First, nativism among the urban working classes was very limited. Second, there was no institutional support for nativism among working-class groups. Organized labor consisted predominantly of immigrant workers and leaders. Third, both the overwhelming numbers and the skill levels of the foreigners made it impossible for native Argentine workers to exclude them or discriminate against them. And fourth, the non-elite nativism expressed in the presentations of the popular theater of Buenos Aires emphasized negotiation of differences between the working-class foreigners and natives, not exclusion.

World War I temporarily stopped the massive overseas migration of the preceding decade, but the resumption of immigration after the war combined with the revival of labor strikes and protests rekindled the elites' fears of foreign agitators and the efforts on the part of some to restrict immigration. In February 1919, a congressman introduced a bill to restrict immigration, but it never became law. In July 1922 another congressman proposed legislation that was the first effort to exclude immigrants on the basis of nationality or race. It denied entrance to Negroes, Chinese, and Indians as well as to those who were mentally, morally, or physically inadequate. This bill likewise failed to become law.[46] In 1924, Carlos Nestor Maciel published his anti-Italian polemic, *La italianización de la Argentina,* in which he attacked southern Italians as inferior and urged the adoption of restrictions similar to those just enacted in the United States.[47] Yet until the worldwide Depression of the 1930s, the Argentine government never placed general legal restrictions on immigration. The idea of immigrants as civilizers and transformers remained stronger throughout this period than the various concerns provoked by immigration.

U.S. Policies and Attitudes

Immigration was not at first of major concern to those who established the new North American nation, but nativism soon became a significant if cyclical phenomenon within the society. The Constitution of the United States, in striking contrast with the Argentine Constitution of 1853, included only one short paragraph on immigration, and that paragraph simply prohibited Congress from interfering with migration or the importation of people being accepted by the thirteen colonies. Yet an intense nativism, based on fears of foreign radicalism and internal dissent, emerged during the 1790s and culminated in the Alien and Sedition Acts of 1798. Similarly, with the influx of increasingly larger numbers of immigrants during the 1830s, 1840s, and 1850s, and the intensification of the sectional conflicts that led to the Civil War, nativism resurged in the 1850s. And nativism resurfaced a number of times during the decades leading up to the national restriction laws of the 1920s.[48]

Although the states rather than the federal government regulated immigration for the first century of the country's existence, in 1876 the U.S. Supreme Court declared this unconstitutional. As a result, the federal government became increasingly involved in immigration. In 1882, Congress—at the urging of New York State—passed the first national immigration law, which established a head tax of $.50 to defray the expenses of regulating and caring for immigrants, and which excluded foreign convicts (except those convicted of political crimes), lunatics, idiots, and those likely to become public charges. The governors of the states were to determine who would administer the law locally.[49]

In 1882, Congress also enacted the Chinese Exclusion Act and in so doing for the first time prohibited the entry of a group of foreigners on the basis of nationality. Anti-Chinese sentiments had developed gradually in California over the preceding two decades, but it was not until 1876, when both the Republican and Democratic parties supported restrictions on the Chinese, that the issue became a national one. A congressional inquiry led to the law of 1882, which suspended the admission of all Chinese labor for ten years and prohibited Chinese from becoming naturalized citizens.

When this law expired, it was extended for additional ten-year periods both in 1892 and 1902.[50]

Working-class nativism, which was of limited significance in Argentina, emerged in the United States during this period. At the first public general meeting of the Knights of Labor in 1878, the members upheld their internationalist principles and—despite pressure to do so—did not include in their preamble any restrictionist statement on the importation of foreigners. Under the leadership of Clarence T. Powderly, the Knights opened their doors to all producers, native and foreign alike, and grew rapidly. Yet the increasing numbers of foreign workers who were competing for jobs with members of the Knights made the latter question their previous stand. In 1883 they first supported the idea of legislation forbidding the importation of contract labor. Their efforts helped bring about the alien contract labor law of 1885 (the Foran Act), which made it unlawful "in any way to assist or encourage the importation of aliens under contract to work in the United States."[51]

Thus, during the 1880s, immigration restriction legislation was confined to the Chinese Exclusion Act and the Contract Labor Law, but, as John Higham pointed out, "For the first time in American history . . . a sizeable section of opinion made the momentous and troubling discovery that the United States confronted the social ills of the Old World."[52] Although nativists of the 1880s ignored for the time being the growing number of "new immigrants," they were able to create widespread sentiment that something should be done to limit immigration.[53]

By the 1890s, the Italians and other "new immigrants" who were arriving in ever larger numbers became the focus of anti-foreign sentiments. In December 1889, both the Senate and the House created committees on immigration. The investigations carried out by these committees indicated that immigrant agents and steamship companies were frequently violating existing laws. This revelation provided the impetus for new legislation. Although the resulting Immigration Law of 1891 codified existing legislation, provided for better inspection, and established full federal control over the regulation of immigration, it focused on the selection of individuals coming to the country rather than the restriction of all immigration.[54]

The multiyear depression that began in 1893 stimulated the growth of anti-immigration organizations and increased pressure on the two major parties to restrict immigration. The American Protective Association (APA), established in Clinton, Iowa, in 1887, expanded from seventy thousand members in 1893 to perhaps as many as two and a half million members in 1896. It supported public as opposed to parochial schools, immigration restriction, and slowing down the process of naturalization. The main concern of the organization's leaders, however, was Catholicism, and, as the Immigration Commission *Reports* noted, the APA lobbying efforts were "directed against immigrants only as they were Catholics."[55]

The Immigration Restriction League of Boston, however, proved much more successful in mobilizing sentiments for restriction and in working with congressmen and senators to enact legislation. It focused exclusively on the adoption of a literacy test to screen immigrants, and thereby to keep out what it considered to be undesirable foreign elements. The league joined forces with longtime restrictionist Henry Cabot Lodge, who in December 1895 introduced in the Senate a literacy bill drafted by the league. The Lodge Bill was passed after some modification by both houses of Congress in February 1897, but President Grover Cleveland vetoed it. Of greatest significance for us, the Literacy Bill, as the Immigration Commission noted, was "especially aimed at southern and eastern European immigrants."[56] The bill failed to become law at this time, but it represented the beginning of a campaign that culminated in success two decades later.[57]

Although the return of prosperity after 1897 diminished the general fears of immigration, the restrictionists continued their efforts and gradually gained additional supporters among the working class. The American Federation of Labor (AFL), representing the elite skilled workers, became an increasingly important voice for restriction. Beginning in 1904, when organized business attacked the growing labor movement and put a stop to labor's recent limited success, the AFL turned to restriction with new vigor. It not only supported the continued exclusion of Asians and increasing restriction against the "new immigrants" (whom its leaders viewed as inferior, strikebreakers, and "pliant dupes of the employers"), it also concentrated its efforts on obtaining the passage of a literacy bill. From this time on, the popular nativists joined forces with the patrician nativists to bring about general restriction.[58]

Until the twentieth century, most Americans assumed that their society would automatically assimilate immigrants. At the turn of the century, however, many began to question this assumption and therefore to support new approaches to handle the large number of immigrants. The positive response was an effort to Americanize the newcomers through education and stricter requirements for naturalization. The negative side was restriction.[59]

Between 1903 and 1910, Congress passed several laws that systematized the process of naturalization and gradually raised the barriers against entering immigrants. It twice increased the head tax, substituted the word *alien* for *immigrant*, extended the definition of alien to cover cabin class as well as steerage passengers, added anarchists to the list of those to be excluded, and made the steamship companies fully responsible if they brought inadmissible immigrants to the country. Perhaps most important, it created the Immigration Commission whose *Reports* would have a major impact on subsequent immigration legislation.[60]

The Immigration Commission, organized on April 22, 1907, under the chairmanship of Senator William P. Dillingham, produced a massive forty-one-volume set of reports that provided the justification for the restrictive legislation of the next two decades. Although the study was based in part on extensive and useful field investigations and on original data from the census of 1900, the bias against the "new immigration" with which the commission approached its task can clearly be seen throughout it.[61] Thus the *Reports* presented the old immigration as one of permanent settlers from the "most progressive sections of Europe," who dispersed throughout the country, brought their families, became citizens and learned English, and contributed to "the prosperity and well-being of our people." In sharp contrast, it portrayed the new immigration as single males who were temporary unskilled laborers from the "less progressive and advanced countries of Europe," "far less intelligent than the old," who concentrated in cities, and who took "a considerable part of their earnings out of the country."[62] In short, the new immigrants were stereotyped and depicted as inferior to the old immigrants in virtually every respect and as nationalities that should be restricted from entering the United States in the future.

On the basis of the *Reports*, the commission urged that the quantity and quality of future immigration permit effective assimilation even if this meant slowing down the pace of industrial expansion. Specifically the commission recommended the deportation of criminals, those who became a public charge, and other undesirable aliens; the strict enforcement of all laws that gave preference to relatives of immigrants already in the country; various means "to protect the immigrant against exploitation, to discourage sending savings abroad, to encourage permanent residence and naturalization, and to secure better distribution of alien immigrants throughout the country"; the continued exclusion of Asians; and the restriction of unskilled labor. And finally, the commission reviewed different methods of restricting immigration—a literacy test, a national quota system, the exclusion of unskilled workers without families, the limitation of arrivals at any port, a fixed minimal money requirement for entry, and an increase in the head tax. The commission concluded that the literacy test was "the most feasible single method of restricting undesirable immigration."[63]

Although many of the popular and patrician nativist groups had testified before the Immigration Commission and had their sentiments reflected in the Immigration Commission *Reports*, the impact of the *Reports* was heightened by additional factors. At about the same time the eugenics movement, based on the idea of selective breeding to improve the population, began to catch the imagination of the general public. By 1906, the leaders of the Immigration Restriction League were pointing out that restriction was a way to influence positively the future racial composition of the population. Since they believed in the superiority of the Anglo-Saxon race, they sought to limit the entrance of what they considered to be inferior Italians and other southern and eastern Europeans. Between 1910 and 1914, popular magazines such as the *Saturday Evening Post* began to publish articles supporting the ideas of the new pseudoscience of heredity and attacking the new immigrants. In the process, these ideas gained greater currency among the general public. Perhaps the most influential American publicist of the movement was Madison Grant, a New York patrician and founder of the New York Zoological Society, who strongly believed that the current mixture of races in America would destroy the country's racial purity and its cultural values. Grant's major work, *The Passing of the Great Race*, seemed to sum up the fears of nativists and others, and to provide further justification for the exclusion of the new immigrants.[64]

Nativism reached a new intensity by the beginning of World War I. The economic recession of 1913 and 1914 heightened the fears of native workers that immigrants threatened their jobs. Catholicism became an issue in the 1914 New York gubernatorial election, and in other places and situations as well. Violent conflicts broke out between native-born Americans and immigrants in various areas of the country. Confidence in the ability of the United States to assimilate the immigrants faded further.[65]

In New York City, hostility toward the Italians reached a peak during the half dozen or so years before World War I. Increasingly, most Americans stereotyped Italians as ignorant, volatile, "priest ridden," dishonest, dirty—as criminals and strikebreakers who clustered in urban ghettos and who refused to assimilate. Sicilians were specially singled out for scorn as swarthy mafiosi, as transients who came and went at the beck and call of agents and padroni.[66]

The anti-Italian sentiment was also manifested in local discriminatory legislation designed to exclude Italians from certain jobs. Although in 1894 and 1895, New York State temporarily excluded all aliens from jobs on state and local public works projects, it was some years later before a body of exclusionary legislation was enacted into law. In 1909, New York made citizenship a requirement for becoming a lawyer or a detective. In 1914, the New York State Supreme Court upheld a law excluding aliens from employment on public works, a law that was aimed at Italians working on the subways. The following year citizenship was made a requirement for obtaining licenses as public cartmen, junk dealers, and peddlers, all occupations that included many Italians.[67]

A number of factors in addition to the large and sudden influx of Italians into New York City contributed to the development of these views. Italian workers, whose provincialism, self-reliance, transiency, and lack of urban skills made them difficult to organize, initially antagonized American labor by frequently acting as strikebreakers. In addition, the small minority of northern Italians in New York, unlike their proportionately much larger counterpart in Buenos Aires, sought to distance themselves from the southern masses upon whom they too looked down, and thus contributed to the negative perception of the Italians.[68]

In 1900, King Umberto of Italy was assassinated by an Italian anarchist who had lived in Paterson, New Jersey. A few years later the term *Black Hand* became commonplace in New York City as newspapers sensationalized every incident of crime and violence involving Italians. And in 1909, Detective Joseph Petrosino of the Italian Squad of the New York City Police was assassinated in Palermo while investigating the links between Sicilian criminal elements and the Italian community in New York.[69]

Given the hostility toward the Italians and the other new immigrants, it is perhaps surprising that the national restrictionist movement failed for so long to achieve its goal. The first literacy bill had been introduced into Congress in 1895 and was vetoed by President Cleveland in 1897. Despite growing support, subsequent attempts to enact the legislation into law also failed. Between 1910 and 1917, Congress passed and sent to the president three literacy bills, all of which were vetoed.[70]

A literacy bill was finally enacted into law in 1917 over the veto of President Wilson, but it did not produce the results desired by its proponents. A twentieth-century low of only 110,000 immigrants entered the country in 1918, but by 1920 the number had rebounded to 430,000, and in 1921 jumped to 805,000. The Red Scare of 1919 along with the resumption of large-scale migration rekindled the fears of many native Americans. The *Saturday Evening Post,* the *Atlantic Monthly,* and other leading popular magazines demanded more effective restriction. As a result, Congress turned to another method of restriction suggested by the Immigration Commission in 1910, a national quota system.[71]

The Johnson Act of 1921 and the National Quota Act of 1924 translated the quota system into law. The former bill limited the number of yearly entrants to 3 percent of the foreign born of that nationality at the time of the census of 1910 and the total number of Europeans to 350,000. The Quota Act of 1924 further restricted immigration. It provided that only 2 percent of the foreign born of each nationality in the country at the time of the 1890 census would be admitted annually and the total of Europeans would be reduced to 150,000.[72]

The 1924 bill was written specifically to produce a drastic reduction in the number of Italians and other new immigrants who could enter the country. The shift in the 1924 legislation from the 1910 to the 1890 census as the base for determining the nationality quotas produced the results desired by the nativists; a major reduction of southern and eastern European immigration and a sizeable though relatively much smaller reduction among northwestern Europeans and Germans. The annual quota for Italians, for example, was reduced from 40,000 to 3,660, whereas the quota for Germans was reduced only from 69,330 to 45,700.[73] The message was clear. Italians and the other southern and eastern European immigrants were not wanted in the United States.

❦

What emerges from this review of the two host societies is that the Italians in Buenos Aires encountered a more favorable situation in which to attempt to realize their goals than did their counterparts in New York City. The economy, the social structure, the culture, and the size and development of the Italian community were more advantageous to the Italians in Buenos Aires. Only the political system was a comparative plus for the Italians in New York, and even in this case they were slow to capitalize on this advantage. Perhaps most important, the Italians were perceived in essentially positive terms as important contributors to the development of Argentine society, whereas in the United States they were viewed for the most part in negative terms. Argentine nativism was primarily confined to some sectors of the elites and never sufficiently widespread to undermine the consensus in favor of immigration. In the United States, however, there was significant popular as well as elite nativism. As the immigrants sought to adjust to their respective environments, the differing characteristics of the host societies gave the Italians in Buenos Aires a relative advantage over those in New York City.

Part I of this book has set forth the Italian and the New World contexts in which migration unfolded. It has also described the process of moving from the villages of origin to the two destinations abroad. Especially important within this ongoing drama was the interplay between individual Italians and the larger impersonal structures they encountered, which constrained the choices they could make.

The Atlantic economy was among the most important of these. On the one hand, it created the economic pressures and dislocations within Italy that led so many to emigrate overseas. On the other hand, it was responsible for the economic opportunities in the receiving societies that attracted the migrants. The pace, concentration, and relative numerical strength of the two migrations as well as the nature of the respective receiving societies were also important. The social networks, which mediated between individuals and the larger structures, became significant structures as well.

Yet individual Italians responded to these structural realities in different ways. The choices they made—their creative coping—therefore led to different outcomes. They chose to emigrate or not, to go to Buenos Aires or New York or some other destination, to live in a particular neighborhood, to take a particular job, to associate with particular people, and to stay abroad or return home. And the stage upon which they acted out the migration drama—the multiple structural contexts in which the individual immigrants found themselves—would change with time as the immigrants began the complicated phase of adjustment.

Part II

The Adjustment of the Italians in Buenos Aires and New York City

When the Italians got off the boat in Buenos Aires or New York City, they began the process of adjustment.[1] Their goal was to prosper in their new environments, and they immediately sought to find jobs, places to live, and people with whom to socialize. As they took their first steps, they relied on such informal institutions as family and neighborhood. Those who remained longer or indefinitely frequently participated in formal immigrant and host society institutions to further their interests. Although they were living in unfamiliar environments defined by the social, political, and cultural structures described in the preceding chapters, the Italians were able to make meaningful decisions about work, residence, social life, and institutional participation.

The process of adjustment involved the use of resources the immigrants had brought with them. As they negotiated their way in the new environment, they found a tension between the old and the new. On the one hand, they had their traditional cultures and institutions, their fellow villagers, and their old social networks. On the other, they faced new cultures and institutions, new people, and new social networks. The continuing interaction over time of resources brought from the village and the new host society's structures modified both.

Because personal networks tied each individual to virtually all the various phases of the adjustment process, these networks were among the most important resources the immigrants brought with them and continued to rely on thereafter. Networks were first created in the villages of origin. In the process of migration and adjustment some of the old networks continued, others ceased to exist, and new ones were also established. The continually evolving personal networks were crucial for the immigrants in finding jobs and housing, in participating in immigrant and host society institutions, and in prospering abroad.

In the six chapters of this part I examine how the Italian immigrants went about adjusting to their new environments, how successful they were in this endeavor, and how the adjustment of the Italians in Buenos Aires compared to the adjustment of those in New York. How rapidly and successfully did the Italians in the respective cities find jobs, places to live, and people with whom to socialize? What were their patterns of occupational and residential mobility? And in what ways did they use institutions to help them protect their interests and achieve their goals?

4

Fare l'America

Fare l'America—to make it in America—was the single most important reason for nearly all of the Italians to migrate.[1] Migration was an investment made by an individual and his or her family, and everyone expected an immediate or at least a long-term return on that investment. The cost of passage and initial settlement, the disruption and separation of the family, and the inevitable hardships were accepted because the eventual rewards would compensate for these sacrifices. Everything depended on doing well economically in the chosen New World destination. The minimal initial expectation was to make ends meet, but success depended on making a surplus.

The significance of the surplus was that it permitted the immigrants to achieve the objectives for which they had come. The most common of these were to improve their standard of living in Buenos Aires or New York, to send money home for the purchase of a relative's ticket to America or to help support the family, to take their savings back to Italy and live a better life there, or perhaps some combination of the three. Oreste Sola, for example, used the surplus he earned to improve his standard of living in Buenos Aires, but he also sent money home to pay for his brother Abele's passage and to support his parents in retirement. Oreste's cousin Abele, on the other hand, worked hard for twelve years at his dairy business in Buenos Aires and then returned home with his savings to improve his standard of living in Valdengo. Ida Sola and her husband, Eugenio Cerruti, sent very little if anything back to Italy. Instead, they bought a house, a car, and other items to improve the family standard of living in Paterson and Haledon.

The Italian immigrants consciously or unconsciously developed economic strategies designed to achieve their objectives.[2] When people left

Italy, most assumed they would return home, and therefore initially pursued a short-term economic strategy. Because their primary concern was to make money quickly and to return home with their savings, they had little incentive to invest abroad and thereby to improve their standard of living in the New World. In response to the particular and changing circumstances they encountered in Buenos Aires and New York, some modified their initial objectives and consequently the strategy they followed to achieve them. These immigrants decided to stay abroad for a longer time, or even permanently; they increasingly developed and pursued a long-term economic strategy of investing most or all of their surplus in their present and future well-being in their new home. Oreste Sola, for example, left Italy with the intention of returning to Valdengo; he wrote about doing so for many years. Nevertheless, he increasingly adopted a long-term economic strategy of investing his earnings in his own future in Buenos Aires, especially after the death of his parents.

This is not to suggest that all Italian immigrants developed one or the other strategy and exclusively and consistently pursued it while abroad. Regardless of their initial intent, the immigrants' economic strategies emerged gradually in a more complex fashion as they interacted with and adjusted to their surroundings abroad. The important point is that the collective economic decisions and actions of the individual Italians in Buenos Aires and New York produced distinctive patterns regarding the development and pursuit of short- or long-term economic strategies. Which of the strategies predominated among Italians in the respective cities had important implications for their adjustment. Where most pursued a long-term strategy, they invested in homes and education and immigrant institutions. In contrast, however, where most pursued a short-term strategy, they saved to invest at home rather than building a future abroad. And, as will be discussed in Chapters 7 and 8, the long-term strategy better lent itself to the development and maintenance of an effective immigrant institutional structure capable of meeting the needs of the individual members of the community.

My task in this chapter, therefore, is not only to evaluate the economic performance of the Italians in Buenos Aires and New York and to determine how successful they were but also to gain an understanding of the economic strategies they developed and the broader implications of their choices. Specifically I examine the factors that affected whether or not Italians made a surplus, how they spent this surplus, and the choice of strategies they adopted to *fare l'America.*

Whether or not the immigrants made a surplus was influenced by a number of things. Among the most important were certain structural factors over which they had little if any control: the number and kinds of jobs available and the levels of prices and unemployment. Wages were partially structural and partially not; in some cases workers were able to influence wages by organizing and threatening to restrict the availability of labor. There were other matters, however, that were clearly within the power of the immigrants to control. They could choose their destinations and therefore the labor market they would enter. In addition, they could increase their income by deciding to find a second job, to put additional family members to work, and to take in boarders. They could also increase their savings to some extent by spending less on such items as rent, food, and clothing. Finally, they could determine how and where they would spend their surplus.

To evaluate the economic performance of the Italians in Buenos Aires and New York and to determine how successful they were, I explore the influence of these structural and cultural variables on the immigrants' ability to earn and save. In the rest of this chapter I describe the nature of the respective labor markets, the opportunities each offered, and how the Italians found jobs and participated in the labor markets. To estimate real incomes, I compare wages with the cost of living, and determine what, if any, supplemental income the immigrants made. A review of family budgets documents the spending and consumption patterns of some Italians, and provides the best basis for estimating how many of them managed to earn a surplus. And finally, I explore the questions of short- and long-term economic strategies and achievement.

The Labor Markets of Buenos Aires and New York City

The respective labor markets of Buenos Aires and New York City had evolved over time and would continue to change in the future. During the decades surrounding the turn of the past century, they could be described by a number of general traits. One of the most significant characteristics of the labor markets in both cities was the rapid growth in new jobs. For example, in the Buenos Aires of 1914, there were 40,000 additional jobs in commerce, 170,000 in industry and artisanal pursuits, and 54,000 for unskilled day laborers that had not existed nineteen years before.[3] Similarly, there were 68,000 additional jobs as clerks and 63,000 for day laborers in the New York of 1900 that had not existed in 1880.[4]

The long-term growth in jobs during the period fluctuated, however, reflecting the ups and downs of the respective business cycles of the two countries. In Buenos Aires, the labor market expanded especially rapidly during the two major economic booms of 1884–1889 and 1905–1912.[5] The labor market in New York also expanded dramatically during the 1880s, the first years of the new century, and during the half dozen years preceding World War I.[6] The decrease in jobs available that came with each down cycle in the economies was temporary, and more than made up for in the subsequent recoveries. In both cities, the overall trend from the 1880s to World War I was one of greatly expanding job opportunities.

A second characteristic of the respective labor markets was the demand for specific types of workers. Although the general occupational structure of the two cities was fairly similar at the turn of the century (Table 16), the job opportunities for incoming immigrants were somewhat different. The primary openings in the industrially developed and commercial economy of New York were for semiskilled factory workers, unskilled day laborers, and for minimally skilled individuals in the personal services sector. There was limited room for additional skilled artisans and white-collar workers because preceding immigrants and natives filled most of these jobs.[7] The commercial-bureaucratic city of Buenos Aires, on the other hand, needed not only unskilled and semiskilled labor for service jobs and construction but also skilled artisans, merchants, and other white-collar workers, as well as some professionals.[8] The demand for labor was great in both cities, but there was relatively more opportunity and less competition for skilled artisans and white-collar workers in Buenos Aires than in New York.

Several other characteristics of the labor markets were of importance. Both cities offered considerable opportunity for women to be employed, and approximately one-quarter of the paid labor force was female. In Buenos Aires, women worked primarily in personal service and the clothing industry, with only a few in white-collar jobs in commerce and education.[9] Women in New York, however, not only worked in personal services and clothing but also found greater opportunities in such white-collar jobs as clerks, bookkeepers, stenographers, and salespersons (Table 16).

Finally, foreigners were a large part of both labor markets, but especially so in Buenos Aires. There they made up nearly three-quarters of the active workforce. In transportation and industrial and manual arts, as well as in the day labor sectors, they accounted for an even higher percentage. In New York City, just under half the workers were foreigners, but in the areas of personal service and day labor they represented more than 60 percent of the total (Table 16).

Finding a Job: Padroni and Personal Networks

Italian immigrants found jobs in these labor markets through a variety of informal and formal mechanisms. Chief among the informal mechanisms were the various personal networks of friends, relatives, and paesani. These networks were often supplemented by responding to want ads in newspapers and "help wanted" signs in local stores and factories.

Table 16. Occupational structure of Buenos Aires and New York City

Occupational categories[a]	Buenos Aires (1895)			New York (1900)		
	Active population[b] (%)	Foreign born (%)	Male (%)	Active population[b] (%)	Foreign born (%)	Male (%)
Unskilled and semiskilled	**23.9**[c]	**75.0**	**53.0**	**24.0**	**62.9**	**58.4**
Personal service	14.3	67.0	24.0	17.1	60.7	42.5
Day labor	9.6	87.0	96.0	6.9	68.3	98.0
Semiskilled and skilled						
Transportation	**7.6**	**81.0**	**99.6**	**5.5**	**38.7**	**99.0**
Skilled						
Industrial and manual arts, manufacturing and mechanical	**34.4**	**81.0**	**77.5**	**36.1**	**55.7**	**74.8**
Non-manual (white collar)						
Commerce, trade, and service	**22.3**	**65.3**	**95.5**	**28.0**	**35.5**	**84.0**
Others[d]	**11.8**	**54.1**	**69.0**	**6.4**	**30.0**	**24.5**
City totals	**100.0**	**73.0**	**77.0**	**100.0**	**49.0**	**75.0**
N	305,000			1,470,000		

[a] To facilitate comparison, I have rearranged the descriptive census categories to approximate the skill categories used throughout the text.

[b] These totals include all job-holders aged fourteen or older in Buenos Aires and ten or older in New York.

[c] The figures in boldface represent the totals within each category.

[d] This category includes those in agriculture, the professions, and miscellaneous.

Sources: Argentina, *Censo 1895*, 2, pp. 47–50; 3, pp. 272–273; U.S. Bureau of the Census, *Special Reports: Occupations at the Twelfth Census* (Washington, D.C., 1904), pp. 634–640.

In addition, Italians found jobs through agencies of various sorts. Some private agencies were in fact an extension of the informal networks that specialized in job placement; they were run by local labor bosses (*padroni*), most of whom operated on a small scale without an office or a license. The padroni nevertheless performed an essential function as intermediaries for many of the newly arrived who knew nothing of the local language and were unfamiliar with the job market. Other, more formal placement agencies were run by immigrant protective societies and by Argentine and U.S. businessmen. The Italian and Argentine governments also became involved in job placement.[10]

In New York, the Italian padroni were the major source of job procurement until the early years of the twentieth century. John Koren, a special investigator for the Department of Labor, estimated in 1897 that well over half of the adult male Italians in the city owed their jobs to these labor bosses. Most padroni were small-time operators who placed a few workers at a time, but some regularly supplied large numbers to contractors and corporations. A combination of factors led to the gradual decline of the padrone system during the first decade of the century. A number of immigrant aid societies and the Italian government set up alternative placement agencies. In 1904, the State of New York, alarmed by the abuses of the padrone system, passed legislation to regulate and control employment agencies. As the Italians became more familiar with the labor market, they depended less on the padroni. By 1914, George Pozzetta concluded, the padrone system had nearly disappeared.[11]

Italians in New York also resorted to more informal mechanisms to find jobs. Immigrants migrated as part of personal networks, but during the 1890s and early years of the century, the networks were not as frequently used for job placement as the padroni. As the Italian community grew in numbers and more immigrants had direct knowledge of the local job situation, informal personal networks became increasingly important in job placement. A study of 1,095 Italian working women conducted in 1912 and 1913, for example, reported that the overwhelming majority "had obtained work through either relatives or friends."[12]

In Buenos Aires, Italians also found jobs through both personal networks and agents, but the nature and relative importance of these placement mechanisms differed from the New York pattern. At first the labor market was less organized than in New York and informal mechanisms predominated. Shipley found that prior to 1900 most immigrants obtained jobs through friends, relatives, and want ads in newspapers. Oreste Sola, for example, was helped by his godfather in finding a job; he in turn assisted his brother. Early on, the Argentine government also took steps to help immigrants find jobs. In the late 1860s, it created a job placement service at the docks. However, because 97 percent of those placed by the government were sent to the interior of the country, this service was of little use to those who wanted to stay in Buenos Aires.[13]

Although the informal mechanisms continued to be important throughout the period, after 1900 the labor market was more formally organized. Around the turn of the century, multipurpose, town-of-origin–based agencies with offices in a village in Italy as well as in Buenos Aires were active among the immigrants, and undoubtedly helped a number find jobs. In the well-documented case of the Agnonesi, for example, several such agencies arranged trips to Buenos Aires with increasing frequency in the late 1890s. Most certainly assisted in job placement. Less than a decade later, the involvement of these agencies in the migration process declined. After World War I, they ceased to be a factor.[14]

In addition, Argentine businessmen, labor unions, and the Argentine government organized placement agencies during the early years of the century. A private Argentine employment agency was first established in 1904. By 1912, there were fifty, placing 170,000 workers annually. The private agencies, however, mostly found jobs for workers outside the city. Labor unions entered the placement service at the same time, but never became as important as the private agencies. Although a free government placement service was authorized in 1907, it was not actually established until 1913. At first it played a secondary role to the private agencies, but by the end of the war it surpassed them in importance.[15]

The evidence suggests an important difference in the predominant mechanisms of job recruitment between the two cities. The Buenos Aires Italians relied more on informal networks and less on padroni than their counterparts did in New York. These mechanisms of job placement undoubtedly overlapped, but the influence of the padroni was considerably greater in New York. This difference can in part be explained by two things: first, the greater cultural dissimilarities between the Italians and the host society in New York and, consequently, the greater need for a knowledgeable mediator to help with job placement; and second, the more temporary residence and the emphasis on immediate earnings of the New York Italians.[16] Both of these factors made the padroni more essential in New York.

Italian Participation in the Labor Markets

The Italians participated in the respective labor markets in different ways. Most important, those who went to Buenos Aires were more influential in all sectors of the labor market and obtained more jobs at the higher end of the skill hierarchy than those in New York. This higher level of participation came about primarily because of the respective pace, size, and concentration of the two migrations as well as the differing job opportunities for incoming immigrants.

Italian men in New York were concentrated primarily in a relatively few blue-collar occupations at the lower end of the skill hierarchy. In 1900, nearly a third of all Italian working males at least ten years of age were employed as unskilled laborers. In addition, 14 percent were semiskilled barbers, waiters, and bootblacks, 15 percent skilled shoemakers, masons, and tailors, and 11 percent small merchants and peddlers. The remainder (27 percent) held a wide variety of mostly semiskilled and skilled jobs. The much smaller number of Italian women working outside the home were even more concentrated in a few occupations: over half were employed in the garment industry, 12 percent in manufacturing (artificial flowers, candy, tobacco), and 13 percent in domestic and personal services.[17]

In a few of these occupations the Italians in New York were overrepresented in relation to their percentage of the city's population, but they never were a numerically large enough group to be a major presence in the labor market as a whole. Italian men, who represented 6.7 percent of the active male population, made up nearly 25 percent of all day laborers, 55 percent of male barbers, 97 percent of bootblacks, 34 percent of shoemakers, and 18 percent of masons. Italian women, who constituted 3.3 percent of the active female population, accounted for 25 percent of all female tailors, 5.6 percent of seamstresses, and 4.0 percent of dressmakers.[18] Nevertheless, they remained a small fraction of the overall workforce.

This occupational pattern in New York changed gradually over the next three decades. Unskilled laborers, working on the subways and other public works, remained the major occupational category of Italian males, with barbers, tailors, and shoemakers a distant but consistent second cluster. The percentage of Italian unskilled laborers increased until 1916, but gradually decreased thereafter. These changes reflected the immigration of many unskilled male workers in the fifteen years before World War I, and the subsequent movement of some out of this category into semiskilled, skilled, and in a few cases, non-manual occupations.[19] Although the picture regarding Italian women is less complete, it is clear that they continued to be important in the clothing industry and other consumer industries such as candy, tobacco, and artificial flowers.[20] Thus Italians in New York were relatively numerous in a few occupations (men as unskilled laborers, women in the garment industry), but, given their small overall numbers, were not a major influence in the labor market.

In Buenos Aires, on the other hand, the substantially larger percentage of Italians in the total population, the greater percentage of skilled workers, the less developed state of the economy, and the limited number of native artisans, industrialists, and merchants all enabled the Italians to

participate more extensively and to exert more influence in the labor market—especially in the industrial and commercial sectors—than did those
in New York. Significantly, as early as 1887, the Italians, who constituted
32 percent of the total population, had a remarkable presence in industry;
they made up 52 percent of the workers and 57.5 percent of the owners!
In commerce, they represented 40 percent of the employees and 17 percent
of the owners. Native-born Argentines, in contrast, who represented 47
percent of the total population, constituted only 20 percent of the workers and owners in commerce, and 16 percent of the workers and less than
10 percent of the owners in industry.[21] By 1909, the percentage of Italian
workers and owners in industry had declined to approximately 37 and
40 percent respectively, most likely because second-generation Italians
were recorded as Argentines. The percentage of Italian workers in commerce also declined slightly, but that of Italian owners more than
doubled.[22] In Buenos Aires, Italians were a considerably more significant
presence in commerce and industry throughout the period than they were
in New York.

We can sum up participation in the labor market by looking at the relative distribution of Italians in the more general categories of white- and
blue-collar occupations in the two cities. Kessner's sample data for 1905
show that four out of every five Italian household heads in New York
(80 percent) were blue-collar workers (Table 17). The remaining one in five
(20 percent) held a white-collar job. Only 2 percent of the total were in high
white-collar occupations. In Buenos Aires as in New York, most Italians
worked in blue-collar jobs, but the total was somewhat less (71 percent versus 80 percent). Within the blue-collar category in Buenos Aires, a significantly higher percentage than in New York (40 percent versus 22 percent) were skilled. Although those with white-collar occupations were in
the minority in both cities, a greater percentage of Italians in Buenos Aires
were white-collar workers (31 percent versus 20 percent) and many more
were, as mentioned earlier, owners of small industrial and commercial establishments. Finally, the percentage of high white-collar jobs in Buenos
Aires, though small, was twice as large as that in New York (4 percent versus 2 percent); there were significant numbers of Italians among the religious, health, education, and fine arts professions, and especially among
engineers and architects.[23]

In both cities, most Italian men and women participated in the blue-
collar sector of the labor market as servants, day laborers, and artisans. But
the working Italians in Buenos Aires were a relatively more skilled blue-
collar and white-collar population than their counterparts in New York,
and they were the single most important group in large sectors of the economy. The participation of the Italians in the labor markets of the two cities
thus differed considerably.

Table 17. Occupational distribution of Italians in Buenos Aires and New York City

Occupational categories	Buenos Aires (1895) Active population[a] (%)	New York (1900, 1905) Active population[a] (%)
Unskilled	**15.6**	**41.9**
Servant	5.6	2.6
Laborer	7.1	37.1
Semiskilled	**15.6**	**16.3**
Cook	4.6	n/a
Barber	1.6	7.6
Bootblack	n/a	3.0
Skilled	**39.5**	**21.8**
Tailor, seamstress	7.8	13.0
Shoemaker	5.0	4.9
Mason	4.9	2.7
Non-manual (white collar)	**29.3**	**20.1**
Commerce	9.8	7.5
Peddler	2.2	.5
Employee (clerk, sales)	5.0	1.9
N	2,233	1,015

[a] Definitions of active population are the same as in Table 16.
Sources: (Buenos Aires) I took a sample of 3,000 Italians in six census districts from the manuscript census schedules of 1895. Of these, 767 had no occupation and are excluded from the calculations. (See Appendix, section 3, and Table 45.) (New York) For the main categories, I used a 1905 sample of heads of households in Thomas Kessner, *The Golden Door: Italian and Jewish Immigrant Mobility in New York City, 1880–1915* (New York, 1977), p. 52; and for the occupations within the categories I used U.S. Bureau of the Census, *Special Reports: Occupations at the Twelfth Census,* pp. 634–640.

Real Income: The First Step in Creating a Surplus

Real income, the actual value of what an individual or family earned from all sources, was the most important factor that determined whether or not the Italians in Buenos Aires and New York City were able to create an economic surplus. Although they could reduce expenses somewhat by underconsumption, the income side of the equation provided the greatest potential source for creating and expanding a surplus. To calculate the real income of the Italians in Buenos Aires and New York, we need to compare wages and prices to establish real wages, to evaluate the impact of unemployment and underemployment on yearly income, and to estimate the amount of supplementary revenue earned.

Much has been written on wages and prices in the United States and New York City and on Argentina and Buenos Aires at the turn of the past

Table 18. Real wages in Buenos Aires and the United States,
1882-1914

Year	Buenos Aires (in pesos)		
	Cost of living index	Police patrolman[a] real wages	Bagley worker[a] real wages
1882	65	36.00	30.50
1886	65	45.00	36.00
1890	95	32.00	30.30
1896	117	41.00	33.60
1900	95	58.00	56.70
1903[b]	100	55.00	65.34
1907	122	49.00	46.00
1912	130	60.00	55.90

Year	United States (in dollars)[c]		
	Cost of living index	Manufacturing workers[d]	
		Real wages	Index real wages
1890	91	$1.58	77
1895	84	1.64	80
1900	84	1.77	87
1905	88	1.88	92
1910	95	1.99	97
1914[b]	100	2.04	100

[a] Monthly wages.
[b] Base years.
[c] There are no figures for New York City specifically. The national averages are included only as a general indicator of real wages in the rapidly growing New York economy.
[d] Daily wages.
Sources: Roberto Cortés Conde, El progreso argentino, 1880-1914 (Buenos Aires, 1979), pp. 226-237; Albert Rees, Real Wages in Manufacturing, 1890-1914 (Princeton, N.J., 1961), pp. 74, 120-127.

century. Although there has been some disagreement as to what real wages actually were, the best evidence indicates that there was a long-term rise in real wages in both countries and cities. For Buenos Aires and New York, the increase during the three decades preceding World War I was at least 30 percent (Table 18).[24]

Yet these data obscure the considerable fluctuations in real wages at the individual level and tell us very little about how well the Italian immigrants in the two cities did.[25] Furthermore, the real wages of Italians depended on the point within this period at which they entered the respective labor markets. If real wages were moving up when an individual migrated, obviously he or she had a better chance of doing well than if they were going down.

To go beyond the general patterns and gain a better understanding of the real income of the Italians, we need to examine the wage and salary ranges within the respective labor forces of New York and Buenos Aires. Wages paid to blue-collar workers in both cities varied considerably according to industry, location, skill level, sex, and age. At the top of the wage hierarchy were skilled males, followed by unskilled males, skilled women, unskilled women, and children. The highest-wage industries paid approximately twice the amount of the lowest. Skilled males generally earned at least twice the income of unskilled males, women generally earned somewhat less than unskilled males, and children earned about half of what women did. In a few occupations—such as tailors and seamstresses—there was a greater parity between the pay of skilled men and women, although women always received less than men with equivalent skill and seniority.

In New York City in 1907, for example, a skilled bricklayer received $.70 per hour, a skilled carpenter $.63, an excavating laborer $.22, and a plaster's laborer $.38.[26] In addition, the average yearly salary of the New York working women studied by the Immigration Commission was $279 compared to $563 for the men.[27] Thus in New York City, skilled males made approximately twice the income of unskilled males and the average yearly income of all males was twice that of women.

In Buenos Aires there was a similar though not identical wage hierarchy. A skilled mason in 1908, for example, made 5.00 to 5.50 pesos per day or approximately twice the 2.50 to 2.80 of his unskilled assistant (called a peon). A skilled worker in a sandal factory earned 4.00 to 4.50 pesos per day, about 60 percent to 80 percent more than a peon, who made 2.50, and just about twice the 2.00 to 2.50 of women workers. Skilled women in the clothing industry, however, made nearly the same pay as the men.[28] Shipley concluded on the basis of his exhaustive study of Buenos Aires wages between 1912 and 1930 that the distances between the categories were slightly less than those indicated by these data. He found for the later period that skilled males made only between 43 percent to 67 percent more than unskilled males, and 59 percent to 72 percent more than females. And the pay of skilled men was about twice that of unskilled women and children.[29] These data indicate a substantial but somewhat smaller earning gap between skilled and unskilled and male and female workers in Buenos Aires than in New York.

Equally important as wages earned was number of days worked. In both cities, seasonal, cyclical, and structural unemployment was a constant con-

Table 19. Unemployment in New York City and Buenos Aires

| Year | New York City | | New York State | |
	June 30 (%)	December 31 (%)	March 31 (%)	September 30 (%)
1897			30.6	13.8
1900			20.0	13.3
1902			13.6	5.7
1904	16.9	17.8	27.6	9.8
1906	6.8	12.8	9.9	5.7
1908	33.3	27.7	35.7	22.5
1910	19.4	29.6	16.1	13.6
1913	26.5	46.5		

| Year | Buenos Aires | |
	Shipley calculations of unemployment (%)	Men 14+ without occupations or unspecified (censuses) (%)
1887		11.6
1895		7.2[a]
1904		6.5
1909		5.2
1914	15.3	5.1[a]
1917	30.1	
1920	16.8	
1923	17.5	

[a] Includes only those without occupations.

Sources: (New York) U.S. Department of Labor, Bureau of Labor Statistics, *Bulletin,* 109, pp. 19, 172; Melvyn Dubofsky, *When Workers Organize: New York City in the Progressive Era* (Amherst, Mass., 1968), p. 164, note 37 summarizes data of the New York State Department of Labor. (Buenos Aires) Roberto Cortés Conde, *El progreso argentino,* pp. 196–197; Robert E. Shipley, "On the Outside Looking In: A Social History of the *Porteno* Worker during the 'Golden Age' of Argentine Development, 1914–1930" (Ph.D. dissertation, Rutgers University, 1977), pp. 75 and 346ff.; Buenos Aires, *Censo 1887,* 2, p. 47; 1904, p. 63; 1910, 1, p. 60; Argentina, *Censo 1895,* 2, p. 50; Argentina, *Censo 1914,* 4, p. 212.

cern for almost all workers. Those at the lower end of the skill and wage hierarchies were the most vulnerable. Nevertheless, Oreste too was unemployed from time to time. The fluctuations and variations in unemployment and underemployment make it difficult to determine with complete accuracy its extent in the two cities. The statistics in Table 19 are nevertheless indicative. The New York City and New York State data indicate wide fluctuations in unemployment within most years and significant ups and downs over time. The level of unemployment ranged from around

10 percent in good years such as 1906 to over 25 percent during economic recessions.[30] A special study of unemployment in New York City in the beginning of 1915 noted that 16.2 percent of the wage earners were unemployed and that many more were underemployed.[31]

In some industries, most workers regularly endured unemployment and underemployment. A 1914 U.S. Labor Department survey of the dress and shirtwaist workers in New York City, for example, documented the instability of employment within this branch of the garment industry. "There are about six months of activity," the author of the report explained, "four in the spring and two in the fall, half of them carried on under extreme, almost feverish, pressure, followed by an equal period of subnormal activity with almost complete stagnation for one month in the year." He went on to say, however, that in general the employers tried to retain as many workers as possible by keeping them at least partly employed during the slow season. The result of this practice was that annual wages were much lower for most than the weekly wages during the busy season multiplied by fifty-two. Thus a worker who earned $15 a week during the busy season, in fact only earned an average weekly salary of $10.94 calculated on a yearly basis.[32]

Although there were similar patterns of seasonal, cyclical, and structural unemployment in Buenos Aires, the data are not as complete and informative. Díaz Alejandro argues that, with the exception of minor cyclical unemployment, "Argentina can be characterized as a full employment economy" for the period 1860–1930 as a whole.[33] The evidence to support such a statement, however, is less than convincing. Shipley has shown that from 1913 to 1930, unemployment was at least 15 percent or more. By 1917, unemployment had reached crisis proportions before again declining in the 1920s.[34]

There is, however, no such definitive study for the period before 1913 in Buenos Aires. Some unemployment clearly existed due to seasonal and cyclical fluctuations, but the evidence is insufficient to determine the precise extent of it. Table 19 provides the census data from 1887 to 1914 for the number of males fourteen and older who reported that they were either without occupation or did not specify an occupation. The 1895 figure of 7.2 percent without occupations is a reasonable minimal estimate of unemployment at that time, but the equivalent figure for 1914—5.1 percent—considerably underestimates the reality.[35] A reasonable estimate of general unemployment in Buenos Aires prior to World War I would be in the range of 7 percent to 10 percent in good years and twice that amount in times of crisis.

Temporarily unemployed immigrants sometimes returned to their original country or remigrated to another country abroad, but this exodus did not solve the problem for those who remained in Buenos Aires or New

York. Whatever immigrants attempted to do about it, unemployment and underemployment were a constant part of the labor economy. Few could count on secure year-round employment. During the war, unemployment was severe in both countries, but before 1913 the situation was somewhat less threatening in Buenos Aires than it was in New York City.

In addition, immigrants in both cities supplemented their income earned outside the home in a number of ways. About a fifth of the Italian immigrant households in New York City had boarders and lodgers. Members of approximately 10 percent of immigrant households engaged in homework, doing dressmaking, sewing, tailoring, and laundry. The income earned from taking in boarders and homework was fairly small, but often critical for the family to make ends meet. Most important, it enabled women and children to remain at home and still contribute to the family budget.[36]

The statistical data on boarders, lodgers, and homework among immigrants in Buenos Aires is very scanty, but it does suggest an even greater reliance on income from boarders than in New York. Data from one census district in Buenos Aires in 1895 indicates that perhaps twice as many Italian immigrant families took in boarders as in New York. Shipley states that homework, especially related to the garment industry, was significant among immigrants in Buenos Aires as well.[37] Supplemental income was important to immigrant families in both cities, but it was never very large. The major source of income was compensation for work outside the home.

How well Italians did in Buenos Aires and New York depended on the skills they brought with them, the opportunities available in the labor markets, where they fitted into the respective wage hierarchies, the stability of their jobs, and their supplemental income. As noted earlier, the large majority (70 percent to 80 percent) of Italians in both cities entered the labor market as blue-collar workers. Nevertheless, those who went to Buenos Aires had certain advantages that enabled them to do relatively better than their counterparts in New York. They came as a more skilled labor force and met much less competition from native workers, and were able to take advantage of the greater opportunities for skilled artisans and small businessmen in the commercial and industrial sectors.

Although the economies of both cities expanded during this period, the Italians fitted into the wage hierarchies in different ways. A larger proportion of Italians in Buenos Aires were skilled and white-collar workers. In New York City, skilled and white-collar workers were for the most part English-speaking northern Europeans or Americans, who were fairly well paid and relatively secure in their jobs. In Buenos Aires, skilled and white-collar workers were also fairly well paid and had relative job security, but many of them were Italians. The semiskilled and unskilled in both cities earned minimal wages, lacked job security, and lived at the margin of poverty. Both in New York and Buenos Aires they were increasingly southern and eastern Europeans. Thus, because of where they entered the wage hierarchy and because of the greater opportunity for occupational mobility, Italians in Buenos Aires were in the long run able to do relatively better economically than those in New York.

Family Budgets: Determining
Consumption Patterns and Surplus

Family budgets can tell us two things: whether Italians actually made ends meet or showed a surplus or a deficit, and specifically how they spent their money. Both are important for our analysis of making it in America. Immigrants had little if any influence on the amount they were paid, on the cost of the things they needed to buy, or on the severity of unemployment. They did, however, decide how to spend or not spend the money they earned. The decisions they made regarding expenditures were, after real income, the second most important factor in determining whether or not they would have a surplus at the end of the week, or month, or year. In this section, I therefore examine the existing data on family budgets in the two cities.

There are a number of studies that estimate the annual or weekly income necessary to sustain a working-class family in New York and Buenos Aires.[38] All assume a minimal budget, full employment, and no savings. Although in every case the number of families examined was small and it is not always clear how representative the samples were, the minimal survival income figures establish a useful standard by which to measure the relative success of the Italians.

The best studies of New York City—those of Chapin (1909) and the New York State Factory Investigating Commission (1915)—provide data based on direct observation of families in various income groups. They establish the necessary minimal annual budget at $825–$877 for a family of four to six (father, mother, and two to four children), $506 for a single man, and $467 for a working woman.[39]

Chapin's study is especially useful because it distinguishes the families by nationality. Of the 391 families he studied, 69 were Italian. Fifty-seven of these Italian families had annual incomes between $600 and $1,099 and were examined in detail (Table 20). More than half (52.5 percent) fell below the minimal annual income of $825 deemed necessary by Chapin to support themselves, and only a quarter (26.5 percent) had incomes above $900, an amount which he felt was "probably" sufficient to maintain a "normal standard."

Table 20. Italian family income-expense data, New York, 1908 (57 Italian families earning $600–$1100/year)

Yearly income	
Amount	Percentage in range
$600–$699	28.0
$700–$799	24.5
$800–$899	21.0
$900–$999	16.0
$1000–$1099	10.5
	100.0

Family expenditures		
Category	Range (%)	Average (%)
Rent	19–22	21.1
Food	48–52	49.6
Clothing	11–16	12.2
Fuel and light	4–6	4.8
Carfare, insurance, health	3–4	3.6
Sundries	8–11	8.7
		100.0

Family budgets		
	57 Italian families (%)	318 families studied (%)
Balanced budget	25	36.5
Budget surplus	58	36.5
Budget deficit	17	27.0

Source: Robert C. Chapin, *The Standard of Living among Workingmen's Families in New York City* (New York, 1909), pp. 62–65, 88, 229.

The Immigration Commission, which studied the annual income of 336 Italian families during the same period, came up with fairly similar results. The average annual Italian family income was $688, and 70 percent earned less than $750, a sum well below the necessary minimum of $825 established by Chapin.[40] The Immigration Commission found a somewhat greater percentage of Italian families with incomes below the minimal rate for survival because its sample was drawn from two exclusively working-class districts. Nevertheless, both studies support the same conclusion: a large proportion (58 percent to 75 percent) of Italian families in New York earned less than the minimal budget deemed necessary to support a family of four to six, and an additional number (15 percent to 20 percent) were in the marginal zone between sufficient and insufficient budgets. On the basis of this evidence, it would seem that few Italian families were making ends meet, let alone producing a surplus.

Yet Chapin's data on balanced budgets suggest otherwise; 58 percent of the Italian households reported a budget surplus, and only 17 percent reported a deficit (Table 20). This was the highest percentage with a surplus budget and the lowest percentage with a deficit budget of any group studied. Similarly, the percentage of Italian families with a surplus was considerably above the average for all 318 families Chapin studied, and the percentage with a deficit considerably lower.[41]

Chapin explains this fact by suggesting a difference in the "American standard of living" and that of the southern European. His data do indicate that the Italian families were willing, at least temporarily, to send their children to work at an early age, to accept crowded living accommodations, to take in boarders, and to skimp on clothing in order to make ends meet and to save. Whereas 56 percent of all Chapin's families were below his standard in terms of food, clothing, or shelter, or some combination of the three, 65 percent of the Italian families fell below these levels. The large majority of Italian families that were below his standard were underclothed and overcrowded. The one category they did not cut back on was food.[42]

Chapin's data make it clear that individual choices regarding consumption played an important part in whether a family budget was balanced, showed a surplus, or showed a deficit. He notes that some groups were able to begin saving on incomes below his minimal standard of $825. The Italians and other southern and eastern Europeans were able to begin saving on incomes as low as $700 or $800, whereas Americans, Irish, and Germans did not begin to save until they had family incomes above $900 or $1,000.[43]

Because there are no similar studies on Italian family budgets for Buenos Aires, we are compelled to estimate the situation of the Italians in that city on the basis of more general data for all workers. The Department of Labor conducted a number of surveys of family budgets in Buenos Aires between 1913 and 1928 that give us a good indication of how working-class families in general fared.[44] Since the Italians were a substantial portion of the working class, these figures provide at least some indication of their situation during this period.

The proportions of expenses for food, clothing, and rent for a working-class family in Buenos Aires were very similar to those for New York City

Table 21. Family income-expense data, Buenos Aires, 1897–1925

	Family expenditures, 1897–1918	
Category	Range (%)	Average (%)
Food	42–70	50
Rent	13–35	22
Clothing	7–17	13
Other	7–25	15
Total		100

Family budgets		
	1913	1914
Balanced budget	31	30
Budget surplus	47	53
Budget deficit	22	17
(Deficit with one worker)	(23.7)	(22.5)
(Deficit with one+ workers)	(20.4)	(11.8)
Total[a]	100	100

Size family male wage earner could support, 1914			
	Full Employment (26 days/month)	¾ Employment (20 days/month)	½ Employment (13 days/month)
Skilled or semiskilled	4 people	3 people	1 person
Unskilled	2 people	1 person	

[a]Numbers involved: 1913, 221; 1914, 156.
Sources: (Family expenditures) Conde, *El progreso argentino*, pp. 284–287, conveniently summarizes the extensive data of eleven Department of Labor and three other studies of family expenditures. (Family budgets) Argentina, Departamento Nacional del Trabajo, *Boletín*, 33 (Buenos Aires: January 1916), p. 205; see also pp. 203–211. (Family sizes) Shipley, "On the Outside Looking In," pp. 187–188, 191–192; see also pp. 173–200.

Italians (Tables 20 and 21). In both groups, half of all income was spent on food, 21 percent to 22 percent on rent, 12 percent to 13 percent on clothing, and 15 percent to 17 percent on other needs.[45] Most important, the percentages in the two cities with family budget surpluses and deficits were also quite close. In both cases approximately half had surpluses and less than a quarter had deficits.

Shipley presents a more textured picture by taking into consideration skill levels and unemployment. He points out that although nearly half the working-class families studied showed a budget surplus and an additional 20 percent balanced their budgets, such a positive position was possible primarily for families of skilled workers and for others who were willing to underconsume. In addition, he emphasizes the importance of family size and unemployment on the ability to meet budgets.[46] Table 21 shows that in 1914 a skilled male wage earner could support a family of four people if he was continuously employed (26 days a month), but he could support only three people if he worked three-quarters of the time (20 days a month). An unskilled male wage earner, however, could support only a family of two if he were fully employed, and of one (himself) if he worked three-quarters of the time.

Shipley concludes that workers of both sexes could generally make ends meet if they were single. With families of any size, however, they had to be skilled or rely on other sources of income to do so. Given the average family size in Buenos Aires of two adults and five children, most workers had to supplement their income consistently. For the approximately half of the working class who held unskilled jobs, it was difficult to make ends meet.

Several examples will help illustrate the complexity and variation of the workers' economic situations. In one family consisting of a man, his wife, and seven children, the husband—a skilled smelter—earned 112.50 pesos per month. His daughter earned 25.00 pesos as an ironing woman working thirteen to fourteen hours daily. Total wage income was thus 137.50 pesos per month. The family expenses, however, were 185.50 pesos—leaving a deficit of 48.00 pesos. The report does not explain how the family made up the difference, but presumably it did so by taking in boarders, or perhaps by drawing on savings. On the other hand, a single male port worker living in a boarding house showed a budget surplus. He earned 100.00 pesos per month and had expenses of 67.50 pesos.[47]

Yet even if two men made the same amount of money and had the same size family, the way they spent their money could result in a budget surplus or deficit. In a skilled smelter's family of four, the husband made 100.00 pesos per month and the family expenses were 124.00 pesos. The apparent deficit was 24.00 pesos. If the wife took in a boarder or did laundry it would have been less. On the other hand, a port worker with the same size family earned the same amount and yet had a surplus at the end of the month. He earned 100 pesos and had expenses of 93.05 pesos, which produced a surplus of 6.95 pesos.[48]

For several reasons the information on working-class families is indicative of Italian families, although we have no direct evidence on Italian family budgets in Buenos Aires. First, the Italians were a substantial proportion (approximately a third) of the city's workforce. Second, they were more skilled than their counterparts in New York and therefore as a group better paid and less vulnerable to unemployment. And third, we know they were willing to underconsume in order to save. I estimate that approximately half of the Italians in Buenos Aires were able to save some money.

In both cities during most times, perhaps 50 percent of the Italian working-class families were able to show a surplus, and an additional 25 percent were able to balance the family budget. To obtain this favorable economic situation, however, they needed two or more workers in the family, supplemental income from boarders and homework, and considerable underconsumption. In times of economic recession or even less-than-full employment, these percentages dropped considerably, especially for the more vulnerable unskilled workers. Yet the difficulties should not obscure the critical fact that many did manage to save something.

Long-Term Measurements of Economic Success

The data on long-term economic success are important because they suggest that the Italians in the two cities developed different economic strategies. In New York before World War I, where there was a higher percentage of unskilled workers, most Italians followed a short-term economic strategy that emphasized immediate financial returns and the repatriation of much of their earnings to Italy. The majority of the Italians in Buenos Aires, on the other hand, adopted a long-term strategy of economic gain that involved investing much of their surplus in improving their standard of living where they were.[49]

To support this hypothesis, I will examine the evidence on occupational mobility, home ownership, remittances, and the value and some of the activities of the immigrant institutions in Buenos Aires and New York. Occupational mobility can be analyzed at the group or the individual level, and to the extent possible, we will look at both. Group mobility involves comparing the occupations of all working Italians in a city at two different times, and will show us whether there were more or fewer workers in any specific skill category than there had been ten or twenty years before. The problem with this approach is that we have no way of knowing if the Italians at the beginning of the period were the same ones at the end.

Individual mobility analysis enables us to determine what happened to the same individual over time. My assumption is that the longer an individual Italian was in New York or Buenos Aires, the more likely he or she was to learn English or Spanish, to acquire other occupational skills, to learn how to take advantage of potential job opportunities, and thus to experience occupational mobility. To prove this assumption requires the systematic tracing of individuals as Thernstrom and others have done for various towns and cities in the United States.[50] The problem here is that during the period under study, large numbers of individuals left both cities between censuses and thus can not be traced.

Kessner found at the group level that there was a higher percentage of Italians in New York City who were semiskilled and skilled workers in 1905 than there had been in 1880, and a corresponding decrease in the percentage of unskilled and low white-collar workers. Semiskilled workers increased from 6.9 percent to 16.3 percent of Italian household heads, skilled workers increased from 13.1 percent to 21.8 percent, unskilled workers declined from 53.1 percent to 41.9 percent, and low white-collar workers declined from 24.9 percent to 17.8 percent. Thus there was significant upward group mobility within the blue-collar class, but at the same time there was a decline in the percentage of Italians among the white-collar class.[51]

Turning to an examination of individual mobility, Kessner's traces of 312 individual Italians between 1880 and 1915 confirm these conclusions. He notes significant individual upward mobility from unskilled to semiskilled occupations, some upward mobility from semiskilled to skilled, but limited mobility from blue-collar to white-collar jobs.[52] This pattern of mobility reflected the segmentation of the New York labor force and the consequent difficulty of moving into the skilled and white-collar sectors.[53]

There is no equivalent body of direct data for Buenos Aires with which to document the occupational mobility of Italians in that city. Only two of the six censuses spanning the years from 1869 to 1914 broke down occupations by nationality, and in the two cases that did (1887 and 1909), occupations were listed by nationality in only a few categories. In addition, the twenty-six years separating the two available manuscript censuses (1869 and 1895) preclude meaningful tracing.

We must therefore construct the Italian mobility patterns with indirect evidence and fragmentary direct evidence. Let me begin with several general points. First, the rapid growth in every sector of the active population between 1895 and 1914 created considerable space for mobility; during this nineteen-year period the active population increased more than two and a half times (from 305,000 to 792,000). Although the percentage of foreigners in the active population declined slightly (from 73 percent to 65.4 percent), the absolute number of foreigners more than doubled (from 223,000 to 518,000).[54]

Second, Italians were the largest of the foreign groups in Buenos Aires; in 1895 they represented 53 percent of all foreigners in the city, and 39 percent in 1914. Given the overwhelming percentage of Italians who were of working age, there is no reason to doubt that they were at least as heavily involved in the active population as their representation within the foreign population would indicate.[55] Thus we can project that there were at least 118,000 Italians in the active labor force in 1895, and 200,000 in 1914.[56]

This evidence indicates the probability of significant long-term Italian occupational mobility in Buenos Aires during the decades before World War I. The direct evidence on the participation of Italians in commerce from the 1887 and the 1909 Buenos Aires censuses mentioned earlier strengthens the case.[57] Between these two years, the proportion of Italian owners of commercial establishments increased from 17 percent to 38 percent; the actual number of owners rose from 115 to 10,875. At the same time, although the proportion of Italian commercial employees decreased slightly from 39.7 percent to 35 percent, the absolute number nearly tripled, from 13,000 to 38,000. Italian overrepresentation among owners and employees of commercial establishments by 1909, coupled with the rapid expansion of the commercial sector, strongly suggests that a considerable number moved up from blue-collar to commercial jobs and from commercial jobs to ownership. Those who moved up were replaced by more recent, less skilled, and less experienced immigrants.

There was considerable occupational mobility among Italians in both cities, but these patterns differed to some extent. In New York, mobility was primarily from unskilled to semiskilled jobs and, to a lesser extent, from semiskilled to skilled. Although the evidence on Buenos Aires is less complete, it indicates that there was similar or greater mobility within the blue-collar sector, and in addition, there was some significant mobility into and within the white-collar sector. The relatively greater mobility of Italians in Buenos Aires reflected a more fluid labor market, greater opportunity, and the development and pursuit of a long-term economic strategy of investment in their future in that city.

The Buenos Aires Italians' integration into the labor market at a higher level and their greater subsequent occupational mobility would suggest that in the long run they invested more in their adopted city than did those in New York. To substantiate this, however, we need to look at such indicators as where Italians invested their surpluses as home ownership, the wealth and functions of immigrant institutions, and remittances.

Table 22 presents the existing data on home ownership in both cities. The evidence for Buenos Aires is overwhelming; Italians in increasing numbers were able to purchase houses and to do so in greater proportions than Argentines. Between 1887 and 1904, the proportion of Italians among all home owners increased from 36 percent to 45 percent while that of Argentines declined from 44 percent to 30 percent. At the same time, the

Table 22. Italian home owners in Buenos Aires and New York City

	Buenos Aires				
	All home owners (%)			Proportion of population who owned homes (%)	
Nationality	1887	1904	Nationality	1887	1904
Argentines	44.3	30.3	Argentines	7.5	4.8
Italians	35.6	44.6	Italians	9.0	16.1
Others	20.1	25.1	All nationalities	8.0	8.7
Total	100.0	100.0			
$N =$	34,715	82,540	$N =$	433,375	950,891

	New York City, 1908		
Nationality	Number in survey[a]	Number owning homes	Percentage owning homes
Italians	524	7	1.3
Germans	200	3	1.5
Hebrews	330	0	.0
Total foreign born	2,261	14	.6

[a] Heads of households.

Sources: (Buenos Aires) Buenos Aires, *Censo 1887,* 2, p. 142; Buenos Aires, *Censo 1904,* pp. 106, 119–120. (New York) U.S. Immigration Commission, *Reports,* 26, p. 209.

proportion of Italians who owned homes increased from 9 percent in 1887 to 16.1 percent in 1909 and that of Argentines dropped from 7.5 percent to 4.8 percent.[58]

The only data available for New York City come from the Immigration Commission, and show that just 1.3 percent of the 524 Italian heads of households surveyed owned their own homes (Table 22). This figure is certainly low for the entire city—the sample comes only from Manhattan. Italians living in the other boroughs, especially Brooklyn, were more likely to be home owners. Even if we estimate that at best the proportion of Italian home owners was in the range of 7 percent to 8 percent, this figure would still be about half what the percentage was in Buenos Aires in 1904. By this measure, the Italians in Buenos Aires did considerably better at the time than those in New York City.

Information on mutual aid societies in the two cities further supports the idea that the Italians in Buenos Aires invested more locally than did

Table 23. Remittances sent from Argentina and the United States to Italy, 1884–1914

| | Value of money orders and bank drafts[a] (in millions of lire) | | | |
| | Argentina | | United States | |
Year	Money orders	Bank drafts	Money orders	Bank drafts
1884–1902	7.32		82.46	
(Annual average)	.41		4.58	
1902–1914	3.76	97.7	1,071.00	431.70
(Annual average)	.31	8.14	89.25	5.97

| | Per capita value of money orders and bank drafts (in lire)[a] | | | |
| | Argentina | | United States | |
Year	Money orders	Bank drafts	Money orders	Bank drafts
1890			33.2	
1895	.5			
1900			15.7	
1910			98.8	
1914	.5	7.20		27.74

[a]These figures include only the money orders sent under the auspices of the officially recognized Banco di Napoli.

Sources: Commissariato Generale del'Emigrazione, *Annuario Statistico della Emigrazione Italiana dal 1876 al 1925* (Rome, 1926), pp. 1647–1648, 1657–1659; and Warren Dean, "Remittances of Italian Immigrants: From Brazil, Argentina, Uruguay and U.S.A., 1884–1914," *Occasional Papers* (New York University, 1974), No. 14.

those in New York. In 1908, the value of the Italian mutual aid societies in Buenos Aires was approximately five times greater than the value of those in New York. In addition, the mutual aid societies in Buenos Aires established more than a dozen schools, enrolling perhaps as much as 40 percent of the Italian school-age children who attended schools. The investments in mutual aid societies and schools in Buenos Aires were a clear commitment to a future there.[59]

And finally, the data we have on the remittances sent back to Italy to meet various family obligations and to invest in a future there—though not complete—provide important additional evidence to indicate the predominance of different economic strategies among the Italians in the two cities (Table 23). There were several ways for the immigrants to get their money back to Italy. Some carried it themselves or had friends do it for them. In addition, there were two formal ways to send remittances home: one by postal or telegraph money orders and the other by bank drafts. The Italian government published the data on postal and telegraphic money orders cashed in Italy from all overseas sources starting in 1873, and on the officially authorized bank drafts sent through the Banca di Napoli starting in 1901.

There are several problems with this set of data. In addition to being somewhat incomplete, it is not broken down by cities within countries. However, because the Argentine and U.S. figures show such extraordinary differences, and because Buenos Aires and New York contained such large concentrations of the Italians within their respective countries (34+ percent and 27+ percent), the data provide a reasonable basis on which to estimate the situation in the two cities. Furthermore, although the Italian government believed that immigrants used money orders almost exclusively, some, such as Oreste Sola and his brother, Abele, sent money home by bank drafts. This practice was especially true in Argentina.[60] Businessmen as well used the banks, but unfortunately there is no breakdown between immigrants and businessmen in the data.

What stands out in these figures is the much greater amount of money, both in absolute and per capita terms, sent back from the United States compared to Argentina (Table 23). In the period from 1884 to 1902, Italians in the United States sent home postal orders amounting to 11 times as much money as Italians in Argentina sent this way. From 1902 to 1914, they sent home 285 times the amount! The data on drafts of the Banca di Napoli for the 1902 and 1914 period show that Italians in the United States sent home considerably more money this way too than did those in Argentina. The per capita figures for money orders reveal a similar difference. The average per capita value of money orders from Argentina was .5 lira compared to 33, 16, and 99 lire from the United States. The per capita value of Banca di Napoli drafts in 1914 was one-quarter that sent from the United States.

These data on remittances demonstrate that Italians in the United States and New York were able to save considerable sums. Equally important, the data also show that the Italians sent much of this money home rather than investing it in their temporarily adopted country and city. The Italians in Buenos Aires may have saved as much or conceivably even more than those in New York, but they invested more of it locally. We know, for example, that although Oreste and Abele Sola sent home a great deal of money, they spent even more in Buenos Aires.

The information I have presented on long-term economic achievement and investment—occupational mobility, home ownership, wealth and commitment to education of the mutual aid societies, and remittances—makes most sense in the context of distinct economic strategies on the part of the Italians in Buenos Aires and New York. In New York the predominant emphasis was on immediate financial returns, whereas in Buenos Aires it was on long-term gain. The savings were never great in either case, nor can we state conclusively that one group was able to save more than the other. What the evidence does indicate is that those in New York sent much of their savings home, while those in Buenos Aires invested more of theirs in the future where they were.

What did the Italians in Buenos Aires and New York City achieve economically during the decades preceding World War I, and how do the results in the respective cities compare? On the basis of the evidence presented in this chapter, I can make several points. The experiences of the Italians in the two cities were similar in a number of ways. The long-term expansion of jobs in both places created substantial employment opportunities. Although in absolute terms the wages for workers were higher in New York, so was the cost of living. As a result, real wages were essentially the same, although unskilled workers probably could earn somewhat more in New York than in Buenos Aires. The most important determinant of a worker's earning power was where he or she fitted into the job hierarchy; skilled workers made approximately twice as much as unskilled workers, men made twice as much as most women, and so forth. In both cities, the Italians spent similar percentages of their income on food, rent, and clothing. And finally, Italians were excellent savers. As a result, during most years approximately half of them were able to produce a budget surplus and another quarter made ends meet.

At the same time, there were important differences between the Italians in the two cities. Because there was a greater demand for skilled and white-collar workers in Buenos Aires, Italians in that city were initially able to find jobs higher up on the skill and wage hierarchies. In addition, there was greater fluidity in the Buenos Aires labor market and thus relatively greater subsequent occupational mobility. Largely because of the contextual differences, Italians in the two cities also spent their economic surpluses differently. In New York, most adopted a short-term economic strategy that emphasized immediate return to Italy, and they sent or carried with them much of their surplus. In Buenos Aires, on the other hand, most developed and pursued a long-term economic strategy. Much of their surplus was spent on home ownership, mutual aid societies, schools, and businesses. Relatively little, compared to New York, was sent home.

Many of the Italians in both Buenos Aires and New York managed to produce at least small surpluses and in this sense were successful in making it in America. However, the Italians in Buenos Aires did better in the sense that by investing locally they created an effective institutional structure to facilitate their adjustment and to improve their standard of living there. Those in New York who returned to Italy may have prospered back home on the basis of their earnings abroad. But those who remained in New York prior to World War I had fewer community resources to help them adjust. The remarkable fact is that in both cities so many Italians were able to earn some surplus and thus successfully to *fare l'America*. Because they chose to use these surpluses in different ways, however, they produced different outcomes.

Residence Patterns and Residential Mobility

In addition to obtaining a job, one of the most immediate and important tasks for the Italians who went to Buenos Aires and New York City was finding a place to live.[1] Where the immigrants lived was important for a number of reasons. The availability, cost, condition, and location of housing influenced their opportunities to save. It also affected the extent of their interaction with family, other Italian immigrants, and members of the host societies. Once they established themselves, immigrants frequently changed residence within the city or moved on to another destination. The nature of this mobility had an impact on home ownership, institution building, and community formation. Residence was thus crucial to the adjustment process.

Many factors influenced residence patterns. In their search for housing—as in their quest for jobs—the immigrants confronted important structural factors over which they had little control: the location of jobs, the availability and cost of housing, the size and growth of the cities, and the availability and cost of transportation. In addition, a number of cultural and individual variables influenced their choice of where to live. Among them was the desire to be both near work and kin and fellow paesani, the perception of immigration as temporary or permanent, the willingness to underconsume in order to save, the attitude toward home ownership, and host society prejudice and discrimination. These variables interacted in various combinations. Some influenced both initial settlement and subsequent local and outward mobility. Others were important only to one of these parts of the ongoing search for housing.

One of the major problems confronting historians who wish to analyze the settlement patterns of Italian immigrants abroad is that village, local region, and provincial identities were more influential than any overall Italian identity in the decision of where to live. Except for a small minority of intellectuals and political activists, the concepts of a united Italy and of Italian nationalism had little meaning for most Italian immigrants at the turn of the past century. It was within the receiving society—where North Americans and Argentines frequently grouped those from the Italian peninsula together as one nationality—that most Italians began to think in terms of a national identity. Thus, to understand the residence patterns of Italians in the two cities, we need to explore their behavior in terms of the local regions and especially the villages from which they came.

To study the residence patterns of the various Italian subgroups, it is essential to use sources that link individual Italians from specific villages to their exact addresses in Buenos Aires and New York City. Neither the manuscript nor the published census data, with rare exceptions, include town of origin and therefore are not useful for this type of analysis. The result is that few have studied the crucial Italian subgroup residence patterns in either Buenos Aires or New York City.[2] An important contribution of this chapter therefore is that it is based on data—New York City naturalization records and Buenos Aires mutual aid society records—that locate individuals in both the sending and receiving contexts, thus permitting us to document with precision such subgroup residential behavior.[3]

The collective results of the ongoing search for housing in the two cities created distinct patterns of residence. In this chapter I will describe and compare these evolving patterns, explain why they developed as they did, and suggest their influence on adjustment.

Italian Residence Patterns in Buenos Aires and New York

From the general citywide perspective, there was a striking difference between the pattern of settlement of Italians in Buenos Aires and New York; in the former they were fairly evenly dispersed throughout the populated areas, whereas in the latter they were concentrated in a few locations. In 1895, at least 19 percent of the inhabitants in each of the Buenos Aires census districts were Italian born, with the exception of Districts 2 and 4 at the very center of the city. And even in the districts that were the exceptions, Italians were 10 percent of the population. In addition, no one district accounted for more than 8.7 percent of the total Italian population. Nine of the twenty census districts had 5 percent or more of the total Italian population.[4]

There was, nevertheless, some clustering among Italians within Buenos Aires. This clustering can best be shown by dividing the city into three areas: the core, the core-periphery, and the outlying area (Map 2). In 1895, 36 percent of the Italians lived within the core, while 44 percent lived in the

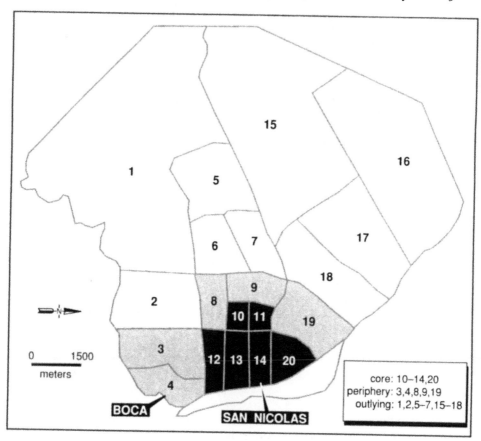

Map 2. Buenos Aires census districts and areas

core-periphery (Table 24). A somewhat smaller percentage of the Italians than of the population as a whole (36 percent of the Italians versus 42 percent of the total population) lived in the core, while a somewhat larger percentage (44 percent of the Italians versus 38 percent of the total population) lived in the core-periphery. Italians were generally dispersed throughout the areas where the city's total population resided, but were somewhat overrepresented in the districts of the core-periphery surrounding the center city.

As the city grew over the next decade, the Italian and the total population gradually shifted outward; as of 1904 both populations had declined by approximately 8 percent in the core and had increased by 10 percent in the outlying districts. The largest number of Italians (41 percent) still

Table 24. Relative location of total population and Italian population in Buenos Aires

Area	1895 (%)	1904 (%)	1914 (%)
Core			
Total population	42	33	22
Italian population	36	29	17
Core-periphery			
Total population	38	38	37
Italian population	44	41	31
Outlying area			
Total population	19	29	50
Italian population	19	19	51

	Definition of each area by census districts	
Area	1895	1904–1914
Core	1–8, 13–16, 18, 19	10–14, 20[a]
Core-periphery	9–11, 19, 21, 27, 28	3, 4, 8, 9, 19[b]
Outlying area	12, 17, 22–26	1, 2, 5–7, 15–18[c]

[a] 8% smaller than in 1895.
[b] 7% smaller than in 1895.
[c] 8% larger than in 1895.
Sources: Figures calculated on the basis of Argentina, Censo 1895; Argentina, Censo 1914; and Buenos Aires, Censo 1904.

resided in the core-periphery. The relationship between the Italian and the total population remained essentially the same.

In contrast to those in Buenos Aires, the Italians in New York concentrated in only two of the five boroughs that after 1898 made up the city.[5] In 1900, 66 percent lived in Manhattan and an additional 26 percent in Brooklyn (Map 3 and Table 25).

Within Manhattan the first Italians had settled in the Mulberry District and gradually had spread into neighboring wards below Fourteenth Street and to East Harlem on the Upper East Side (Map 3). In 1890, 73 percent of the Italians lived below 14th Street, clustering in the Mulberry District and its surrounding wards, and an additional 10 percent lived in the East Harlem community. Two adjacent wards alone (6 and 14) accounted for more than 42 percent. Only six of the twenty-two wards had 5 percent or more of the total Italian population of Manhattan (Table 26). Italians in New York gradually moved out from the Mulberry District and East Harlem, and some settled in the areas between the two major colonies. But up to World War I, Italians remained concentrated in Manhattan and, within Manhattan, below 14th Street and in East Harlem.

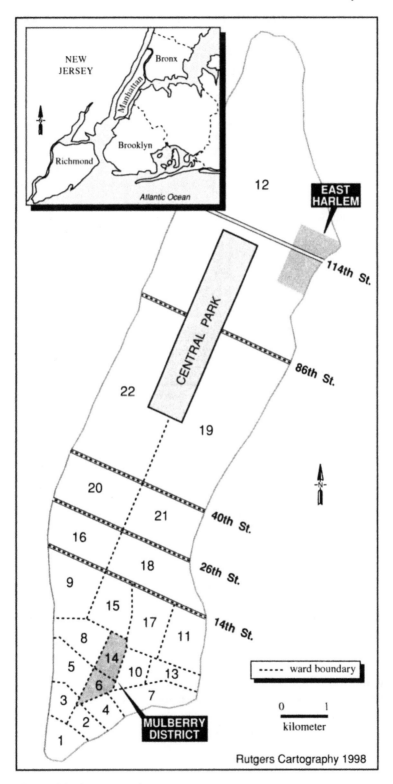

Map 3. Manhattan wards

Table 25. Relative location of total population and Italian population of New York City

	1900		1910		1920		1930	
	Total (%)	Italian (%)	Total (%)	Italian (%)	Total (%)	Italian (%)	Total (%)	Italian (%)
Manhattan	54	66	49	59	41	47	27	27
Brooklyn	34	26	34	30	36	35	37	44
Bronx	6	5	9	7	13	10	18	15
Queens	4	2	6	3	8	5	16	11
Richmond (Staten Island)	2	1	2	1	2	2	2	3
	100	100	100	100	100	99	100	100
Total population in 000s	(3,437)	(145)	(4,767)	(340)	(5,620)	(390)	(6,930)	(440)

Sources: U.S. Census, 1910, 1, pp. 824, 827–829, 856; U.S. Census, 1920, 2, pp. 788, 849, 904; U.S. Census, 1930, 2, pp. 548–551.

Table 26. Concentration of Italians in Manhattan (first and second Generations)

Area	Italian population, 1890 (%)	Italian population, 1930 (%)
Below 14th Street	73	40
14th–86th Street	13	22
Above 86th Street	14	38
	100	100

Sources: U.S. Department of Interior, Bureau of the Census, Vital Statistics of New York and Brooklyn, 1885–1900 (Washington, D.C., 1901), pp. 230–237; William B. Shedd, Italian Population in New York (New York, 1934).

Although citywide Italian settlement differed significantly in Buenos Aires and New York City, an examination of Italian subgroups reveals a considerable similarity in patterns; in both cities, Italians clustered in specific areas according to village and, to a lesser extent, regional and provincial origin.

The data presented in Table 27 indicate regional and provincial clusters within the eight districts of Buenos Aires, accounting for more than three-quarters of the mutual aid society members in my sample. Scholars frequently divide Italy into four large regions: the North, the Center, the

Table 27. Distribution of Italian mutual aid society members in eight Buenos Aires districts, by region and province, 1904

| Districts[a] | Regions[b] | | Provinces[c] | | Total Italian society members (%) | Total Italian population (1904) (%) |
	North (%)	South (%)	Calabria (%)	Genoa (%)		
9	5.6	3.0	3.6	5.7	4.7	8.0
10	5.4	4.8	9.1	7.4	5.3	4.3
12	4.0	4.2	3.6	4.1	4.6	5.3
13	6.2	6.6	3.6	8.3	6.1	4.0
14	22.0	30.7	38.2	18.0	23.6	5.7
18	10.6	4.8	0.0	10.7	8.2	7.2
19	14.4	11.4	10.9	14.9	13.4	7.5
20	9.0	15.1	21.8	8.3	11.5	4.6
Total for 8 districts	77.2	80.6	90.8	77.4	77.4	46.9
(N) =	(499)	(166)	(55)	(102)	(1,509)	(228,000)

[a]See Map 2 for location of districts.
[b]For location of Italian regions see Map 1.
Source: Buenos Aires Mutual Aid Society Records (see Appendix).

South, and Sicily. Here we will examine only the North and South because the overwhelming majority of Italians in the sample came from these two regions.

There were northern and southern Italians in considerable numbers in all eight districts, and especially in Districts 14, 19, and 20. What is indicative of regional clustering, however, is that northern Italians were overrepresented (compared to all Italian society members and to the total Italian population) in Districts 18 and 19 and in neighboring District 9, while southern Italians were overrepresented in Districts 14 and 20.

At the provincial level, 60 percent of the Calabrians (those from the neighboring provinces of Catanzaro, Cosenza, and Reggio di Calabria) clustered in Districts 14 and 20.[6] In contrast, immigrants from the province of Genoa were more evenly distributed throughout the area; seven of the eight districts contained 5 percent or more of the total Genovese population in the sample, compared to only four out of eight for the Calabrians.

Provincial and regional clustering also existed in Manhattan, as Table 28 illustrates. The largest percentage of those from all regions of Italy lived below 14th Street, but the percentage that lived between 14th and 86th

Table 28. Distribution of naturalized Italians in Manhattan, by selected regions and provinces, 1906–1921

Regions[a]	All naturalized Italians (%)	North (%)	South (%)	Sicily (%)
Below 14th Street	47.8	44.7	48.4	48.2
14th–86th Streets	25.8	43.5	19.4	30.0
Above 86th Street	26.4	11.7	32.7	21.8
(N) =	(1,635)	(239)	(894)	(427)

Provinces[a]	Genoa (%)	Naples (%)	Salerno (%)	Palermo (%)	Messina (%)
Below 14th Street	77.7	37.5	43.8	43.8	45.9
14th–86th Streets	13.3	25.0	15.4	36.5	22.2
Above 86th Street	8.9	37.5	40.8	19.7	31.9
(N) =	(45)	(160)	(130)	(203)	(72)

[a]For location of Italian regions see Map 1.
Sources: New York City Naturalization Records (see Appendix).

Streets and above 86th Street varied considerably. Forty-four percent of the North Italians lived between 14th and 86th Street, especially on the West Side, but relatively few lived above 86th Street. Southern Italians, in contrast, concentrated above 86th Street, and those from Sicily on the East Side between 14th and 86th Streets.

Table 28 also shows several distinct provincial clusters in New York. Seventy-eight percent of the Genovese lived in four wards below 14th Street. Those from the province of Naples concentrated in two areas, one below 14th Street and the other in East Harlem above 86th Street. Immigrants from the province of Salerno similarly resided in clusters below 14th Street and in East Harlem, but they concentrated in a different area below 14th Street than did the Neapolitans. Sicilians, as noted earlier, concentrated primarily on the East Side. Sixty percent of those from the province of Messina, however, clustered in Wards 17 and 18 and in East Harlem, while immigrants from the western Sicilian province of Palermo established a major settlement in Ward 19 between 40th and 86th Streets as well as a lower Manhattan cluster.

Village-based clusters, which reflected the influence of personal networks, were the most important of all the Italian subgroups. A detailed examination of several specific areas within the two cities enables us to indicate the location of some village clusters and their relationship to provincial groupings. The Boca—a center of the maritime industry in Buenos Aires lying at the mouth of the Riachuelo River several miles to the south of the central business district (Map 2, District 4)—was, in 1904, 33 percent Italian born; a similar percentage were second-generation Italians.[7] Ligurian sailors and political exiles (those from the provinces of Genoa, Savona, and La Spezia) came to the Boca in the early nineteenth century. Although the population became more diversified by the end of the century, Ligurians continued to dominate the life of the district. In fact, the language in the majority of homes, in business, and in public discourse remained Ligurian until the early decades of the twentieth century.[8]

The manuscript schedules of the 1895 census and the membership lists of the mutual aid societies from the 1890 to 1910 period tell us where within the Boca the Ligurians lived. What these records show is that the Ligurians, who by 1904 had lived in the Boca for many years, were dispersed throughout the area. The entire Boca district was, to a considerable extent, a large Genovese cluster. There were, nevertheless, subclusters of other more recently arrived Italians interspersed among the Ligurians. Immigrants from the small Adriatic fishing village of Sirolo-Numana had by 1890 established three distinct settlements within the Boca: one in the area of Calles La Madrid and Necochea, a second six blocks west in the area of Calles Olavarria and Hernadarias, and a third on the Isla de la Boca (Map 4). Some of the Sirolesi moved to Quilmes, a satellite colony about eighteen kilometers and several railroad stops to the south.[9] In addition, there were clusters of immigrants from Ortona on Calle Necochea near Calle Pinzon, and from Stromboli and the Sicilian fishing village of Giardini on the Isla de la Boca.

Village-based clusters were as important in the San Nicolás district located in the center of Buenos Aires (Map 2, District 14) as they were in the Boca. Although the 21 percent of Italian born in San Nicolás was substantially lower than that in the Boca, Italians clustered in the blocks on the north and west sides of the district. Migrants from the village of Agnone (Campobasso) had established a colony in the area of Calles Montevideo and Cordoba by as early as the mid-1870s. A second Agnonese colony was subsequently formed in the area of Calles Maipu and Cordoba just a few blocks to the east (Map 5). The Bagnaresi (Bagnara, Calabria) apparently arrived in the San Nicolás district somewhat later than the Agnonesi, but by 1890 had established a colony in the vicinity of Calles Viamonte and 25 de Mayo. A smaller group of Bagnaresi settled in the 1100 block on Calle Cerrito. In contrast, the older immigrants from Genoa and Torino were more dispersed within the district. Although they resided primarily in areas outside the centers of Agnonese and Bagnarese settlement, they did not apparently form one or two main clusters.[10]

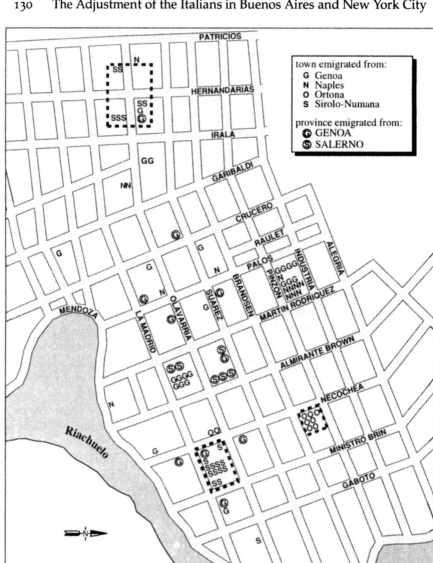

Map 4. Italian clusters in the Boca

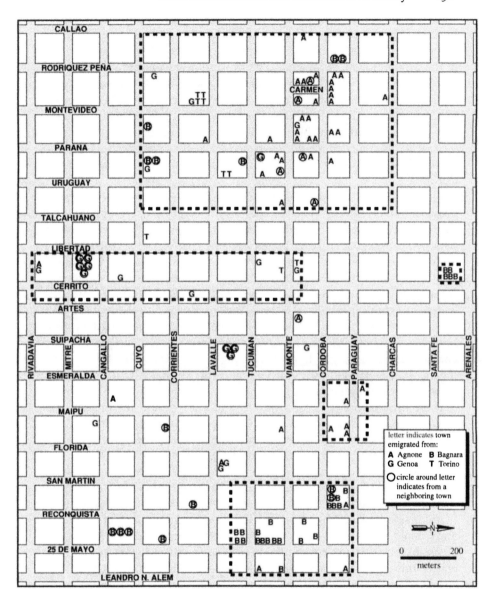

Map 5. Italian clusters in San Nicolás

No single regional group dominated San Nicolás as did the Ligurians in the Boca. The data, however, suggest the existence of smaller regional clusters within the district. In addition to the twenty-one Agnonesi who lived in the Montevideo-Cordoba area, there were other immigrants from the provinces of Campobasso and Naples who also shared this space (Map 5). Similarly, there were other immigrants from Calabria and Cosenza who lived in the heart of the Bagnarese community around Calles Reconquista and Viamonte, and in the blocks just to the south. Also, immigrants from Genoa, Torino, and Alessandria formed at least one cluster in the eight blocks along Calles Cerrito and Libertad between Calles Rivadavia and Cordoba.

Village-based clusters, which served as focal points for more extended provincial and regional clusters, were as important in New York City as they were in Buenos Aires. Italians first appeared in significant numbers in what would subsequently become known as the Mulberry District in the early nineteenth century (Map 3). For the most part they were political exiles—professionals, artisans, and workers—who came from the Ligurian coast and from other areas of northern Italy. By 1855 there were approximately one thousand Italians in New York (compared to eleven thousand in Buenos Aires), most of whom lived in the Five Points area of the future Mulberry District. Over the next thirty-five years, the colony grew in size and became increasingly diversified in regional composition. By 1890, the Italians had expanded into Ward 14, and the Mulberry District had become 44 percent Italian born. Most of these Italians were from the South.

The naturalization records from 1906 to 1921 permit me to delineate some of the village clusters in the Mulberry District, in East Harlem, and in the surrounding areas. For example, twenty-nine of the thirty-six Genovesi (81 percent) for whom we have data lived below 14th Street, and twenty of them lived in nearby clusters to the south and west of Washington Square. Similarly, the immigrants from Naples settled in a series of clusters within New York City. Forty-nine percent lived below 14th Street. Many resided in the Mulberry District; fourteen in the area of Mulberry and Canal and another eight in the area of Mulberry and Broome several blocks to the north (Map 6). Still others lived in mini-clusters in adjoining wards. Immigrants from Salerno and the western Sicilian town of Sciacca also lived in clearly defined clusters.

As in Buenos Aires, village clusters in New York were the focal points for more extensive provincial and regional clusters. For example, immigrants from the Ligurian coast concentrated in the Five Points area of Ward 6, where there was a cluster of Genovesi. Similarly those from the provinces of Naples and Salerno lived in the same areas as those from the towns of Naples and Salerno (Map 6). The same was true with immigrants from most other major towns and provinces.[11]

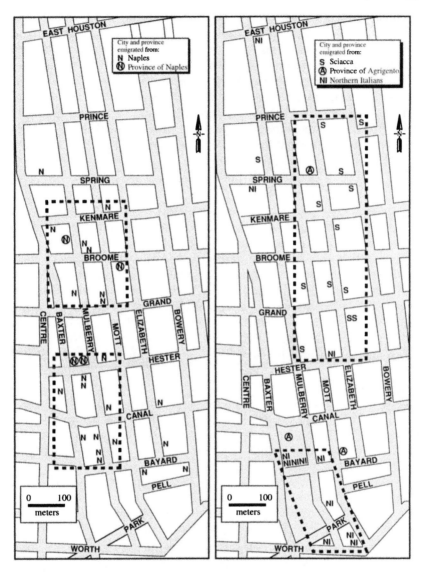

Map 6. Village clusters in the Mulberry District

Italians settled in East Harlem between First and Third Avenue and 104th and 120th Street in an identical pattern. Several individuals from the North Italian town of Piacenza lived in the area of 105th Street and Second Avenue, and they were joined by other northern Italians (Map 7, cluster 4). Similarly, immigrants from the town and province of Palermo clustered in the area of Second and Third Avenue and 107th Street, those from the town and province of Naples between First and Second Avenue and 112th and 120th Street, and those from the town and province of Potenza between 116th and 119th Street and Pleasant and First Avenue (Map 7, clusters 2, 1, 3). Although many residents from a particular city and province in Italy concentrated in a local neighborhood, there were always some who lived in other parts of East Harlem.

The preceding evidence suggests several important conclusions. Italians as a group settled in distinct patterns in Buenos Aires and New York City. In Buenos Aires, where they represented approximately a quarter of all inhabitants, they were dispersed fairly evenly in the areas where the total population of the city resided, and constituted at least 10 percent of the total population in every census district. In both 1895 and 1904, the largest percentage of Italians was located in the core-periphery districts surrounding the central business district, and the smallest percentage in the outlying area. In New York City, in contrast, the Italians were concentrated in two main areas, the Mulberry District and surrounding wards, and in East Harlem.

At the local level, however, the patterns of residence were very similar. Italians in both cities settled in village-based clusters formed by personal networks. These networks frequently were the focal points for provincial or regional clustering. Those from the North of Italy, who had resided longer in the two cities, tended to be more dispersed than the recently arrived southerners.

Developing Patterns

Once they had found places to live, many of the Italians in Buenos Aires and New York moved frequently. Some left to return to Italy or to go to new destinations abroad. Others moved within the metropolitan areas. Of those who moved within their adopted city, some went from the central districts to the outlying areas, while others moved locally within a neighborhood.

The available evidence indicates that very large numbers left both cities, especially during the decades before 1900. We know, for example, that approximately 40 percent of the Italians in Buenos Aires and 50 percent of those in New York returned to Italy (Table 10)[12] In addition we know

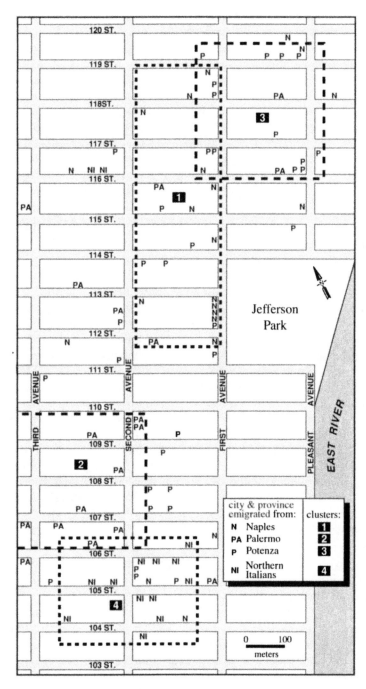

Map 7. Italian clusters in East Harlem

that both cities—but especially New York—served as way stations for many Italians destined for other parts of the country. In a residential trace of 449 Italian families living in New York in 1880, Thomas Kessner found that 92 percent were not there ten years later. A similar trace of New York Italians between 1905 and 1915 showed that during this latter decade a somewhat smaller but still very substantial number (72 percent) had moved out of the city.[13] Unfortunately there is no study for Buenos Aires equivalent to that of Kessner's residential trace of New York Italians. Nevertheless, the data on return migration and other more impressionistic evidence make it clear that in both cities large numbers of Italians moved out.

Italians also moved frequently within the two cities. I have already shown that Italians in Buenos Aires at first settled almost completely within the core and the core-periphery of the city. By 1914, large numbers had moved to the outlying districts (Table 24). While only 19 percent lived in the outlying districts in 1895, nineteen years later—as the total population grew and moved outward—51 percent of the Italians resided there.

Italians in New York also first settled in the central areas of the city below 14th Street in Manhattan, and then gradually expanded into East Harlem and the areas in between. Compared to the Italians in Buenos Aires, however, New York Italians started moving to the outlying areas of the city at a later date. In 1900, 66 percent of the Italians lived in Manhattan. Only by 1920, after World War I, did more than half of them live in the other boroughs (Table 25).

In addition to this movement outward, the Italians also frequently moved more locally within their neighborhoods. My sample of 554 Italians naturalized in Manhattan in 1921 shows that by this time those who were remaining in the city were moving but not very far.[14] Table 29 presents the results of comparing the addresses of these 554 Italians at the time they declared their intentions to become naturalized citizens (1915–1916) to their addresses in 1921 when they in fact were naturalized. Fifty-eight percent of the Italians sampled changed residence during this five- to six-year period. Of those who changed residence, however, 63 percent moved only a short distance. This relative locational stability can be illustrated even more dramatically if the figures are combined on those who did not move with those who moved locally. Seventy-eight percent either did not move or moved within twelve blocks of their original residence. Furthermore, 93 percent of those who were in the Mulberry District in 1915–1916 and 92 percent of those who were in East Harlem were still there in 1921. By the end of World War I, the Italian colony of New York consisted of locally mobile but more permanent city residents.

My samples of mutual aid society records indicate similarly high residential mobility among Italians in Buenos Aires. These data also demon-

Table 29. Mobility of naturalized Italians in Manhattan, 1915–1916 to 1921

	Number	Percentage
No move	218	42
Move one or more times	302	58
Move within 6 blocks	(158)	(30)
Move 7 to 12 blocks	(31)	(6)
Move 12+ blocks[a]	(113)	(22)
Total sample[b]	520	100
No move		42
No move + move within 6 blocks		72
No move + move within 12 blocks		78

[a]Of the 113 individuals who moved more than twelve blocks, 63 moved within Manhattan, 21 moved from one borough to another within New York City, and 29 moved to Manhattan from outside of New York City.

[b]The sample is of 554 Italians who were naturalized in the District Court of the United States, Southern District of New York, in 1921. For 34 of them, however, one address—either in the declaration of intention in 1915–1916 or in the petition for naturalization in 1921—was missing, making it impossible to trace mobility. I have excluded these 34 from the analysis, and thus the total is 520.

Source: New York City Naturalization Records.

strate that, as in New York, those who changed residence generally did not move very far. Table 30 presents the results of address changes of a sample of 377 members of the Unione e Benevolenza between 1895 and 1901. It shows that 45 percent, as opposed to 58 percent in New York, moved one or more times during this six-year period. Yet 62 percent of those who changed residence—almost the identical percentage as in New York—moved within twelve blocks. Similarly, 83 percent either did not move or moved locally in Buenos Aires, compared to 78 percent in New York. Ninety percent of those who were in the Boca at the beginning of the period and 86 percent of those in San Nicolás were there in 1901, compared to figures of 93 percent and 92 percent for those who resided in the Mulberry District and East Harlem.

Residential mobility, measured by the naturalization and mutual aid society data, was extensive in both cities, but was somewhat higher among Italians in Manhattan than among those in Buenos Aires. Most of this difference can be explained, however, by the fact that the Buenos Aires data are from the 1895–1901 period, which preceded the decade of rapid Italian movement to the outlying areas of the city. These data, along with Kessner's information and the published censuses, all indicate that Italians moved frequently within both cities between 1890 and 1920.

Table 30. Mobility of Unione e Benevolenza members in Buenos Aires, 1895–1901

	Number	Percentage
No move	209	55
Move one or more times	168	45
Move within 6 blocks	(64)	(17)
Move 7–12 blocks	(41)	(11)
Move 12+ blocks	(63)	(17)
Total sample[a]	377	100
No move		55
No move + move within 6 blocks		72
No move + move within 12 blocks		83

[a] The sample (377 individuals) is an 8.5 percent random sample of the 4,000 members of the Unione e Benevolenza recorded in the Libri d'inscrizione dei soci, 1895–1901.

Yet there was a significant difference in the nature of this mobility in the two cities. In 1890, residential mobility among New York Italians was overwhelmingly movement outside the city. Twenty-five years later, many more of the moves were to destinations within the city; some moved to the other boroughs of the city but what is important is that most made only local moves. Although New York had initially been a way station for Italians going to other parts of the United States, increasingly it became a more permanent residential location.

At the end of the nineteenth century, residential mobility among Buenos Aires Italians was already more confined within the city, and this pattern most certainly held true thereafter. Italian immigrants going to the interior did pass through Buenos Aires, and some who resided there temporarily did return to Italy. However, the city was never primarily a way station; Italians in Buenos Aires made frequent local moves, but the city always had a larger stable Italian population than New York did. At the same time, Italians in Buenos Aires moved to the outlying areas of the city at an earlier date and in greater numbers than in New York.

Explanations of the Residence Patterns

Although a number of influences determined where an individual would live, both the nature and location of work and the desire to live close to one's place of employment were among the most important. Italians, especially the large majority who worked long hours for low pay, lived near their places of employment. In New York, the largest percentage initially resided below 14th Street in Manhattan—where, as late as 1906, 67 percent of all factory jobs were located. Pratt's 1911 study of population congestion in New York shows that Italian male workers, more than any other group living below 14th Street, walked to work (55 percent) or spent the minimal amount—ten cents or less—on carfare (34 percent). The percentage of Italian female workers who walked to work or paid the minimal carfare was even higher.[15] Industry and commerce did move increasingly to Brooklyn, especially after World War I, and this shift enabled some Italians to move out of Manhattan and still be close to work.

Industry and commerce were concentrated in the central area of Buenos Aires, but to a lesser extent than in New York. Small artisan shops dominated a large part of Buenos Aires industry until the 1930s, and this kind of industry did not need a great deal of space, complex marketing, or special transportation. As a result, there was no tendency to group these workshops in particular locations. The large food processing and agricultural-products plants, however, were located in the center of the city and increasingly in the area to the south. Buenos Aires, nevertheless, was not an island with limited space, and the immigrants therefore could spread out to a greater extent and still be close to their jobs. As industry and commerce moved to the outlying parts of the city after 1900, so too did some of the Italians who until then had lived in the center.[16]

Some occupations were clustered in certain areas of both cities; those who were employed in these occupations frequently lived in the same areas. Unskilled laborers were to be found fairly evenly distributed in the same areas where the Italian population in general was located (Table 31). The same distribution was essentially true for carpenters, tailors, clerks, and businessmen. Cooks and waiters, on the other hand, clustered in patterns that did not reflect the general distribution of the Italian population. In New York, 61 percent of the cooks and 72 percent of the waiters in the naturalization sample lived between 14th and 86th Streets on the West Side (Wards 16, 20, and 22) where many restaurants were located. Similarly in Buenos Aires, 79 percent of the cooks and 100 percent of the waiters in the mutual aid society sample resided in the core and especially in Districts 14 and 20. Sailors in Buenos Aires concentrated in the Boca (38 percent) and in the three central districts (12, 13, 14) next to the docks (52 percent).

The housing market also had a significant impact on the choice of initial residence and subsequent moves. The overwhelming bulk of rental housing was located in the central areas and it was in short supply in the outlying districts. Immigrants, most of whom lacked the funds to buy a lot or

Table 31. Distribution of Italians by occupation

Occupation (N in NYC) (N in BA)	New York City				Buenos Aires			
	Below 14th (%)	14th–86th (%)	Above 86th (%)	Other clusters (Districts = %)	Core (%)	Periphery (%)	Outlying (%)	Other clusters (Districts = %)
Unskilled laborer (188) (70)	63	18	19	(6, 14) = 30	50	33	17	(14, 20) = 34
Cook (23) (14)	35	61	4	(16, 20, 22) = 43	79	14	7	(14, 20) = 64
Waiter (49) (10)	20	72	8	(16, 20, 22) = 51	100	0		(14, 20) = 60
Carpenter (21) (68)	57	10	33		41	38	21	
Tailor (113) (26)	58	18	24		77	8		(14) = 35
Clerk (66) (52)	47	23	30		50	27	23	
Business (general) (63) (152)	57	29	14		46	34	20	
Total NYC sample	48	16	25	Total BA sample	44	28	28	

Sources: New York City Naturalization Records; Buenos Aires Mutual Aid Society Records.

to finance home construction, were therefore initially limited to this type of housing in the central districts. The growth of the population in the center in turn led to a shortage of housing and to the development of crowded and often unhealthy tenement houses.[17]

Although most Italians could not initially afford to buy property and construct a house, home ownership—especially in Buenos Aires—appeared to be one of the important objectives of those who settled more permanently in the two cities. In Buenos Aires, where by 1904 many Italians had lived for some time, 16 percent of the Italian population—compared to 9 percent of the total population—owned a home (Table 22). Stated in other terms, Italians, who in 1904 represented 24 percent of the city's population, were 45 percent of all home owners. Furthermore, four of the six districts with the highest proportions of Italian population were also those with the highest percentage of Italian homeowners (4, 8, 9, 18). By 1914, the percentage of Italian home owners had increased even more, especially in the outlying districts.

New York City data on property ownership is fragmentary but nevertheless suggestive. As discussed in the preceding chapter, the 1909 Immigration Commission survey of 524 Italian households in Manhattan indicates that only 1.3 percent of the heads of families owned homes. Even if this figure misses the relatively small number of Italians in the outlying boroughs where home ownership was more possible, the percentage of home ownership was proportionately still most certainly far below that in Buenos Aires. To the Italians in New York, most of whom emphasized more immediate economic returns and the repatriation of their surpluses to Italy, home ownership in their host city was less important than it was to those in Buenos Aires. The desire to own a home was, therefore, less of an influence on residence patterns in New York.

The ability to save and obtain credit determined patterns of outward mobility more than initial settlement, but it was important to both processes in different ways. As explained in detail in the preceding chapter, savings were influenced by economic success, the individual's reasons for migrating, the economic strategy he or she pursued, and the availability of credit, among other things. In Buenos Aires, the Italians were relatively higher up on the wage hierarchy, and their long-term economic strategy led them to invest surplus capital there. In addition, their ability to buy a home was increased when, during the first decade of the century, extended monthly payment mortgages became more available.[18] Many New York Italians, on the other hand, intended to return to Italy from the outset. They sent their surplus earnings home and consequently had less desire to invest in a building lot or a home. It was the middle-income Italians who were better able to save and obtain credit, and there were relatively more of them in Buenos Aires than in New York.[19] Those who decided to remain in New York waited to move out of Manhattan until they could save enough to buy a house. For most, this was not possible or considered desirable before World War I.

The influence of transportation on residence was complex, and it differed in the two cities. Although the transportation system affected where an immigrant might move, it did not necessarily determine the timing of this move. In New York, elevated trains began to run from the Battery to Harlem in 1881, which clearly facilitated the development of the East Harlem Italian colony. By the early 1900s, however, the subway system connected Brooklyn, Queens, and the Bronx with Manhattan, yet the major outward movement in New York did not occur until after World War I.[20]

In Buenos Aires, there was a closer short-term association between the development and cost of transportation and the movement of Italians to the outlying districts. The rail system had linked various parts of the city by 1900, but it was not until the introduction of the electric streetcar and the major reduction of fares in the early 1900s that Italians in large numbers began to move to the outlying districts.[21]

Family, kinship, and paesani networks also influenced residence patterns. Already established individuals frequently provided a temporary place to stay for new immigrants and then assisted them in finding more permanent lodgings. Because members of these networks wanted to be in close proximity, they sought housing in the same areas. Oreste Sola, for example, lived with his godfather in Buenos Aires for several years. When Abele arrived in the city, he moved into the apartment of his brother, Oreste, and continued to live with him and his wife, Corinna, for many years. Ida Sola likewise lived for a time with relatives when she first came to New York.

Movement outward was also influenced by these personal networks. For example, following the establishment of the original colony of Sirolesi in the Boca as noted earlier, a second colony developed in the nearby town of Quilmes. The two areas were linked by a network of kin and paesani. This linkage undoubtedly encouraged those who sought and were able to move out to select Quilmes as their destination. Similarly in New York a colony of Cinisi lived in the area of 6th Street and Avenue A in Manhattan. Other Cinisi resided in clusters in the Bowery, Harlem, and Brooklyn.[22] It is reasonable to assume that the relationship between the Cinisi colonies in Manhattan and Brooklyn was similar to that of the Sirolesi colonies in the Boca and Quilmes, and that when the Cinisi moved out of Manhattan many chose the Cinise section of Brooklyn as their destination.

And finally, personal considerations caused Italians to move frequently. The birth of a child or the arrival of relatives from Italy compelled some families to seek larger quarters. The loss of a job, illness, or an economic downturn forced others to find cheaper accommodations. Or the chafing of grown children under the dominant authority of a parent might make still others look for an alternative situation.

The location and availability of jobs, the concern to live near work, the housing market, the desire to own property, the ability to save, the availability of transportation, the existence of personal networks, the individual economic strategies, and various other personal considerations all influenced residence patterns. Some of these were more important in determining initial settlement, while others were more significant in determining subsequent moves. And some were crucial to both parts of the process. The location and availability of work, the housing market, and the existence of kin and paesani networks were of primary importance for initial settlement patterns. The desire to own property, the ability to save and obtain credit, the availability of transportation, and the existence of personal networks were significant for subsequent mobility.

Several points emerge from this analysis of the settlement patterns in the two cities. First, at the citywide level, Italians in Buenos Aires were evenly dispersed, while those in New York were concentrated in a few areas. This difference was due primarily to the distinct nature and location of commerce and industry, to differing geographical settings, and to the percentage of Italians in the respective populations. Second, although Italians moved frequently in both cities, significant movement to the outlying areas occurred at different times; in Buenos Aires the Italians began to move to the outlying districts in large numbers during the decade before World War I, but in New York they did not do so until after the war. This difference was the result of the distinct economic strategies followed by the Italians in the two cities and the consequent decision to invest surplus in the host society or send it home, and the respective positions of the Italians in the job hierarchies. And third, the settlement patterns were, nevertheless, very similar at the sub-Italian level. Italians clustered on the basis of village, and to a lesser extent, provincial and regional ties. This, in turn, was determined by the common influence of immigrant networks.

Italians found housing with relatively little difficulty in both cities, but because the resulting settlement patterns differed in some important ways, they exerted distinct influences on the respective processes of adjustment. First, the Italians in Buenos Aires were more permanent than those in New York in the sense that although they moved frequently, more of them did so within the city. Thus a larger number of long-time Italian residents were available in Buenos Aires than in New York to support a formal institutional structure, which I will discuss in Chapters 7 and 8. In addition, Italians in Buenos Aires moved in greater percentages and at an earlier time to the outlying areas of the city. In these outlying areas, there was more opportunity for property and home ownership. Both these distinctions fitted within the respective economic strategies pursued by most Italians in Buenos Aires and New York. In this sense, residential patterns were part of the larger effort of the immigrants to achieve specific social and economic goals.

6

Family, Household, and Neighborhood

Italian immigrants in Buenos Aires and New York City lived and acted within a number of overlapping institutional spheres of varying importance to their lives—those of the family and household, the local neighborhood, the Italian community, and the host society community, among others. As the immigrants sought to reconstruct their lives in a new environment, they relied in different ways on these institutions to facilitate and cushion the process of adjustment. To the extent that these institutions incorporated the immigrants and met their needs, they established parameters within which individuals made decisions about their own lives. Yet involvement was a two-way process. Not only were the immigrants affected by these institutions, they also influenced in varying degrees the nature and goals of these entities.

Although these institutional spheres overlapped, I will for the purposes of analysis divide them into two categories: on the one hand, the informal, more immediate institutions of family, household, and local neighborhood, and on the other hand, the formal, legally recognized institutions of the broader Italian community and the host society. In this chapter, I will examine the former. In the subsequent two chapters, I will look at the latter.

The most immediate of these institutional spheres for the immigrants were those of the family, the household, and the neighborhood. Relations among members of all three were similarly founded on direct personal contact, but in each the nature of the individuals' bonds to one another differed. The family was based on reciprocal blood and marriage relationships created in Italy and extended by the act of migration to Buenos Aires and New York. Most immigrants had their closest ties and greatest loyalty to the members of their family—whether in Italy or the New World or both, and it was to the family that they generally turned for help in times of need.

I am using the term *household* to refer to a group of individuals who shared a residence and consumed food together. The household generally included at least one family, but others—such as unrelated boarders or additional unrelated families—sometimes lived within it as well. Thus, although some scholars have treated household and family as identical, in fact this was not always the case.[1] The two frequently coincided, but family often extended beyond household and household sometimes included individuals who were not family members. The distinction is important in the study of migration because immigrants frequently used family and household in different ways as they adjusted to their new environments.

The attachment to neighborhood developed as a result of economic and social contacts outside the immediate family and household. Some of these contacts were with transplanted kin and fellow paesani from the villages of origin, but many were also completely new. The ties to neighbors varied according to the functions they fulfilled. Generally they were less intimate and more likely to be of an instrumental nature than those to the family and household. Nevertheless, the familiarity of the local neighborhood, the recognition it offered its members, and the functions it served often recreated a village atmosphere and provided an important reference point for individual immigrants within the larger metropolitan area. The local neighborhood thus often became the new focal point from which the immigrants moved outward into the New World.

My concern in this chapter is to evaluate how in both New York and Buenos Aires individual immigrants' experiences were influenced by and in turn influenced family, household, and neighborhood.

Family and Household

Both families and households were important in the adjustment process. Most migrants, as was the case for Oreste and Ida Sola, saw themselves as part of a family located in Italy and abroad to which they were tied by bonds of blood, marriage, loyalty, reciprocal obligations, and tradition. Decisions by individuals regarding migration were generally made within the context of the family and with family goals in mind. Migrants also lived in a household abroad to which they were tied by the pragmatic bonds of shared residence and mutual assistance, and often by the bonds of family as well.

The extensive body of literature on family history makes it clear that families and households adopted different forms in response to the demands for survival and self-preservation in specific places and times.[2] In some situations, the *simple* or *nuclear* family and household (father, mother, and children) best served the members' needs. In others, the *extended* or *complex* family and household (nuclear plus some combination of additional kin such as grandparents, uncles and aunts, siblings, cousins, and in-laws) was most appropriate. Sometimes family and household were identical. Other times they were not.

The purpose of this section is to examine the ways in which Italian family and household forms and functions changed during the migration to Buenos Aires and New York City, and how these adaptations facilitated the immigrants' adjustment. I first look briefly at the family and household in Italy during the second half of the nineteenth century. Then I examine them in the two respective New World cities and compare their experiences.

Family and Household in Italy

When investigating the nature of family and household in Italy, we must begin by confronting two myths: one, that the nuclear family household was the predominant Italian form throughout its history and, two, that family members had no meaningful ties outside the nuclear family household.[3] The recent literature on household and family in Italy during the second half of the nineteenth century refutes both these contentions. It emphasizes instead the diversity in family type produced by economic and demographic factors and by cultural norms and practices.[4] Extended or complex family households were common and perhaps even predominated in many areas of Italy, and could be found in the same areas where there were also nuclear family households.

In the extensive sharecropping areas of central and parts of northern Italy, extended family households were common. Landlords, who sought the maximum yearly return on their land, were anxious to rent to families with the greatest number of adult workers. At the same time, the growth of agrarian wage labor in the eighteenth and nineteenth centuries led to the presence of nuclear family households as well. Thus "the large multiple-family household system of the sharecroppers coexisted with the smaller, usually nuclear families of their agricultural wage-laborer neighbors in nineteen-century central Italy."[5]

Although the nuclear family household predominated in much of southern Italy, in Sicily and Sardinia—where agrarian wage labor and a market economy were the norm, there was family and household variation based on age of marriage and personal service before marriage. In Sardinia, for example, many unmarried young people worked for a period of time as servants in other houses, and both men and women married late. In Sicily and much of southern Italy, on the other hand, individuals did not generally work as servants in other houses before marriage, and they married earlier than in Sardinia.[6]

Evidence from the Molise suggests that in terms of household forms, it may have been a transitional area. There, complex households were found with greater frequency than in Sicily and the South, but were not as prevalent as in the Center and North.[7] The patrilineal joint family, in which more than one child brought a spouse to live in the parental household, was, according to Douglass, the social ideal in Agnone and the surrounding towns of the Molise, even though the frequency of its existence at any given time (between 7.2 percent and 11.4 percent) was not nearly as high as among the sharecroppers of the Center-North. What Douglass shows, however, is that a life course analysis of the evidence indicates that 52 percent of families attained the joint family ideal at some point.

The important conclusion is that there was no single Italian household type in the second half of the nineteenth century. Family systems were complex and varied according to specific local economic and political conditions, customs, and traditions. It is therefore misleading to assume that the nuclear family household was the predominant type in nineteenth-century Italy. Instead there were many different kinds of household types—nuclear and extended in different forms—in the various regions of Italy and also within the same communities. And even in areas where the nuclear family household predominated, certain kinds of social ties outside the nuclear family were important.

Whatever its particular composition, the fundamental functions of the Italian family at all times were survival and self-preservation.[8] Each new generation in turn assumed these responsibilities, and its actions were guided by these goals. The family was a reproductive unit that brought children into the world and cared for them until they were able to start families of their own. In addition, the family was an economic unit that managed collective financial, human, and material resources to ensure both survival and the availability of inheritance and dowries for the children to establish families. It allocated jobs, regulated demands on resources, and oversaw the process of passing on collective wealth. Furthermore, the family was a social unit that on the one hand educated children and socialized them to the cultural norms of the community and on the other hand tied its members to larger social networks of kin, neighbors, and friends.

The relationships between the members of the family were determined by mutual obligations and responsibilities that varied over the life course of its members. The father and husband was the dominant figure in the family, who assigned economic roles to family members and assumed the major responsibility for providing support. His authority was for the most part unchallenged, at least openly. Nevertheless, the mother and wife controlled the domestic sphere and the routine management of household resources. In addition, she managed kin relations, illnesses, childbirth, death, and the selection of marriage partners for her sons. Women were also important to varying degrees in work outside the home; in this sphere they apparently were the greatest contributors in central Italy and to a lesser extent in the North and the South.[9] The children were expected to work to contribute to family resources from an early age and to respect their parents' wishes. This relationship changed when the children grew up, got married, and left the home, but even then the parents—like Luigi and Margherita Sola—assumed that their children would support them in their old age.

The family thus was central to the lives of most individuals throughout Italy, but its structure and functions varied according to circumstances. The process of migration would bring about changes within the family and household that facilitated the immigrants' adjustment.

Family and Household in New York City and Buenos Aires

The family proved to be an enduring but flexible institution that responded to the new sets of circumstances and needs created by migration.[10] Families continued to play a major role in the lives of those who migrated; family members, wherever they might have been located physically, remained to a greater or lesser extent tied to each other and most continued to assume some if not all of the responsibilities and obligations of such membership.[11] Thus, for example, for many years both Oreste and Abele Sola consistently sent money home from Buenos Aires to support their parents in retirement.

Although the family survived migration and in many cases prospered as a result of it, the moves affected the family. Some impact was inevitable given the migration of some family members and not others and the different economic and social contexts of the two receiving societies. The nature of existing data imposes many limits on our effort to determine what happened to the family in the migration process and how it facilitated adjustment. The aggregate snapshots provided by censuses in both countries leave out important information, mask the diversity and complexity of family life, and provide no basis for measuring change over time. Critical manuscript census schedules are available in Argentina only for 1895, and even then there is no indication of the relationships of family members to each other or of the extent of households. Although manuscript schedules are available for New York City, high rates of mobility make it difficult to trace individual families from census to census.

In addition, there is considerably more scholarly work on the Italian immigrant family in New York City than in Buenos Aires, a factor that makes comparison difficult. This section therefore is an exploratory effort that will suggest answers to some of the important questions regarding family, household, and migration, and I hope it will indicate directions for future research to confirm these arguments. The focus will be primarily on family and household composition and on the roles of family members, because the effects of migration were quite visible in these areas and because there are sufficient data with which to explore them.

One of the results of the selective process that took place during migration is that the Italian populations in Buenos Aires and New York differed from those in Italy. Since fewer children and older people initially made the voyages across the Atlantic, the percentage of Italian working-class adults in the total Italian population was considerably higher in the two New World cities than in Italy. In addition, substantially more men migrated than women, creating an initial imbalance between the sexes. Furthermore, Italians abroad were only a minority of the total population of the cities in which they resided. And finally, the Italians in Buenos Aires and New York were more mobile than those in Italy.[12]

Despite the difficulties created by imbalanced age and sex structures, by being a numerical minority, and by considerable geographical mobility, the Italians maintained their families and continued to create new ones. Of the large number of adult Italian immigrants in the two cities, most were either married or widowed. Two out of every three adult men and more than four out of every five adult women in Buenos Aires were married or widowed both in 1895 and in 1914. The more limited data on New York suggest a similar pattern there (Table 32).[13]

In addition to the evidence that at least 60 percent of the adult Italians in both cities were married, partial data suggest that most married Italians in these two cities were living with their spouses. Approximately four out of five married Italians in three central districts of Buenos Aires in 1895 lived with their spouses.[14] In New York in 1900, an even higher percentage of married Italians who lived on two blocks of Elizabeth Street occupied nearly entirely by Italians lived with their spouses. Ninety-five percent of the households on these blocks had a husband present. A much larger sample of Italian households in Greenwich Village five years later showed that 93 percent had a husband present.[15]

Not only did the Italian family survive migration, but high Italian endogamy rates and large numbers of children born to Italian parents during the decades before World War I served to perpetuate the family in Buenos Aires and New York.[16] Italian men and women married primarily Italian spouses. During the thirty-five year period from 1882 to 1917, Italian women in Buenos Aires overwhelmingly chose Italian men as marriage partners, although the incidence of such marriages gradually declined from 90 percent to 75 percent over the period. Italian men, of whom

Table 32. Marital status of adult Italians in Buenos Aires and New York City

| | Buenos Aires | | | | New York City | |
| | 1895[a] | | 1914[a] | | 1920[a,b] | |
Marital status	Male (%)	Female (%)	Male (%)	Female (%)	Male (%)	Female (%)
Single	35	12	35	14	25	14
Married	61	76	61	70	71	76
Widowed	4	12	4	15	4	9
	100	100	100	100	100	100

[a] The 1895 figures include all Italians sixteen years of age and older; the 1914 and 1920 figures include those fifteen and older.

[b] These figures must be used with caution since they include all Italians living in New York, Chicago, Detroit, Milwaukee, Boston, and Rhode Island. I present them because there is nothing else available. What makes them indicative of New York City is that the Italians of New York City represented 72.4 percent of the total of the five cities and one state.

Sources: Argentina, Censo 1895, 2, pp. 28–29; Argentina, Censo 1914, 2, p. 421; Niles Carpenter, Immigrants and Their Children (New York, 1969), pp. 424–427.

Table 33. Indicators of marriage patterns of Italians in Buenos Aires

| | Buenos Aires | | | |
	1882–1886 (%)	1893–1897 (%)	1903–1907 (%)	1913–1917 (%)
Italian women with:				
Italian men	90	86	80	75
Argentine men	4	7	12	17
Other men	6	7	8	8
	100	100	100	100
Italian men with:				
Italian women	73	67	56	49
Argentine women	22	25	34	37
Other women	5	8	10	14
	100	100	100	100

Sources: Samuel L. Baily, "Marriage Patterns and Immigrant Assimilation in Buenos Aires, 1882–1923," Hispanic American Historical Review, 60, 1 (February 1980), pp. 40–42.

there were considerably more, were somewhat less endogamous than the women. At the beginning of the period, 73 percent of the Italian men married Italian women; this figure declined to just under 50 percent thirty-five years later (Table 33).[17]

Unfortunately we do not have the actual percentages of marriage partners by nationality for New York. Indirect evidence, however, suggests a similarly high degree of intramarriage among Italian men and women in that city. The 1900 census data on the parents of U.S.-born children of Italian descent (one or both parents Italian-born) show that more than 93 percent of Italian fathers were married to Italian mothers. Twenty years later (1920), we see that for every 1,000 Italian mothers, 971 were married to Italian fathers, whereas for every 1,000 Italian fathers, only 828 were married to Italian mothers. These data exclude married Italians who did not have children, but this number was not very large.[18]

Italians in both Buenos Aires and New York married predominantly Italian spouses during the half century before World War I, even though there were fewer Italian women than men in these two cities. What made this possible was that Italian men frequently sent home for a bride if one was not available, or they made the trip back to their home town to marry a local woman.

In addition to high rates of endogamy, high numbers of births to Italian women in both cities provided the basis for the perpetuation of the Italian family in subsequent generations. In 1887, Italian women in Buenos Aires represented 25 percent of all women, yet produced 42 percent of all births. Similarly, in 1904, they constituted 20 percent of all women and produced 33 percent of all births.[19] This high number of births created a substantial—though impossible to define precisely—second generation of Italians in Buenos Aires.[20] In New York City, Italian women constituted less than 7 percent of all women in 1910 and 1920, and yet produced approximately 20 percent of all births (Table 34). Here, fortunately, we have the data on second-generation Italians to establish the point with precision. In New York in 1910, there were 341,000 first-generation Italians born in Italy and an additional 204,000 people born abroad of Italian parents. By 1920, the number of first-generation Italians grew to 391,000 and the second generation increased to 412,000.[21]

The Italian family survived immigration and continued as a vital force in the lives of its members, but in the process it also changed. The important questions are how much and in what ways did it change, and were there significant differences between the experiences in Buenos Aires and New York City?[22] To answer these questions I will turn to the evidence on household and family composition and on the roles of individual family members.

Household and family composition of Italian populations in both cities in the New World reflected in part the dynamics of the process of migration. Most men, whether or not they were married, initially migrated without female family members. After some time, if they decided to settle, the men would call for their wives or find a suitable woman abroad or in Italy to marry. At the same time they would encourage and assist other kin of their own generation (brothers and sisters, brothers- and sisters-in-law,

Table 34. Births to Italian women in Buenos Aires and New York City (percentage of all births)

	Buenos Aires		New York City	
Years	Births[a]	Italian women as % of all women	Births[a]	Italian women as % of all women
1882–1886	42	25 (1887)		
1892–1896	37			
1902–1906	33	20 (1904)		
1910			22	< 7
1912–1914[b]	23			
1915			21	< 7
1920			19	< 7

Notes:
[a] These figures slightly understate the actual number of births to Italian women because they are based on births to Italian females married to Italian males. If data were available on the relatively small number of Italian females married to non-Italian males and on illegitimate births, I estimate the figures would increase in each case by between 3 percent and 5 percent.
[b] Births were not listed by nationality of parents after 1914.
Sources: Buenos Aires, Dirección General de Estadística, Anuario estadístico de la Ciudad de Buenos Aires, 1882–1923, 25 vols. (Buenos Aires, 1882–1925); Ira Rosenwaike, Population History of New York City (Syracuse, N.Y., 1972), p. 182; U.S. Census 1910; U.S. Census 1920.

cousins) to come join them as well, thus expanding their peer group within the family household. Later they would have children and call for close kin of older and younger generations (parents, maiden aunts, nieces and nephews), restoring a more traditional multigeneration composition to the family household. Change depended on where individuals were in the course of the migration process, but since during the decades before World War I there were always new immigrants who were joining those already in Buenos Aires and New York, there were always families and households at various stages in the process.

Although in both cities the nuclear structure predominated as the preferred form among Italian-headed families, some households were at least temporarily extended during migration to create what Modell and Hareven have called the "malleable household."[23] The malleable household emerged in Buenos Aires and New York—as elsewhere in immigrant-receiving societies—because of the presence of young immigrants who needed a place to stay, crowded and expensive housing markets, immigrant families who needed the income provided by boarders, and a preference among Italians to be with kin and paesani. Some boarders were related to the family with which they resided, but many of them were not.

In New York during the first decade of the twentieth century, approximately two-thirds of the Italian households located below 14th Street in

Table 35. Composition of Italian-headed households, New York City, 1900–1915

	Baily	Gabaccia		Gutman	Immigration Commission[a]	
	1900 (%)	1905 (%)	1915 (%)	1905 (%)	1910 A (%)	1910 B (%)
All Italian households						
Nuclear	65	61	81	60	77[b]	62[b]
Extended	33	37	19	34	23	38
Other[c]	2	2		6		
	100	100	100	100	100	100
Italian households with						
Boarders	18	8	7	21	22	18
Relatives	16	12	9	23		
Multiple conjugal units	15	17	3			31
Servants	0	0	0	0	0	0
Average household size	5.0	5.3		4.6	5.8	
Number of households studied	246	1,555	1,722	3,166	421	524

[a] The data in Immigration Commission column B include partner households (multiple conjugal unit households). The data in Immigration Commission column A do not.
[b] These percentages refer to single family as opposed to nuclear family households. The Immigration Commission defined single family households as including "the immediate family with, perhaps, a near relative on the same footing as a member of the immediate family, but with no boarders or lodgers." (U.S. Immigration Commission, *Reports*, 26, p. 199.) The other sources refer to the nuclear household of husband, wife, and unmarried children; husband and wife; or single parent and unmarried children.
[c] Other includes single adults, unrelated individuals, and unmarried brothers and sisters.
Sources: (1) Baily data come from the manuscript federal census of 1900 and include all 246 Italian-headed households (1,235 individuals) on Elizabeth Sreet between Broome and Spring Streets. (2) Gabaccia data come from the manuscript New York State censuses of 1905 and 1915. For 1905, they included 1,555 Italian-headed households in Ward 14 (8,249 individuals). For 1915, they include 1,772 households (8,846 individuals). I wish to thank Donna Gabaccia for generously sharing this information with me and giving me permission to use it here. See also Donna Gabaccia, *From Sicily to Elizabeth Street: Housing and Social Change among Italian Immigrants, 1880–1930* (Albany, N.Y., 1984), p. 59. (3) Gutman data come from the manuscript New York State census of 1905 and include 3,116 Italian-headed households (14,300 individuals) in the Greenwich Village area (parts of Wards 6, 14, and 15). See Herbert G. Gutman, *The Black Family in Slavery and Freedom, 1750–1925* (New York, 1976), Appendi: B. (4) Immigration Commission data come from its survey of households headed by southern Italians (said to contain 2,427 individuals) on Elizabeth Street between Spring and Houston Streets and on East 114th Street between First and Second Avenues. The survey figures, however, are confusing and should be regarded with caution. The commission refers at times to 421 households and at other times to 524 (including partner households) without explaining the difference in these base figures. In addition, the 31 percent (162) of partner households it refers to do not add up to the difference between the two columns. See Immigration Commission, *Reports*, 26, pp. 163–165 and 198–202. (5) See also Miriam J. Cohen, *Workshop to Office: Two Generations of Italian Women in New York City, 1900–1950* (Ithaca, N.Y., 1992), p. 94. which provides figures on the number of households with boarders similar to those of the studies cited here.

Manhattan were nuclear and the other third extended (Table 35). The extended households were created by the addition of various combinations of boarders, relatives, and other conjugal units. According to most sources, boarders were part of nearly one-fifth of all households and more than half of all extended households. Somewhat fewer relatives and mul-

Table 36. New York City Italian households with
boarders as percentage of all Italian households according
to length of residence of heads in the United States

Length of residence (years)	Immigration Commission data (1910) N (%)	Baily data (1900) N (%)
1–4	97 (27)	72 (28)
5–9	112 (24)	57 (24.5)
10+	211 (19)	117 (9.5)
All	420 (22)	246 (18)

Sources: See Table 35.

tiple conjugal units (two or more co-residing nuclear family units) extended these households. These categories obviously overlapped, as when
a relative was a boarder.

Although the development of the malleable household was an important adjustment strategy of approximately a third of the Italian families in
New York during the first decade of the century, it was a temporary strategy. Gabaccia's data present a significant decline in the extended family
household by 1915 (Table 35). In addition, data on Italian households both
in 1900 and 1910 show that the percentage with boarders declined the
longer the head of the household had been in the United States (Table 36).
The newly arrived immigrant nuclear family, the immigrant men in New
York without their wives, and the young single men and women created
the malleable household because it served their mutual purposes. As time
passed and the needs of the more established parties changed, the relative
number of extended households declined.

If the malleable household was temporary, its impact on social relationships was not. As Gabaccia has documented, in Sicily only those who assumed the social and economic roles of dependents (children, older relatives) could be part of the household and share its private space. In New
York, however, boarders ate and slept in the household and "a peer group
of non-resident kin and friends also joined the family in its private space
[the kitchen] for casual socializing."[24] The changes in household composition and their impact on social relations thus were important accommodations to migration and urbanization in New York City.

The nature of the Buenos Aires data makes it especially difficult to distinguish one household from another, and thus impossible in most cases
to document with certainty household composition.[25] Fortunately I have
some data from two census districts that will permit me to begin to explore
this important but neglected subject.

Table 37. Composition of Italian-headed households and families, Buenos Aires, 1895

Households (District 15)		Families (District 20)	
Type	(%)	Type	(%)
Nuclear	32	Nuclear (complete)[b]	65
Extended	62	Nuclear (incomplete)[b]	7
Other[a]	6	Extended and multiple	8
Total	100	Families without nucleus	3
Extended with boarders	40	No family[b]	17
Extended with relatives	30		100
Extended with multiple conjugal units	18		
Extended with servants	27		
Average household size 7.4		Average family size 4.2	

[a] "Other" includes single adults, unrelated individuals, and unmarried brothers and sisters.

[b] "Complete nuclear" family is a husband and wife with or without children whereas the "incomplete nuclear" family is a husband or wife with children. "No family" is an individual without wife or children who lives with other unrelated individuals.

Sources: Argentine Census 1895, manuscript schedules for Districts 15 and 20. Stephanie Bower collected the District 15 data for her own work and graciously shared the part of it on Italian families with me. It is a select sample made up of the 20 percent (245) of Italian households in District 15 whose heads filled out their own separate census forms and returned them to the census taker. These 245 Italian households were located in seventy-two of the eighty-three *manzanas* (blocks) in the district. The data on District 20 consist of a 24 percent (1,346) random sample of Italian families in the census collected by Cacopardo and Moreno. For purposes of selection they defined Italian families as all families in which at least one member was Italian. See Maria Cristina Cacopardo and José Luis Moreno, "La familia italiana en la Argentina de fines del siglo XIX," in Cacopardo and Moreno, *La familia italiana y meridional en la emigración a la Argentina* (Naples, 1994), pp. 32, 34, 68.

In a pioneering work, Cacopardo and Moreno provide the only published data on Italian family composition and migration to Argentina at the turn of the past century. Their research is of special interest to us because they examine the Italian family in the Boca district of Buenos Aires (Table 37). According to their data, in 1895, 72 percent of the Italian families in the Boca were nuclear and only 8 percent extended. The remaining 20 percent were families without a nucleus or not families at all. On the basis of this evidence, the authors conclude that the endogamous nuclear family was the most efficient type of family organization to facilitate the adaptation of Italian immigrants in urban areas. They further conclude that the nuclear family was adopted in urban Argentina even by those who came from extended families in Italy.[26]

Although the nuclear composition predominated among Italian *families* in Buenos Aires, as the Cacopardo-Moreno study indicates, the same was not necessarily so among Italian *households*. The needs of immigrants often led them to extend their households at least temporarily to boarders, relatives, and even other conjugal units. Unpublished data on Italian households for District 15 of Buenos Aires show this quite dramatically (Table 37). According to this evidence, nearly two-thirds of the Italian households were extended, and only one-third were simple nuclear families living by themselves. These malleable households included overlapping groups of boarders (in 40 percent of the households), relatives (in 30 percent), and multiple conjugal units (in 18 percent).

We must be cautious in extrapolating from these data to all Italians in Buenos Aires. The District 15 sample is selective and it reflects a population of somewhat higher socioeconomic status than that of the Italians citywide. On the basis of my evaluation of this and the other relevant data, I would argue that the District 15 figure for extended households is high for all Buenos Aires Italians, and that for nuclear households somewhat low. A more reasonable estimate would be approximately 47 percent to 49 percent nuclear, 45 percent to 47 percent extended, and the remaining 4 percent to 8 percent made up of single adults, unrelated individuals, and unmarried brothers and sisters.[27]

Using my estimates to compare Italian household composition in Buenos Aires with that in New York, we note that in the former substantially more Italian households were extended; in Buenos Aires approximately 13 percent more of the Italian households were extended than in New York (46 percent to 33 percent).

In New York, two-thirds of the households were simple nuclear and one-third extended. In Buenos Aires, 48 percent were simple nuclear and 46 percent extended. In addition, the percentage of all households with boarders and relatives was considerably higher in Buenos Aires than it was in New York. The percentage with multiple conjugal units was about the same in both cities. Another striking difference indicated by the District 15 data is that some Italian households in Buenos Aires included servants, whereas none of the Italian households in New York did (See Tables 35 and 37).[28]

Thus it is reasonable to argue that Italian households in Buenos Aires were more frequently extended and somewhat larger than their counterparts in New York, included more boarders and relatives, and sometimes included servants. In other words, if the average extended Italian household in New York consisted of a mother, father, two children, and one or two boarders, the average extended Italian household in Buenos Aires was made up of a mother, father, two children, two or three boarders, and in some cases a servant.

Not only did family and household composition change in response to migration, so too did some of the roles and functions of family members. The family continued to satisfy the basic needs of its members in Buenos Aires and New York; it continued as a reproductive, economic, and social unit. Yet given the new circumstances in which it functioned, the way the family met these needs often differed from the way it had operated in Italy.

One important change already noted was the introduction of boarders and nonresident kin and friends into the private space of the household for casual socializing. Many of the changes in the functioning of the family and its members were related more directly to economic activity. In most cases moving from traditional rural economies to urban market economies meant that family survival was based to a much larger extent on wage labor and cash than before. Although immigrant families had been economically vulnerable in Italy, in times of crisis they could usually subsist on their own resources. In Buenos Aires and New York, however, wages were low for most Italian men; there was nothing to fall back on when faced with irregular employment and unemployment. Security, survival, and any hope of saving depended even more on cooperation under the direction of the father and husband. Each member had to contribute a share. The pay of daughters and sons was turned over to the family manager. The family was the fundamental economic unit.[29]

The father and husband continued to be the main economic support of the family in Buenos Aires and New York. The majority of men who had been peasant farmers in Italy generally worked at low-paying construction and factory jobs in New York and Buenos Aires. Artisans and small merchants could only sometimes find similar employment abroad; they were more likely to do so in Buenos Aires than in New York.[30]

The economic activity of women changed even more. Both in Buenos Aires and New York, there were greater opportunities for female workers in factories, and many more women began to work outside the household for money. They worked primarily in the garment, confectionery, and artificial flower industries in New York, and in the garment, confectionery, match, and cigarette industries in Buenos Aires. In both cities, single women were most likely to follow this pattern, but in Buenos Aires more single and married women worked outside the household (Table 38).[31]

Women also found themselves operating in a new consumer society. They had to pay the rent, negotiate with merchants each day for food and clothing, and decide which of the many new products to buy or not to buy. Ewen skillfully portrays the challenges these immigrant women faced in terms of the plethora of new household consumer items (kitchenware, canned foods, furniture) available in New York. In the New World, she notes, the mother was responsible for securing goods in the marketplace as opposed to producing them at home.[32]

Thus, during migration and adjustment, the family remained an important resource for the immigrants to draw upon because it modified its form and its members' roles in response to the needs created by the new situations. These changes took place both in Buenos Aires and New York, but

Table 38. Italian women working in Buenos Aires and New York City according to marital status (age 16 or older)

Marital status	Buenos Aires, 1895		New York City, 1905 (%)
	District 3 (%)	District 5 (%)	
Married women working	38	37	7[a]
Single women working	62	80	46
Widows working	54	60	
N (total)	(170)	(212)	

[a]There were 188 single women in Cohen's study. Cohen believes that due to underreporting, the 7 percent figure is somewhat low. This is supported by Odencrantz, who found that 24 percent of the mothers in her 544 families worked outside the home. Louise C. Odencrantz, *Italian Women in Industry: A Study of Conditions in New York City* [New York, 1919], p. 20.

Sources: (Buenos Aires) Baily's six-district sample of the manuscript schedules of the Argentine census of 1895. For a discussion of this sample, see Appendix. (New York) Cohen, *Workshop to Office*, pp. 52, 90.

there were some differences in the extent of these change in the two locations. Most notably, in Buenos Aires the extended family household was more common, and the percentage of women working outside the home was greater. In New York the role of the women who managed the household resources was more complex and demanding. These were differences of degree, however. The most significant changes that took place in the family and household were common to Italians in both cities.

Neighborhood

The local neighborhood was the most immediate and important sphere of social and economic activity beyond the family. As such, it was another critical space in which Italian immigrants adjusted to life in Buenos Aires and New York. It was generally the principal focus of their existence outside the home. The street provided an important context in which individuals could interact with each other. Living quarters were crowded and usually restricted to family members. The street served as playground, market, information center, and as the entrance to stores, cafés, and other institutions. Here people were recognized and known, and this acknowledgment added meaning to their lives. For example, one day Oreste Sola was stopped on the street by a man he had never seen before but who recognized him because he looked so much like his father. For most, the neighborhood was a familiar reference point from which they viewed the larger metropolis.

Neighborhood in Buenos Aires and New York had several interrelated meanings.[33] First of all it was a geographical space. Living in a common physical setting with other people was essential, but the extent of this space and the number of people who lived in it could vary considerably.[34] In addition, neighborhood was also an economic and social space. The neighbors often worked in the geographical location, purchased their food there, and obtained other daily necessities and services. They recognized and acknowledged business and other acquaintances with whom they came into contact and they socialized with close friends and relatives. These spaces often overlapped. Within any geographical space, there were many individual and group networks that defined different social and economic configurations. The greater the density of people per acre, the more likely it was that there would be multiple social and economic neighborhoods within the same physical space.

Various institutions often contributed to the residents' sense of being part of a specific neighborhood. Especially important among these were local businesses such as the grocery store and the butcher shop. In exchange for regular patronage these stores extended credit to their customers, thus creating special economic ties between the owners and the residents. Sometimes the owner of a local store also sold steamship tickets, sent money to Italy, wrote letters, and performed other services related to communicating with home. Furthermore, the neighborhood might include a pharmacy, a doctor, a lawyer, a bakery, and some cafés and social clubs. And in most there might be schools, churches, and mutual aid societies. What is important is that neighborhoods varied enormously; each had its own specific cluster of institutions.[35]

Italian neighborhoods in Buenos Aires and New York were not the same as the neighborhoods the immigrants had come from in the villages of Italy. As Gabaccia has demonstrated, the Italian immigrants could not recreate identical Old World neighborhoods in the New World any more than they could recreate identical family and household structures.[36] The act of migration brought about too many changes for that to be possible. First, most moved from rural villages to the urban environments of Buenos Aires and New York. Second, there were different people in the new neighborhoods. Where before there had been only the inhabitants of the village of origin, now there might be a cluster of such people, but also Italians from other villages and provinces of the country, other foreigners, as well as native Argentines or North Americans. As we have seen in the preceding chapter, although Italians successfully settled in village- and province-based clusters, there were always people who were neither family members nor paesani who lived in the new geographical neighborhood. As the immigrants tried to recreate an environment like the village they had left, they had to establish new ties and create new social networks.

The Italian neighborhoods in Buenos Aires and New York and the immigrants' sense of belonging to them were an important influence on their lives at first, but the relative impact of the neighborhood most certainly declined over time. Scobie argues that the local neighborhood (*barrio* or *cuadra*) in Buenos Aires was the principal focus of the lives of the immigrants outside the home until 1910, but after that competition with the forces of the larger city reduced its importance. He singles out the reduction in streetcar fares as most influential in this transformation.[37] In New York City, streetcars, subways, movies, and amusement parks had a greater impact at an earlier period, and may have diminished the influence of the local neighborhood sooner than in Buenos Aires.[38] Nevertheless, there is no doubt that in both cities before World War I, the local neighborhood was important to the Italian immigrants as a familiar refuge to help them adjust to their new environment.

The core of most immigrant neighborhoods in Buenos Aires and New York was the clustering based on village and province of origin described in Chapter 5. Often these clusters were reinforced by institutions such as mutual aid societies, social clubs or cafés, and travel agents that were also based on village of origin. At the same time, the Italian villagers shared some things in common with those from other villages in Italy, other foreigners, and natives who lived in the same local geographical space—churches, schools, fire companies, and citywide mutual aid societies, among other institutions and organizations. As a result, the members of these village-of-origin social networks soon became involved in some of the broader-based networks within the local area. Thus each individual in the neighborhood felt simultaneous ties and loyalties to family, kin, and paesani, as well as to a variety of broader, non-village-of-origin social networks.

A closer look at some specific local Italian neighborhoods in the two cities enables us to see the complexity of these ties. The Mulberry District was the older and more densely settled of the two major Italian areas in Manhattan. Originally settled primarily by Ligurians and other northern Italians, the colony grew rapidly during the latter part of the nineteenth century, and as it did, it became more densely settled and diversified. Within this heavily Italian district there were many smaller village- and province-of-origin-based neighborhoods.[39]

Map 8 indicates some of the Italian businesses and organizations within a fifteen-block area in the heart of the Mulberry District during the first decade of the twentieth century. Italians and their children made up nearly three-quarters of the population. The density in this highly congested area was just over five hundred people per acre.[40] In addition to some of the Italian doctors, lawyers, pharmacists, undertakers, banks, and restaurants, the map includes at least twenty-three of the local mutual aid societies. There were many Italian grocery stores, butcher shops, bakeries, and cafés in the area as well. Just beyond this fifteen-block area were

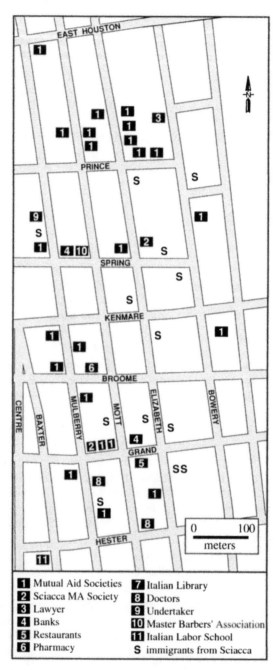

Map 8. Mulberry District neighborhood in New York City

several churches that held services in the basement for Italians. Nearby was the Banca Italo-Americano, the Libreria Italiana, and the offices of *Il Progresso Italo-Americano,* all owned by Barsotti. Not included in the map are the non-Italian institutions and organizations such as churches, public schools, the police, fire companies, banks, and stores.

All these organizations and institutions were part of different yet overlapping Italian sub-neighborhoods within this fifteen-block area. For example, one of these neighborhoods was formed by people from the Sicilian town of Sciacca. Map 8 indicates the location of the Sciacca mutual aid society at 186 Elizabeth Street as well as a number of immigrants from Sciacca who resided in the four blocks of Elizabeth Street between Hester and Prince Street.[41] On the basis of this evidence, we can easily envision a Sciacca-based social network geographically located within these four blocks on Elizabeth Street and reinforced by the mutual aid society plus specific grocery stories, bakeries, banks, and pharmacies that these people patronized. There were many such village-of-origin-based clusters with mutual aid societies and other organizations and institutions that constituted distinct but overlapping sub-neighborhoods.[42]

Italians in significant numbers began to settle in East Harlem later than they had in the Mulberry District.[43] Some seeking more space and lower rents moved there from the Mulberry District, but others came directly from Italy. Increasingly, those from southern Italy predominated. By 1900, the Italians and their children represented approximately two-thirds of the population of the area bounded by First and Third Avenues and 104th and 120th Streets. One of the attractions of the area was that it was less densely populated than the Mulberry District; the total population in the nine blocks in the center of East Harlem shown in Map 9 was only 337 per acre compared to 508 in the Mulberry District. Given the diversity of the Italian population, it is not surprising that there were numerous smaller neighborhoods based on village- and province-of-origin clusters just as there were in the Mulberry District.[44]

In his insightful micro study of Italian Harlem, Orsi stresses the importance of the block and the town and province of origin for the residents of the area. Streets were the extensions of homes. People—often from the same place in Italy—generally kept to their own block. And block clubs presided over the local neighborhood. This neighborhood, according to Orsi, "was a recognizable world—not static, not particularly stable, but dependable enough."[45]

Although there was this strong attachment to the block in which one lived, Orsi argues that there also was a sense among the inhabitants of some wider identification with Italian Harlem. Neighborhood boundaries were defined, but people nevertheless moved around. One institution that

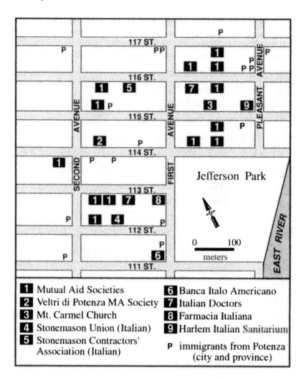

Map 9. Italian East Harlem neighborhood in New York City

fostered this identification with the larger area was the Church of Mount Carmel on 115th Street and the Madonna del Carmine that it housed. In 1881, immigrants from Polla in the province of Salerno established a mutual aid society named after the protectress of their town, the Madonna del Carmine. The annual celebration of the Madonna quickly became a community-wide affair for East Harlem's southern Italians, especially after 1884 when the statue was housed in the newly completed church of Mount Carmel. Such common institutions and festivals plus geographical separation created among many a sense of Italian Harlem's isolation from the rest of Manhattan.[46]

Some of the Italian institutions and organizations in the nine blocks surrounding the Church of Mount Carmel are indicated on Map 9. The pattern is similar to that of the Mulberry District. In addition to the church, there were several Italian doctors, pharmacists, and banks, a sanitarium, and at least fifteen mutual aid societies and organizations. The importance of these societies to the formation of neighborhood is illustrated here by the Veltri di Potenza Society, located at 307 E. 114th Street (Map 9, #2). On the same block I have located three families from Potenza and eleven additional families in the remaining seven blocks of the area.[47] There were grocery stores, bakeries, cafés, and other stores in the block that defined this neighborhood, but clearly the social space of the immigrants from Potenza extended beyond the block. Along with the Potenza neighborhood, there were many other neighborhoods of immigrants from different villages and regions that overlapped with each other.

The two Buenos Aires Italian neighborhoods—San Nicolás and the Boca—were similar in many respect to the New York City neighborhoods, but also differed in some ways. San Nicolás, in the center of the city, was approximately one-third Italians and their children, about half the percentage of Italians in the two New York City districts. In addition, the population density was considerably lower than in New York.[48] Nevertheless, the Italian population was diverse and the village-of-origin clusters similarly provided the basis for sub-neighborhoods here as well.

The Agnonesi, one of the many village clusters that occupied the San Nicolás area along with other foreigners and Argentines, illustrate the importance of village of origin as a significant basis for the formation of neighborhood (Map 10).[49] Most of the Agnonesi attended the Church of Our Lady of Carmen, were members of the Agnonese Circolo Sannitico and the Italian-wide society Colonia Italiana, sent money back to Agnone through the Marinelli Agency and bought goods in the wine store next door, and patronized the Nicola Pharmacy, all within a few blocks of each other in the Barrio del Carmen. The leading families of the Agnonese community (Map 10, #10–14) lived in the same area as twenty-five other Agnonese families whose specific addresses I have been able to identify.[50] There were many food shops, professional offices, cafés, and businesses of Agnonesi that were used by the residents.

The Barrio del Carmen was one of the main concentrations of Agnonesi in Buenos Aires, but Italians from Genoa, Torino, Naples, and other towns also lived in this area. The presence of institutions such as the Primo Circolo Napoletano and the Colonia Italiana at the edges of the barrio is evidence of this Italian regional diversity. Furthermore, there were Spaniards, other foreigners, and Argentines also living in the barrio. Here as well as in the Mulberry District and East Harlem, the village-based core of individuals who patronized a series of organizations and businesses was an important part of each neighborhood, but there were many overlapping sub-neighborhoods in the same geographical space, as there were in New York.

The Boca was the most distinctive of the four Italian neighborhoods under discussion here. Until the mid-1860s, the Boca was physically isolated from the center of Buenos Aires by the lack of good connecting roads and no railroad link at all. Furthermore, there were no churches, schools, fire

Map 10. Barrio del Carmen in Buenos Aires

stations, and other similar institutions.[51] Although the relative physical isolation and the lack of outside services contributed to the inhabitants' self-reliance and consciousness of being a distinct part of the city, it was the ability of the Ligurians to establish their social and economic hegemony—built on a common culture of place of origin, Ligurian language, and maritime occupations—that most clearly defined the area. By the end of the 1850s, Italians and their children living at home represented 53 percent of the Boca population, and Ligurians made up more than 85 percent of the Italians.[52] The Italian population gradually became more diversified, but the Ligurians maintained their hegemony at least until the 1880s. After that, other loyalties—such as an Italian national identity focused on September 20th and other patriotic celebrations, and an Argentine identity

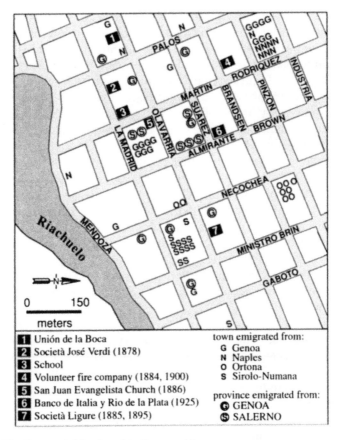

Map 11. The Boca neighborhood in Buenos Aires

based on participation in national political parties—increasingly attracted the residents of the area.[53]

Lorenzo Ferro, a third-generation Ligurian resident of the Boca who was born in 1905, described to me the pervasiveness of the Ligurian culture until the end of the past century.[54] Most children, he explained, did not speak Spanish until they went to school. "The common language was Genovese. In the great majority of houses they spoke only Genovese modified by some Argentine words." Merchants who were Jewish, Spanish, or Syrian all spoke Genovese, he noted. Indeed, there were several periodicals published in Genovese.

Many of the most important institutions of the community were located within a few blocks of each other, reflecting both Ligurian hegemony and the existence of other groups of Italians (Map 11). The Società Ligure,

founded in 1885 and moved to Calle Olavarria 261 in 1895, brought together hundreds of the leading members of the Ligurian community and
was a major force within the larger Boca community. Other institutions—
the Unión de la Boca, the Società José Verdi, and the Volunteer Fire Company—included Ligurians, but also many Italians from other areas as
well. The Church of San Juan Evangelista (1886) also brought together
Italians from many areas. These latter institutions helped reinforce the
broader sense of the Boca as one large neighborhood separate from the rest
of Buenos Aires.

At the same time, it is clear that smaller neighborhoods or sub-neighborhoods based on village-of-origin clusters existed in the Boca just as
they did in the other three Italian areas under discussion. Map 11 indicates
the location of fifteen families that we can identify as having come from
Genoa and the Ligurian coast. Yet within the same area there were nine
families from Naples and Salerno and a pocket of twelve from the Adriatic
town of Sirolo-Numana.[55] They most certainly shopped in local grocery
stores and bakeries, patronized particular cafés, and were attended to by
local doctors, pharmacists, and perhaps shipping agents from their respective towns of origin.

Ferro provides some important observations about the nature of the local neighborhoods. The *almaceneros* (grocery store owners), he stressed,
were very respected people in each local neighborhood because everyone
in the block patronized them. What was most important was that they sold
their goods on credit and the customers paid them back on a monthly basis. Other important local merchants, according to Ferro, were the *verduleros* (vegetable peddlers) and the *lecheros* (milkmen) who came daily to
the house. The verduleros were Italian, but the lecheros were Basques who
spoke Genovese.[56]

We are fortunate to have unusually detailed information on one city
block in the Boca, which illustrates more clearly the composition and functioning of the local neighborhood (Map 12)[57] Ninety-one people lived in
this block, of whom 37 percent were Italian born and a total of 74 percent
were either Italian born or children of Italian-born parents. Within the
block there was a pharmacy, a bakery, a shoe store, a barbershop, a tin
shop, a bookstore, and a cigarette factory, all of which were owned by Italians. Just around the corner was a butcher shop also owned by an Italian.
The six of these owners for whom we have data had lived in the Boca for
an average of 11.6 years. Of the forty-five men and women who listed occupations, at least 80 percent worked right in this block. Unfortunately we
do not know if the Italians living in this block came predominantly from
one village in Italy or if they were members of the Società Ligure or any
other institutions. Yet given the pattern of village-based clusters, it would
not be surprising to see one or more in this block too. Even so, this block

Address	Use	Resident	Owner	Length of Residence
	LA MADRID			
1402	Pharmacy, home	Italian	Italian	17 years +
1410	home	Italian	Italian	?
1414	home	Uruguayan	?	?
1418	home	Greek	?	?
1422	Business, home	Argentine	Argentine	
1440	Bakery, home	Italian	Italian	15 years +
1450	Bookstore, home	Italian	Italian	7 years +
1454	Shoeshop, home	Italian	Italian	13 years +
1462	home	Austrian	?	4 years +
1466	home	Italian	?	12 years +
1468	home	Russian	?	?
1472	Tinsmith, home	Italian	Italian	8 years +
1478	Barber, home	Italian	?	?
1484	Business, home	Swiss	Swiss	?
	Cigarette Factory, home	Italian	Italian	?
corner 1083	Butcher, home	Italian	Italian	10 years +
	MENDOZA			

Left margin labels: 1400 block, ADMIRANTE BROWN, corner

ADDITIONAL DATA ON THIS NEIGHBORHOOD

total population	91
males	62%
Italian born	37%
Italian born + children	74%
occupations: women (4)	servants, cook, cigarette maker
men (41)	shoemaker (6), clerk (6), cigarette maker (4), pharmacy (3), baker (3), student (3), blacksmith (3), business (3), miscellaneous (7)
number of adults (16+)	51 (56% of total population)
adults married	49%
home owners (adults)	35% of adults (16+)

Sources: República Argentina, Tercer censo nacional (1895), Manuscript Schedules for Buenos Aires, vol. 610, booklets 609–626 (District 20, Manzana 112).

Map 12. A city block in the Boca, Buenos Aires

does illustrate the way many people could concentrate much of their daily activity within a very small geographical area.

At the same time a number of institutions, according to Ferro, created a special feeling of solidarity in the Boca. Chief among these were the Unión de la Boca and the Volunteer Fire Company. Even the Società Ligure, whose membership was restricted to those from that area of Italy, served to foster identity with the Boca as a whole. And finally, he noted, Italian doctors from various villages in Italy had such a sense of community that they contributed their services to all Boca residents at minimal cost.

One final insight of Ferro is important. The people of the Boca, according to him, had multiple identities and loyalties. His father, for example, was the son of Ligurian parents and he had married a Ligurian woman, yet he was *"muy Argentino."* His father, Ferro continued, was proud to be a member of both the Società Ligure and the Unión de la Boca, and he spoke Genovese, Tuscan, and Spanish. What better evidence of multiple and overlapping identities could there be?

The Boca was somewhat different from the other three neighborhoods in its size and cohesiveness. To a lesser extent, there was something of this broader neighborhood identification among Italians in East Harlem. Geographical separation was important in both cases, but in the Boca the unique factor was the ability of one group—the Ligurians—to establish its economic and cultural dominance over the broader neighborhood and thus for a considerable period of time to foster a special sense of identity among the residents.

Nevertheless, the most important initial basis of neighborhood in all our examples was the village-of-origin-based cluster, supported in most cases by additional institutions and organizations. These clusters constituted a familiar niche from which the members could begin to engage the inhabitants of the larger neighborhood and the cities. Many of these sub-neighborhoods overlapped with each other in the same geographical space. The strength of neighborhood ties varied from group to group and over time. Gradually the tie to the neighborhoods diminished, but initially the neighborhood, like the family, was an important, familiar, and supportive niche that facilitated the adjustment of the Italian immigrants to Buenos Aires and New York.

The informal institutions of family, household, and neighborhood served the Italian immigrants well as they reconstructed new lives in Buenos Aires and New York City. Their strength lay in the fact that they were familiar and immediate Old World institutions that could be modified to facilitate adjustment to new situations abroad. The malleable household was a logical extension of Italian family forms, even though it was a different structure and redefined former concepts of private space. Similarly, the village-of-origin core was the logical basis for the development of local neighborhoods abroad even though the new neighborhoods were inhabited by a very different mixture of people from those the immigrants had left behind.

Although there were some differences in the modifications of family, household, and neighborhood among the Italians in Buenos Aires compared to those in New York, the similarities between these two cases were most important. More Buenos Aires Italian families were extended and more women worked outside the home there than in New York, but in both cities the biggest change was in the creation of the malleable household. New York Italian neighborhoods were more densely populated and homogeneous than were those in Buenos Aires. Nevertheless, in both cities what is most notable is that Italian neighborhoods were constructed around village-of-origin cores that served as points of entry into the larger neighborhoods and the cities.

Informal local institutions functioned in very similar ways in Buenos Aires and New York City. The significant differences in the nature and functioning of institutions were among the formal institutions I discuss in the next two chapters.

Formal Institutions before the
Mass Migration Era

In addition to living and acting within the immediate, informal institutional spheres of family, household, and local neighborhood, Italian immigrants in Buenos Aires and New York participated at least to some extent in formal, legally recognized institutions.[1] Some of these organizations were established and maintained by their own ethnic community, while others belonged to the host society. Formal Italian ethnic institutions were organized and controlled by members of the respective Italian communities. They included legally recognized Italian mutual aid societies, newspapers, business associations, churches, hospitals, immigrant aid societies, and social clubs. Formal host society institutions were organized and controlled by members of the host society (non-Italians) and generally included local and national political organizations and governments, labor unions, churches, business associations, public schools, and immigrant aid societies.

The extent to which the Italians participated in one or the other group of institutions, or in some combination of the two, affected the nature and speed of their adjustment. A well- developed Italian institutional structure was a major resource available to the immigrants; it facilitated their efforts to get jobs, find places to live, establish meaningful social relations, defend their interests, and improve working and living conditions. The absence of a well-developed Italian formal institutional structure forced the immigrants to rely on whatever assistance they might get from informal institutions or on frequently less accessible and receptive host society formal institutions.[2] Thus it is important to explore how extensive the respective institutional structures were as well as the patterns of Italian participation in them.

This chapter and the one that follows take up several interrelated questions: Which formal institutions did the Italians in Buenos Aires and New

York City participate in and when? Why did they become involved in these institutions and not others? Who organized and controlled these institutions and what were their goals? Did the patterns of institutional participation among the Italians in the two cities differ and if so how and why? And what was the impact of these patterns of institutional participation on the adjustment of the Italian immigrants? In this chapter, I discuss the establishment and early development of Italian immigrant institutions and the participation of Italians in both ethnic and host society institutions during the pre–mass migration era. Chapter 8 examines the changes in these patterns during the subsequent period of mass migration.

Buenos Aires before 1880

During the first half of the nineteenth century, thousands of Italians arrived on the shores of the Rio de la Plata. Some were northern Italian farmers who settled in agricultural colonies both in Argentina and Uruguay. Others, involved in maritime pursuits, went to the area when commerce on the Ligurian coast began to decline; they rapidly gained control over coastal and river shipping and trade. A few became wealthy merchants providing produce to Buenos Aires and supplies to the armies fighting for control of the region. And finally, a small but significant group of political exiles, who for the most part settled in the cities, also immigrated. With the overthrow of the anti-foreign dictator Juan Manuel de Rosas in 1852, an increasing number of Italians arrived in Argentina from Italy. Many who had temporarily resided in Montevideo crossed the river to Buenos Aires. As a result, by 1856, there were eleven thousand Italians living in Buenos Aires, representing a substantial 12 percent of the total population of the city.[3]

Immediately after the fall of Rosas in 1852, the Italians of Buenos Aires began to build organizations to meet their needs, defend their interests, and support the political and military activity of those fighting for the unification of Italy. In 1853, they established the Società di Beneficenza per L'Ospedale Italiano for the purpose of collecting funds and building a hospital in Buenos Aires. The society, initiated with the support of the local consul of Victor Emmanuel II, was, with a few exceptions, supported by all sectors of the Italian community. The hospital was not completed for twenty more years, but during most of these two decades the project served as a focal point for the community.[4]

Mutual aid societies, however, were the most important formal institutions for the immigrants in Buenos Aires during this period—many more Italians joined these societies than any other kind of organization.[5] Some societies restricted membership to those from a certain village or region of

Italy, while others restricted it to those living in a specific neighborhood of the city. Still others were formed by workers in the same occupation. Finally, some were broadly based and brought together individuals from all parts of Italy. All of them sought to provide at a minimum essential death, sickness, and unemployment benefits for their members in addition to creating a congenial social environment.

The Unione e Benevolenza, the first Italian mutual aid society in Argentina, was established in 1858. Many of its founders were political exiles, forced to migrate during the upheavals of 1848–1849, and avid supporters of the republican cause of Giuseppe Garibaldi and Giuseppe Mazzini. Equally important in the long run, the seven initiating members came from six different provinces in the North of Italy and one from the South, and they opened membership to all Italians. Among those who joined the organization between 1858 and 1862 approximately 90 percent came from northern Italy, of whom nearly three- quarters were from the provinces of Genoa, Como, Milan, and Pavia alone. Many were skilled artisans, sailors, merchants, and small shopkeepers. Only a few were unskilled workers or professionals (Table 39).

The intense political struggles between republicans and monarchists within the Italian community inevitably complicated, but did not stop, the development of institution building.[6] The Unione e Benevolenza started with 53 founding members in 1858 and successfully recruited approximately 2,800 members by the end of 1860. The society divided in 1861, and the dissident monarchists withdrew and established their own organization, the Nazionale Italiana. Although the conflict temporarily reduced the membership of the Unione e Benevolenza to about 1,100, it recovered quickly. By 1863, the organization was able to buy land on which to begin the construction of a large building to serve as its permanent headquarters.

In 1864, there was a second important division within the Unione e Benevolenza that once more led the defeated dissidents to withdraw and establish their own society.[7] This time the split was between moderate republicans, who increasingly accepted the legitimacy of the king of Italy, and the radical republicans who continued to challenge the right of the House of Savoy to rule Italy or to represent the Italians in Argentina. The struggle became so intense that it ended up in the courts. The judge required the establishment of a provisional executive committee to oversee new elections. In these elections, the moderate republicans won overwhelmingly. The radical faction withdrew to establish the Società Repubblicana degli Operai Italiani. Shortly thereafter, the Unione e Benevolenza reaffirmed its apolitical character and attempted to separate Italian politics and mutualism.

The reaffirmation of apolitical mutualism, however, did not immediately end the competition between the republicans and monarchists within

Table 39. Place of birth and occupations of new members of the Unione e Benevolenza, 1858–1862 and 1888

Place of birth	1858–1862 (%)	1888 (%)
Northern Italy	91.5	68.0
Central Italy	4.0	5.0
Southern Italy	4.5	12.0
Buenos Aires or Montevideo	.0	15.0
	100.0	100.0

Occupations	1858–1862 (%)	1888 (%)
Unskilled	2.0	8.0
Semiskilled (cooks, sailors)	32.5	16.0
Skilled (masons, carpenters, blacksmiths)	48.5	49.0
White collar (employees, merchants, businessmen)	15.0	22.0
Miscellaneous	2.0	5.0
	100.0	100.0
N (total)	(263)	(218)

Sources: The data represent a 9.4 percent random sample from the list of new members of the Unione e Benevolenza (see Appendix). See also Samuel L. Baily, "Las sociedades de ayuda mutua y el desarrollo de una comunidad italiana en Buenos Aires, 1858–1918," Desarrollo Económico, 21, 84 (January–March 1982), pp. 497, 505. Cibotti categorizes these workers according to economic sectors rather than skill as I have done. She found that 44.5 percent of these new members in the early period were in the secondary sector and 47.5 percent were in the commercial and service sector. See Ema Cibotti, "Mutualismo y política en un estudio de caso: La sociedad "Unione e Benevolenza" en Buenos Aires entre 1858 y 1865," in Fernando J. Devoto and Gianfausto Rosoli, eds., L'Italia nella società Argentina (Rome, 1988), pp. 241–265, especially p. 253.

the Italian community of Buenos Aires. The struggle continued, though in a muted and controlled form that permitted the mutual aid societies to focus more attention on the immediate needs of their members. Although an attempt in 1867 to reconcile the Unione e Benevolenza and the Nazionale Italiana failed, the moderate republicans and the monarchists learned during these years to coexist with each other, to share support of the celebration of many Italian patriotic occasions, and to focus on the economic and social needs of their members.[8]

Nor did apolitical mutualism mean that the Italian organizations operated in isolation from Argentine politics. The pioneering work of Ema Cibotti and Hilda Sábato has demonstrated that the Italians not only had important ties with Argentine political groups, but that moderate and radical republicans as well as monarchists attempted to use these ties to advance their own causes.[9]

The Argentine political system in the half century before 1912 was based on rule by a small elite and lack of direct participation by the large majority of the population.[10] In a system such as this, the Italians operated as pressure groups seeking to influence political decisions by petitions and demonstrations and other nonelectoral means. At the end of 1878, for example, the government instituted a sales tax on liquor, tobacco, and cards. The merchants of the city, many of whom were Italians, organized an effort to have the tax repealed. They presented a petition to the authorities and also organized a public protest meeting attended by more than thirty thousand people. The Italian-language newspapers were in the forefront of the anti-tax effort. A week after the protest meeting, the government accepted the proposal of the merchants and the tax, for the time, was rescinded. The issue came up again in the following year and again the merchants fought it with similar results.[11]

The Italian elites had close ties with the Argentine liberals who dominated the country after the overthrow of Rosas, and especially with Bartólome Mitre, governor of the independent province of Buenos Aires during the 1850s, and then—from 1862 to 1868—president of a reunited Argentina. Many Italians had fought beside the Argentine liberals to overthrow Rosas and also had fought along with Mitre to defend the province of Buenos Aires. In addition, the size and growing economic importance of the Italian community made it a significant pressure group within the Argentine political system.[12]

Although Mitre and his followers were sympathetic to the Italian republicans, following the unification of Italy under the king in 1860 they became more equivocal in their support of the republican cause. After 1860, they in effect supported both Italian factions in Argentina, but clearly accepted the reality of the king's control of Italy. This pragmatic position of the Mitre government strengthened the hand of the moderate Italian republicans in their fight with the radicals and in the emergence of apolitical mutualism.

Under the pragmatic, apolitical mutualism of the moderate republicans, the Unione e Benevolenza grew and provided new services for its members. In 1867, for example, when the large new headquarters that had been started four years before was completed, the society opened its first primary school and library. The establishment of a primary school responded to an important need of many in the Italian community of Buenos Aires. In the 1860s, few public schools existed and private and religious schools were limited, expensive, and for ideological reasons unacceptable to some. It would be two more decades (1884) before the Argentine government would pass a law to establish obligatory and free primary education and begin to construct the necessary schools. Thus, by providing schools, the Unione e Benevolenza and other mutual aid societies were meeting a growing need of the Italian community that was not met by the host society.

The monarchist-dominated Nazionale Italiana experienced numerous difficulties during the 1860s, but, with the support of the Italian consul, managed to grow slowly and to obtain a membership of approximately seven hundred by the end of the decade. It also established a school in 1866 and its members devoted considerable time and effort to collecting funds for the building of the Italian Hospital.

Although two major crises of the 1870s—the yellow fever epidemic of 1871 and the economic depression of 1873 to 1877—slowed the growth of the Unione e Benevolenza and the Nazionale Italiana, they had already established several significant precedents for future Italian organizations. Both societies were national and cosmopolitan in that they supported the unity of Italy and opened their membership to people from all parts of Italy. In addition, both developed extensive programs that served the educational and health as well as the insurance, legal, and social needs of their members. Using this model of organization, the rapidly growing Italian community of Buenos Aires created ten new mutual aid societies during the 1870s.[13] By 1879, the seven largest, wealthiest, and most influential Italian mutual aid societies to be created in Buenos Aires before World War I had been established as nationalist institutions with extensive functions open to all Italians.

During the same decade there were also new developments within the mutualist movement that reflected the growing size and diversity of the Italian population. Most important, localism (*campanilismo*) became increasingly significant. The first village-of-origin society, with membership restricted to those from a specific Italian village or area, was established in 1876 (the Lago di Como). Many other such societies were to be organized in subsequent decades. In addition, in 1879 Italians living in the Belgrano area of Buenos Aires organized the first neighborhood society. This organization would grow to a membership of four thousand by 1910. And finally in 1879, the Unione e Benevolenza organized a women's branch, thus formally incorporating women into the mutualist movement.

The growth of the mutual aid societies was accompanied by the creation and development of other immigrant institutions. Italian-language newspapers were perhaps the second most important of them. Although no one could join a newspaper as he or she could a mutual aid society, tens of thousands of Italians scanned their columns in search of job and housing information, community activities, survival tips, news of Italy, and other information of use to them as they sought to adjust to life in their new surroundings. The larger, more permanent, and more influential of these papers strongly supported Italian unity and thus helped to break down the village and regional loyalties of many of the immigrants.[14]

The first Italian-language newspaper was established in the 1850s, with dozens of others starting publication in subsequent years. Most, however, had limited circulation and did not last very long. Many papers appeared as the result of personality clashes and political differences among the small circle of Italian editors and publishers. These men usually knew each other well, fought and competed intensely, and often shifted from paper to paper. Virtually all the newspapers were involved in Italian politics and thus provided an arena for political expression and action outside the mutual aid societies.[15]

In 1876, Basilio Cittadini founded *La Patria*, the most important and by far the most widely circulated Italian-language newspaper in Argentina until it ceased publishing in 1931. Within a year of its founding, *La Patria* changed its name to *La Patria Italiana*, and nearly two decades later became *La Patria degli Italiani* (1893). In 1869, Cittadini, a bright young lawyer and correspondent for *Il Secolo* of Florence, had been sent to Buenos Aires to become editor of *La Nazionale Italiana*. He was involved in the creation of *L'Operaio Italiano* in 1872 and four years later left *L'Operaio* to establish *La Patria*.

La Patria was a liberal, anticlerical, moderate republican morning daily that over time became increasingly sympathetic to the Italian monarchy. Cittadini had arrived in Buenos Aires a radical republican and initially had used his newspapers to support this cause. Yet for a number of reasons his republicanism became more moderate over time. Among them were the reality of a united Italy under the monarchy and the growing pragmatism within the Italian community toward political matters. In addition, he began during this period to develop close ties with the Argentine and Italian governments and with the Italian elites of Buenos Aires.

The content of *La Patria* increasingly reflected the more immediate economic and social interests of its readers. The editors interpreted Argentine society for Italian immigrants, defended their various interests, arbitrated some of their disputes, and often spoke for them as a community. The bulk of the paper was devoted to news about Italy and information on how to survive and prosper in Buenos Aires. The front page usually contained several stories about Italian domestic affairs and foreign relations, as well as some important stories about Italians in Argentina. The inside pages focused on a wide variety of subjects. Much attention was given to working and living conditions. Another section was devoted to Italian commerce and industry in Argentina. One of the most important parts of the paper was the section containing letters to the editor seeking advice and assistance. About a quarter of the total space was devoted to advertising, most of which was for Italian patent medicines, steamship companies, banks, and agencies.

During the late 1870s and the 1880s, La Patria competed successfully with L'Operaio Italiano for the support and readership of the rapidly growing Italian community, and gradually became the major foreign-language newspaper in Argentina. By 1887, it had obtained nearly twice the circulation of its chief rival and had become one of the four leading dailies of Buenos Aires.[16]

Several important ethnic organizations besides mutual aid societies and newspapers developed in the 1870s. In 1872, a group of leading Italian businessmen formed the Banco de Italia y Rio de la Plata. The bank became the leading financial and business institution of the immigrant community from this date on. In the same year, the Italian Hospital started serving the community. And in 1873, the prestigious social club, the Circolo Italiano, opened its doors and brought together under one roof six hundred leading members of the city's Italian elite.[17]

The most important Italian institutions in Buenos Aires were closely tied to each other by common interests and by the personal networks of their leaders. Many of the leaders of the mutual aid societies were wealthy merchants, businessmen, and lawyers who were an integral part of the Italian elite.[18] Thus a mutual aid society leader might be on the board of the Banco de Italia y Rio de la Plata, active in the Italian Hospital, closely associated with a newspaper, a member of the Circolo Italiano, and active in several other mutual aid societies. These connections were important for the growth and development of the mutual aid societies and the other ethnic institutions of the community. The societies needed loans from the banks to finance their buildings and services, and the banks needed the deposits of the society members. The societies wanted direct contacts with the newspapers in order to guarantee access to the broader Italian community and to publicize their activities and positions. The newspapers needed the support of the societies and their members. The societies needed the Italian Hospital to care for their members; the Italian Hospital needed the societies to finance its operation. The Circolo Italiano provided an informal and exclusive meeting place for the most successful and active members of the elite.

Many such personal networks developed before 1880 and continued to function subsequently. For example, Achille Maveroff, a wealthy businessman and founder of the newspaper La Nazione Italiana, was president of the Unione e Benevolenza (1868–1871), president of the Italian Hospital Committee, one of the founders and then president (1872–1875) of the Banco de Italia y Rio de la Plata, and a leading member of the Circolo Italiano. Similarly, Basilio Cittadini, the founder of La Patria, had been active with other newspapers and was the first secretary of the Banco de Italia y Rio de la Plata, active in the leadership of several mutual aid societies, and a member of the Circolo Italiano.

Another network developed around individuals associated with the newspaper *L'Operaio Italiano*. Giuseppe Solari, a major shareholder in the paper, was president of the Unione e Benevolenza from 1877 to 1879 and again in 1883. From 1889 to 1891, he was president of the Italian Hospital. Annibal Blosi, president of the Unione e Benevolenza from 1880 to 1882, was director of *L'Operaio Italiano* until his death in 1888. He was also active in the Italian Hospital, a lawyer for the Banco de Italia y Rio de la Plata, and a member of the Circolo Italiano.

By 1880, an integrated elite of successful merchants, businessmen, and professionals controlled the extensive and wealthy Italian institutional structure of Buenos Aires. This elite had overcome the political divisions that for a time had threatened to fragment the mutual aid societies and other ethnic institutions. Its members had come together in support of a united Italy, in defense of the Italians of Buenos Aires, and in pursuit of economic success.

The important question is how well this extensive, highly organized, and wealthy formal institutional structure served the Italian community as a whole. Obviously the elites who led these organizations looked after their own professional and business interests and benefited from their involvement.[19] But approximately two-thirds of the Italians in Buenos Aires were blue-collar workers. Most of the semiskilled and skilled workers among them participated in some or all of these institutions, but few of the 15 percent to 20 percent of the Italian working population who were unskilled did. For example, although 83 percent of the new members of the Unione e Benevolenza in the 1858–1862 period were blue-collar workers, only 2 percent were unskilled. In 1888, 73 percent were blue-collar and 8 percent unskilled (Table 39).

Any class tensions within the Italian community, however, were minimal or at least muted, and for several reasons did not at this time produce open conflicts. Although the elites in the community firmly controlled the immigrant organizations, for the most part they ran these institutions in an efficient and professional manner and were thus able to offer significant benefits to many blue-collar workers. Furthermore, their power was limited to some extent by the fact that there were many low white-collar and skilled workers in the mutual aid societies.

The issue is important and deserves further scholarly attention. What is necessary to point out here is that there was a relative difference between the Italian elites in New York and Buenos Aires in terms of how they used their power within their respective communities. Those in Buenos Aires were for the most part well-educated and professional leaders who believed it was in their best interests to provide a wide variety of services to a broad range of the Italian community. I am not suggesting that they were selfless individuals, but they did use the institutional structure to help meet the needs of the large number of working-class Italians in Buenos Aires who participated in these organizations.

Before I move on to a detailed examination of the Italians in New York, I need to make one final point: host society institutions in Buenos Aires were of limited importance to the Italian immigrants during this period. Existing schools and hospitals were inadequate to meet the needs of the rapidly growing Italian population. Only a few skilled workers were organized in labor unions. The church had limited human and financial resources, provided few services, and was of little significance to the generally anticlerical Italian community. Political concerns regarding Buenos Aires were expressed through the Italian leaders and occasionally more directly through demonstrations and petitions, but they were not expressed by participating directly in elections and Argentine political parties. In the subsequent period of mass migration, however, participation in these host society institutions would become more significant.

Italian participation in formal institutions in Buenos Aires before mass migration was primarily confined to an interrelated set of ethnic institutions created by the community itself and controlled for the most part by a comparatively responsive Italian business and professional elite. They included the large cosmopolitan mutual aid societies with their schools, several daily Italian-language newspapers, a major bank, a hospital, and a prestigious social club. This extensive institutional structure fostered widespread immigrant participation in formal Italian institutions, and, for the time, the integration of individual Italians into a citywide Italian community as opposed to a host society community.

New York before 1890

A number of Italians came to New York during the first half of the nineteenth century. By the 1850s, the city's Italian community of approximately one thousand was in some respects similar to that of Buenos Aires. It was a settlement composed in part of political exiles who had remained in New York and had found jobs as journalists, lawyers, and small businessmen. In addition, the small community also included professionals and artists (musicians, sculptors, engravers) who migrated with the intention of permanent settlement, and the skilled and semiskilled workers (tailors, vendors, saloon keepers) who occasionally found their way to the city during this early period. Most came from Liguria and other parts of northern Italy.[20]

There were, as I discussed in preceding chapters, several significant structural differences between the Buenos Aires and New York Italian communities. In 1850, the New York community was just under a thousand individuals, less than one-tenth the size of the Buenos Aires community. Furthermore, this number in New York constituted only the tiniest fraction of the total population of the city—.01 percent. The Italian community grew very slowly over the next two decades, in part because of limited immigration, and in part because the new migrants—increasingly from the South—used New York as a way station to other parts of the United States. In New York before the 1890s, there were fewer permanent Italians than in Buenos Aires who were available to create and develop immigrant institutions of any size, wealth, and influence.

Nevertheless, this relatively small Italian community was large enough to support some institutions before the 1890s. The first Italian-language newspaper, *L'Eco d'Italia*, which began publishing as a weekly in 1849 and became a daily in 1883, was an important source of communication within the early community. Later, and especially around the turn of the century, there were many other Italian-language newspapers published in New York. Most were of short duration and small circulation.

The newspaper with the largest circulation and the one that was most long-lived was *Il Progresso Italo-Americano*. Tuscan businessman Carlo Barsotti established the paper in 1879 because of his anger when *L'Eco d'Italia* did not give sufficient attention to a letter he had sent to the editor. Barsotti had begun operating boarding houses for Italian immigrants in New York City during the early 1870s. He used this business as a base for a successful career in labor contracting and banking. *Il Progresso* was inconsequential for a few years, but in 1882—when Barsotti hired the professional journalist Adolfo Rossi as editor—circulation began to increase. By 1890, there were 6,500 copies of the paper printed each day, and circulation grew rapidly thereafter.[21]

Il Progresso built its leading position among Italian-language dailies providing information needed by the recently arrived immigrants. Page one of the four-page daily was perhaps the least useful, being generally devoted to major news about Italy, New York, and the United States. Of greater relevance to most immigrants was the information contained in the rest of the paper. At the bottom of page one were notices of arriving and departing boats and other shipping news. The second page consisted of announcements of mutual aid society meetings, reports on community events, and frequently a list of Italians who had letters waiting for them at the New York Post Office. The section of classified ads must have been of special interest. In nearly every issue of the paper during this period there were a variety of ads from employers and labor agents in need of workers, men seeking wives, and proprietors anxious to sell grocery stores, barber shops, restaurants, and saloons.[22]

A few examples of classified ads provide a sense of the importance of the paper both to the newly arrived immigrants and to those who had been in the country some time. An educated man of thirty with a good job was seeking to correspond with a young Italian woman—born in New York of Italian parents—with regard to marriage. An Italian employer or agent in Jersey City was looking for experienced carpenters to work in New York or outside the city. The owner of a ten-room, two-story Brooklyn house with basement, just twenty-five minutes from New York and suitable for two families, wanted to sell his home. The owner of a newly furnished barber shop connected to two habitable rooms wanted to sell the business because, after twelve years, he was returning to Italy. A Washington, D.C., businessman wanted four young Italians to sell fruit from handcarts and preferred those from the southern provinces of Avellino and Salerno.[23]

Over half of the paper consisted of commercial ads for Italian businesses, professionals, and goods of presumed interest to the immigrant community. Scanning these columns of advertisements one could locate banks, boarding houses, steamship agents, food and wine stores, restaurants, doctors, pharmacies, and a wide range of medical cures, among other things, all within the Italian communities of New York. Frequently a number of services were offered by the same business in the same ad. The Hotel Firenze at 65 W. Houston Street in lower Manhattan, for example, offered individual or shared rooms with food, but it also had a billiard parlor, a wine shop, and an agency for the purchase of railroad and steamship tickets.[24]

In addition to providing useful information to its readers, *Il Progresso* promoted the business and personal interests of its publisher. Among the ads that appeared regularly on page two were those for the Banca Italo-Americana and the Libreria Italiana, both owned by Barsotti. The bank headquarters were at 2 Center Street, but it also had branches at 31 Mulberry Street, 72 Thompson Street, and at 2209 First Avenue in Harlem, as well as a branch in Naples. The bank offered to send money to any Italian post office, to sell railroad and steamship tickets for anywhere in Europe or the United States, to pay 5 percent a year on savings accounts, to loan money on objects of value, to serve as a notary public, and to give free legal advice and service. The paper also frequently listed the arrival of "our immigrants," with towns of origin and the agents who had arranged the trip in conjunction with Barsotti's bank.[25]

Il Progresso also served the personal as well as the business interests of its owner. Barsotti was one of the *prominenti* who constituted the elite of the growing Italian community of New York City. The prominenti were the small number of successful and wealthy immigrants who established their control over the immigrant masses by providing some of the social and economic services their fellow countrymen needed (job placement, boarding houses, banks to send savings home, and so on) and felt they could not, at least initially, get elsewhere. The prominenti, according to Pozzetta, generally had limited education and were conservative in social outlook and self-serving.[26] One might argue that all elites are at least to some extent self-serving, and those in Buenos Aires were no exception. However, the New York Italian elites were less educated and progressive in social outlook than those in Buenos Aires.

It is therefore not surprising that Il Progresso reflected these attitudes of Barsotti and the prominenti. It was, for example, generally, though not always, opposed to labor and social reforms. Barsotti was most concerned about his business interests and his own prestige and public image. If reforms that might benefit the mass of working-class Italian immigrants threatened these things, he opposed them in his paper. Thus he could condemn the high child mortality rate and the white slavery trade in New York City, announce the meetings of Italian shoemakers, tailors, and bricklayers, and give sympathetic coverage to a tram strike, since these things did not conflict with his personal and business interests. But at the same time he opposed all efforts to reform labor recruitment and banking practices, and spoke out against organizations created to protect immigrant workers from labor bosses.[27]

A comparison of Barsotti with Basilio Cittadini, founder and director of La Patria in Buenos Aires, helps clarify this point. Cittadini was an experienced professional journalist committed to a number of social causes. La Patria consistently reflected its director's commitment to serve the interests of the broader Italian community of Buenos Aires, including those of the working class. Barsotti, on the other had, was a businessman involved among other things in job placement and banking. He had little concern for the working class and the broader Italian community of New York. As a result of the difference between their owners, the leading Italian-language newspapers in Buenos Aires and New York served their respective communities in distinct ways.

Italians in New York also organized mutual aid societies during this period, the first—the Unione e Fratellanza—in 1858, followed by two in the 1860s, five in the 1870s, and at least several dozen more in the 1880s. Unfortunately, we know very little about the nature of these early societies and how they operated.[28] Was the Unione e Fratellanza led by Italian republicans who were businessmen and professionals as was the case with the Unione e Benevolenza in Buenos Aires? What was the occupational and regional composition of the membership? Was there a monarchist group within the organization, and, if so, how did the leaders deal with the

Table 40. New York City–area Italian mutual aid societies, 1858–1886

Society[a]	Date created	Members (1884)	Comments
Unione e Fratellanza (N.Y.)	1858	270	Largest net worth
Tiro al Bersaglia (N.Y.)	1866	80	
Antonio di Padova (N.Y.)	1869	150	Incorporated by P. Ledwith
Firenze (N.Y.)	1873	160	President (1884) A. Podesta
Operaia di Mutuo Soccorso (N.Y.)	1874	260	President (1884) L. V. Fugazy; originally called Club Lombardo
Legione Garibaldi (N.Y.)	1874	90	Incorporated by Fugazy; southern Italians
Unione e Fratellanza (Hoboken)	1876	76	
Fraterna (N.Y.)	1877	108	Merchants, most from Sicily; incorporated by Fugazy; large net worth
Mazzini (N.Y.)	1870s	400	Workers and industrialists
Italian Rifle Guard (N.Y.)	1880	105	
Cavour (Newark, N.J.)	1881	115	
Società Beneficenza Italiana (N.Y.)	1882	60	President (1884) Fugazy
Vittorio Emanuele (N.Y.)	1883	40	
Cuochi e Pasticcieri (N.Y.)	1883	70	Incorporated by Fugazy
Italia (Brooklyn)	1880s	120	

[a]The list includes the fourteen societies for which I have data. There were approximately forty-five societies in all.

Sources: "L'elemento italiano rappresentato nelle associazione di New York, Brooklyn, Hoboken, e Newark, 1884," Archive of the Center for Migration Studies, New York; Il Progresso Italo-Americano, 8/16/1886 and 9/3/1886.

republican-monarchist political conflicts? Did the consul of the House of Savoy attempt to influence the organization and, if so, how successful was he? We simply do not have sufficient evidence to provide very complete answers to these questions.

Nevertheless, the information in Table 40, used in conjunction with that published in the Italian-language press, is suggestive of several points of comparison with the mutualist movement in Buenos Aires. Given the limited size of the Italian community of New York before 1880, it is not surprising that the first mutual aid societies were small (five reported 160 members or fewer and the other three had memberships of 260, 270, and 400), had limited resources, and—perhaps because host society institutions such as schools were more fully developed in New York—restricted their activities to traditional mutual aid functions (death, sickness, and unemployment benefits, social activities, and patriotic celebrations). Half of the societies were based on town or region of origin in Italy. The others were open to all Italian males.[29]

Undoubtedly the political struggles between the republicans and the monarchists that were so evident in Buenos Aires existed to some extent in the Italian community of New York, but there is little information to document the precise nature of this conflict or its ebb and flow within the mutualist movement. The names of some of the societies—Legione Garibaldi, Mazzini, Vittorio Emanuele—indicate the importance of Italian political issues to at least some, yet there is no available evidence of the fratricidal fighting that took place within the Unione e Benevolenza of Buenos Aires in the 1860s. If there were political tensions within the mutualist movement, they did not prevent the various societies from cooperating to celebrate Italian holidays, to coordinate protest movements, and to form a loose regional confederation—the Società Italiane Unite, with members in New York, Brooklyn, Hoboken, and Newark—to plan these occasions.

Rather, the divisions within the mutualist movement seemed to have been based more on personal rivalries among the prominenti, who used positions of leadership within the societies to further their own business and personal interests. As Table 40 indicates, for example, Louis V. Fugazy—a leading immigrant banker, labor contractor, and notary public—was active in the creation and operation of a number of the early mutual aid societies, and this involvement expanded over the years. It is not hard to envision that membership in a Fugazy-dominated mutual aid society might well become the means for obtaining a job and various other services through Fugazy's banks and agencies. Also positions of leadership within these multi-class societies might well be used to control or minimize any threat by organized workers to the business interests of the prominenti.[30] Other prominenti were active in the mutualist movement as well, and the competition among them for control of the societies inevitably led to conflicts.

During the 1880s, when the Italian community grew from twelve thousand to forty thousand, the ethnic institutional structure expanded as well. Italian immigrants, increasingly from the South, created dozens of small village- or local-area-based mutual aid societies, and some of the older societies took new initiatives to help the immigrants. As in the 1870s, however, the prominenti were involved in the establishment and operation of many of these new societies, apparently used the organizations for their own purposes, and fought among themselves.

In 1882, for example, a few of the older societies established the Società Italiana di Beneficenza (Italian Beneficent Society) to help the new arrivals and less fortunate members of the Italian community. Fugazy was elected president of the new society. The Italian consul in New York, Gian Paolo

Riva—alarmed by the poor and deteriorating conditions in which the masses of Italians in New York lived and frustrated by what he considered the ineffectual response of the Beneficent Society—established the Italian Home Society. Riva needed help to fund and operate the Italian Home, however, and turned to Barsotti, Felice Tocci (editor of *L'Eco*), banker Giovanni Lordi, and other prominenti not associated with Fugazy's Italian Beneficent Society. The money was raised and the Italian Home—with a small hospital, relief and immigration bureaus, and a school—opened in January 1891. The Italian Home Society survived until 1896, but it divided the Italian community and created a conflict that diverted time and resources from the needs of the increasing numbers of immigrants.[31]

A more successful initiative among some of the leaders of the Italian ethnic community during this period was the establishment in 1887 of the Italian Chamber of Commerce. At first of limited membership, the chamber of commerce succeeded by the end of the century in attracting a majority of the Italian businessmen in New York. It also became an organizational base for entry into local politics, as I will discuss in the next chapter.[32]

Many Italians in New York did not participate in formal institutions during the pre–mass migration era, but—as in Buenos Aires—most of those who did confined their activity to the community's ethnic institutions. Unlike those in Buenos Aires, however, a few in New York initiated their own special ways of participating in such host society institutions as the Catholic Church and organized labor. In so doing, they laid the foundations and methods for much greater participation of this type during the period of mass migration.

The Catholic Church, apparently fearful of rekindling nativist reactions, was slow in responding to the needs of the growing numbers of Italian immigrants in New York City. Although there was at first opposition to the creation of Italian parishes as a means of incorporating immigrants into the church, in fact a number of such parishes and missions were established before the mid-1890s, including Our Lady of Mt. Carmel in East Harlem (1884) and St. Joachim (1888) and Our Lady of Loretto (1891) on the Lower East Side. For some time, however, many were duplex parishes shared with others. The Irish controlled these churches and the Italians were in the humiliating position of being forced to worship in *la chiesa inferiore* in the basement. This situation sometimes endured for many years. For example, although an Italian parish was established at our Lady of Mt. Carmel Church in East Harlem in 1884, the Italians were confined to the basement for thirty-five more years, until 1919.[33]

The Irish-American Church in New York differed significantly from the church and the practice of religion to which the immigrants were accustomed in Italy. The Irish clergy spoke English, placed considerable importance on fundraising for parish projects, and stressed the doctrinal tenets of the church. The southern Italian immigrants were suspicious of the church hierarchy, which in Italy had been allied with the landowners. They were unfamiliar with contributing to the support of priests, church buildings, and parochial schools. Theirs was a more immediate religion that focused on personal relationships with God and the saints. It was, as Orsi explains, a folk religion that involved street processions, festivals, and a distinct worldview. The inevitable misunderstandings and conflicts alienated many Italians from the institutional church. In addition, there were too few priests to care for the growing numbers of immigrants.[34]

A few groups within the church, however, made special efforts to reach out to the Italian immigrants. In 1888, the first Scalabrini fathers arrived in New York City to begin helping the immigrants. The next year Mother Cabrini and six of her Sisters of the Sacred Heart arrived in New York, and shortly began their pioneering work at Columbus Hospital. The Missionaries of St. Charles founded the St. Raphael Society for the Protection of Italian Immigrants in 1891.[35]

In general, however, church participation by the Italian immigrants was limited during this period. Pozzetta cites a church census of 1884 that found that only twelve hundred of the city's fifty thousand Italians were regular participants in church services. He estimates that between 60 percent and 75 percent had no church connections or very minimal ones.[36] Although the formal structure of the Catholic Church in New York was not an institution of significance for most Italian immigrants during this period, the establishment of the ethnic parish as a way to incorporate the immigrants would prove to be of major importance in the future.

In addition, this period witnessed the initial participation of some Italians in working-class organizations. Italian workers and political radicals (anarchists, syndicalists, and socialists) came to the United States and were active on a small but significant scale in the development of some of these organizations. As far back as 1872 there was an Italian section of the First International. But for the most part, Italian workers organized themselves in occupation-based mutual aid societies and these—like many other mutual aid societies—were often controlled by the prominenti. In 1883, Italian cooks and pastry makers organized a mutual aid society that was incorporated by L. V. Fugazy. Several years later, Italian barbers, garment workers, bricklayers, shoemakers, and musicians organized similar societies. The barbers and several other groups affiliated with the Knights of Labor. These organizations generally did not last very long, and most Italian workers before 1900 remained unorganized. Nevertheless, these Italian-controlled organizations established, in a manner similar to the Italian parishes of the church, an important precedent for the future incorporation of the immigrants into the labor movement.[37]

The Italian community of New York had, by the beginning of mass migration in the early 1890s, created a limited formal institutional structure of mutual aid societies, Italian-language newspapers, and a chamber of commerce. In addition, those Italians who were involved in any formal institutions during this period confined their activity for the most part to the mutual aid societies and the Italian-language newspapers. Host society institutions played only a marginal role in the immigrants' lives. Because the formal institutional structure of the Italian population in New York was not extensive, the level of community participation in it was comparatively low. Italians in New York met their needs primarily through the family, the unregistered and unlicensed banks and labor agents, and various other informal institutions.

❦

As the discussion in this chapter shows, although the Italians in both Buenos Aires and New York City organized formal ethnic institutions during the pre–mass migration period, these institutional structures were very different. Those of the Buenos Aires community were significantly more developed, participation of the Italians in them much greater, and their assistance in the process of adjustment therefore more extensive. For the most part Italians in New York turned to informal institutions for help in adjusting to the new environment.

A number of reasons explain these differences. The much greater size and duration of the Italian community in Buenos Aires provided a critical mass at a much earlier date with which to construct a formal ethnic institutional structure. In addition, the mutual aid societies in Buenos Aires were more inclusive, larger, wealthier, and thus better able to provide a broader range of services.

Furthermore, the leaders of the Buenos Aires organizations were more educated, more inclusive in social outlook, and relatively less self-serving. Certainly they looked after their own interests and benefited from their roles within the mutual aid societies and other organizations, but the class dynamics among Italians differed in the two cities. As I discussed in Chapter 3, Italians in Buenos Aires developed a three-class community whereas in New York they developed an essentially two- class one. Because of this, power was relatively more evenly distributed among the Buenos Aires Italians and within the mutual aid societies. This distribution in turn enabled skilled and white-collar workers to exert greater influence within these societies and to moderate the positions of the elites.

Finally, the different economic strategies pursued by the majority of Italians in the respective communities help explain why those in Buenos Aires were able to build a more extensive formal institutional structure during this period. In these early years, New York was a way station for the many who passed through or who stayed only a few years. Their goal was to maximize short-term profit and return home with as much as they could. Paying dues to support a mutual aid society or other formal institution did not, from this perspective, make much sense. The greater permanence and the willingness to invest in long-term economic returns of those in Buenos Aires helped foster the development of an extensive and helpful formal institutional structure there.

8

Formal Institutions during the Mass Migration Era

Although the patterns of Italian institutional participation that had emerged by the beginning of mass migration provided a crucial foundation for subsequent developments, new circumstances in Buenos Aires and New York also influenced the way the immigrants became involved in formal institutions. The most significant new factor was the dramatically increasing number of individuals within the Italian communities. Between 1887 and 1914, the Italian community of Buenos Aires grew from 138,000 to 312,000. In New York, it started at a much smaller size, but grew even more rapidly—from 40,000 in 1890 to 370,000 in 1914. How would the existing institutions incorporate the enormous number of newcomers and help them meet their needs and achieve their goals? What new institutions would the immigrants and others create in response to these needs?

In this chapter, I explore these new avenues of institutional participation as well as the limits imposed upon immigrant participation by the members of the host society. I also describe developments within the formal ethnic institutions. And finally, I evaluate the impact of the patterns of participation on the adjustment of the Italians in the two cities.

Buenos Aires, 1880–1914

The arrival of hundreds of thousands of additional immigrants between 1880 and 1914 created new problems and posed new challenges for the Italian community of Buenos Aires. The rapid increase in numbers of Italians in need of help presented the first challenge. Could the mutual aid societies and other ethnic institutions expand sufficiently to incorporate the new members of the community? Second, the economic success and well-developed institutional structure of the Italian community raised concerns among some within the Argentine elites regarding the assimilation of the immigrants. In addition, the rise of a labor movement dominated by Italians and other foreigners presented a third challenge to the hegemony of the elites within the Italian community and the host society as well.

Former Argentine president Domingo F. Sarmiento (1868–1874), although a major supporter of immigration, came increasingly to perceive the Italian mutual aid societies, schools, and press as obstacles to assimilation.[1] He expressed these concerns especially forcefully in early 1881, when a number of the Italian mutual aid societies with schools (the Unione e Benevolenza and the Nazionale Italiana among others) organized the First Italian Pedagogical Congress in Buenos Aires. The members of the congress sought to unify scholastic rules and procedures and to stimulate the further growth of Italian schools. Although they discussed ways to maintain and strengthen the "national" (Italian) character of the education, they also responded to Argentine criticism by adding the Spanish language and Argentine history and geography to the curriculum.[2]

Sarmiento was not satisfied with the proposed reforms and in the newspaper *El Nacional* denounced the idea of educating students "Italianly." "What is this then to educate 'Italianly?'" he inquired. "To conserve or create in the child's mind the cult of the patria that he does not know, that he probably will not know, dislodging from his natural sentiments that which compels him to love the land in which he was born?"[3] Sarmiento continued to attack the Italian institutions in a similar manner until his death in 1889 (see Chapter 3).

Although there are insufficient data to determine precisely what percentage of Italian school-age children living in Buenos Aires went to Italian schools, we do know that between 1867—when the first schools began to operate—and 1895, no more than three thousand students attended these schools at any one time. However, I estimate that these students represented a significant proportion of the rather limited Italian school-age population—perhaps 20 percent to 30 percent of the primary school population of the city's Italians, and as much as 40 percent to 50 percent of the Italian children who attended schools. Such figures, even if only approximately accurate, lent support to Sarmiento's concerns.[4]

Sarmiento's attacks united the Italian community leadership in defense of its presence in and contributions to Argentina. And the Italian immigrant institutional structure he attacked continued to expand, aided by economic prosperity and increased immigration.

Mutual Aid Societies

The 1880s began a period of considerable growth in the mutualist movement. Italians established twenty-one new societies during the decade—

including, for the first time, a number of southern Italian village and regional societies (Unione Meridionale, Primo Circolo Napolitano). The
larger and older societies also grew rapidly during the 1880s. The Unione
e Benevolenza, for example, obtained its maximum school enrollment of
1,125 in 1883 and its maximum membership of 6,300 in 1888. The Education Law of 1884—which established free, compulsory public elementary
education—was not fully implemented until the early 1900s, but even so,
the increasing availability of free public schools did diminish the enrollment in the Italian schools. Between 1883 and 1885, for example, enrollment in the four schools of the Unione e Benevolenza declined from 1,125
to 754.[5]

The Italian mutualist movement continued its expansion in the 1890s,
when thirty-five more societies were established. Nearly two-thirds of
these organizations were either village-regional or neighborhood societies. After 1900, however, the pace of growth of the movement slowed
down. During the first decade of the twentieth century, just five new mutual aid societies were created.

By 1910, there were seventy-four or seventy-five Italian mutual aid societies in Buenos Aires with approximately fifty-two thousand members
(Table 41). Women made up 17 percent of the total membership. Thirteen
societies maintained schools with a combined enrollment of approximately two thousand students. The large majority of the societies (81 percent) had less than one thousand members. Among this number were all
of those based on village and region or neighborhood with the exception
of two: Italiana of Belgrano and Ligure of the Boca.

The large, inclusive multipurpose societies—though few in number—
attracted the most members and had by far the greatest net worth. The
fourteen largest societies accounted for two-thirds (66 percent) of the total
membership and nearly four-fifths (78 percent) of the total net worth.
There was an even greater concentration of members and wealth among
the top half of this group; the seven largest societies had nearly half
(47 percent) of all members and 71 percent of the total net worth.

For the purposes of comparison with New York, it is important to emphasize that the Buenos Aires mutualist movement developed on two levels.[6] On the one hand were the small number of larger and long-established
societies, which had most of the membership and wealth. They were open
to all Italians and performed a wide variety of functions; they ran most
of the schools and were an important source of economic support for the
Italian Hospital and other community endeavors. The leaders of these
multi-class societies were Italian nationalists, businessmen, and professionals who believed they were serving the best interest of the broader Italian community. On the other hand were the numerous but relatively small
village-regional and neighborhood societies, most of which had been es-

Table 41. Italian mutual aid societies in Buenos Aires, 1908 (14 largest societies)

Society	Date founded	Members in 1908	Schools (students)	Net worth (in lire)
Beneficenza per l'Ospedale	1853	3,334	No	3,365,000
Unione e Benevolenza	1858	3,764	Yes (247)	924,000
Nazionale Italiana	1861	3,906	Yes (195)	633,000
Unione Operai Italiani	1874	3,125	Yes (278)	532,000
Colonia Italiana	1877	3,250	Yes (195)	262,000
Italia Unita	1878	3,227	Yes (163)	213,000
Patria e Lavoro	1878	1,146	Yes (91)	81,000
Unione e Benevolenza Femminile	1879	1,201	No	30,000
Margherita di Savoia	1879	1,436	Yes (68)	99,000
Italiana (Belgrano)	1879	3,866	No	314,000
Italia	1883	1,812	Yes (100)	151,000
Ligure (Boca)	1885	1,904	Yes (70)	30,000
Nuova Italia	1889	1,000	No	70,000
Giuseppe Garabaldi	1890	1,620	No	152,000
Total for 14 societies		34,591	9 (1,407)	6,856,000
Total for 7 largest societies		24,472	5 (1,078)	6,243,000
Total for all 74 societies		52,498	13 (1,967)	8,740,000

Source: "Le società italiane all'estero nel 1908," Bollettino dell'Emigrazione, 24 (1908), pp. 2–8. Bollettino del Ministero degli Affari Esteri, 124 (April 1898), pp. 1–8, and 369 (December 1908), pp. 1–154, provide the most complete data. The figures, however, vary slightly from those of several other sources. See Emilio Zuccarini, I lavori degli Italiani nell República Argentina (Buenos Aires, 1910), pp. 153–156; Buenos Aires, Censo 1904, pp. 212–235; Argentina, Censo 1914, 10, pp. 306–307; and Samuel L. Baily, "Las sociedades de ayuda mutua y el desarrollo de una comunidad italiana en Buenos Aires, 1858–1918," Desarrollo Económico, 21, 84 (January–March 1982), pp. 490–491.

tablished in the 1880s and 1890s. The two groups of societies often shared members and interacted with each other, but the large societies always predominated in the mutualist movement and thus were in a better position to impose their vision of the community on new arrivals.

In sum, the Italians of Buenos Aires had by 1910 created a large, wealthy, and effective mutualist movement. The 43,000 men on the membership rolls represented about three of every ten adult Italian males in Buenos Aires (28 percent of 154,000) and the 9,000 women about one in every ten (9 percent of 97,000) adult Italian females.

The decade following 1910 presented a special challenge for the Italian mutual aid societies of Buenos Aires. As members aged, they needed more services. This increased need for services placed greater demands on financial reserves. The smaller, more recently established societies—which had limited financial assets and were often less well managed—were especially vulnerable, but even the larger societies could not completely escape these pressures. Many of the societies were therefore prepared to explore formal consolidation and unification as a possible solution to their problems.

Previous efforts to unite the movement formally had failed due to political differences, localism, and personal rivalries among leaders. Several efforts undertaken during World War I also failed. Nevertheless, a more successful unification movement, designed to consolidate a number of societies into one centrally administered organization, began within the Unione e Benevolenza during the same decade. In 1916, approximately a dozen societies joined with the Unione e Benevolenza to form the Associazione Italiana di Mutualità ed Istruzioni. With the subsequent addition of six other societies, the Associazione Italiana consolidated eighteen societies into one organization—four of the largest societies, a number of the village-regional societies both from the North and the South of Italy, and a few of the neighborhood societies. The Associazione Italiana, which is still in existence, has been the center of Italian mutualism in Buenos Aires since 1916.

Italian-Language Newspapers

The Italian-language newspapers also expanded during the period of mass migration and exerted considerable influence on both the old and newly arrived immigrants.[7] Under the directorship of Basilio Cittadini during the first decade of the century, the leading newspaper *La Patria* expanded from six to twelve pages and dramatically increased its regular circulation from about fifteen thousand to an estimated forty thousand.[8] Special editions had more pages and a much larger circulation. For example, the edition to commemorate the inauguration of the monument to Garibaldi in June 1904 had twenty-five pages and a circulation of sixty thousand. These figures made *La Patria* in the early 1900s the third- or fourth-largest daily newspaper of any kind in Argentina, trailing only the Argentine dailies, *La Prensa* and *La Nación*, whose regular circulations were ninety-five thousand and sixty thousand respectively.[9]

The precise influence of *La Patria* is difficult to measure, but there is considerable evidence to suggest that the paper exerted a major leadership role within the community. Humberto Nelli uses the formula of four to one in determining the readership based on circulation of Italian-language newspapers in the United States at the same time.[10] If we apply this formula to *La Patria* in 1904, the readership would be approximately 160,000, or 70 percent of the city's population of 228,000 Italians. This figure most certainly overstates the real readership of *La Patria*, but it is reasonable to estimate that approximately half the Italian population were readers of the paper.

Perhaps as significant as circulation and readership figures is the internal evidence in the newspaper, which suggests the importance of *La Patria* within the Italian community. Almost all of the mutual aid societies, clubs, schools, and other institutions announced meetings and communicated the results of those meetings in the pages of *La Patria*. It was an important transmitter of information about and interpreter of Argentine society. Furthermore, the paper was the most important defender of the Italian immigrants and the self-appointed guardian of the Italian language and Italian culture in general. And its intense Italian nationalism and community-wide perspective served to break down the village and provincial loyalties many immigrants brought with them.

In addition, the paper performed several more unusual functions that increased its influence. In 1900, *La Patria* established free legal aid and medical clinics. Five years later, it opened an agricultural clinic. Although the medical service was limited to subscribers, the legal and agricultural advice was offered to all Italians. These services gave the paper something of the character of a mutual aid society.[11]

The paper also served as an arbiter of disputes and a spokesman for the Italian community. In March 1901, for example, the striking shoe workers of the Italian-owned Pagola and Martinez factory came to the offices of *La Patria* to explain their grievances. The paper printed the grievances and urged the Italian owner and workers to settle the strike quickly so as to avoid police intervention. Similarly, *La Patria* was deeply involved in the school crisis of the early 1900s. In the first decade of the twentieth century, financial pressure threatened the continued existence of many Italian schools and stimulated a heated debate within the community over their importance and necessity. Early in 1906, the Nazionale Italiana closed one of its three schools in Buenos Aires. Many of the students came to the paper to protest the closing. Cittadini took up their cause, insisted that it was "the duty of all Italians to see that these schools do not disappear," and approached the Italian government for financial help.[12]

One of the reasons that the paper was able to play such an important role was that Cittadini had influence not only in the Italian community of Buenos Aires but also with the Italian and Argentine governments. In the school crisis, for example, he approached the Italian government for help. When in mid-1902, an Italian in the custody of the Buenos Aires police died as a result of a beating, it was Cittadini who was granted an interview with Argentine President Julio Roca to resolve the matter. And it was Cittadini who received the highest honor Argentina could bestow on an editor of the foreign-language press—he was elected vice president of the Argentine press association.[13]

Along with the growth and expansion of mutual aid societies and newspapers, various additional Italian business and financial institutions emerged during the period of mass migration. In 1884, the leading Italian businessmen in Buenos Aires established the Camera Italiana de Commercio to represent their collective interests; it became a major influence within the community. In addition, before the end of the 1880s, Italians created two more Italian-Argentine banks—the Nuevo Banco Italiano and the Banco de Roma y Rio de la Plata—to support the financial needs of the growing Italian business community and the financial services demanded by the ever-increasing number of immigrants.

Host Society Institutions

Although Italian institutions developed and expanded successfully during the period of mass migration, Italians also began to participate in increasing numbers in some host society institutions. The extent of this participation, however, varied from institution to institution. Few became involved in the church or in Argentine politics. Large numbers became active in organized labor. What is significant is that Italian immigrants as a group made their first sustained attempts to participate in host society institutions. These efforts resulted in an important change from the earlier pattern of participation primarily in ethnic institutions. Not only were Italians becoming more involved in host society institutions, in the process of doing so they also frequently worked in cooperation with other ethnic groups.

The Church

The Catholic Church expanded its efforts to involve the Italian immigrants, but for a number of reasons achieved only limited success before World War I. First, the leaders of the Italian community were for the most part strongly anticlerical and discouraged such participation, even though increasing numbers of the new arrivals were from the southern parts of Italy and more receptive to religion, if not to the institutional church. Second, the liberal and anticlerical Argentine governments of Julio Roca (1880–1886, 1898–1904) and his political partners greatly restricted the nonreligious activities of the church. In addition to eliminating the church from the public schools (Educational Law of 1884), the Roca regime, by instituting civil registries, encroached on the church's traditional role of recording marriages and deaths. The government also took steps to re-move the church from politics. And third, since the church in Rome con-sidered Argentina a Catholic country, it made only a minimal effort to send priests to serve the immigrants. This neglect placed an enormous burden on the limited human and financial resources of the Argentine church.[14]

The church was not a central part of the lives of most Italian immigrants in Buenos Aires, especially before 1900. As in New York, however, a few dedicated Salesian and Scalabrini fathers made special efforts to involve the immigrants and help them meet their needs. The Scalabrini fathers were never as successful as they were in New York; they withdrew from Argentina in 1906. The Salesians, however, accomplished considerably more than the Scalabrinis, but much of what they achieved was in the in-terior of the country and not in Buenos Aires.[15] Most Italian immigrants in the capital were not active in the church or its affiliated organizations. Even the growing number of those from the South of Italy who were more religious often did not center their religious practices within the church. At least some immigrants created and joined lay religious organizations, which had no contact with the clergy.[16] Although the Italian immigrants and their children were essential to the later expansion of the Argentine church, before World War I the church was never strong enough in human and financial resources to challenge the predominant role of the mutual aid societies and their leaders among the Italian immigrants of the city.

Politics

The nature of Italian participation in Argentine politics did not change significantly during the period of mass migration from 1880 to 1914.[17] As during the preceding period, elections were of limited importance in the political system.[18] Although the 1869 Argentine law of citizenship and nat-uralization legally entitled foreigners to become citizens and vote after two years of residence, very few Italians did so. In 1895, a meager 0.2 per-cent of the total foreign-born population of Buenos Aires was naturalized; by 1914, the number had only increased to 2.3 percent.[19] The census data are not broken down by specific nationalities, but, given these extremely low naturalization figures for all foreigners and the fact that Italians rep-resented half the foreign born, it is obvious that most Italians were not be-coming Argentine citizens and voting in national elections. Instead, they continued to operate as pressure groups seeking to influence national po-litical decisions by demonstrations, petitions, and personal contacts with leading Argentine politicians.

Some Argentines and Italians nevertheless made periodic attempts to involve the immigrants directly in politics. Although generally unsuccessful, these efforts illustrate many of the problems that relegated Italians to the sidelines of national and municipal electoral politics. For example, in 1896 the Agnonese colony in the Barrio del Carmen held a banquet to honor the Italian ambassador to Argentina and invited two Argentine national deputies who lived in the area.[20] The two deputies had established ties with different Italian groups in the city and were anxious to involve Italians in Argentine politics. At the dinner they urged the Agnonese leaders to put forth a candidate for the next municipal council election. The leaders proposed Giovanni Carosella, a thirty-eight-year-old businessman from a leading Agnonese family who had lived in Argentina for ten years and was married to an Argentine of Italian parentage. The candidate, however, was not well known among the older North Italian immigrant groups or the national Argentine political leadership. Although Carosella was elected, the election was challenged on the grounds that the candidate did not have full command of Spanish. Behind closed doors, the municipal council gave Carosella a written examination in Spanish, an exam that he failed. New elections were held in which there was no Italian candidate.

Frustrated by attempts such as this to penetrate the Argentine political system, the leaders of the dynamic Agnonese colony increasingly turned their attention to the Italian institutional structure. Many Agnonesi joined the Colonia Italiana, the large and wealthy mutual aid society whose headquarters were located nearby in the San Nicolás area. By 1898, five of the organization's council members, including Giovanni Carosella, were Agnonesi. In the following decade, an Agnonese became president of the organization.[21]

Clearly the focus of Italian political activity in Buenos Aires was either the ethnic institutional structure or informal protests, rallies, and petitions. A few Argentines of Italian descent did, however, manage to become successfully involved in Argentine politics. Carlos Pelligrini became president of Argentina in 1890.

The political career of Alfredo Demarchi illustrates another such exception. Demarchi, a member of one of the most distinguished Italo-Argentine families, was born in Buenos Aires in 1857. His grandfather, who had arrived in 1830, was the first Italian consul general to Argentina. His uncle was a president of the Banco de Italia y Rio de la Plata. Demarchi, a great promoter of Italo-Argentine industry, established two textile mills and a chemical company. He became a director of the Banco de Italia y Rio de la Plata in 1884 and later served as its vice-president, and he was vice-president (1903, 1908–10) and president (1904–1907) of the major Argentine industrial organization, the Unión Industrial Argentina.

What is unique about Demarchi is that during much of his adult life he also held important elected and appointed Argentine offices. He was elected to the Municipal Council of Buenos Aires in 1893 and a year later he was elected to the National Congress, where he served until 1914. In 1915, he returned to Italy to fight in the war.[22]

Despite exceptions such as Pelligrini and Demarchi, Italians and Argentines of Italian descent generally did not participate in Argentine politics before 1912. The passage of an electoral law in that year provided for obligatory secret voting and marked the beginning of an important change in the situation. Henceforth, elections were of much greater significance. Italians immediately began to move into the political system. After the 1912 election brought a number of Italians to the provincial legislature of Santa Fe, *La Patria* proclaimed that the victories marked the rise of a new generation of politicians made up in large part of people of Italian descent.[23] Yet, it was not until World War II that Italians obtained large numbers of political offices.

Organized Labor

During the first decade of the twentieth century, labor organizations provided Italian immigrants with a working-class institutional alternative to the multi-class mutual aid societies. Tens of thousands took advantage of this new option. Undoubtedly many individuals joined both mutual aid societies and labor unions, but the rise of working-class organizations with significant Italian leadership presented a challenge to the hegemony of the mutual aid societies within the Italian community.

Labor organization in Argentina was largely a product of the mass migration that began in the 1880s. Foreigners provided the ideologies, the leadership, and the majority of members of the country's early labor unions. In the first decade of the twentieth century, approximately three-quarters of the labor leaders and two-thirds of the union members were foreign born, and these workers were employed primarily in small industry, manual arts, and transportation.[24]

The first attempts of the immigrant workers to organize were, as in New York, mutual aid societies that recruited members from a specific occupation. Before 1880, none of these organizations was particularly effective in defending the interests of the workers. With the mass immigration of the 1880s, however, thousands of new workers arrived in Buenos Aires and other Argentine cities and began to form new militant, class-based organizations. Toward the end of the 1880s, rapid inflation and the resulting erosion of real wages prompted a series of strikes and prepared the way for the establishment in 1890 of the country's first labor federation.[25]

During the 1880s and 1890s, Italians were active in many working-class organizations and groups. Among the most important organizers were political radicals from Italy such as Errico Malatesta and Ettore Mattei who accompanied the immigrants. In Italy since the 1870s, a series of popular protests had manifested growing class consciousness and militancy among an increasing number of workers and peasants. Middle-class anarchists, socialists, and syndicalists frequently provided the ideologies of organization and resistance for these popular uprisings. Repression by the Italian government of these movements in Italy forced a number of the leaders to emigrate, some for relatively short stays until it was safe to return home, others to remain abroad permanently.[26]

In 1890, the Italians were not as significant as the German Socialists among the leaders of the embryonic labor movement, but they contributed a substantial number of leaders and workers to almost all working-class organizations. During the 1890s, they became increasingly important as leaders of the various short- lived labor federations, and in the first decade of the twentieth century they became the most important single leadership element within the working class.

Italian immigrants successfully participated in the organization of Argentine labor because there was a good fit between their experience in Italy and the kind of labor movement that emerged in Buenos Aires. Given the restricted nature of the Argentine political system, it is not surprising that the direct action of the anarchists and the revolutionary unionism of the syndicalists held greater appeal to the immigrants than the socialists' call to naturalize and change the system by participation in essentially meaningless elections.

In 1901, the workers of Buenos Aires and a few interior cities met to create Argentina's first significant labor federation, the Federación Obrera Regional Argentina (FORA). Nevertheless, competition continued among anarchists, syndicalists, and socialists, and there were several additional splits within the labor movement. Less than a year after its establishment, the FORA became an exclusively anarchist organization. In 1903, the socialist and syndicalist workers established a rival labor federation, the Unión General del Trabajo (UGT), but it soon became exclusively syndicalist.

These two organizations (the FORA and the UGT), which at the peak of their influence in 1906 represented perhaps 70 percent to 80 percent of the approximately fifty thousand organized workers in the city and maybe as much as 50 percent of the workers in small industry and manual arts, provided militant leadership for the labor movement until the government repression of June 1910 temporarily ended their activity.[27] Between 1902 and 1910, the FORA and the UGT led a number of general strikes, some of which involved as many as 200,000 workers. Their affiliates participated in hundreds of individual strikes. As a result of this action and the prosperity of the period, real wages of skilled and semiskilled workers increased, their hours decreased, and rents in some working-class districts were lowered.[28]

Italians were equally strong within both major federations. Approximately half of the members of the executive committees and a similar proportion of the general memberships of these organizations were Italians. The Buenos Aires Municipal Census of 1904 lists about a dozen Italian labor organizations with a membership of ten thousand. Keeping in mind that Italians were among the members of many other labor unions and that they represented half of the foreign population, it is reasonable to estimate that they constituted about half of the approximately fifty thousand organized workers in the city.[29] Although government repression temporarily curtailed the workers' organizations in 1910, many had gained valuable experience and developed a working-class culture that enabled them to revive the labor organization at the end of the next decade.[30]

The emergence of a strong class-based radical labor movement challenged the ethnic-based mutualist movement for the loyalty of Italian workers in Buenos Aires. Tens of thousands of Italians were members of labor organizations, and many more supported the general strikes and protests. Many of these same workers were also members of the multiclass mutual aid societies. The labor movement stressed the class interests of the Italian workers, while the mutualist movement stressed ethnic loyalty. Inevitably the two at times conflicted.[31]

Although we know very little about the interaction of class and ethnicity within the Italian community of Buenos Aires, a pioneering article by Romolo Gandolfo provides some insight into this issue.[32] Gandolfo argues that because large numbers of Italian workers and tenants had Italian employers and landlords, there was considerable tension within the Italian community. Since many of these employers and landlords were members and frequently leaders of the same mutual aid societies as their employees and tenants, the mutual aid societies became potential arenas of intraethnic conflict. Yet he concludes that before World War I both the labor leaders and the Italian elites avoided exploiting class tensions: the labor leaders were fearful that such action might produce an ethnic backlash that could weaken labor organizations, and the Italian elites refused to acknowledge the existence of intra-ethnic conflict because it belied the ethnic unity upon which they depended to maintain their positions.

Both class and ethnicity were important to the Italian workers, and because of this, there were intra-ethnic tensions within the Italian community of Buenos Aires. Ethnicity brought Italians together in immigrant organizations, but it also facilitated Italian labor leaders' efforts to attract Italian workers to class-based organizations. What is significant is that before World War I, class-based labor organizations—in which Italians participated extensively as leaders and members—could not overcome the hegemony of the traditional elites over the Italian community. The Italian institutions remained strong and the appeal to ethnicity effective.

One other host society institution needs to be mentioned here because of the important role Italians played within it. In 1887, a number of Italian businessmen joined their counterparts of other nationalities to establish what would become the Argentine equivalent of the National Association of Manufacturers, the Unión Industrial Argentina (UIA). Although not an Italian institution, before 1900 those with Italian surnames accounted for a third of the membership and leadership of the UIA. After 1900, this representation increased to about half.[33] The Italians were essential to the development of this major industrial organization in Argentina, in much the same way as they were to the development of organized labor.

New York City, 1890–1914

The Italian community of New York grew extremely rapidly in the decades after 1890, and especially after 1900. In New York, unlike Buenos Aires, mass migration overwhelmed the existing Italian institutional structure. The new immigrants needed mutual aid societies and other institutions to help meet their basic needs, but the existing ethnic institutions were not numerous or wealthy enough to absorb and guide the new arrivals. Most Italian immigrants had no choice but to fall back on informal institutions for help as they had in the past, and increasingly to look outside the ethnic community to the host society for assistance.

Mutual Aid Societies

There was a rapid proliferation of mutual aid societies—from several dozen in the mid-1880s to more than three hundred by 1910. Some scholars believe the number was substantially higher, perhaps in the thousands.[34] Two surveys of Italian mutual aid societies abroad published in the *Bollettino dell'Emigrazione* offer the best available data on the subject.[35] The 1908 survey listed twenty-five mutual aid societies in Manhattan and Brooklyn, with approximately 4,400 members. Because it did not include some of the older and wealthier societies (the Unione e Fratellanza, La Fraterna, and the Legione Garibaldi), this was only a partial list. The subsequent survey of 1910 recorded a more realistic number of 338 societies.

The 1908 survey, though missing a great many societies, is nevertheless useful because it contains information that, combined with other, more impressionistic data, enables me to estimate membership and net worth of the 338 societies reported in 1910. The average size of the twenty-five societies listed in 1908 was 175 members. Using this figure as the average for the 338 societies in 1910 yields a total membership of approximately 45,600. Similarly, the average net worth of the twenty-five societies in 1908 was 10,700 lire, but other data suggest that this is probably more than twice the actual average. Assuming that the average net worth was more in the range of 5,000 lire, I project a total net worth for the 338 societies of 1,690,000 lire.[36]

This information indicates several significant differences between the mutualist movements in Buenos Aires and New York. Nearly all of the New York societies were recently established, small, poorly financed and managed, and limited to immigrants from the same town or region of Italy. The average size of the mutual aid societies in New York (175 members) was much smaller than in Buenos Aires (709 members), and the average net worth of the New York societies (5,000 lire) was but a fraction of that of the societies in Buenos Aires (118,000 lire). The precise figures may vary to some extent from these estimates, but even if the actual New York figures were double what I have projected, it would not alter the basic conclusion. The larger and better organized Buenos Aires societies had many times the resources with which to meet the needs of the Italians in the city than their counterparts did in New York.

Furthermore, divisiveness based on personal rivalries and Old World ties increasingly characterized the New York movement. Although a few of the older societies were open to all Italians and probably attempted to represent the community as a whole, they never were large or wealthy enough to establish effective leadership of the mutualist movement. Unfortunately, membership lists, minutes of the executive committee and general assembly meetings, financial reports, and other data that are available on the Buenos Aires societies do not apparently exist for New York. We thus know much less about the New York societies. Given the Italian social structure of New York, however, it is likely that in many societies the members were unskilled and semiskilled workers. We know that the leaders were generally successful labor contractors, bankers, and professionals. For example, Louis V. Fugazy (discussed in the preceding chapter) was during these years involved in the incorporation of perhaps as many as a hundred such societies and was the president of at least several dozen.[37]

Whatever the limitations of the societies, they met some needs or immigrants would not have created and joined them. Unemployment, sickness, and death benefits, however limited, were essential. So too were the close ties with leaders who, as labor agents and small bankers, could facilitate the search for jobs and the sending of money and tickets back to Italy. The societies also provided a setting for socializing with fellow villagers.

A few of the older and larger societies, supported by the Italian-language newspapers, provided a basis for coordinating community-wide celebrations and meetings to defend common interests. Throughout the period, the newspapers repeatedly referred to the United Italian Societies of New York, Brooklyn, Hoboken, and Newark, but this simply indicated joint activity rather than a functioning organization. Beginning in 1905, a number of societies joined the National Order of the Sons of Italy, and that organization gradually developed broad influence within the community.

The New York mutualist movement lacked the large and wealthy community-wide societies that in Buenos Aires provided the leadership for the Italian community, and as a consequence never had the human and financial resources to incorporate and to provide very much guidance and assistance to the mass of newcomers. The pre–mass migration mutualist movement was generally overwhelmed by mass migration. Italians in New York organized hundreds of small village and regional mutual aid societies, which reinforced the localism and fragmentation of the community. Most Italians did not join mutual aid societies, or if they did, they remained more isolated within their local societies and less involved in any broader community than their counterparts in Buenos Aires.

The Press

The Italian-language press also grew during the period of mass migration, provided information that helped the immigrants adjust to their new environment, and by sometimes focusing on community-wide issues and supporting Italian nationalism, did help overcome some of the isolation and localism of the new arrivals. At the same time, however, it continued to serve the narrow business and personal interests of the newspaper owners. In some cases the papers could combine their own interests with those of the broader Italian community, but as I discussed in Chapter 7, when the two were in conflict the former were paramount.

By 1914, there were more than a half dozen large commercial dailies including *L'Eco d'Italia, Il Progresso Italo-Americano, Bolletino della Sera,* and *Corriere della Sera.* Circulation and revenues increased as the Italian community grew. For example, the largest of the newspapers, *Il Progresso Italo-Americano,* increased its circulation from 6,500 in 1890 to more than 80,000 in 1914.[38]

The Italian-language press continued to print a good deal of news about Italy, to defend Italians in New York and other parts of the United States, and to provide practical information on jobs and available apartments. However, unlike its Buenos Aires counterpart, it also championed some new causes that facilitated the immigrants' participation in host society, as opposed to ethnic, institutions.[39] For example, in September 1894, *Il Progresso* began a two-month-long series on "Italians in American Politics." The articles urged Italians to register and vote, and to stimulate interest the paper conducted a mock election to determine whom the readers would most like to see as a potential Italian candidate. Nearly fourteen thousand votes were cast for twenty-one prominent Italians. The winner was the successful fruit dealer, politician, and leading force within the Italian Chamber of Commerce, Antonio Zucca.[40]

Il Progresso continued throughout the period to urge Italians to register and vote every November when elections were scheduled to be held, and it generally supported the overwhelmingly Irish candidates of Tammany Hall and the Democratic Party. In early November 1907, as part of its yearly effort to encourage Italians to register and vote, *Il Progresso* featured an article on the recently enacted (June 29, 1906) federal naturalization law and included the entire printed text of the document translated into Italian.[41]

One final ethnic institution needs to be mentioned. In 1896, a group of businessmen established the first major Italian-American bank, the Italian Savings Bank, in the heart of the Bowery colony. Hundreds of "Italian Banks" had appeared and disappeared in New York for many years. Most were unregistered and were run by padroni, boarding house owners, and saloon keepers. In 1897, only six—including the Italian Savings Bank—had legal status under the laws of New York State. There was no control or regulation of the others and many immigrants were taken advantage of and lost money. As a result, the Italian Savings Bank, which provided a new level of protection and security, developed rapidly. By 1904, it had more than seven thousand accounts.[42]

Host Society Institutions: Developing the Ethnic Niche

Given the limited development and functions of the formal institutional structure in the Italian colony, the more narrowly self-serving nature of the leadership, the rapid and extremely large influx of immigrants, and the resulting inability of the community to meet the newcomers' basic needs, it is not surprising that a number of non-immigrant-run institutions attempted to assist the immigrants. Prominent among these groups was the Italian government and its representative in New York, the Italian consul.

The Italian government continued to try to help the immigrants as it had previously in 1888 when the Italian consul had taken the leadership in establishing the short-lived Italian Home. It was, as Stabili notes, the ties of the Italian elites (prominenti) to the labor agencies and banks, and their resulting refusal to do anything to protect the immigrants from the abuses of the padroni, that pressured the Italian government into action.[43]

In 1901, a group of well-to-do Americans also bypassed the traditional immigrant leadership to create the Society for the Protection of Italian Immigrants. The Protective Society, led by President Eliot Norton and

Recording Secretary Sarah Moore but supported financially in part by the Italian government, again sought to provide an alternative to the padrone labor contracting system and to the "steerers" who attempted to direct the arriving immigrants to specific boarding houses. It set up a labor bureau, published a list of approved boarding houses, and hired its own agents to meet the immigrants when they arrived at the Battery. The society subsequently expanded its services to provide legal advice and financial assistance.[44]

The Protective Society was the first effective and enduring organization created to help the new immigrants. It assisted over seven thousand individuals during its first two years of existence. By 1906, it provided aid for more than thirteen thousand yearly. Because of its success and its avowed purpose of providing an alternative to some of the business interests of the local Italian leaders, the society was attacked by the prominenti.[45]

The Benevolent Institute, also established in 1901 and supported in part by the Italian government, worked closely with the Protective Society during the next decade or so before World War I to assist the immigrants. Under the dedicated leadership of Celestino Piva, the institute provided food, clothing, and temporary shelter for newly arrived Italians who needed the help. In addition, Piva sought to provide medical assistance through small dispensaries and, by 1912, was successful in opening an Italian hospital on East 83rd Street. Piva worked independently of the local Italian prominenti, but the community nevertheless made a considerable effort to support the construction of the hospital. In 1907, for example, the mutual aid societies sponsored festivities associated with the celebration of September 20th, raising $3,626 for the benefit of the hospital. Similar events in subsequent years raised additional funds for the cause.[46]

Thus the Italian government, supporting non-immigrant-led or controlled efforts, made a small contribution to meeting at least the most pressing needs of the new immigrants, but its efforts benefited only a small portion of the mass of new arrivals.

The Catholic Church

The Catholic Church during the era of mass migration expanded on the foundations established during the preceding period to reach and incorporate Italian immigrants. Its greatest success was the creation of more Italian parishes, the ethnic niches that encouraged immigrants to participate in the church. Yet scholars disagree as to how successful this effort was, especially before World War I. Sylvano Tomasi argues that the church, through the creation of Italian national parishes, encouraged the immigrants to develop a sense of Italian-American identity, absorbed them into the mainstream of American Catholicism, and enabled them to take their place in the larger pluralistic American society. Thus for him the Italian national parishes were the "focal points" of the Italian community, and the church was able to integrate the Italians into American society.[47]

Tomasi provides supporting data on the expansion of these Italian national parishes in New York. In 1899, there were fourteen Italian churches and chapels served by 38 Italian priests in New York and Brooklyn. Twenty-nine years later, in 1918, the numbers had increased dramatically to seventy churches and chapels, 175 Italian priests, 750,000 members, fifteen parochial schools, and 10,000 students. By 1920, there were approximately 800,000 Italian-speaking individuals in New York City, of whom more than 90 percent, according to Tomasi, were members of Catholic churches.[48]

Yet was the ethnic parish "the most relevant institution supporting the immigrants in their encounter with the surrounding groups and the dominant society" during the period of mass migration before World War I, as Tomasi suggests?[49] A number of other scholars raise serious questions as to the validity of this assertion. Specifically, they challenge the statement that most Italians were active participants in the Catholic Church and even the statement that for those who were active participants, the church was "the most relevant" institutional influence in their lives.

Tomasi's critics generally agree with him that religion was important to most Italian immigrants in New York, but assert that this did not mean they were active participants in the formal institutional church. As noted in the preceding chapter, the immigrants brought with them a tradition of a personal, popular religion and a wariness of the institutional church and its priests. In New York City they confronted a church dominated by the Irish, who stressed doctrinal tenets and financial support for parish projects rather than a personal relationship with God and the saints. In addition, though the number of Italian priests increased substantially, it was inadequate from the beginning.[50]

Baptisms, weddings, funerals, and the feasts to honor the saints were important to Italian immigrants, but attending Sunday Mass and financially supporting the Irish-controlled institutional church was not necessarily so. Paul McBride, in a thoughtful review of Tomasi's book, uses Tomasi's own data to make the point. Church reports of ten New York Italian parishes in 1929 and 1930 indicate that attendance at Sunday Mass fluctuated between 15 percent and 75 percent, and similar records show that at the Lady of Mt. Carmel parish in Italian Harlem, 44 percent of the members attended Sunday Mass in 1926 and only 33 percent in 1929.[51]

In an informative study based on dozens of interviews with members of the Lady of Mt. Carmel Parish, Robert Orsi defines popular religion as the integration of the rituals and symbols of the institutional church with the people's traditional values and perceptions of reality as expressed in events like the annual feast of the Madonna of 115th Street. Yet he too notes that his informants consistently made the distinction between religion and the church, that going to Sunday Mass was not so important, that they considered themselves religious people and Catholics, that they faithfully attended baptisms, weddings, and funerals, and that they went to church on the feast days of the saints they were named for.[52]

In the years before World War I, the complex and evolving relationship between the Italian immigrants and the institutional church varied from individual to individual. For those involved, the Italian parish was a significant influence in their lives. For some, the church was less important than other institutions. And for still others, the American church played no part at all in their lives. But for most Italians, the church was not "the most relevant institution" in which they participated. As George Pozzetta concludes, the majority gave up formal religion.[53] However, the Italian national parish created an ethnic niche that in later years expanded dramatically to became a major mechanism for the participation of Italians in host society institutions.

Politics

As with the church, relatively small numbers of Italians became involved in local politics prior to World War I, but those who did created important organizational precedents for the much broader participation of Italians in the future. Most southern Italians shunned politics during this period because of their lack of familiarity with the political system, their traditional distrust of government, their localism, and for many, the presumed temporary nature of their stay in New York. In addition, in politics as in so many other institutions, they confronted Irish-controlled organizations whose leaders were initially unsympathetic to Italians and did not encourage their participation.

A number of things, however, favored the gradual incorporation of Italians into the local political structure at an earlier period than in Buenos Aires. Elections played an important role in the New York City political system. The need to win elections and to attract voters thus provided the small but growing number of Italian-American citizens with a potential— if not yet actual—political resource.

In addition, by the turn of the century, well-organized and effective political machines—whose leaders were willing to accommodate to some extent the diverse social and economic groups of the city—had come to play an increasingly important role in politics. The formation of Italian political clubs affiliated with these machines was an important initial step in the long-term process of Italian incorporation into the political system in New York. In a manner similar to the role played by ethnic parishes in the church, Italian political clubs proved over time to be the most effective mechanism with which to recruit Italians into the political system.

As the Italian community of New York grew in size and became more permanent, some of its members became involved first with the Republican and then the Democratic organizations. In the 1890s, the Republicans organized dozens of political clubs, such as the Italian-American Progressive Republican Club and the Italian Republican League, in Italian districts. In 1894, the Republicans nominated the editor of one of the Italian-language newspapers as a candidate for local office, and subsequently nominated other Italian-Americans as candidates for various offices. None, however, were successful until 1906, when A. C. Astarita was elected a city alderman.[54]

One naturalized Italian, James March (Antonio M. Maggio), developed a successful career as a Republican political leader. March moved to New York in 1880 and began working for the Erie Railroad. In 1885, he was made overseer of the railroad and put in charge of several thousand workers. After a brief and frustrating experience in politics with Tammany Hall, March joined the Republican Party, moved up in its ranks, and in 1894 was elected Republican leader of the 6th Assembly District. Shortly thereafter he was appointed warden of the port of New York by Governor Theodore Roosevelt, and in 1904 he was elected Republican presidential elector.[55]

Initial relations between Tammany Hall and the Italians were strained. In the early 1890s, the Irish-dominated organization showed little interest in attracting Italian voters. Yet the growing numbers of Italians—and the Republican efforts to recruit and organize them—stimulated the Democrats to begin to organize Italian political clubs as well and to seek the support of the Italian-language newspapers. The Italian Democratic Political Club was organized in 1892, and many others followed.

Antonio Zucca's political career illustrates the process of the initial incorporation of Italians into the Democratic Party. Zucca, the winner of *Il Progresso's* mock election in the fall of 1894, declined at that time to run for public office. In a letter to the paper, he thanked those who had voted for him and explained why they should vote for others: he had no ambitions at all for a public career, his business affairs would not permit him to become involved in politics, and he lived in a district that completely lacked an Italian element and therefore he could not win an election. He went on to urge Italians to register and vote because, due to the recent exposure of corruption within Tammany Hall, the elections would be much closer and thus the Italian votes would be more important to the political parties. He concluded that the Democratic Party was still the most vital force in New York City politics, that Italians should join and create a strong nucleus within it, and that then the party leaders would nominate one or two Italian Americans for public office.[56]

Three years later (in 1897), Zucca changed his mind and was the successful Democratic candidate for coroner of New York City. Zucca had organized the Italian Political Association, joined the Executive Committee of Tammany Hall, and taken on the presidency of the Italian-American Democratic Association. In addition, he was at different times president of the Italian Chamber of Commerce, of the Italian Savings Bank, and of the Italian Benevolent Association. This network of political and business associations was essential to his successful political career. In 1904, he was elected to the New York Board of Assessors; two years later he was elected president of this board.[57]

Tammany Hall was increasingly interested in incorporating the growing number of Italians in the city during the decade before World War I.[58] The first tangible results of this interest came during the administration of Tammany reform mayor George B. McClellan Jr. (1903–1909). In 1904, Democrat Peter Acritelli, treasurer of the Italian Chamber of Commerce, was elected coroner of New York and a number of Italian Americans were appointed to political jobs (deputy chief of licenses, municipal assessor, superintendent of the tenement house department). In addition, McClellan did not enforce a Republican-sponsored state law that made foreigners ineligible for municipal jobs. And in 1905, a Republican governor vetoed a bill to make October 12 a legal holiday.[59]

Tammany Mayor William Gaynor (1909–1913) provided additional evidence of the Democrats' interest in the Italian vote. When Gaynor ran for mayor in 1909, he actively sought and received Italian support; he praised Italy, attacked the Republicans as restrictionists, and supported hiring of foreign labor for public works. As a result, after his election, he appointed an Italian American of Sicilian parents, John J. Freschi, as magistrate. In 1912, the prominenti established an Italian-American Gaynor Club to support the mayor's reelection.[60]

March, Zucca, and a few others, though exceptional, laid the institutional foundations for subsequent Italian-American political participation. They established Italian political clubs as ethnic niches through which Italians might participate in politics. However, before World War I, the numbers of naturalized Italians and Italian voters remained small. Foerster states that only 16 percent of the southern Italians were naturalized compared to 33 percent of the other foreigners. It is important to note, however, that this 16 percent was eight to ten times greater than the percentage of naturalized Italians in Buenos Aires at the same time. Alberto Pecorini states that in New York in 1911 only fifteen thousand Italians out of a population of nearly a half a million actually voted.[61] But Italians began joining political clubs as they came to understand the practice of local politics, realized the benefits of participation, and were encouraged to do so by fellow Italians.[62]

Organized Labor

As with politics, Italian participation in organized labor developed slowly during the decades before World War I. With mass migration, increasing numbers of Italians moved into the labor market of New York City, especially into unskilled and semiskilled public works, construction, waterfront, and garment industry jobs (see Chapter 4). Few Italians, however, joined unions before 1900. During the first decade of the twentieth century, the problems that prevented Italians from organizing were overcome to some extent, and by World War I a significant minority were active in the labor movement.

There were many reasons why most Italians took some time to begin to participate in the working-class movement. The large number who were unskilled workers generally lacked experience with labor organizations, frequently assumed their stay in New York was temporary, and encountered hostility from many established unions. There was little reason or incentive for them to join labor organizations. In addition, there were insufficient numbers of experienced Italian-speaking labor organizers to educate the workers about the advantages of unionism and to facilitate their entry into the unions. And the Italian community, initially dominated by labor contractors, bankers, and businessmen, only gradually came to realize the vital role to be played by organized labor and to support their fellow countrymen and women when they went out on strike.[63]

Some Italians did, however, organize. Skilled craftsmen organized first and then gradually some of the semiskilled and unskilled workers. In most cases, Italians who organized did so by creating Italian sections within the larger union structures in much the same way as Italians created ethnic parishes within the church and Italian political clubs within the Republican and Democratic parties. Italian-speaking organizers generally played a major role in the successful recruitment of Italian workers and the establishment of the Italian sections.

In contrast with Buenos Aires—where Italians dominated the labor movement—the British, Irish, Germans, and other older immigrant groups controlled organized labor in New York. These older immigrants frequently were prejudiced against Italians and at first did not seek to incorporate them into their unions. They could not, however, ignore the skilled Italian craftsmen—the shoemakers, masons, bricklayers, tailors, carpenters, barbers, and so on—who were becoming increasingly numerous within the New York City labor force. When Italian craftsmen were excluded from established unions, they began to create their own organizations. Confronted with dual unions, the craft unions of the AFL actively began to organize the Italians. Yet even when skilled Italians were accepted into the unions, they were often poorly treated. Meetings were conducted in English, and Italians rarely became part of the union leadership.[64]

The large majority of unskilled common workers, however, remained outside the American labor movement. An important reason for this was that before 1900, the padroni controlled a good part of the Italian workforce in New York City (see Chapter 4).[65] As the padrone system declined in importance during the first decade of the century, unskilled Italian workers began to organize and strike. Italian-speaking leaders and the creation of separate Italian unions and Italian sections within established unions were essential to the success of this process.

As Rudolph Vecoli has shown, Italian radicals played an important part in developing a militant working-class culture in the United States and in providing leadership for working-class organizations. During the three decades preceding World War I, many of the leaders of the Italian anarchist, socialist, and syndicalist movements spent some time in the New York area (New York City, Hoboken, Paterson) speaking to workers, publishing newspapers, organizing political groups, and participating in strikes and other forms of popular protest and resistance.[66]

Nevertheless, the Italian radical movement in the United States at first had limited success in recruiting the mass of Italian workers to its ranks. Anti-organizational and organizational anarchists, revolutionary and democratic socialists, and syndicalists spent much of their energy fighting among themselves. In addition, the large majority of immigrants resisted their teachings and calls to action. Yet, as Vecoli concludes, "The radicals did comprise a substantial stratum of the Italian workers. It was this militant minority which provided the grassroots leadership as well as the active rank-and-file supporters in the coming labor struggles."[67]

❦

The respective patterns of Italian formal institutional participation in Buenos Aires and New York City during the half century before World War I differed in important ways. In Buenos Aires during the pre–mass migration period before 1880, the Italians developed an extended, wealthy, and powerful immigrant institutional structure around a handful of large mutual aid societies, open to Italians from all parts of the peninsula, which provided multiple services (schools, hospitals, medical clinics, job placement) for their members. The leaders of these societies were part of an elite that established Italian-language newspapers, the Italian Hospital, Italo-Argentine banks, the Italian Chamber of Commerce, and social clubs, among other institutions. There was very limited participation among Italians in nonimmigrant institutions such as the church and the political parties.

The main focus of Italian formal institutional participation in New York during the pre–mass migration period before 1890 was also on immigrant institutions and on mutual aid societies. However, the New York Italians produced a more limited overall formal institutional structure and their mutual aid societies were smaller, had fewer resources, and provided significantly fewer services than their counterparts in Buenos Aires. Italian-language newspapers never effectively or consistently represented the interests of the broader immigrant community.

With mass migration after 1880, the Italian community in Buenos Aires expanded its mutual aid societies, banks, clubs, and other organizations to accommodate the new arrivals. Although some Italian groups attempted to participate in Argentine electoral politics, these attempts were blocked by the native elites. This rebuff in turn served to reinforce the Italian community's focus even more on the mutual aid societies and other immigrant institutions. However, the mutual aid societies were challenged to some extent for the loyalty of the Italian immigrants by the growing activity of the labor movement. Italians were the most important single leadership element within the Argentine labor movement of the first decade of the twentieth century, and this leadership provided an important link between labor and the incoming immigrants. Thus the ethnic institutional structure, supplemented by an Italian-dominated labor movement, provided the main formal organizations in which Italians in Buenos Aires participated. For the most part, the immigrant institutions absorbed the new migrants who entered the city each year, although by the middle of the first decade of the new century, this task was becoming increasingly difficult to do.

The New York Italian institutional structure expanded after 1890 in an attempt to meet some of the demands of the new immigrants. However, it lacked the strong foundation that existed in Buenos Aires so it never was able to keep up with the new demands. The community was fragmented and unable to absorb the newcomers. Non-Italian groups attempted to meet at least some of the needs of the immigrants, but they too were overwhelmed by the demands. Nevertheless, during this period some within the Italian community were able to move into the Catholic Church, local politics, and the labor movement by creating ethnic niches for themselves there. In so doing, they provided a foundation for increased participation in these host society institutions in the future.

These patterns of institutional participation affected the Italians' adjustment process in the two cities. The well-developed Italian immigrant structure in Buenos Aires and the less developed one in New York certainly were important contributing factors to the more rapid and complete adjustment of the Italians in Buenos Aires. In Buenos Aires, extensive resources to help the immigrants were available, and the individuals who extended them generally shared the same language and customs—the same worldview—as those who were seeking help. In New York, the resources to help were less extensive—and even when they were available, those who offered them were generally members of the host society who did not speak Italian or any of its local dialects and did not understand much about Italian culture.

At the same time, the self-interest of the Italians in things Argentine dictated that they move beyond the ethnic community to explore participation in host society institutions. Members of the Italian elites and some small businessmen, for example, were interested in participating in Argentine politics. Perhaps the situation would have developed differently had they been able to do so, but the Argentine elites refused to let them. The result was to turn the attention of these Italians even more inward to the Italian community.

In addition, self-interest on the part of working-class Italians moved them beyond the immigrant institutions to form class-based labor organizations. This move was easy because Italians and other foreigners already dominated the leadership and rank and file of this host society institution. However, in joining class-based unions, the Italian workers did not cease to participate in the ethnically based mutual aid societies. During the period before the war, they apparently saw no major conflict in participating in both.

These two attempts to move beyond the Italian institutional structure of Buenos Aires failed, for different reasons, to weaken it. Throughout the period, the Italian elites successfully maintained their hegemony over the Italian community. This hegemony was due partly to the elites' relatively progressive social views and their efforts to represent the broader interests of the community. It was also due partly to the limits placed on Italian participation in nonethnic institutions by the host society, and partly to the workers' willingness to participate simultaneously in the multi-class ethnic institutions and the class-based labor organizations. The continued hegemony of the Italian elites meant that they primarily influenced the adjustment of the Italians in Buenos Aires.

In New York, where the formal ethnic institutions were inadequate to meet the needs of the immigrants, Italian immigrants turned to other options of institutional participation. One was to resort to informal local institutions for assistance. This option fitted the short-term economic strategy that most adopted and pursued, resulting in the continued fragmentation of the community.

Gradually, however, New York Italians came increasingly to participate in various host society institutions. The process was slow due to the strong ties of localism among the Italians and to opposition—and even hostility—on the part of those who controlled the host society institutions. The Irish and other established immigrant groups looked down on Italians and blocked their entrance wherever they attempted to participate—in the church, in politics, and in organized labor. As the Italian community became more permanent and familiar with the local society, self-interest motivated its members to explore participation in all these institutions. Where given the opportunity to develop ethnic niches within these larger host society institutions—the Italian parish, the Italian labor local, and the Italian political club, the immigrants began to participate.

This type of participation remained somewhat limited during the pre–World War I period, but it developed the mechanisms for expanded participation in the future. As a result, adjustment in New York was predominantly influenced by host society as opposed to formal ethnic institutions, and by informal ethnic institutions.

9

Constructing a Continuum

Although the fourteen million Italians who migrated overseas during the four decades preceding World War I went to multiple destinations on five continents, more chose Buenos Aires and New York City than any other places in the world. As a result, by 1914 the Italian communities in these two cites numbered more than 300,000 individuals. The primary goal for most who went there was to do better economically than they had done in Italy. Whether temporary or more permanent migrants, they needed to adjust to some extent to their new environment to obtain their objective. At a minimum they needed to get a job and find a place to live. If they remained longer, they needed friends with whom to socialize and institutions to articulate and protect their interests.

In the preceding chapters, I have set forth a detailed description and explanation of the respective patterns of adjustment of the Italians in Buenos Aires and New York. Most notably, I have shown that the Italians in Buenos Aires at the turn of the past century adjusted more rapidly, effectively, and completely than those in New York. In this concluding chapter, I extend my analysis to other cases in an effort to develop broader patterns of adjustment and explanation. To clarify the comparison of all the cases, I first summarize the evidence that best describes and explains the respective patterns in Buenos Aires and New York. Then I examine Italian migration to three additional New World cities—San Francisco, São Paulo, and Toronto.

To facilitate a systematic comparison I summarize in each of the five cases the most important variables that indicate the nature and extent of adjustment under the general rubrics of economic activity, residence patterns, and organizational activity. In addition, I summarize the factors of primary importance in accounting for the various patterns of adjustment by looking at three interrelated clusters of variables: the skills, resources, and attitudes the immigrants brought with them; the characteristics of the receiving societies and of the environment the immigrants found upon arrival; and the changing nature of the immigrant communities and host societies over time.

There is a trade-off when shifting from the detailed analysis of the type presented on Buenos Aires and New York in the preceding chapters to the condensed analysis that follows. Summarizing the information and presenting it in this schematic way inevitably sacrifices some of the complexity and the nuances of the examples. However, it enhances my ability to make systematic comparisons, to determine similarities and differences, to identify patterns, and to explain what caused the different outcomes. Both types of analysis are, in my opinion, necessary. The purpose of this chapter is to demonstrate what comparison can do to enhance our understanding of Italian immigrant adjustment.

The Adjustment of Italians in
Buenos Aires and New York City

Let me begin by summarizing the evidence I have presented that defines the distinct patterns of Italian adjustment in Buenos Aires and New York City.

Economic activity. In both cities, approximately 50 percent of the Italians managed to earn a surplus in good years, but they developed different economic strategies and spent their surpluses in different ways. In Buenos Aires, most Italians pursued a long-term strategy of spending their money in that city to improve their standard of living there. In New York, on the other hand, most followed a short-term strategy of saving as much as possible in the shortest time and returning to Italy. Thus more of the money earned by Italians stayed in Buenos Aires than in New York; this increased savings rate strengthened local Italian community resources and facilitated the adjustment of future immigrants in the South American city.

In Buenos Aires, Italian workers and owners dominated the vital commercial and industrial sectors of this rapidly growing city throughout the period under consideration; in New York, the Italians, although numerous in a few specific occupations, were never a major presence in any sector of the economy. In addition, although most Italians in both cities were blue-collar workers, a higher proportion in Buenos Aires were skilled workers, white-collar workers, and owners of small industrial and commercial establishments. Italians in both cities experienced some upward occupational mobility. In New York, however, this mobility was confined to movement within the blue-collar sector, whereas in Buenos Aires at least some were able to move from blue-collar to white-collar occupations as well. Finally, Italians in Buenos Aires played a much more significant role in organizations of workers and employers; they were essential contributors to the development of the organized labor movement and were a significance presence in the establishment and growth of the major businessmen's association, the Argentine Industrial Union.

Residence patterns. Although in both cities many Italians first settled in crowded, low-rent central districts, Italians were more evenly dispersed throughout Buenos Aires, while in New York they were concentrated in two areas of Lower Manhattan and East Harlem. This pattern reflected greater discrimination against Italians in New York. Living conditions, poor in both cities, were somewhat better in Buenos Aires—where only one-quarter of the Italians lived in congested and frequently unhealthy tenement houses—than in New York, where tenements sheltered three-quarters of them. The population density in the New York Italian districts was approximately 50 percent higher than it was in the most densely settled districts in Buenos Aires. Per capita property ownership was also considerably higher among Italians in Buenos Aires than in New York. And finally, Italians in Buenos Aires moved earlier than those in New York to outlying areas where there was less congestion, better living conditions, and greater opportunity to buy homes.

Organizational activity. Italians were active in a variety of institutions and organizations that could articulate their needs, protect their interests, and help them achieve their goals. In Buenos Aires, many of these organizations were highly developed formal immigrant institutions that commanded greater resources and were more representative of the diverse elements of the community than was the case in New York. For example, the mutual aid society movement started in the mid-nineteenth century in both cities but subsequently developed very differently. In New York, the overwhelming majority of societies were small (under five hundred members), poorly financed and poorly managed, and generally confined to members from one town or region in Italy. In Buenos Aires, on the other hand, a number of large societies (one thousand members and more) were open to all Italians and provided leadership for the movement. These societies had substantial financial and physical assets and provided extensive services for their members. The divisive influences of localism, politics, and personal rivalries were present to some extent in Buenos Aires, but the leadership of the societies overcame these disruptions and developed a relatively united and effective mutualist movement by 1914.

Informal local institutions were also of major importance to Italians in both cities. In New York, however, they were for most the only institutions in which they participated. In Buenos Aires, on the other hand, informal local institutions were complemented by the extensive formal immigrant institutional structure.

Thus, as reflected in economic activity, residence patterns, and organizational activity, the Italians of Buenos Aires adjusted more rapidly, effectively, and completely by 1914 than those of New York.

How do we account for the different patterns of adjustment? Some of the variables—time, objectives of migration, informal social networks, host society economic opportunity, absolute size of immigrant community, and nationality—were common to both cases. As a result, these factors are of less significance than others in explaining the outcomes. Let me therefore summarize the other factors that are of primary importance in accounting for the different patterns of adjustment, first for Buenos Aires and then for New York City.

What the immigrants brought with them to Buenos Aires. Most important among these factors were relatively high occupational and organizational skills, greater expectations that migration was to be permanent, and the well-developed informal social networks of kin and paesani that played such a critical role in helping immigrants find jobs and housing and in developing the institutional structure to protect their interests.

One word of explanation needs to be interjected here. In the Introduction, I suggested that nationality was a control variable that remained constant in both cases. In fact, however, it became clear in the process of research that the Italians who went to Buenos Aires and New York were not the same; more from the North, who had higher occupational and organizational skills, went to Buenos Aires, whereas a larger number of those from the South, who had lesser skills, went to New York. Thus the area of origin from within Italy of an individual migrant becomes in most though not all cases a surrogate for degree of skill. As a result, nationality ceases to be a constant and becomes an explanatory variable. What is important here is that being Italian is constant to all of our immigrants, but since most northerners had higher occupational and organizational skills than did most southerners, regional and provincial origin becomes an important explanatory variable.

What the immigrants found when they arrived in Buenos Aires. As compared to New York, Buenos Aires offered a less industrialized economy that provided greater opportunity for employment in skilled and white-collar jobs. In addition, an essentially positive attitude on the part of the government and host society toward the Italians minimized discrimination. Moreover, Buenos Aires contained a Latin culture of language, religion, and values that was more familiar to the Italian immigrants.

The Italian immigrant community of Buenos Aires reached a critical mass many years before the onset of mass migration; by 1880, it had a wealthy and well-developed institutional structure capable of facilitating the adjustment of the newcomers. In addition, Italians were a significant percentage of the total city population (more than 20 percent throughout), which helped strengthen community efforts. Furthermore, the Italians had only one other large immigrant group, the Spanish, with which to compete. The only major restriction on immigrant opportunity was in the area of electoral politics, but this limitation did not hinder their economic progress.

Subsequent developments in Buenos Aires. The gradual pace of subsequent migration to Buenos Aires was of critical importance because the slower rate of immigration made it much easier for both the Italian and host society communities to help the immigrants adjust to their new environment. So too was the relatively more dynamic and representative nature of the Italian elite and the more inclusive relations among Italian subgroups from various regions and villages. And finally, because many Italians adopted a long-term economic strategy that included investing in and creating a better life in Buenos Aires, their commitment obviously strengthened the community and its ability to meet the needs of the immigrants.

Turning to New York, we find that the most important variables that explain the adjustment pattern in this city are essentially the inverse of those that explain Buenos Aires.

What the immigrants brought with them to New York. Those Italians who went to New York came with relatively lower occupational and organizational skills than those who went to Buenos Aires. They also brought with them higher expectations that migration would be temporary, a less extensive social network structure, and a greater reliance on agents to get to the New World and padroni to find employment.

What they found when they arrived in New York. New York had a more highly developed industrial economy that restricted employment opportunities for the Italians primarily to the lower levels of the skill and wage hierarchies. It also had an unfamiliar English-speaking culture in which to work and live and an essentially negative host society attitude toward the immigrants. The Italian institutional structure in New York at the beginning of mass migration in 1890 was relatively limited, the Italians represented a small percentage of the total city population, and there were a half dozen other immigrant groups—many of which were long-established— with which they had to compete for jobs and resources.

Subsequent developments in New York. Among the most important changes over time was the concentrated arrival during the fifteen years from 1900 through 1914 of three-quarters of the total migration for the whole period (1860–1914). This number overwhelmed the capacity of the immigrant institutions to assist the newcomers. In addition, other immigrant groups with which the Italians had to compete for jobs and recognition continued to arrive in large numbers. Furthermore, the two-tiered Italian social structure, a highly self-serving elite, and poor relations among Italians from different villages and regions—especially northern

Italians' efforts to disassociate themselves from southern Italians—undermined efforts to unite the community and defend its interests in the face of hostility and discrimination on the part of other immigrant groups and the host society.

It is important to emphasize that the more limited adjustment of the Italians in New York did not necessarily mean they failed to achieve their primary objective. The point is that to achieve the goal of almost all—to save as much as possible quickly and return home—limited adjustment was sufficient. They did not want to invest and build an institutional structure in New York. Rather they wished to send money home to Italy and invest in a future there. This short-term, maximum-return strategy worked for many in New York, but in Buenos Aires most Italians could not pursue their long-term strategy of investing their resources there without adjusting more completely.

In the end, Italians in Buenos Aires during this period had the advantage in adjusting (compared to their counterparts in New York) because of their greater skills and resources, broader economic opportunity, earlier establishment of a critical mass, larger relative population, and lower levels of competition from other groups. It also was important that they had a host society that viewed them in essentially positive terms, a well-developed and wealthy immigrant institutional structure, a gradual pace of migration, and an elite that provided positive leadership for the entire community.

Many New York Italians succeeded in producing a surplus and in the short run unskilled workers most likely saved more in New York than in Buenos Aires. Yet the adoption of a short-term strategy had important consequences for them. Formal immigrant institutions during this period were weak because they never had the community resources to become truly effective. The immigrants, as a result, had to rely much more on padroni and on informal social networks for jobs and assistance. For those who did remain in New York, there was little formal institutional help in defending their interests and little assistance in pursuing their goals. In the post–World War I period, the Italian community would become more permanent, and Italians would gradually work their way into positions and influence. Before World War I, however, their adjustment was less effective and complete than that of their counterparts in Buenos Aires.

The Adjustment of Italians in Other New World Cities

On the basis of my in-depth study of Buenos Aires and New York City I have been able to identify inductively a number of variables that describe and explain adjustment in these two cases. In this section I apply these variables to new cases.

This comparison of the adjustment of Italian immigrants in urban destinations in other countries in the Americas during the same time period enables me to set forth a tentative continuum of Italian immigrant adjustment. Buenos Aires, I believe, represents the polar case of most rapid, effective, and complete adjustment. New York represents the polar opposite. The three additional cases I briefly examine all fall somewhere in between the two poles: San Francisco is closer to Buenos Aires, Toronto is closer to New York, and São Paulo is somewhere in the middle.

Two caveats are in order. First, as I move from the polar cases toward those that fall in between, the relative distinctions will frequently be less pronounced and therefore more difficult to identify and summarize. In addition, the three new cases I am presenting are of necessity very brief and obviously are not based on the extensive primary research that I have done on Buenos Aires and New York. Thus this five-case comparative analysis can only be suggestive and conceptually stimulating rather than definitive.

My intention is to encourage others to apply these concepts to their own work, to modify and revise them, and in so doing to increase our understanding of immigrant adjustment in urban settings all over the world. Specialists on the Italians in San Francisco, São Paulo, and Toronto will be able to offer more nuanced pictures of the Italian experience in these cities. Those familiar with Italians in other cities and those studying urban immigrants of any nationality might suggest where their cases fit on the continuum.

San Francisco

Italian migration to California began with the Gold Rush of 1848. San Francisco, a tiny village of 800 people, was transformed into an instant city of 50,000. A handful of Italian merchants, some from South America, were attracted to the city in the beginning, and gradually other Italians followed them. Ships from Genoa established passenger service to San Francisco in the 1850s and the transcontinental railroad was completed in 1869. Both facilitated the arrival of more Italians. The number, small at first, increased steadily over time. Northern Italians, especially Ligurians, predominated during the early years. In the 1880s and early 1900s, when the numbers grew most rapidly, many southern Italians were among the immigrants. By World War I, the Italian community counted approximately 20,000 members in a city of nearly 450,000 people (Table 42).[1]

Most scholars writing about the Italians in the United States argue that San Francisco's Italians did better than their fellow countrymen who went

Table 42. Italian Population of San Francisco, São Paulo, and Toronto, 1850–1920

Year	San Francisco		São Paulo		Toronto	
	Italian population	Percentage of total population	Italian population	Percentage of total population	Italian population	Percentage of total population
1850	35	0.1				
1860					17	
1870	1,691					
1872			203	7		
1880	2,491					
1886			5,717	12		
1890	5,212					
1891					570	0.3
1893			45,457	35		
1900	7,508	2.2				
1901					1,156	
1902					4,000	1.9
1906			100,000	33		
1910	16,918	4.1				
1911					4,873	
1913					14,000	3.7
1920	23,924	4.7	92,000	16		

Sources: Deanna Paoli Gumina, *The Italians of San Francisco, 1850–1930* (New York, 1978), pp. 3, 35; Rose Doris Scherini, *The Italian American Community of San Francisco: A Descriptive Study* (New York, 1980), p. 3; Franco Cenni, *Italianos no Brasil* (São Paulo, 1958), pp. 170ff.; Estado de São Paulo, Comissão Central de Estadística, *Relatorio 1887* (São Paulo, 1888), pp. 9–23; Estado de São Paulo, Repartição de Estatística e Archivo, *Relatorio 1894* (São Paulo, 1894), pp. 64–119; Estado de São Paulo, *Annuario estatística 1944* (São Paulo, 1948); and John E. Zucchi, *Italians in Toronto: Development of a National Identity, 1875–1935* (Montreal, 1988), p. 44.

to such eastern cities as New York, Boston, and Chicago. These observations coincide with my view that the adjustment of the Italians in San Francisco was fairly rapid, effective, and complete, and was much closer to the Buenos Aires pattern than to that of New York City. I examine the same factors for San Francisco that I used to indicate the nature and extent of adjustment in Buenos Aires and New York City—the Italian community's economic activity, residence patterns, and organizational activity—to support this argument.

Economic activity. Although most Italians in San Francisco were blue-collar workers in service, commercial, transportation, or small manufacturing jobs, a sizeable minority were involved and did especially well in truck farming, fishing, grape growing, and wine making. What is important about these latter pursuits is that although they occupied a relatively small number of Italians directly, they created an Italian economic niche and contributed significantly to what one author refers to as the "chemistry then forming in the colony," which facilitated economic success among many.[2]

This chemistry involved a considerable degree of cooperation among workers and owners, including the mutual economic support of fellow Italians. Cooperative farms in local truck gardens allowed newcomers without resources to start off as hired hands and eventually buy into the enterprise. The establishment of the Colombo Produce Market (1874) provided Italian farmers and fishermen with a collective outlet for their products. Italian liquor dealers and restaurants sold locally grown Italian wine. Italian bankers loaned money to Italians to buy homes and stores. This mutually beneficial cooperation was especially evident in the year following the 1906 earthquake. Much of the community's largest and most important settlement, the North Beach, was in ruins, and Italians joined together to rebuild the area. Italian banks provided building loans to home owners and businesses, while Italian masons and construction workers did the rebuilding.

To a much greater extent than in New York—though perhaps not quite as much as in Buenos Aires—Italians in San Francisco participated in the development of the local economy. Most important, they were a major presence in agriculture and fishing, which they used as ethnic economic niches to expand into other areas. They owned banks and other businesses, and they cooperated in many cases to help each other get established. They created protective organizations such as that of the fishermen and the truck farmers in the 1860s, that of the agricultural retailers and workers in the 1870s, and a chamber of commerce in the 1880s. White-collar workers were certainly not as large a percentage of the population as in Buenos Aires, but there were more skilled workers and small businessmen than in New York.

Residence patterns. Italians lived in two major clusters and one minor settlement in San Francisco but, as in Buenos Aires, at least some lived in all parts of the city. Thus they were more intermingled with other immigrants and with Americans than were those in New York. Italians moved frequently, as they did in both New York and Buenos Aires, but primarily within the local area and within the city. Most came first to the North Beach area, and then, as they accumulated more resources and gained familiarity with their new environment, they moved to other parts of the city.

Organizational activity. Scholars disagree on the success of the Italians in terms of their community organizations. Cinel stresses the problems: lack of effective leaders, strength of local and regional ties, splits within the

Table 43. Italian societies in San Francisco and São Paulo, 1898 and 1908

| | San Francisco | | São Paulo | |
	1898	1908	1898	1908
Number	67	60	46	170
Members	5,820	2,087	4,532	8,213
Capital (in millions of lire)	0.871	0.858	0.458	2.053
Italian population[a]	7,000	15,000	60,000	110,000

[a]Population estimates based on data in Table 42.
Sources: Bollettino del Ministero degli Affair Esteri, 124 (April 1898), pp. 1–8; 369 (December 1908), pp. 1–154.

mutualist movement, failure to support the Italian hospital, and so on. Fichera, on the other hand, points to the cooperative efforts in economic activity mentioned earlier and to the development of Italian banks and businesses. My view is closer to that of Fichera. Italian cooperation in the economic sphere was real and served as a catalyst to development in other areas. In addition, although mutual aid societies in the beginning were restricted to individuals from a particular region, they were numerous enough to accommodate most of the new immigrants. Only in the first decade of the twentieth century, when immigrants from towns without mutual aid societies in San Francisco came in substantial numbers, was there any kind of a problem. The first mutual aid society was established in 1858, the second a decade later, but there were four new ones in the 1870s, seven in the 1880s, and eight in the 1890s. By 1898 there were sixty-seven such organizations listed by the Italian consul (Table 43). Also, two community-wide newspapers—L'Italian and La Voce del Popolo—and a school were established in the 1880s. The Italians in San Francisco managed by the 1880s to create a fairly adequate if not entirely united institutional structure, which was able to meet many of the needs of most new immigrants.

To explain the San Francisco pattern of fairly rapid, effective, and complete adjustment, let me return to the clusters of variables I used to explain the Buenos Aires and New York cases: what the immigrants brought with them, what they found, and the subsequent developments in their new home.

What they brought with them. One of the most striking features of the San Francisco Italians compared to those of New York and the other major cities of the United States is that the majority of them came from the North of Italy. They were a population with greater skills and resources and more experience with organizations. Most, according to Cinel, intended to return home, but many in fact stayed. That many stayed was in part the result of self-selection due to the greater distance and cost of San Francisco compared to New York, but it was also the result of encountering a more hospitable and rewarding environment.

What they found. Italians obviously found economic opportunity in all the cities I am discussing, but what is important is how this opportunity differed from place to place. The California economy was heavily agrarian and San Francisco was at an earlier stage of industrialization and urbanization than New York. The Italians arrived as the economy was developing and found, much as they did in Buenos Aires, that they could compete on a more or less equal basis with Americans and the other immigrants who were there. It was a developing frontier area with a less rigid social structure than that found in the longer-settled areas of the Northeast. The presence of Mexicans and Asians may also have worked to the Italians' advantage in terms of host society perceptions. Americans looked down on Mexicans and Asians and frequently discriminated against them, whereas they regarded Italians as "white."[3] Thus the Italians were perceived at least in relatively neutral terms if not in as positive terms as in Buenos Aires.

As in New York, the dominant English-speaking American culture in San Francisco was not very familiar to the Italians, but it may help explain why they cooperated with each other economically. Along with greater economic opportunities, increased cooperation among those Italians who did not speak English and who were unfamiliar with the environment in which they were then living enabled them to use various ethnic niches to adjust. The new immigrants entered San Francisco society through the respective mutual aid, workers', and business organizations, and often together were better able to learn about the new society.

In San Francisco, immigrant organizations developed early and reached a level sufficient to be able to accommodate the considerable numbers of newcomers who entered the city in the late 1880s and 1890s. Data on mutual aid societies indicate the early relative success of the San Francisco societies compared to those of New York.[4] The wealth of these San Francisco organizations by 1898 was a remarkable .871 million lire, just slightly less than the .902 million lire for New York. Most significantly, this wealth represented 116 lire for every Italian in San Francisco compared to 6.2 lire for those in New York. Even though the per capita wealth of the Italian societies decreased during the next decade, it still remained far ahead of that of New York. The San Francisco Italian community was small in size and, as in New York, its members had to compete with the Irish, Germans, and other immigrant groups as well as the Americans. But the expanding economy, the lack of discrimination, and the resources of the Italian community made this a more equal and largely successful competition.

Subsequent developments. One of the most important characteristics of Italian migration to San Francisco is that the pace was fairly gradual throughout. Table 42 indicates the growth from a handful of merchants in 1850 to 2,491 individuals by 1880, 5,212 by 1890, 7,508 by 1900, and 16,918 by 1910. The spurts of growth in the 1880s and early 1900s were limited enough so that the overall pace remained sufficiently gradual for the institutions to be able to absorb the newcomers. The elite may not have provided unified leadership of this community, but the business elite were dynamic enough to foster cooperation based on mutual self-interest. Most notable were men like Andrea Sbarboro and Amadeo R. Giannini, who provided leadership for the economic growth of the community. There were divisions within the community, but there was enough cooperation to make it work. And over time regional groups began to think more in terms of being Italian as opposed to identifying primarily with their village of origin.

The things that seem especially important in explaining the nature and extent of San Francisco Italians' adjustment by World War I were the skills and resources of the immigrants, the permanency of a sizeable part of the community, and the emerging economy, which offered numerous opportunities for immigrants to participate more or less as equals. The immigrants also benefited from economic cooperation within the community, a sufficiently large and wealthy organizational infrastructure to facilitate the adjustment of the new arrivals, positive or at least neutral host society perceptions, and the gradual pace of migration.

São Paulo

Italians were by far the largest group of immigrants to Brazil, making up more than half of the total during the decades preceding World War I. They also concentrated in the city and state of São Paulo, where their numbers made them a major presence in both the rural and the urban workforce. Italian immigration to São Paulo began in the late 1870s and reached massive proportions during the fifteen years following the abolition of slavery (1888) and the overthrow of the monarchy (1889). The migration was unique among the cases in this study in that the Paulista planters and the government subsidized it in an effort to provide the labor to replace the recently freed slaves on the coffee plantations. Massive Italian migration ended in 1902 when the Italian government, concerned with the poor treatment of its citizens on the coffee plantations in São Paulo, prohibited future subsidized migration to Brazil. Nevertheless some Italian migration continued to São Paulo at a slower rate thereafter.[5]

The Italians in São Paulo, who frequently noted that their community was not as well developed, well organized, or wealthy as that of the Italians in Buenos Aires, might have felt differently if they had instead compared themselves to the Italians in New York.[6] Had they done so, they would have realized that the nature and extent of their adjustment by 1914 was somewhere in the middle between that of their two large sister communities; it was not as rapid, effective, and complete as in Buenos Aires, but it was more rapid, effective, and complete than in New York. The following evidence on economic activity, residence patterns, and organizational activity summarizes this case.

Economic activity. The rapid development of the coffee industry during the second half of the nineteenth century combined with the abolition of slavery provided great opportunity for immigrant workers on the coffee plantations and in the growing cities as well. São Paulo was not as industrially developed as Buenos Aires at that time. Nevertheless, the export-driven economy, with a large service sector and an embryonic industrial sector, was more comparable to that of Argentina than to that of the United States. As the largest immigrant group, the Italians were a major presence in the workforce, both on the plantations and in the city of São Paulo. In São Paulo, most were blue-collar workers, but many were skilled artisans and some were white-collar workers. The rapid growth of the city and the demand for workers at all levels of society provided opportunities for those with the requisite skills to advance. Occupational mobility was certainly higher than in New York, although how much so is not entirely clear. And the Italians were, like those in Buenos Aires, among the initiators and leaders of the organized labor movement.

Residence patterns. There are few data on São Paulo regarding residence, but the data we do have suggest a pattern more similar to that of Buenos Aires than of New York. Italians were approximately one-third of the city's population from 1890 onward and were more evenly distributed throughout the city than was the case in New York. This pattern of more even distribution indicates in part less discrimination against the Italians than in New York. Population density per city block was most certainly lower in São Paulo than in New York. Thus housing was at least less crowded if not much better in other respects. There is some data on home ownership among Italians in São Paulo. Here we find the Italians between their Buenos Aires and New York counterparts: in 1902 5.5 percent of the Italians in São Paulo were home owners compared to 12.6 percent in Buenos Aires in 1904, and between 2 and 3 percent in New York.[7]

Organizational activity. There was considerable organizational activity among the Italians in São Paulo, but it began at a later date and the institutions never became as extensive and wealthy as in Buenos Aires. Although the first Italian mutual aid society was established in 1878, the real growth of community organizations did not take place until the late 1880s and the 1890s during mass migration. As Table 43 shows, by 1898 there were forty-six societies with 4,532 members and capital of .458 million lire. In absolute terms this growth was far behind Buenos Aires in all categories, but also somewhat behind both San Francisco and New York. If we calculate the per capita amount of this institutional wealth for the total Italian population in 1898, New York and São Paulo are about even; the former had 6.2 lire per Italian and the latter 6.1 lire. The 1908 figures show a doubling of members and of capital for São Paulo. São Paulo also had a number of schools and several community-wide newspapers established in the beginning of the 1890s.

To explain this intermediate pattern of adjustment in São Paulo let us again return to our three clusters of variables: what the Italians brought with them, what they found when they arrived, and what happened subsequently.

What they brought with them. The majority of the Italians who went to São Paulo came from the North of Italy, as was the case in Buenos Aires and San Francisco. One would therefore expect that they would have greater occupational and organizational skills and financial resources than those in cities such as New York populated primarily by southern Italians. In São Paulo, however, the usual correlation between regional origin and level of skills and resources did not hold. The significant factor here was that the government provided free passage and help in settling for families who would come to work in São Paulo. As a result of the subsidy, individuals were able to migrate who would otherwise have been unable to do so. These immigrants were more likely to be permanent than those in New York for two reasons related to subsidization: they came with their families—as the terms of the subsidy required—and many, at least for some time, did not have the money to return home. The data on Brazil show a significantly lower Italian return rate than from the United States or Argentina. There are no data on Italian repatriation from the city of São Paulo, but it seems most likely that the Italian rate of return from São Paulo was no higher than the Brazil-wide figure of about 30 percent.[8]

What they found. The Italians encountered a rapidly expanding agricultural and commercial export economy in São Paulo that offered them considerable opportunity. As was the case in Buenos Aires, the native middle class was neither numerous nor well developed, which made it possible for newcomers to obtain jobs higher up the skill and wage hierarchies than in New York. Also, Italians were confronted with less discrimination than in New York and Toronto. If they were not perceived in as positive terms as in Buenos Aires, they nevertheless were not seen in the more negative terms of New York. During the period of mass migration, the Brazilian elite viewed Italian migration as an important way to reduce labor costs on the coffee plantations. At the beginning of mass migration in the late 1880s, the Italians found a small immigrant institutional structure more equiva-

lent to that of New York than to that of Buenos Aires. The Italian population of the city quickly reached one-third of the total and remained at this
level at least up to World War I. Also as in Buenos Aires, there was only
one other major immigrant group, the Portuguese in this case, with which
to compete.

Subsequent developments. The pace of Italian migration to São Paulo was
uneven. Migration started slowly in the 1870s, became massive in the late
1880s, and remained so until 1902, when the Italian government forbade
continued subsidized migration to Brazil. Three-quarters of the total number of Italian immigrants who came to Brazil during the forty years before
World War I did so during the fifteen years from 1887 through 1902. This
sudden influx in such a short period of time—so similar to the situation in
New York—clearly strained the capabilities of the immigrant institutions
to absorb them and facilitate adjustment. The Italians of São Paulo did,
however, develop a community-oriented elite, the various regional groups
within the community were able to work together, and northern Italians
predominated—all factors that were more similar to Buenos Aires than to
New York.

Thus the Italians in São Paulo present a mixed pattern of adjustment.
Their environment was more like Buenos Aires in terms of the nature of
the receiving society and economy (more opportunity at the middle and
top of the wage and skill hierarchy, late industrialization, less discrimination), the large relative numbers of Italians compared to the host society
population, and the greater permanency of the Italian community. As individuals, they were more like those who went to New York in terms of
overall skill levels and resources. The São Paulo Italian migration was
unique, however, in one important respect; the government provided free
passage to families and this permitted a population with fewer skills and
resources than the populations that developed in Buenos Aires and San
Francisco.

Toronto

The Toronto Italian community was the smallest and least well established of any of my cases at the time of World War I.[9] Its small size and later
development make it more difficult to evaluate and compare according to
my framework of analysis.[10] The community did not reach five thousand
until approximately 1905. Even then, perhaps half of these individuals
were temporary residents who used Toronto as a way station to other
places. Considerable, though not really mass, migration during the decade
before World War I created a community of fourteen thousand individuals by 1913, of whom nine thousand were permanent residents (Table 42).

Most of the indicators suggest that the Toronto Italians' pattern of adjustment was close to that of New York and was slower and less complete than in Buenos Aires, San Francisco, or even São Paulo. Nevertheless, it was apparently relatively effective for the small number who were there. I present the evidence for this case in terms of economic activity, residence patterns, and organizational activity as I have for the other cases.

Economic activity. The Italians were so few in number that they never became a major presence in any sector of the commercial, financial, and small manufacturing economy of Toronto. Most were unskilled laborers or tradesmen serving their fellow Italian villagers. Few at first were in the emerging larger industries, but some did serve as strikebreakers in the metallurgic industry between 1898 and 1905. Italian protective organizations were few in number. The Circolo Operai was established in 1903, but Italians were not instrumental in the development of the labor movement or of business organizations.

Residence patterns. Initially the Italians concentrated in the downtown St. John's Ward—known simply as the Ward—and then some moved west to the College-Grace and to the Dufferin-Davenport areas. The Sicilians settled in an area east of the Ward. The settlement pattern was one of high concentration like New York, apparently reflecting discrimination, as opposed to the more dispersed patterns of Buenos Aires, San Francisco, and São Paulo. Before World War I, there is little evidence of residential mobility to the outlying areas of the community. Unfortunately, we have no information on property ownership. Toronto, in a manner similar to New York during the 1880s and 1890s, was a way station through which many sojourners and temporary migrants passed on their journeys to other places, and to which considerable numbers returned for the winters. As the figures in Table 42 indicate, the Italian population of Toronto in 1901–1902 was approximately four thousand, but three thousand of this number were temporary residents. Similarly, the population a decade later was approximately fourteen thousand, but still five thousand of them were temporary residents.[11]

Organizational activity. Italians in Toronto were slow to develop an organizational structure. The first mutual aid society was established in 1888, but the next two were not founded until 1902 and 1903. The first Italian-language newspaper was published in 1908, the same year an Italian parish was created in the Ward. This small institutional structure was neither powerful nor wealthy. Nevertheless, given the small numbers of immigrants and the temporary residence of many, it seemed able for the most part to serve many of the needs of the community.

To explain this pattern of adjustment, let me again turn to the things the Italians brought with them to Toronto, what they found, and the subsequent developments they encountered there.

What they brought with them. Toronto's Italians were overwhelmingly from southern Italy and came with the economic resources and occupational and organizational skills to be predicted from that origin. Many were temporary sojourners who had followed village chains to a number of U.S. cities and then to Toronto. They worked in various parts of Canada during the summer months and returned to Toronto in the winter. Given the recentness of arrival and the temporary nature of much of the population, it is not surprising that padroni played a large part in recruitment and job placement.

What they found. The economy was based on commerce, finance and business, and small manufacturing. Italians worked as unskilled labor in construction, in service occupations, and to a very limited extent in the skilled building and manufacturing trades. As in New York, they found many of the skilled and white-collar jobs already occupied by Canadians and other, earlier arriving immigrant groups. The culture of the dominant English society—language, religion, values—was not familiar to the Italians. In addition, Italians seem to have been perceived in relatively negative terms, in a manner similar to that experienced by Italians in New York. Furthermore, immigrant organizations were recent and few in number.

Subsequent developments. The pace of migration picked up considerably in the decade before World War I, creating some pressure on the limited capabilities of the institutional structure to help the immigrants, but the overall numbers still remained small. Intragroup relations seem to have been fairly good, probably because almost all of the Italians were from regions of the South. They seemed to identify, to find jobs and housing, and to socialize in terms of their village or region of origin, especially if there was a local mutual aid society available.

The Toronto Italian community is difficult to place on my continuum of adjustment because of its late establishment and its relatively small size in 1914. Yet in terms of the measurements we have been using, Toronto's Italians were slow to adjust. They worked primarily in unskilled labor jobs for which they had been recruited by padroni. The padroni and the village-based mutual aid societies were at the center of economic life, and the Italians confined themselves to this small community. Unlike the situation in San Francisco, discrimination in Toronto on the part of the dominant English-speaking community served to reinforce this isolation and to restrict both occupational and residential mobility. Competition with other groups further limited opportunities.

&

Systematically comparing these five cases enables me to sharpen the focus on what explains the respective patterns of adjustment. Table 44 summarizes the data in schematic form.

Table 44. Key variables associated with respective patterns of adjustment

Variable	More rapid, effective, and complete ←————— ADJUSTMENT —————→ Less rapid, effective, and complete				
	Buenos Aires	San Francisco	São Paulo	Toronto	New York City
What they brought with them					
Expectations of permanency	Higher	Higher	Higher	Lower	Lower
Social and economic skills and resources	Greater	Greater	Lesser	Lesser	Lesser
What they found					
Opportunities in skilled and white-collar jobs and in small business	Greater	Greater	Greater	Lesser	Lesser
Italian community	More developed	Medium developed	Medium developed	Less developed	Less developed
Language and religion	Similar	Dissimilar	Similar	Dissimilar	Dissimilar
Host attitude	More positive	More positive	More positive	Negative	Negative
Subsequent developments					
Pace of migration	Spread out	Spread out	Concentrated	Concentrated	Concentrated
Time of critical mass	Early	Late	Middle	Late	Middle
Absolute size	Large	Small	Large	Very small	Large
Relative size	Large	Small	Large	Very small	Small
Resulting strategy	Long term	Long term	Long term	Short term	Short term

One way to link the variables is to look at the nature of the opportunity the immigrants encountered and how the other variables increased or decreased it. In all five cases, there was opportunity, but the Italians adjusted more rapidly, effectively, and completely where there were certain kinds of opportunities and the possibility of taking advantage of them. What the cases of more rapid, effective, and complete adjustment (Buenos Aires and San Francisco) had in common were a commercial and financial economy with an industrial sector in the early stages of development and a predominance of northern Italians. These two cases both show greater permanency of population, more effectively organized immigrant institutions and leadership, more positive host society perceptions, and a more gradual pace of migration than the other three.

Italians adjusted more rapidly, effectively, and completely in host societies where skilled and white-collar jobs and opportunities in small business were available. To take advantage of these opportunities, the immigrants needed appropriate skills and resources, minimal competition from native and other foreign workers, and minimal discrimination. Immigrants also adjusted more effectively where the Italian community was sufficiently developed to help them defend their interests and where the pace of migration was gradual. These things were reinforced with the adoption by many of a long-term strategy of investing most savings in the host society.

What stands out among the cases of slower, less effective, and less complete adjustment (New York and Toronto) is a more highly developed commercial-financial-industrial economy whose skilled and white-collar jobs were already occupied by natives or immigrants who had arrived earlier. These cases also display negative host society perceptions, discrimination, relatively late achievement of critical mass, limited development and limited wealth of immigrant organizations, and a concentrated pace of migration. These things in combination defined the limits of the opportunities available to Italians and reinforced the proclivity of most to adopt a short-term strategy of saving and rapid return.

Perhaps what is most important to bear in mind is that each of these cases presents a unique cluster of variables—many, but not all, of which overlap with those of the other similar cases. What is essential is the presence of enough of the key variables to produce the specific outcome. Buenos Aires and San Francisco were not identical. Although they were similar in terms of most variables (permanency, skills, opportunities, host attitudes, pace, and strategies), they differed in terms of language and religion, size, and to some extent in the makeup of the Italian community. Nevertheless, the particular cluster of variables at work in San Francisco produced a pattern of more rapid, effective, and complete adjustment. Here what seemed to be most important were the relative openness of the society, more positive host society attitudes, and the chance for Italians to compete on nearly equal terms with everyone else. Similarity of culture and a large Italian community were not essential in the San Francisco case even though they were present in the Buenos Aires case.

Because New York and Toronto were quite similar in all respects with the exception of size, the pattern of variables associated with less rapid, effective, and complete adjustment is most consistent. There is a high degree of congruence in terms of permanency, skills, opportunities, Italian community, language and religion, host attitude, discrimination, pace, and strategies. Cultural dissimilarity (language and religion) seemed to be of greater significance for these two cases than it was in San Francisco.

São Paulo's intermediate pattern of adjustment serves to clarify further the relative importance of the variables. The kind of opportunity available in São Paulo was similar to that in both Buenos Aires and San Francisco, but the Italians in São Paulo lacked sufficient skills to take full advantage of this opportunity. In addition, cultural similarity did not seem to play a decisive role here. Thus a review of the São Paulo case alongside that of San Francisco suggests that the impact of culture may not be as important as many have suggested. The concentrated pace of migration and the lesser skills and resources of the migrants seem to be what set São Paulo apart from Buenos Aires and San Francisco.

The patterns of Italian adjustment in these five cities provide a range of outcomes that have enabled me to place them tentatively on the adjustment continuum. Yet it may be that Buenos Aires and New York are not the best polar cases or that some of the explanatory variables are of greater or lesser importance than indicated in Table 44. Additional studies of other Italian and other immigrant communities would increase our confidence in the accuracy of the relative positions of the five cases on the continuum.

One of the most original findings of this study is that besides opportunity and skills, pace is the most consistent indicator of outcome. It is clear that pace is important, but we need additional cases to understand more precisely how it works to influence adjustment. Does it operate independently of other variables or is it functioning in tandem with some of them? Is it in all situations an accurate predictor of outcome?

Similarly, additional cases would help us better understand the working of other variables. The position of the immigrant group in the social hierarchy of the host society is an intriguing but little-understood variable. From this study of five cases we see that two of the variables—competition with other groups and host society attitudes toward Italians—are linked to the Italians' position on the social hierarchy. The presence of Asians and Mexicans in San Francisco, of blacks in Brazil, and of a native population in Buenos Aires created situations in which Italians were not the underclass in the social hierarchy. On the other hand, Italians in New

York and Toronto found no such underclass and instead apparently filled this role at the bottom of the social hierarchy. To be fully understood, this issue needs to be studied in more situations.

In addition, I am convinced that size is an important variable that influences outcome, but in these five cases size is not indicative of any specific outcome. Studies of communities of differing sizes would help us learn more about the impact of numbers on outcomes. Similarly we could further explore the importance of culture on outcome if we could find more cases like San Francisco where similarity of culture appeared to be of minimal importance. Finally, we might look at the ways each of these patterns that emerged before World War I has influenced the long-term interaction of Italians and their descendants with the host society.

It is my hope that the variables I have identified and the continuum set forth here will be useful to others as an inductively derived framework for additional systematic comparisons of Italian immigrant adjustment in urban areas. Indeed, this continuum should be useful to those who study the adjustment of any immigrant group as a basis for systematic comparison. It is my belief that only in this way will we be able to comprehend the experiences of Oreste and Ida Sola and the millions of other Italian migrants who went abroad during the decades preceding World War I to the lands of promise. What their stories show is the importance of understanding the global nature of immigration from village of origin to the multiple destinations abroad and the need to compare the immigrants' experiences in a systematic way.

Appendix

1. New York City Naturalization Records

The sample consists of 1,953 Italians who became naturalized in the Federal District Court, Southern District of New York (Manhattan) during selected years between 1906 and 1921: 571 Italians from October 1906 to December 1909, 828 from January 1914 to December 1916, and 554 from January to December 1921. All Italians who were naturalized in the Southern District Court during the specified periods were included. There were other courts in which an Italian could become naturalized (federal courts and municipal courts), and thus some naturalized Italians living in Manhattan were not included in this database. Nevertheless, the large majority of Italians who became naturalized in Manhattan did so in the Federal District Court, Southern District of New York, making this sample representative of the population of naturalized Italians. These records can be found in the Federal Archives in Manhattan.

2. Buenos Aires Mutual Aid Society Records

The primary sample consists of 1,509 individuals who became members of one of four mutual aid societies in Buenos Aires between 1888 and 1913: the Unione e Benevolenza, the Colonia Italiana, the Società Garibaldi, and the Società Volturno. The nature of the data presented certain specific problems that forced me to select certain years rather than others. The most important of these problems was the lack of complete data for various years in some societies. In general, my intent was to make a sample of new members in intervals of ten years. The method I used was a systematic selection in which every *n* name was selected in sequence after the first name had been randomly chosen. The proportion selected for each society differed according to the number of new members in a given year. Nevertheless, when it was possible, I used a minimum of 150 cases per society per year.

Following are some of the specifications for each of the societies:

Unione e Benevolenza. I chose the period 1858–1862 because it comprised the first years of the society's existence, and I selected 263 (9.4 percent) from the total of 2,800 new members, using every tenth name. The first year for which there was complete information for new members was 1888, and I selected 218 of the total of 438 new members for that year. The lists for 1901 indicated only residence in Buenos Aires and not town of birth. From this year I selected 90 of 332 names. In each succeeding case, where there were fewer names in total, I took a higher percentage.

In addition, for the study of mobility I have used a sample of the addresses of 377 (8.5 percent) of the approximately 4,000 members of the Unione e Benevolenza listed in the Libri d'inscrizione dei soci from 1895 to 1901. These books were the only ones I could find that included changes in addresses over time and thus would permit the determination of residential mobility. Here I took approximately every tenth name.

Colonia Italiana. This society was established in 1877, but to facilitate comparison with the other societies I decided to use samples of new members in 1890 (172 out of 650), 1900 (199 out of 199), and 1910 (157 out of 157).

Società Garibaldi. The only information available on this society was that referring to the "*iniziatori*" (24 of 24 in 1890), the "*fondatori*" (116 of 116 in 1890), and the "*benemeriti*" (212 of 212 between 1890 and 1910). These data do not constitute a sample of the new members as is the case with the other three societies. It is difficult to determine how representative these 352 individuals were among the total of 17,000 who became members of the organization during this twenty-year period. Certainly they were representative of the active leadership within the society.

Società Volturno. For this society, which was established in 1893, I made a sample of the new members in 1893 (49 of 49), 1903 (76 of 160), and 1913 (31 of 62).

3. Argentine Manuscript Census Schedules, 1895

I have used two samples of Buenos Aires from the Argentine manuscript census schedules of 1895: a six-district sample, which I did, and a sample of District 15 done by Stephanie Bower.

Buenos Aires Six-District Sample

I made a systematic sample of five hundred adult Italians (aged sixteen or older) from each of six census districts in Buenos Aires, for a total of three thousand individuals. The importance of the samples is that they allow me to break down the following information on individuals by nationality, which is not included in the published volumes: sex, age, marital status, occupation, literacy, property ownership, children, and nationality of spouse. The samples came from the following volume numbers for each district: District 2, vols. 470–476; District 3, vols. 477–484; District 5, vols. 491–497; District 7, vols. 504–509; District 21, vols. 612–618; and District 28, vols. 645–651. The percentage of all Italians in the district that each sample of five hundred represents is as follows: District 2, 33 percent; District 3, 13 percent; District 5, 7 percent; District 7, 11 percent; District 21, 6 percent; and District 28, 6 percent.

Buenos Aires District 15 Sample

Stephanie Bower collected the District 15 data for her own work and graciously shared the part of it on Italian families with me. It is especially important because it is the only evidence we have that indicates household composition with certainty. The question is, how representative is this sample of all Italians in Buenos Aires? It is a select sample made up of the 20 percent (245) of Italian households (1,815 individuals) in District 15 whose heads filled out their own separate census forms and returned them to the census taker. Although this is a select sample, Bower has collected the data from all seventy-two manzanas with Italian residents in the district. (The other eleven manzanas had no Italian residents.)

To evaluate the representativeness of this sample, I have compared the 1,199 adult Italians sampled in District 15 with those in my Buenos Aires six-district sample (see Table 45). In terms of age, the difference between the two samples is minimal; the average age in District 15 was thirty-three while that in the six districts was just three years higher. With regard to occupations, there were some significant differences. More individuals in District 15 were listed as being non-manual and professional, as being in the miscellaneous categories of students and persons of independent means, and as no occupation recorded. In addition, 27 percent of the households in District 15 had servants. Clearly the Italian population of this district was of a higher socioeconomic status than the Italian population of Buenos Aires as represented by the six-district sample.

Table 45. Occupation and age of Italian household members: District 15 compared with other districts (Italians aged 16 and older)

Occupations	District 15 sample (%)	Six-district sample (%)
Unskilled	14[a]	7
Semiskilled	7	18
Skilled	16	26
Non-manual (minus professional)	24	20
Professional	3	2
Miscellaneous	6	2
Without	30	25
	100	100
Average age	33 years	36 years
N (total)	(1,199)	(3,000)

[a] Includes 11 percent household servants.
Source: Manuscript schedules, Argentine Federal Census, 1895.

4. Agnone Archival Records

I consulted all the town of Agnone's passport records from 1885 to 1914. These records are a wonderfully rich, if underutilized, source of information on emigrants. They contain each emigrant's name, father's name, place and date of birth, occupation, migration destination, date of departure, and observations such as whether or not an agent handled the application.

In addition, I consulted the town's marriage records. I included in my calculations all the marriages that took place in Agnone in 1876 (97 marriages), 1886 (122 marriages), 1896 (77 marriages), and 1906 (78 marriages).

Notes

Prologue

1. The history of Oreste and Ida Sola is based on the following sources: Samuel L. Baily and Franco Ramella, eds., *One Family, Two Worlds: An Italian Family's Correspondence across the Atlantic, 1901–1922* (New Brunswick, N.J., 1980); Luciana Benigno and Franco Ramella, "Una famiglia e un paese: La trama dei rapporti in una storia di emigrazione," in Gianfausto Rosoli et al., *Identità e integrazione: Famiglie, paesi, percorsi, e immagini di se nell'emigrazione biellese* (Milan, 1988), pp. 65–105; thirty unpublished letters written between 1916 and 1973 located in the Sola Archive (Vigliano, Italy) and in the Cerruti Archive (Haledon, N.J.); a number of interviews between the author and the children and grandchildren of Ida Sola Cerruti conducted in March and June 1990 in Haledon; census manuscripts and other records in the Municipal Archives of Valdengo and the Biella Archives; and passenger lists of arrivals in New York.

2. The term *paesani* refers to the inhabitants of the same village or cluster of nearby villages, such as those surrounding Biella.

3. Baily and Ramella, *One Family*, p. 34.

4. The term *Biellesi* refers to the residents from the District of Biella and includes individuals from the city of Biella, Valdengo, and all the nearly eighty other towns nearby. The migration of the Biellesi is being documented and analyzed in a pathbreaking multivolume work, *Biellesi nel mondo* (Milan, 1986, 1988, 1990, and so forth), directed by Valerio Castronovo and funded by the Banca Sella and the Fondazione Sella.

5. Baily and Ramella, *One Family*, pp. 67–68.

6. Baily and Ramella, *One Family*, p. 54.

7. Oreste and Ida each had a brother named Abele. I have tried to make it clear to which of the two Abeles I am referring each time, but the reader would do well to keep this identity problem in mind.

8. Baily and Ramella, *One Family*, p. 65.

9. There must have been additional reasons why Andrea was upset with his father, but I have no information on what they might have been.

10. Baily and Ramella, *One Family*, p. 207

11. Postcard from Ida's brother Abele to Ida, November 11, 1951, in the Sola archives, Vigliano.

12. Letter from Ida to her brother Abele, January 6, 1966, in the Cerruti Archive, Haledon.

Introduction

1. Among the most useful historiographical essays on immigration and Italian immigration are John Higham, "Current Trends in the Study of Ethnicity in the United States," *Journal of American Ethnic History*, 2, 1 (Fall 1982), pp. 5–15; Thomas J. Archdeacon, "Problems and Possibilities in the Study of American Immigration and Ethnic History," *International Migration Review*, 19 (Spring 1985), pp. 112–134; Samuel L. Baily, "The Future of Italian-American Studies: An Historian's Approach to Research in the Coming Decade," in Lydio F. Tomasi, ed., *Italian Americans: New Perspectives in Italian Immigration and Ethnicity* (New York, 1985), pp. 193–201; Rudolph J. Vecoli, "Return from the Melting Pot: Ethnicity in the United States in the 1980s," *Journal of American Ethnic History*, 5, 1 (Fall 1985), pp. 7–20; Olivier Zunz, "American History and the Changing Meaning of Assimilation," *Journal of American Ethnic History*, 4, 2 (Spring 1985), pp. 53–84; George E. Pozzetta, "Immigrants and Ethnics: The State of Italian-American Historiography," *Journal of American Ethnic History*, 9, 1 (Fall 1989), pp. 67–95; Kathleen N. Conzen et al., "The Invention of Ethnicity: A Perspective from the USA," *Altreitalie*, 2, 3 (April 1990), pp. 37–62; Ewa Morawska, "The Sociology and Historiography of Immigration," in Virginia Yans-McLaughlin, ed., *Immigration Reconsidered: History, Sociology, and Politics* (New York, 1990), pp. 187–238; Rudolph J. Vecoli, "Introduction," in Rudolph J. Vecoli and Suzanne M. Sinke, eds., *A Century of European Migration, 1830–1930* (Urbana, Ill., 1991), pp. 1–14; Samuel L. Baily, "Immigration," in Peter N. Stearns, ed., *Encyclopedia of Social History* (New York, 1994), pp. 340–344.

2. The classic statement of this view is Oscar Handlin's Pulitzer Prize–winning book *The Uprooted* (New York, 1951).

3. Rudolph J. Vecoli's article, "Contadini in Chicago: A Critique of *The Uprooted*," *Journal of American History*, 51, 3 (December 1964), pp. 404–417, initiated the reassessment of the assimilationist model. Subsequent works continued the reassessment and clarified the pluralist model. See, for example, Josef J. Barton, *Peasants and Strangers: Italians, Rumanians, and Slovaks in an American City, 1890–1950* (Cambridge, Mass., 1975); Kathleen N. Conzen, *Immigrant Milwaukee* (Cambridge, Mass., 1976); John W. Briggs, *An Italian Passage: Immigrants to Three American Cities, 1890–1930* (New Haven, 1978); Virginia Yans-McLaughlin, *Family and Community: Italian Immigrants in Buffalo, 1880–1930* (Urbana, Ill., 1982); Dino Cinel, *From Italy to San Francisco: The Immigrant Experience* (Stanford, 1982); Olivier Zunz, *The Changing Face of Inequality: Urbanization, Industrial Development, and Immigrants in Detroit, 1880–1920* (Chicago, 1982); Samuel L. Baily, "The Adjustment of Italian Immigrants in Buenos Aires and New York, 1870–1914," *American Historical Review*, 88, 2 (April 1983), pp. 281–305; Donna Gabaccia, *From Sicily to Elizabeth Street: Housing and Social Change among Italian Immigrants, 1880–1930* (Albany, N.Y., 1984); John Bodnar, *The Transplanted: A History of Immigrants in Urban America* (Bloomington,

Ind., 1985); Kerby A. Miller, *Emigrants and Exiles: Ireland and the Irish Exodus to North America* (New York, 1985); Gary R. Mormino and George E. Pozzetta, *The Immigrant World of Ybor City: Italians and Their Latin Neighbors in Tampa, 1885–1985* (Urbana, Ill., 1987); Donna Gabaccia, *Militants and Migrants: Rural Sicilians Become American Workers* (New Brunswick, N.J., 1988); Peter Kivisto and Dag Blanck, eds., *American Immigrants and Their Generations* (Urbana, Ill., 1990); Yans-McLaughlin, *Immigration Reconsidered* (1990); and Samuel L. Baily, "The Village Outward Approach to the Study of Social Networks: A Case Study of the Agnonesi Diaspora Abroad, 1885–1989," *Studi Emigrazione*, 29, 105 (March 1992), pp. 43–68.

4. Diego Armus, "Diez años de la historiografía sobre la inmigración masiva a la Argentina," *Estudios Migratorios Latinoamericanos*, 2, 4 (December 1986), pp. 431–460; and Fernando J. Devoto, *Movimientos migratorios: Historiografía y problemas* (Buenos Aires, 1992). The pioneering scholarly journal *Estudios Migratorios Latinoamericanos*, founded in 1985 by the Centro de Estudios Migratorios Latinoamericanos of Buenos Aires and edited by Luigi Favero and Fernando J. Devoto, regularly publishes articles that deal with various aspects of Argentine and Latin American immigration historiography.

5. Gino Germani, *Política y sociedad en una época de transición: De la sociedad tradicional a la sociedad de masas* (Buenos Aires, 1962); and José Luis Romero, *A History of Argentine Political Thought* (Stanford, 1963). See also Gustavo Beyhaut et al., "Los inmigrantes en el sistema ocupacional argentino," in Torcuato S. Di Tella et al., *Argentina, sociedad de masas* (Buenos Aires, 1966), pp. 85–123; Manuel Bejarano, "Inmigración y estructuras tradicionales en Buenos Aires," in Torcuato S. Di Tella et al., *Los fragmentos del poder* (Buenos Aires, 1969), pp. 75–159; and Oscar Cornblit, "Inmigrantes y empresarios en la política argentina," in Di Tella et al., *Los fragmentos del poder*, pp. 389–438.

6. Armus, "Diez años"; Samuel L. Baily, "Marriage Patterns and Immigrant Assimilation in Buenos Aires, 1882–1923," *Hispanic American Historical Review*, 60, 1 (February 1980), pp. 32–48; Samuel L. Baily, "Las sociedades de ayuda mutua y el desarrollo de una comunidad italiana en Buenos Aires, 1858–1918," *Desarrollo Económico*, 21, 84 (January-March 1982), pp. 485–514; Samuel L. Baily, "Patrones de residencia de los Italianos en Buenos Aires y Nueva York: 1880–1914," *Estudios Migratorios Latinoamericanos*, 1, 1 (December 1985), pp. 8–42; Fernando J. Devoto and Gianfausto Rosoli, eds., *La inmigración italiana en la Argentina* (Buenos Aires, 1985); Fernando J. Devoto and Gianfausto Rosoli, eds., *L'Italia nella società Argentina* (Rome, 1988); Devoto, *Movimientos migratorios*; Fernando J. Devoto and Eduardo J. Miguez, eds., *Asociacionismo, trabajo e identidad étnica: Los Italianos en América Latina en una perspectiva comparada* (Buenos Aires, 1992); Herbert S. Klein, "The Integration of Italian Immigrants into the United States and Argentina: A Comparative Analysis," *American Historical Review* 88, 2 (April 1983), pp. 306–339; and Mark D. Szuchman, *Mobility and Integration in Urban Argentina: Cordoba in the Liberal Era* (Austin, Tex., 1980).

In her perceptive and stimulating critique of the cultural pluralist paradigm as used in Argentina—"El pluralismo cultural en la Argentina: Un balance crítico" (presented at the 2 Jornadas del Comité Internacional de Ciencias Históricas, Comité Argentino, Paraná, Entre Rios, 1988)—Hilda Sábato rightly points out that Germani and Romero were more nuanced in their writings than either their supporters or their critics acknowledge. I was fortunate enough to work with both men in the 1960s and 1970s, and I want to acknowledge my intellectual debt to them. I differ with some of their conclusions, but my work has been significantly influenced by theirs. Although I believe a pluralist paradigm on the whole more closely reflects the reality of the immigrants' experiences in Argentina than does an assimilationist paradigm, I am certain that future scholars will further refine these paradigms and perhaps develop new ones in their efforts to explain the patterns of immigration to Argentina.

7. See, for example, Dirk Hoerder, "Struggle a Hard Battle," in his *Essays on Working-Class Immigrants* (De Kalb, Ill., 1986); Donna Gabaccia, comp., *Immigrant Women in the United States: A Selective Annotated Multidisciplinary Bibliography* (New York, 1989); Gabaccia, *Militants and Migrants*; David M. Emmons, *The Butte Irish: Class and Ethnicity in an American Mining Town, 1875–1925* (Urbana, Ill., 1989); and Hasia R. Diner, *Erin's Daughters in America: Irish Immigrant Women in the Nineteenth Century* (Baltimore, 1983).

8. At the time, northwestern Italy was rapidly industrializing and was an area of both emigration and immigration. For an excellent analysis of this apparent paradox, see Franco Ramella, "Emigration from an Area of Intense Industrial Development: The Case of Northwestern Italy," in Vecoli and Sinke, *A Century of European Migrations*, pp. 261–274. See also Chapter 1 in this work.

9. For a cogent discussion of historians' and sociologists' views on the influence of structural determinants in the migration process, see Ewa Morawska, "The Sociology and Historiography of Immigration," esp. pp. 187–196. The quotation is from p. 193. My own thinking on this subject has been influenced by William B. Taylor's splendid article, "Between Global Process and Local Knowledge: An Inquiry into Early Latin American Social History, 1500–1900," in Olivier Zunz, ed., *Reliving the Past: The Worlds of Social History* (Chapel Hill, N.C., 1985), pp. 115–190.

10. Morawska, "The Sociology and Historiography of Immigration," pp. 187–196.

11. The literature on chain migration and migration networks is extensive. These are some of the more recent works, many of which include extensive bibliographies. Samuel L. Baily, "Chain Migration of Italians to Argentina: Case Studies of the Agnonesi and the Sirolesi," *Studi Emigrazione*, 19, 65 (March 1982), pp. 73–91; Robert C. Ostergren, "Kinship Networks and Migration," *Social Science History*, 6, 3 (Summer 1982), pp. 293–320; Gabaccia, *From Sicily to Elizabeth Street*; John Zucchi, "Occupations, Enterprise and the Migration Chain: The Fruit Traders from Termini Imerese in Toronto, 1900–1930," *Studi Emigrazione*, 77 (March 1985), pp. 68–79; Douglas S. Massey et al., *Return to Aztlan: The Social Process of International Migration from Western Mexico* (Berkeley, 1987); Fernando J. Devoto, "Las cadenas migratorias italianas: Algunas reflexiones a la luz del caso argentino," *Studi Emigrazione*, 24, 87 (October 1987), pp. 355–373; the entire issue of *Estudios Migratorios Latinoamericanos*, 3, 8 (April 1988); Gabaccia, *Militants and Migrants*; the articles of Alejandro Portes and Jozsef Borocz, Monica Boyd, and James T. Fawcett in *International Migration Review*, 23 (Fall 1989); Franc Sturino, "Italian Emigration: Reconsidering the Links in Chain Migration," in Robert Perin and Franc Sturino, eds., *Arrangiarsi: The Italian Immigration Experience in Canada* (Montreal, 1989), pp. 63–90; Silvia Stefanoni, "Catene migratorie e strutture familiari. Un caso italo-australiano, *Studi*

Emigrazione, 27, 98 (June 1990), pp. 255–276; Charles Tilly, "Transplanted Networks," in Yans-McLaughlin, *Immigration Reconsidered*; Jon Gjerde, "Chain Migration from the West Coast of Norway," in Vecoli and Sinke, *A Century of European Migrations*, pp. 158–181; Baily, "The Village Outward Approach"; and Maria Bjerg and Hernan Otero, eds., *Inmigración y redes sociales en la Argentina moderna* (Buenos Aires, 1995), esp. the introductory essays by Franco Ramella and Eduardo Miguez.

12. Baily, "Chain Migration of Italians to Argentina."

13. Massey et al., *Return to Aztlan*, p. 139.

14. Tilly, "Transplanted Networks," p. 87.

15. Scholars continue to explore and debate the nature and functioning of these networks. One of the most insightful discussions of the typology and variations of immigrant networks is Devoto, "Las cadenas migratorias italianas." For a model of what historians might do to analyze networks if they had the sources, see Massey et al., *Return to Aztlan*. In this pioneering work, the authors interviewed a random sample of two hundred individuals from different households in each of four different villages in western Mexico that sent hundreds of migrants almost exclusively to Los Angeles. In addition, they interviewed sixty migrants from these villages who were residing in California at the time.

16. Baily, "The Village Outward Approach"; Bodnar, *The Transplanted*; J. D. Gould, "European Inter-Continental Emigration, 1815–1914," *Journal of European Economic History*, 8, 3 (Winter 1979), pp. 593–679; 9, 1 (Spring 1980), pp. 41–112; and esp. 9, 2 (Fall 1980), pp. 267–315; Dirk Hoerder, "Preface" and "An Introduction to Labor Migration in the Atlantic Economies, 1815–1914," in Dirk Hoerder, ed., *Labor Migration in the Atlantic Economies: The European and North American Working Classes during the Period of Industrialization* (Westport, Conn., 1985), pp. xv–xvi, 3–31; Dirk Hoerder, "International Labor Markets and Community Building by Migrant Workers in the Atlantic Economies," in Vecoli and Sinke, *A Century of European Migration*, pp. 78–107; *International Migration Review*, 23, 87 (Fall 1989), esp. the articles by Aristide R. Zolberg, John Salt, Alejandro Portes and Jozsef Borocz, Monica Boyd, and James T. Fawcett; Ewa Morawska, "The Sociology and Historiography of Immigration," and Virginia Yans-McLaughlin, "Introduction," in Yans-McLaughlin, *Immigration Reconsidered*; Bruno Ramirez, *On the Move: French Canadian and Italian Migrants in the North Atlantic Economy, 1860–1914* (Toronto, 1990); and Eric R. Wolf, *Europe and the People without History* (Berkeley, 1982), pp. 361–363.

17. Hoerder, "International Labor Markets," p. 80.

18. John Gould, "Comments," in *American Historical Review*, 88, 2 (April 1983), p. 335.

19. Rudolph J. Vecoli, "Introduction," in Vecoli and Sinke, *A Century of European Migrations*, p. 2.

20. Raymond Grew, "The Case for Comparing Histories," *American Historical Review*, 85, 4 (October 1980), pp. 763–778. This entire issue of *American Historical Review* is devoted to comparative history, as is the subsequent issue (December 1980). See also George M. Fredrickson, "Comparative History," in Michael Kammen, ed., *The Past before Us* (Ithaca, 1980); and Magnus Morner et al., "Comparative Approaches to Latin American History," *Latin American Research Review*, 17, 3 (1983).

21. Grew, "The Case for Comparing Histories," p. 766.

22. My thinking in this respect has been influenced by John H. Goldthorpe's

stimulating article, "The Uses of History in Sociology: Reflections on Some Recent Tendencies," *British Journal of Sociology*, 42, 2 (June 1991), pp. 211–230. See also the excellent article by Edgar Kiser and Michael Hechter, "The Role of General Theory in Comparative-Historical Sociology," *American Journal of Sociology*, 97, 1 (July 1991), pp. 1–30.

23. Frank Thistlethwaite, "Migration from Europe Overseas in the Nineteenth and Twentieth Centuries," in Herbert Moller, ed., *Population Movements in Modern European History* (New York, 1964), pp. 73–92; and John Higham, "Immigration," in C. Vann Woodward, ed., *The Comparative Approach to American History* (New York, 1968), pp. 91–105.

24. Barton, *Peasants and Strangers.*

25. Ronald H. Bayor, *Neighbors in Conflict: The Irish, Germans, Jews, and Italians of New York City, 1929–1941* (Baltimore, 1978); John Bodnar et al., *Lives of Their Own: Blacks, Italians, and Poles in Pittsburgh, 1900–1950* (Urbana, Ill., 1982); Fernando J. Devoto and Alejandro Fernandez, "Asociacionismo, liderazgo y participación en dos grupos étnicos en areas urbanas de la Argentina finisecular: Un enfoque comparado," in Fernando J. Devoto and Gianfausto Rosoli, eds., *L'Italia nella società Argentina* (Rome, 1988), pp. 190–208; Ewen, *Immigrant Women in the Land of Dollars;* Thomas Kessner, *The Golden Door: Italian and Jewish Immigrant Mobility in New York City, 1880–1915* (New York, 1977); Dedier Norberto Marquiegui, "Revisando el debate sobre la conducta matrimonial de los extranjeros. Un estudio a partir del caso de los Españoles y Franceses en Luján, 1880–1920," *Estudios Migratorios Latinoamericanos*, 7, 20 (April 1992), pp. 3–36; Mormino and Pozzetta, *Ybor City;* Judith Smith, *Family Connections: A History of Italian and Jewish Immigrant Lives in Providence, Rhode Island, 1900–1940* (Albany, N.Y., 1985); and Szuchman, *Mobility and Integration in Urban Argentina.*

26. Cinel, *From Italy to San Francisco;* Gabaccia, *From Sicily to Elizabeth Street.*

27. Briggs, *An Italian Passage;* Gabaccia, *Militants and Migrants.*

28. Baily, "The Adjustment of Italian Immigrants"; Samuel L. Baily, "Cross-Cultural Comparison and the Writing of Migration History: Some Thoughts on How to Study Italians in the New World," in Yans-McLaughlin, *Immigration Reconsidered*, pp. 241–253. Herbert S. Klein focuses on countries rather than cities, but he is one of the few to make cross-cultural comparisons; see "The Integration of Italian Immigrants" and "A integração dos emigrantes Italianos no Brasil, na Argentina, e Estados Unidos," *Novos Estudos CEBRAP*, 25 (1989), pp. 95–117. Leo Spitzer also makes cross-cultural comparisons in *Lives in Between: Assimilation and Marginality in Austria, Brazil, West Africa 1780–1945* (New York, 1989). Robert F. Forester's classic work, *The Italian Immigration of Our Times* (Cambridge, Mass., 1919) includes a wealth of data on Italians in the United States and Argentina—as well as in Europe, North Africa, and the other countries of the Americas—but he was reluctant to make the comparisons. Instead he chose to present the extensive information he had gathered in separate country-specific chapters, leaving it to the reader to make the comparisons. Walter Nugent's admirable, more recent work, *Crossings: The Great Transatlantic Migrations, 1870–1914* (Bloomington, Ind. 1992), is important because it discusses Italians as well as other European immigrant groups in Europe, Argentina, Brazil, Canada, and the United States and makes some useful comparisons. It is, nevertheless, a brief "descriptive synthesis" based

on secondary sources and official statistics, and the author does not use comparison in a systematic way.

29. Nancy Green, one of the few immigration historians to systematically explore the comparative method, provides a good discussion of some of the approaches that have been used implicitly if not explicitly to study comparative migration. See her "L'Histoire comparative et le champ des etudes migratoires," *Annales ESC,* 6 (November-December 1990), pp. 1336–1350; and "The Comparative Method and Poststructural Structuralism: New Perspectives for Migration Studies," *Journal of American Ethnic History,* 13, 4 (Summer 1994), pp. 3–22.

30. In addition to the works cited in notes 20, 22, 28, and 29, I have found the following to be especially useful: Victoria E. Bonnell, "The Uses of Theory: Concepts and Comparison in Historical Sociology," *Comparative Studies in Society and History,* 22, 2 (April 1980); and Theda Skocpol and Margaret Somers, "The Uses of Comparative History as Macrosocial Inquiry," *Comparative Studies in Society and History,* 22, 2 (April, 1980), pp. 174–197. For a detailed discussion of my views of the uses of comparative history, see Baily, "Cross-Cultural Comparison and the Writing of Migration History."

31. The way I construct my comparisons combines elements of the contrast of contexts and the macro-causal analysis approaches of Skocpol and Somers. Where I depart from them is in the scope of my comparison and the use of evidence on which it is based. For an evaluation of "grand historical sociology," see Goldthorpe, "The Uses of History in Sociology," and Kiser and Hechter, "The Role of General Theory." See also Theda Skocpol, "A Critical Review of Barrington Moore's Social Origins of Dictatorship and Democracy," *Politics and Society* (Fall 1973), pp. 1–34. Skocpol has placed greater emphasis on the use of primary data in her more recent work. See, for example, *Protecting Soldiers and Mothers: The Political Origins of Social Policy in the United States* (Cambridge, Mass., 1992).

32. Morawska, "The Sociology and Historiography of Immigration," p. 193.

33. Many scholars distinguish between temporary migrants (sojourners) and permanent migrants (immigrants). The definition of these terms is, however, often imprecise. I use *temporary migrant* to refer to those who left Italy with the intention of returning or who returned within five years, and *permanent migrant* for those who left Italy with the intention of remaining abroad or who did in fact remain there for more than five years. See Gould, "European Inter-Continental Emigration, 1815–1914," 9, 1, pp. 41–112; and Betty Boyd Caroli, *Italian Repatriation from the United States, 1900–1914* (New York, 1973).

Part I. The Italian Diaspora and the Old and New World Contexts of Migration

1. The figures on nineteenth-century European migration, especially for the earlier part of the century, must be considered as approximations and thus used with caution. A good discussion of this problem can be found in J. D. Gould, "European Inter-Continental Emigration, 1815–1914," *Journal of European Economic History,* 9, 1 (Spring 1980), pp. 41–112; and 9, 2 (Fall 1980), pp. 267–315. See also Leslie Page Moch, *Moving Europeans: Migration in Western Europe since 1650* (Bloomington, Ind.: 1992); Walter Nugent, *Crossings: The Great Transatlantic Migrations,*

1870–1914 (Bloomington, Ind., 1992); and Philip Taylor, *The Distant Magnet: European Emigration to the U.S.A.* (London, 1971).

2. Gould, "European Inter-Continental Emigration, 1815–1914," 9, 2, p. 282.

Chapter 1. Italy and the Causes of Emigration

1. The two main sources of emigration data are the Italian government and the governments of the receiving societies. These data do not always agree or cover the same things. In this chapter I use the Italian government data because it alone provides information on the Italian background of the emigrants.

2. A. M. Mussilli, ed., *Nuovo dizionario del comuni e frazioni di comune*, 28th ed. (Rome, 1977).

3. For a detailed and insightful discussion of emigration from each of the areas and regions of Italy, see Francesco Coletti, *Dell'emigrazione italiana* (Milan, 1912), pp. 128–146. Sori provides provincial emigration rates during the 1876–1901 and 1902–1913 periods. See Ercole Sori, *L'emigrazione italiana dall'Unita alla Seconda Guerra Mondiale* (Bologna, 1979), pp. 19–26.

4. John W. Briggs, *An Italian Passage: Immigrants to Three American Cities, 1890–1930* (New Haven, 1978), pp. 5–11.

5. For data on regional variations in the sex and age of the emigrants, see Commissariato Generale dell'Emigrazione, *Annuario statistico della emigrazione italiana dal 1876 al 1925* (Rome, 1926), pp. 155–183.

6. Briggs, *An Italian Passage*, pp. 5–11.

7. Emigrants were defined as those traveling in third class, which included approximately 90 percent of all those who traveled by ship.

8. Most women listed themselves as housewives or as not working even though they may have been engaged at least part time in some work for pay.

9. Sori discusses this process of proletarianization in some detail. See Sori, *L'emigrazione italiana*, pp. 32–39.

10. As Dudley Baines has written recently, the main problem confronting scholars studying the causes of European emigration between 1815 and 1930 is that there is very little reliable direct evidence to document why some left and others not. Therefore scholars interested in this period are compelled to infer individual or group motivations from indirect evidence or from personal testimony (such as letters) whose representativeness is generally impossible to determine. The most reliable indirect evidence on which to infer causation, I believe, is at the local level and must be central in any analysis. Here I part with Baines, who stresses the region as the most appropriate unit of analysis. Clearly one must look at the causation of emigration at multiple levels—local, regional, national, and international—but I would argue that it is essential to begin at the village level. See Dudley Baines, "European Emigration, 1815–1930: Looking at the Emigration Decision Again," *Economic History Review*, 47, 3 (1994), pp. 525–544; Samuel L. Baily, "The Village Outward Approach to the Study of Social Networks: A Case Study of the Agnonesi Diaspora Abroad, 1885–1989," *Studi Emigrazione*, 29, 105 (March 1992), pp. 43–68; Baily, "The Future of Italian-American Studies"; Donna Gabaccia, *Militants and Migrants: Rural Sicilians Become American Workers* (New Brunswick, N.J., 1988), p. 2;

Franc Sturino, *Forging the Chain: Italian Migration to North America, 1880–1930* (Toronto, 1990), p. 2.

11. Rudolph M. Bell, *Fate and Honor: Family and Village, Demographic and Cultural Change in Rural Italy since 1800* (Chicago, 1979), p. 180. For a lucid and insightful analysis of the importance of the family in the migration decision-making process see Sarah F. Harbison, "Family Structure and Family Strategy in Migration Decision Making," in Gordon F. De Jong and Robert W. Gardner, eds., *Migration Decision Making: Multidisciplinary Approaches to Microlevel Studies in Developed and Developing Countries* (New York, 1981), pp. 225–251.

12. Shepard B. Clough, *The Economic History of Modern Italy* (New York, 1964), pp. 66–70; Bell, *Fate and Honor*, pp. 189–190.

13. Philip Taylor, *The Distant Magnet: European Emigration to the U.S.A.* (London, 1971), pp. 108–110, 116–119.

14. Aldo Albonico and Gianfausto Rosoli, *Italia y America* (Madrid, 1994), pp. 247–250; Grazia Dore, "Some Social and Historical Aspects of Italian Emigration to America," *Journal of Social History*, 2, 2 (Winter 1968), pp. 104, 108–110; Emilio Franzina, *Gli Italiani al nuovo mondo: L'emigrazione italiana in America 1492–1942* (Milan, 1995), pp. 156–168.

15. Albonico and Rosoli, *Italia y America*, pp. 251–254; Dore, "Some Social and Historical Aspects," pp. 117–118; Robert F. Foerster, *The Italian Emigration of Our Times* (Cambridge, Mass., 1919), pp. 17, 293; Franzina, *Gli Italiani*, pp. 168–171.

16. Massimo Livi-Bacci, *A History of Italian Fertility during the Last Two Centuries* (Princeton, N.J., 1977), pp. 52–53; Taylor, *The Distant Magnet*, p. 51; B. R. Mitchell, *European Historical Statistics, 1750–1970*, abridged ed. (London, 1978), pp. 5, 10.

17. Clough, *Economic History*, pp. 58–65, 99; Luciano Gafagna, "The Industrial Revolution in Italy, 1830–1914," *Fontana Economic History of Europe*, vol. 4, *The Emergence of Industrial Societies, Part 1* (London, 1973), pp. 279–328.

18. This and the following paragraphs are based on Bell, *Fate and Honor*, 181–192; Dino Cinel, *From Italy to San Francisco: The Immigrant Experience* (Stanford, 1982), pp. 59–65; Clough, *Economic History*, pp. 99–132; Coletti, *Dell'emigrazione*, pp. 130–146; Robert F. Foerster, *The Italian Emigration of Our Times*, pp. 64–82; Denis Mack Smith, *Italy: A Modern History* (Ann Arbor, 1969), pp. 149–162; and Sori, *L'emigrazione italiana*, pp. 69–118.

19. Cinel, *From Italy to San Francisco*, pp. 61–62. This process obviously varied from region to region. In the provinces of Belluno and Udine, more than 20 percent of the rural acreage changed hands during the 1870s alone. See Foerster, *Italian Emigration*, pp. 109–110.

20. Foerster, *Italian Emigration*, pp. 109, 450–452; Commissariato Generale dell'Emigrazione, *Bollettino dell'Emigrazione* (Rome, 1902–1915), 18 (1910), pp. 46–48.

21. Clough, *Economic History*, pp. 114–121; Foerster, *Italian Emigration*, pp. 89–93; Gafagna, "Industrial Revolution," pp. 292–297; and Mack Smith, *Italy*, pp. 152–159, 182.

22. Between 1881 and 1901, the number of landowners per 1000 population decreased by 5.4 percent in Basilicata, 24.8 percent in Calabria, and 17.5 percent in Sicily. See Foerster, *Italian Emigration*, pp. 68–69, 109–111; and Mack Smith, *Italy*, p. 149.

23. The MacDonalds set forth a model in 1963 and 1964 that sought to explain why some Italians chose to emigrate, others remained at home and protested in a variety of ways, and still others accepted the status quo. For them, the most important indicator of high emigration areas was relatively wide distribution of land tenure and the predominance of family-based agricultural systems. See J. S. Mac-Donald, "Agricultural Organization, Migration, and Labour Militancy in Rural Italy," *Economic History Review*, Series 2, 16 (1963), pp. 61–75; John S. MacDonald and Leatrice MacDonald, "A Simple Institutional Framework for the Analysis of Agricultural Development Potential," *Economic Development and Cultural Change*, 12 (July 1964), pp. 368–376; John S. and Leatrice MacDonald, "Institutional Economics and Rural Development: Two Italian Types," *Human Organization*, 23 (1964), pp. 113–118. See also John S. MacDonald, "Some Socio-Economic Differentials in Rural Italy, 1902–1913," *Economic Development and Cultural Change*, 7 (1958), pp. 55–72. A decade later, Josef Barton placed greater emphasis than the MacDonalds on the importance of social structure and on the relationship between the agricultural and nonagricultural sectors of the economy. For him it was the slow decline in artisan manufacturing that limited the resources of the peasants and most critically undermined the stability of the peasant communities. See Josef J. Barton, *Peasants and Strangers: Italians, Rumanians, and Slovaks in an American City, 1890–1950* (Cambridge, Mass., 1975), pp. 27–36, 39–40. Most recently, Donna Gabaccia questioned the MacDonalds' assumption that areas of heavy emigration and rural protest differed significantly from each other. See Gabaccia, *Militants and Migrants*, Introduction and esp. pp. 13, 15, 16; chapter 2 and esp. pp. 20–26; and chapter 3. See also Pino Arlacchi, *Mafia, Peasants and Great Estates: Society in Traditional Calabria* (New York, 1983); Bell, *Fate and Honor*, pp. 178–211; and Briggs, *An Italian Passage*, pp. 1–14.

24. Baily, "The Village Outward Approach."

25. Bell has a good discussion of the importance of these issues. See Bell, *Fate and Honor*, chapter 8 and esp. pp. 180 and 191.

26. In the well-organized town archive there are birth, death, marriage, and tax records dating back to the early nineteenth century, passport records from 1885 to 1953, manuscript censuses, family files, and many other records. The town library has a complete set of various local newspapers that date back to the 1880s. Some church and notary records also exist. Published works on Agnone include Samuel L. Baily, "Chain Migration of Italians to Argentina: Case Studies of the Agnonesi and the Sirolesi," *Studi Emigrazione*, 19, 65 (March 1982), pp. 73–91; Baily, "The Village Outward Approach"; Custode Carlomagno, *Agnone dalle origini ai nostri giorni* (Campobasso, 1965); William A. Douglass, *Emigration in a South Italian Town: An Anthropological History* (New Brunswick, N.J., 1984); William A. Douglass, "The South Italian Family: A Critique," *Journal of Family History* (Winter 1980), pp. 338–359; William A. Douglass, "The Joint-Family Household in Eighteenth-Century Southern Italian History," in David I. Kertzer and Richard P. Saller, eds., *The Family in Italy from Antiquity to the Present* (New Haven, Conn., 1991), pp. 287–303; and Romolo Gandolfo, "Notas sobre la elite de una comunidad emigrada en cadena: El caso de los Agnoneses," in Fernando J. Devoto and Gianfausto Rosoli, eds., *L'Italia nella società Argentina* (Rome, 1988), pp. 160–177.

27. Douglass, *Emigration*, pp. 49–80. I rely heavily on Douglass for the historical

data of pre–1870 Agnone because he is the only person who has carefully worked through the major primary sources. The interpretation of these events and their significance for emigration is mine.

28. *L'Aquilonia*, 1/1/1885, 2/1/1885, 4/16/1885, 1/1/1888, 10/16/1888, 11/1/1888.

29. Although 1,245 passports were issued, I have subtracted the approximately 10 percent (125) who did not actually emigrate and added the approximately 30 percent (336) who traveled on the passports of others. For the actual number of passports issued annually by the Commune of Agnone by destination (1885–1953), see Baily, "The Village Outward Approach," p. 48.

30. Douglas, *Emigration*, p. 93; Carlomagno, *Agnone*, pp. 236–237.

31. Both Carlomagno and Douglass refer to some passport data before 1885, but during several visits I have not been able to locate it in the Agnone Archivio Comunale.

32. Before the early years of the twentieth century, approximately 10 percent of those who had passports did not actually leave home, but from 1905 on the figure jumped to 30 percent. In addition, approximately 30 percent more individuals traveled on others' passports up to 1894, but only 15 percent did so after that date. See Comune di Agnone, "Registri dei passaporti per l'estero, 1885–1900," and "Registro dei passaporti dal 1 gennaio 1907 al 10 maggio 1912." Hereafter referred to as Agnone Passport Records.

33. For the specific data on occupation, sex, and age of Agnone emigrants to New York City and Buenos Aires, see Baily, "The Village Outward Approach," p. 54. Douglass's analysis of the 1901 Census shows a very similar breakdown of the occupations of the Agnonesi living abroad in that year. See Douglass, *Emigration*, pp. 100–101.

34. In each of these three years, there were emigrants (overwhelmingly wives and children) who listed no occupation: 31 percent in 1889, 24 percent in 1899, and 9 percent in 1908. Although it is not entirely clear why the decline occurred, it could indicate either that more women were working, that the work of more women was recorded, or both.

35. Douglass, *Emigration*, pp. 123–125.

36. I use the concept of *social space* as "a unit of socio- economic interaction, often face-to-face" in accordance with the thinking of Franc Sturino. In his study of the Rende area Sturino found that this social space was limited approximately to a ten-kilometer radius from the town of Rende. My own investigations indicate that this figure could extend even further. See Sturino, *Forging the Chain*.

37. Comune di Agnone, *Registri degli atti di matrimonio*, vol. 68 (1876), vol. 79 (1886), vol. 89 (1896), vol. 99 (1906). Number of marriages that took place in each year: 1876, 97; 1886, 122; 1896, 77; and 1906, 78.

38. Douglass, *Emigration*, p. 48. Gould emphasizes the importance of previous emigration and feedback from a given area as one of the major determinants of future emigration. See Gould, "European Inter-Continental Emigration," 8, 3, p. 308.

39. Douglass, *Emigration*, pp. 42–43, and "South Italian Family," pp. 343–344.

40. Douglass, *Emigration*, pp. 59–68. The extensive amount of land devoted to the cultivation of grain remained high at least until 1929 when it was approximately 45 percent. See Istituto Centrale di Statistica, *Cadasto agrario 1929* (Rome, 1935), 63, p. 106.

41. Douglass, *Emigration*, pp. 49–80.

42. Bell, *Fate and Honor*, p. 166.

43. I base this estimate on the figures in the Agrarian Census of 1929. The population of Agnone in 1931 was 9,337, and there is no evidence to suggest that land usage had changed to any significant degree between 1871 and 1929. See Istituto Centrale di Statistica, *Cadasto agrario 1929*, vol. 63, p. 106. See also Douglass, *Emigration*, pp. 59–69.

44. Antonio Arduino, "Schemi particolari di demografia (dal 1532 al 1977) del Comune di Agnone nel Molise," unpublished manuscript.

45. Douglass, *Emigration*, pp. 12–21, 144–158.

46. Douglass, *Emigration*, pp. 86–90.

47. Douglass, *Emigration*, pp. 146–152.

48. Agnone Passport Records. Specific data for three sample years: 1889 (3.8 percent), 1899 (5.2 percent), 1908 (3.7 percent). Arlacchi refers to those who did not fit in as "frictional types." "It is well to remember," he writes, "that it was not only young men integrated into village society at home and bent on returning who emigrated. A certain quota of emigrants came from the 'frictional' types we mentioned earlier: single salaried workers, illegitimate sons and daughters, rebels, deviants, criminals, peasant families 'declassed' by sudden impoverishment. . . . What they had in common was the fact that society had no place for them. In effect, they had been expelled." Arlacchi, *Mafia*, p. 62. See also Vilhelm Moberg's classic novel, *The Emigrants* (New York, 1951), in which he describes the different reasons why sixteen people left Ludjer Parish, Sweden, for the United States in 1850.

49. Arlacchi, *Mafia*, pp. 173–191; Bell, *Fate and Honor*, pp. 193–195; and Coletti, *Dell'emigrazione*, pp. 132, 144.

50. Many scholars from various disciplines have emphasized the importance of social networks to the decision to emigrate. See the Introduction, note 11. On the importance of the family in the migration process see Harbison, "Family Structure and Family Strategy," and also Chapter 6 of this book.

51. I do not have the data to show that agents were or were not used before 1885. It is possible that they were, but—given the fact that so few used agents between 1885 and 1895—it seems most unlikely. The data from 1885 on are based on the passport records, which generally indicated if an individual used an agent. There is some evidence that more informal on-board agents were used, a subject which we will discuss in the next chapter.

52. Timothy C. Del Papa, letter to Samuel L. Baily (7/20/1995) and interview with Samuel L. Baily (8/10/1995). Timothy is the great-grandson of Pietro, has visited Agnone several times, and has collected extensive information on the family. His information includes birth, death, marriage, and passport records, U.S. naturalization records, and numerous interviews with family members in the United States and in Agnone. I wish to thank him for his willingness to share this information with me.

53. Bell's observations on Albareto, one of the four towns he studied in depth, lend support to this speculation. "The family," he notes, "provided each of its children with something, but only one with land. . . . Fathers paid the initial costs of emigration, and sons relinquished claims to the land. Thus disinherited, the emi-

grant worked for his own account, sharing nothing with kin who remained in the village." Bell, *Fate and Honor*, p. 197.

54. Pete Santorelli, taped interview with Samuel L. Baily, 1991. See also the U.S. Ships Passenger Lists for the *Barbarosa*, which arrived in New York on December 26, 1908.

Chapter 2. The Italian Migrations to Buenos Aires and New York City

1. In 1914, approximately 370,000 Italians lived in New York City and 312,000 in Buenos Aires. In São Paulo, the third largest concentration, there were approximately 120,000 Italians.

2. Franc Sturino, *Forging the Chain: Italian Migration to North America, 1880–1930* (Toronto, 1990), p. 78.

3. Although Oreste generally recognized his obligations and did help emigrants from Biella in Buenos Aires, he got tired of doing so and complained to his father. See Samuel L. Baily and Franco Ramella, eds., *One Family, Two Worlds: An Italian Family's Correspondence across the Atlantic, 1901–1922* (New Brunswick, N.J., 1988), pp. 59–63.

4. The literature cited in the Introduction, note 11, provides a large number of examples of the role of personal networks in the migration process.

5. U.S. Senate, Immigration Commission (Dillingham Commission), *Reports* (Washington, D.C., 1911), 41 vols., 4, p. 59. Hereafter referred to as U.S. Immigration Commission, *Reports*.

6. Robert F. Harney, "The Commerce of Migration," *Canadian Ethnic Studies* 9, 1 (1977), pp. 42–55; and Robert F. Harney, *Dalla frontiera alle Little Italies: Gli Italiani in Canada, 1800–1945* (Rome, 1984), pp. 73–91. See also Sturino, *Forging the Chain*, pp. 76–92; U.S. Immigration Commission, *Reports*, 1, 29–30, 2, 375–386, 4, 61–64; and the sections of an informative report by a member of the European Immigration Commission of the U.S. Treasury Department on Italian immigration, Herman J. Schulteis, *Report on European Immigration to the United States of America* (Washington, D.C., 1893), pp. 28–41.

7. Grazia Dore, "Some Social and Historical Aspects of Italian Emigration to America," *Journal of Social History*, 2, 2 (Winter 1968), pp. 99–101, 110–113; Antonio Annino, "El debate sobre la emigración y la expansión a la América Latina en los origines e la ideología imperialista en Italia (1861–1911)," *Jahrbuch fur Geschichte von Staat, Wirtschaft und Gesellschaft Lateinamerikas*, 13 (1976), pp. 192–195, 212; Niccolo Cuneo, *Storia dell'emigrazione italiana in Argentina 1810–1870* (Milan, 1940), esp. pp. 148–155.

8. Sturino, *Forging the Chain*, pp. 76–77.

9. Passports indicate that less than 5 percent of the migrants used agents before 1895, but it is possible that the record keepers did not list agents during this period. The local newspaper *L'Aquilonia* recorded a few cases of groups in 1888 that were organized by Ruggiero Apollonia e Co. See *L'Aquilonia*, 10/16/1888, p. 4, and 11/1/1888, p. 3.

10. This information is based on passport records, which generally indicated sponsorship.

11. The information on the Marinelli family comes from Agnone Family Files (Comune di Agnone, Foglio di famiglia, 1901); Samuel L. Baily, "The Village Outward Approach to the Study of Social Networks: A Case Study of the Agnonesi Diaspora Abroad, 1885–1989," *Studi Emigrazione*, 29, 105 (March 1992), pp. 43–68, esp. pp. 55–56; Romolo Gandolfo, "Notas sobre la elite de una comunidad emigrada en cadena: El caso de los Agnoneses," in Fernando J. Devoto and Gianfausto Rosoli, eds., *L'Italia nella società Argentina* (Rome, 1988), pp. 160–177, esp. pp. 142–144; Dionisio Petriella and Sara Sosa Miatello, *Diccionario biográfico italo-argentino* (Buenos Aires, 1976), pp. 424–425. Ads announcing the services of the Marinelli Agencies in Agnone and Buenos Aires frequently appeared in the pages of *L'Eco del Sannio*. See, for example, *L'Eco del Sannio*, 6/10/1894, p. 4, and 3/20/1913, p. 6. Many other agents who provided services for New York as well as Buenos Aires also advertised in this newspaper.

12. The Italian government attempted to provide help for the migrants by including in the 1901 emigration legislation a provision for the establishment of local emigration committees. These committees were to assist those who wanted to migrate in every way possible. There is little evidence, however, to indicate that these committees actually functioned. Sturino points out that as late as 1907, none of these committees operated in Cosenza. My data show that none were active in Agnone. See Sturino, *Forging the Chain*, p. 76. Arrigo De Zettiry's 1913 guide for Italian migrants to Argentina mentions these committees, but does not say whether or not they actually functioned. See Diego Armus, ed., *Manual del emigrante italiano* (Buenos Aires, 1983), p. 24.

13. Among the most useful accounts that describe the various stages of the move are Armus, *Manual*, pp. 23–49; Broughton Brandenburg, *Imported Americans* (New York, 1903), pp. 123–227; Marta Costa, *Los inmigrantes* (Buenos Aires, 1972), pp. 17–23; Sturino, *Forging the Chain*, pp. 82–92; Philip Taylor, *The Distant Magnet: European Emigration to the U.S.A.* (London, 1971), pp. 131–166; and U.S. Immigration Commission, *Reports*, 37, pp. 5–51.

14. See, for example, Commissariato Generale dell'Emigrazione, *Bollettino dell'Emigrazione* (Rome, 1902–1915), 6 (1902), pp. 3–28; 1905, 2, pp. 3–70; 1905, 10, pp. 3–70; 1905, 21, pp. 3–81; and 1913, 6, pp. 3–130.

15. Taylor states that the cost increased with the length of the voyage, but he does not provide any evidence to substantiate this. See Taylor, *Distant Magnet*, pp. 94–95. As an indication of the actual fares, on ships leaving during the second quarter of 1902, the steerage fare between Genoa or Naples and New York ranged between 165 and 190 lire. The fare on 70 percent of the ships was between 165 and 175 lire, and the average of all ships was 173.8 lire. To Buenos Aires, the range was between 165 and 180 lire; 70 percent of the ships charged between 165 and 175 lire, and the average was 174.6 lire. By 1910, these figures had increased somewhat, but the relative numbers remained nearly the same. See *Bollettino dell'Emigrazione*, 6 (1902), pp. 3–7; 1913, 6, pp. 50–54, 77–79. The difference in fares between New York and Buenos Aires may, however, have been greater a decade before. Schulteis, writing in 1893, reported that fares to New York were $8 less than to Brazil "or any other transatlantic country," with the result that "the majority of the poorer emigrants come to the United States." See Schulteis, *Report*, p. 37.

16. Brandenburg and Sturino among others stress the importance of the groups and of the veterans. See Brandenburg, *Imported Americans*, p. 172, and Sturino, *Forging the Chain*, pp. 82–83.

17. Agnone Passport Records; *L'Aquilonia*, 10/16/1888, p. 4, 11/1/1888, p. 3.

18. Brandenburg and Sturino give excellent accounts of this phase of the trip. See Brandenburg, *Imported Americans*, pp. 118–170, and Sturino, *Forging the Chain*, pp. 84–87. The quotation from the guide is from Armus, *Manual*, p. 30.

19. U.S. Immigration Commission, *Reports*, 37, pp. 7, 22–23.

20. Armus, *Manual*, pp. 34–37.

21. U.S. Immigration Commission, *Reports*, 37, pp. 10–13, 24–29.

22. The Foran Act of 1885 made it illegal to import aliens under contract to work in the United States.

23. Brandenburg provides a particularly vivid description of this arrival process. See Brandenburg, *Imported Americans*, pp. 198–214. For Buenos Aires, see Costa, *Los inmigrantes*, pp. 20–23.

24. Armus, *Manual*, pp. 42–49; Brandenburg, *Imported Americans*, pp. 205–227; Edward Corsi, *In the Shadow of Liberty* (New York, 1937), reprinted as part of the American Immigration Series (1969); Costa, *Los inmigrantes*, pp. 20–23; Sturino, *Forging the Chain*, pp. 90–92; Jorge Ochoa de Eguileor and Eduardo Valdes, *Donde durmieron nuestros abuelos?* (Buenos Aires, 1991).

25. There are several problems in constructing accurate descriptions of these two population movements. First, the available data are limited and often not directly comparable. The Argentine and Buenos Aires censuses provide much more complete and specific data for Buenos Aires than do the United States censuses for New York City. Thus, for some information, I have been compelled to start with the data on Italians in the United States and to estimate the extent to which they represented the situation for Italians in New York City. And second, the various indicators discussed separately in this chapter must be understood to be part of a whole. Often the significance of each is not clear if isolated from the others. The comparisons in at least some cases will be based on partial information and will therefore of necessity be more general than I would like. Yet the total picture enables us to see the most important differences between the Italian migrations to Buenos Aires and New York City.

26. For a full discussion of these institutions, see Chapters 7 and 8.

27. Between August 1911 and August 1912, the Italian government suspended emigration to Argentina because of a dispute over health inspectors on board immigrant ships.

28. For a discussion of business cycles and Italian migration in the United States, see Harry Jerome, *Migration and Business Cycles* (New York, 1926), pp. 196–205.

29. I use ten thousand as a somewhat arbitrary figure to define the critical mass necessary for major institutional development such as mutual aid societies, newspapers, banks, clubs, chambers of commerce, hospitals, and so on. Certainly communities with less than that number had some of these institutions, but roughly ten thousand people seem necessary to support a wide range of institutions and an effective level of development. Whatever the precise figure for the critical mass might be, the ten thousand figure provides a basis to compare the relative growth

of the two Italian communities. The nature of formal institutional development in the two cities is discussed at length in Chapters 7 and 8.

30. We can measure only the total number of Italians who left Argentina or the United States during a given period compared to the number who entered during the same period. We can not measure multiple entries and exits by the same individuals, so the figures given here can only be an approximation for the actual rate of return.

31. Massimo Livi-Bacci, *L'immigrazione e l'assimilazione degli Italiani negli Stati Uniti* (Milan, 1961), p. 35; and República Argentina, Dirección de Inmigración, *Resumen estadística del movimiento migratorio en la República Argentina, 1857–1924* (Buenos Aires, 1925), p. 8. For an insightful discussion of Livi-Bacci's estimates, see J. D. Gould, "European Inter-Continental Emigration, 1815–1914," *Journal of European Economic History*, 9, 1 (Spring 1980), pp. 41–112, esp. pp. 79–91. For a slightly different interpretation of the data, see Klein, "Integration of Italian Immigrants," p. 319.

32. See Gould, "European Inter-Continental Emigration," pp. 91–98; Betty Boyd Caroli, *Italian Repatriation from the United States, 1900–1914* (New York, 1973), pp. 25–50; and Mark Jefferson, *Peopling the Argentine Republic* (New York, 1926), p. 183.

33. Gianfausto Rosoli, ed., *Un secolo di emigrazione italiana, 1876–1976* (Rome, 1978).

34. These census data are not completely comparable since the Buenos Aires figures are for 1895 and 1914 and the New York figures are for 1920. Furthermore, the New York figures for 1900 are taken from a block sample on the lower East Side. See Chapter 6 and esp. Table 33 for additional data and discussion on the subject.

35. Marriage and fertility figures among Italians in Buenos Aires document this growth of the second generation. See Buenos Aires, *Censo 1887*, 2, pp. 418, 425; and Buenos Aires, *Censo 1904*, pp. 24, 91, 96–97, 100. For a fuller discussion of marriage and fertility see Chapter 6.

36. The New York Italian population began to age significantly during World War I, reflecting the later date at which the community reached a significant size. See Table 12.

37. Buenos Aires, *Censo 1887*, 2, pp. 36, 65; Argentina, *Censo 1914*, 3, pp. 12–13, 321.

38. U.S. Immigration Commission, *Reports*, 3, pp. 84–87, 95–96, 131–138; 24, pp. 238–241. Since the literacy figures for Buenos Aires refer to all Italians in the city eight years old or more and the U.S. Immigration Commission figures refer to Italians fourteen years old or more entering the United States or to Italian male heads of households in New York, the actual difference in literacy was even greater.

39. See Table 17.

40. On industrialization and organization in Italy, see Josef J. Barton, *Peasants and Strangers: Italians, Rumanians, and Slovaks in an American City, 1890–1950* (Cambridge, Mass., 1975), pp. 64–67; John W. Briggs, *An Italian Passage: Immigrants to Three American Cities, 1890–1930* (New Haven, 1978), pp. 15–36; Francesco Coletti, *Dell'emigrazione italiana* (Milan, 1912), pp. 130–135, 161–171; Robert F. Foerster, *The Italian Emigration of Our Times* (New York, 1919), pp. 87, 101, 272–273, 402–404; Luciano Gafagna, "The Industrial Revolution in Italy, 1830–1914," *Fontana Economic*

History of Europe, vol. 4, *The Emergence of Industrial Societies, Part 1* (London, 1973), pp. 279–328; and Bianca Gera and Diego Robotti, "L'influenza della tradizione mutualistica piemontese sull'organizazione delle società di mutuo soccorso dei lavoratori italiani in Argentina," in Vanni Blengino, Emilio Franzina, and Adolfo Pepe, eds., *La riscoperta delle Americhe: Lavoratori e sindacato nell'emigrazione italiana in America Latina 1870–1970* (Milan, 1994), pp. 265–276.

41. The more precise data on occupation, sex, and age of the Agnonesi who went to Buenos Aires and New York reinforce the point that the two cities each attracted a somewhat different immigrant population. For these data, see Baily, "The Village Outward Approach," pp. 53–55. For a fuller discussion of occupations, see Chapter 4 of this book.

Chapter 3. What the Immigrants Found

1. Samuel L. Baily and Franco Ramella, eds., *One Family, Two Worlds: An Italian Family's Correspondence across the Atlantic, 1901–1922* (New Brunswick, N.J., 1980), pp. 34–35.

2. For useful general discussions of the development of the two economies, see Melvyn Dubofsky, *Industrialism and the American Worker*, 2nd ed. (Arlington Heights, Ill., 1985); Robert Higgs, *The Transformation of the American Economy, 1865–1914* (New York, 1971); Harold G. Vatter, *The Drive to Industrial Maturity: The U.S. Economy, 1860–1914* (Westport, Conn., 1975), chapters 3 and 9; Roberto Cortés Conde, *El progreso argentino, 1880–1914* (Buenos Aires, 1979); Carlos F. Díaz Alejandro, *Essays on the Economic History of the Argentine Republic* (New Haven, 1970), chapter 1; and Aldo Ferrer, *The Argentine Economy* (Berkeley, 1967), part III. For additional sources, see also Table 15 and Chapter 4 of this book.

3. Díaz Alejandro, *Essays*, p. 10. See also Hilda Sábato, *Agrarian Capitalism and the World Market: Buenos Aires in the Pastoral Age, 1840–1890* (Albuquerque, N.M., 1990).

4. Dubofsky, *Industrialism*, pp. 1–5; Melvyn Dubofsky, *When Workers Organize: New York City in the Progressive Era* (Amherst, Mass., 1968), pp. 1–6; and David C. Hammack, *Power and Society: Greater New York at the Turn of the Century* (New York, 1987), pp. 302–326.

5. James R. Scobie, *Buenos Aires: Plaza to Suburb, 1870–1910* (New York, 1974), pp. 133–137; and Díaz Alejandro, *Essays*, p. 10.

6. Tillman M. Sogge, "Industrial Classes in the United States 1870 to 1950," *American Statistical Association Journal*, 49 (1954), pp. 251–253; Alvin H. Hansen, "Industrial Class Alignments in the United States," *American Statistical Association Journal*, 17 (1920), pp. 417–425; Ronald Story, "Social Class," *Encyclopedia of American Social History* (New York, 1993), pp. 467–482.

7. Scobie, *Buenos Aires*, pp. 208–220; Gino Germani, *Estructura social de la Argentina: Análisis estadístico* (Buenos Aires, 1955), pp. 218–225; Gino Germani, "Mass Immigration and Modernization in Argentina," in Irving L. Horowitz, ed., *Masses in Latin America* (New York, 1970), pp. 289–330; Gustavo Beyhaut et al., "Los inmigrantes en el sistema ocupacional argentino," in Torcuato S. Di Tella et al., *Argentina, sociedad de masas* (Buenos Aires, 1966), pp. 85–123.

8. I use the terms *middle groups* or *middle sectors*—like most Latin American his-

torians—to distinguish these groups from the more cohesive and clearly self-defined *middle classes* of European and U.S. societies. See John Johnson, *Political Change in Latin America: The Emergence of the Middle Sectors* (Stanford, 1958).

9. Germani, *Estructura social*, pp. 218–219; Germani, "Mass Immigration," pp. 303–304.

10. Scobie, *Buenos Aires*, p. 215.

11. See Chapter 4 and esp. Table 17.

12. Hammack, *Power and Society*, pp. 83, 85.

13. Hammack, *Power and Society*, pp. 83, 85; José Luis de Imaz, *La clase alta de Buenos Aires* (Buenos Aires, 1962).

14. Hammack, *Power and Society*, pp. 158 ff., 306–319. In a note to the foreign minister dated October 3, 1904, the Italian ambassador in Washington commented on "the discretely active part" played by Italians in the presidential election of that year and argued that political participation would give the immigrants "an influence, a value." Italy, Ministero degli Affari Esteri (MAE), Serie Política (1891–1916), pacco 360, posizione 74.

15. Hilda Sábato and Ema Cibotti, "Hacer política en Buenos Aires: Los Italianos en la escena política porteña, 1860–1880," *Boletín del Instituto de Historia Argentina y Americana "Dr. E. Ravignani,"* Tercera Serie 2 (1st quarter of 1990), p. 18. Torcuato S. Di Tella describes the political system in essentially the same terms, but he arrives at different conclusions regarding immigrant participation in politics. See Torcuato S. Di Tella, "El impacto inmigratorio sobre el sistema político argentino," *Estudios Migratorios Latinoamericanos*, 4, 12 (August 1989), pp. 218–221. Charles Anderson sets forth a useful generic model of this kind of political system based on "power contenders" with "power capabilities" negotiating and manipulating among themselves. See Charles W. Anderson, "A Conceptualization of Latin American Politics," in Robert D. Tomasek, ed., *Latin American Politics: Studies of the Contemporary Scene*, 2nd ed. (New York, 1970), pp. 4–36. On the lack of development of mass-based political machines see David Rock, *Politics in Argentina, 1890–1930* (Cambridge, 1975), pp. 16 ff. In Buenos Aires and other cities, immigrants who had been residents for at least two years could vote in municipal elections.

16. Carl E. Solberg, "Mass Migration in Argentina, 1870–1970," in William H. McNeill and R. N. Adams, eds., *Human Migration* (Bloomington, Ind., 1978), pp. 146–170.

17. Donna Gabaccia, *From Sicily to Elizabeth Street: Housing and Social Change among Italian Immigrants, 1880–1930* (Albany, N.Y., 1984); Silvano M. Tomasi and Madeline H. Engel, eds., *The Italian Experience in the United States* (New York, 1970), pp. 77–107; Virginia Yans-McLaughlin, *Family and Community: Italian Immigrants in Buffalo, 1880–1930* (Urbana, Ill., 1982).

18. For a full discussion of the Italian communities in the two cities see Chapters 7 and 8.

19. Tulio Halperin-Donghi provides an incisive overview of the development of this widespread pro-immigration ideology in "Para que la inmigración? Ideología y política inmigratoria y aceleración del proceso modernizador: El caso argentino (1810–1914)," *Jahrbuch fur Geschichte von Staat, Wirtschaft und Gesellschaft Lateinamerikas*, 13 (1976), pp. 437–489. See also the excellent article by Fernando Devoto, "Acerca de la construcción de la identidad nacional en un pais de inmi-

grantes, el caso argentino (1850–1930), in *Historia y presente en América Latina: Conferencias Pronunciadas en el Centre Cultural Bancaixa* (Valencia, 1996), pp. 95–126.

20. While most of the elite believed immigration essential to Argentine progress, a plurality of perspectives developed among them regarding the form of incorporation of the immigrants into Argentine society. Tulio Halperin-Donghi provides an excellent introduction to the thought of the main thinkers of this period plus excerpts from their most important works in *Proyecto y construcción de una nación: Argentina, 1846–1880* (Caracas, 1982).

21. Quoted from Robert David Ochs, "A History of Argentine Immigration 1853–1924" (Ph.D. dissertation, University of Illinois, 1939), pp. 37–38.

22. The best sources for following the development of immigration policy are the annual reports (*Memorias* and *Informes*) of the government office in charge of immigration. The name of this office and its affiliation with larger governmental agencies changed several times between 1869 and 1915. In the 1870s, it was called the Comisión General de Inmigración and was a part of the Ministerio del Interior. In the 1880s and most of the 1890s, it became the Departamento General de Inmigración under the Ministerio de Relaciones Exteriores. In the late 1890s, it became the Dirección General de Inmigración under the Ministerio de Agricultura.

23. Donald S. Castro, *The Development and Politics of Argentine Immigration Policy, 1852–1914: To Govern Is to Populate* (San Francisco, 1991), pp. 145–185; Jorge Ochoa de Eguileor and Eduardo Valdes, *Donde durmieron nuestros abuelos?* (Buenos Aires, 1991); and James R. Scobie, *Revolution on the Pampas: A Social History of Argentine Wheat, 1860–1910* (Austin, Tex., 1964).

24. For the text of this law see República Argentina, Ministerio del Interior, Comisión General de Inmigración, *Memoria 1876* (Buenos Aires, 1877). See also Juan Alsina, *La inmigración europea a la República Argentina* (Buenos Aires, 1898), pp. 92–100.

25. In 1887, the population of Buenos Aires was 53 percent foreign born and 32 percent Italian born. Alsina, *La inmigración europea*, p. 132 and Table 9.

26. Fernando Devoto provides a good discussion of the different positions of Alberdi, Sarmiento, and Mitre with regard to the immigrants as civilizers and transformers. See Devoto, "Acerca de la construcción de la identidad nacional," pp. 99–109. See also Halperin-Donghi, "Para que la inmigración?" pp. 466–467. For a detailed discussion of the role of Garibaldi and other Italians in the Rio de la Plata, see Niccolo Cuneo, *Storia dell'emigrazione italiana in Argentina 1810–1870* (Milan, 1940), pp. 140–145, 208–214, 221–229, 253–262.

27. José Hernandez, *Martin Fierro* (Buenos Aires, 1965); Eduardo Gutierrez and José Podesta, *Juan Moreira*, in Juan Carlos Ghiano, ed., *Teatro gauchesco primitivo* (Buenos Aires, 1957); Eugenio Cambaceres, *En la sangre*, 4th ed. (Buenos Aires, 1924). See also Frank Dauster, *Historia del teatro hispanoamericano: Siglos XIX y XX*, 2nd ed. (Mexico, 1973); Halperin-Donghi, "Para que la inmigración?" pp. 458–459, 468–469; Gladys Onega, *La inmigración en la literature argentina, 1880–1910* (Santa Fe, Argentina, 1965); and Luciano Rusich, *El inmigrante italiano en la novela argentina del 80* (Madrid, 1974).

28. Domingo F. Sarmiento, *Obras completas* (Buenos Aires, 1948–1956), 53 vols., 23, *Inmigración y colonización*, and 36, *Condición del extranjero en América*. For a fuller discussion of the school issue, see Chapter 8 of this book. See also Samuel L. Baily,

"Sarmiento and Immigration: Changing Views on the Role of the Immigrant in the Development of Argentina?" in Joseph T. Criscenti, ed., *Sarmiento and His Argentina* (Boulder, Colo., 1992), pp. 131–142; *El Nacional*, 1/13/1881, 1/14/1881; *La Nación*, 1/19/1881.

29. Quoted in José Luis Romero, *A History of Argentine Political Thought* (Stanford, 1963), p. 177.

30. República Argentina, Ministerio de Relaciones Exteriores, Departamento General de Inmigración, *Memoria de 1881–1886* (Buenos Aires, 1886), pp. 74–79. For a detailed descriptive account of the government's immigration organization and policy, see Ochs, "A History of Argentine Immigration," esp. pp. 61, 80–85, and 116–119.

31. Departamento General de Inmigración, *Memoria de 1881–1886*, pp. 5–9; and República Argentina, Ministerio de Relaciones Exteriors, Departamento General de Inmigración, *Memoria de 1888* (Buenos Aires, 1889), pp. 28–29.

32. República Argentina, Ministerio de Relaciones Exteriores, Departamento General de Inmigración, *Memoria de 1890* (Buenos Aires, 1891), pp. 55–56.

33. República Argentina, Ministerio de Relaciones Exteriores, Departamento General de Inmigración, *Memoria de 1891* (Buenos Aires, 1892), pp. 6–9; República Argentina, Ministerio de Relaciones Exteriores, Departamento General de Inmigración, *Memoria de 1893* (Buenos Aires, 1894), pp. 5–6; and República Argentina, Ministerio de Relaciones Exteriores, Departamento General de Inmigración, *Memoria de 1895* (Buenos Aires, 1896), pp. 161–171. See also the other *Memorias* of the Departamento and the Dirección General de Inmigración between 1889 and 1912, plus Juan Alsina, *La inmigración en el primer siglo de la independencia* (Buenos Aires, 1910); and Alsina, *La inmigración europea*.

34. Numerous examples of these efforts to improve their situations are described in Chapter 8.

35. Romero, *Argentine Political Thought*, p. 185; Carl Solberg, *Immigration and Nationalism: Argentina and Chile, 1890–1914* (Austin, Tex., 1970), chapter 3.

36. Samuel L. Baily, *Labor, Nationalism, and Politics in Argentina* (New Brunswick, N.J., 1967), chapters 1 and 2; Samuel L. Baily, "The Italians and Organized Labor in the United States and Argentina, 1880–1910," *International Migration Review*, 1, 3 (Summer 1967), pp. 55–66; and Samuel L. Baily, "The Italians and the Development of Organized Labor in Argentina, Brazil, and the United States, 1880–1914," *Journal of Social History*, 3, 2 (Winter 1969–1970), pp. 123–134. For a more detailed discussion of labor see Chapter 8 of this book. See also Halperin-Donghi, "Para que la inmigración?" pp. 461–464, 473, 478.

37. Halperin-Donghi, "Para que la inmigración?" p. 478. The Italian consul in Buenos Aires in a letter to the Italian foreign minister dated 12/1/1902 stated that although six hundred foreigners had been arrested of whom at least four hundred were Italians, the large majority of them had been released. See Italy, MAE, Serie Política (1891–1916), pacco 323, posizione 58.

38. Halperin-Donghi, "Para que la inmigración?" pp. 478–487; and Devoto, "Acerca de la construcción de la identidad," pp. 109–116.

39. The cultural nationalist Ricardo Rojas also emphasized the importance of patriotic education in creating an Argentine identity. See Devoto, "Acerca de la con-

strucción de la identidad," pp. 115–116; and Solberg, *Immigration and Nationalism,* pp. 136–151.

40. Halperin-Donghi, "Para que la inmigración?" p. 482.

41. Halperin-Donghi, "Para que la inmigración?" pp. 458–459. One of the few physically destructive anti-foreign incidents took place in the provincial town of Tandil several hundred kilometers southwest of Buenos Aires in the beginning of 1871. For details of this incident, see *La Prensa,* January 1–20, 1872; "Textos y documentos para la historia de la cultura. Los asesinatos de Tandil," *Imago Mundi, Revista de Historia de la Cultura,* 1, 2 (December 1953), pp. 77–83.

42. Halperin-Donghi, "Para que la inmigración?" pp. 473–478; Baily, *Labor, Nationalism, and Politics,* chapters 1 and 2.

43. See, for example, one of the most popular Sainetes that deals with the Italian-native theme, Florencio Sanchez, *La Gringa,* in Dardo Cuneo, ed., *Teatro completo* (Buenos Aires, 1941). *La Gringa* was first performed in Buenos Aires in 1904. For more information on the popular theater, see Frank Dauster, *Perfil generacional del teatro hispanoamericano (1894–1924): Chile; Mexico; El Rio de la Plata* (Ottawa, Ontario, 1993), pp. 69–84; and Judith Evans, "Setting the Stage for Struggle: Popular Theater in Buenos Aires, 1890–1914," *Radical History Review,* 21 (Fall 1979), pp. 49–61.

44. For an insightful discussion of the Cocoliche phenomenon see Ana Cara-Walker, "Cocoliche: The Art of Assimilation and Dissimulation among Italians and Argentines," *Latin American Research Review,* 22, 3 (1987), pp. 37–67.

45. Cara-Walker, "Cocoliche," pp. 37–38.

46. Baily, *Labor, Nationalism, and Politics,* pp. 30–38; Ochs, "A History of Argentine Immigration," pp. 196–198; and Rock, *Politics in Argentina,* pp. 160–168.

47. On November 18, 1924, the Italian ambassador to Argentina wrote to the foreign minister about this anti-Italian book but seemed relieved to report, "The book has passed almost unobserved." Italy, MAE, Affari Politici (1919–1930), pacco 806 bis., fasc. 910.

48. For a description of nativism before the 1880s, see John Higham, *Strangers in the Land: Patterns of American Nativism, 1860–1925* (New Brunswick, N.J., 1955), pp. 3–11; U.S. Immigration Commission, *Reports,* 39, pp. 20–22, 95–96.

49. U.S. Immigration Commission, *Reports,* 39, pp. 31–33, 97–98. For the most convenient description of immigration legislation up to 1910, including the texts of all acts, see U.S. Immigration Commission, *Reports,* 39.

50. U.S. Immigration Commission, *Reports,* 39, pp. 67–81, 132–136. On public opinion from 1880–1980, including political party platforms and newspaper and magazine editorials and articles, see Rita Simon, *Public Opinion and the Immigrant: Print Media Coverage, 1880–1980* (Lexington, Mass., 1985); and Rita J. Simon and Susan H. Alexander, *The Ambivalent Welcome: Print Media, Public Opinion and Immigration* (Westport, Conn., 1993).

51. U.S. Immigration Commission, *Reports,* 39, pp. 33–35, 125–126; Dubofsky, *Industrialism,* pp. 59–64.

52. Higham, *Strangers in the Land,* p. 67.

53. The term *new immigrants* was used as a derogatory label during the decades surrounding the turn of the past century by those who wished to distinguish be-

tween the recent arrivals from southern and eastern Europe and the older immigrant groups who had come from northern and western Europe. The use of the term expressed the value judgment that the so-called new immigrants were inferior to the old. See the upcoming discussion on the Immigration Commission.

54. U.S. Immigration Commission, *Reports*, 39, pp. 39–40, 98–100.

55. U.S. Immigration Commission, *Reports*, 39, pp. 80–87; John Higham, *Send These to Me: Jews and Other Immigrants in Urban America* (New York, 1975), pp. 62–63.

56. U.S. Immigration Commission, *Reports*, 39, p. 47.

57. U.S. Immigration Commission, *Reports*, 39, pp. 45–47; Higham, *Strangers in the Land*, pp. 102–105.

58. Gwendolyn Mink, *Old Labor and New Immigrants in American Political Development: Union, Party, and State, 1875–1920* (Ithaca, N.Y., 1986); Dubofsky, *Industrialism*, pp. 64–68, 89–100; Higham, *Strangers in the Land*, pp. 234–235; U.S. Immigration Commission, *Reports*, 39, pp. 49–50.

59. Higham, *Strangers in the Land*, pp. 234–235.

60. U.S. Immigration Commission, *Reports*, 2, pp. 819–827; 39, pp. 51–55, 102–121.

61. It is important to emphasize that although the conclusions and some of the written text reflect this anti–new immigration bias, the *Reports* also include much information that is valuable to scholars. During several years of study, the commission garnered previously nonexistent statistical data from 3.2 million individuals. I have used the *Reports* frequently for data on Italians in New York and the United States.

62. U.S. Immigration Commission, *Reports*, 1, pp. 9–20, 23–48. The quotes are from pp. 13–14, 24–25.

63. U.S. Immigration Commission, *Reports*, 1, pp. 45, 48.

64. Higham, *Strangers in the Land*, pp. 149–157; Simon, *Public Opinion*, pp. 80–83, 211–223.

65. Higham, *Strangers in the Land*, pp. 183–185, 238.

66. Higham states that in general nativism declined in the United States between 1900 and 1912, but Pozzetta makes a strong case that at least for Italians in New York this was not the situation. This and the following paragraphs are based primarily on Pozzetta. See Higham, *Strangers in the Land*, pp. 87–96; George E. Pozzetta, "The Italians of New York City, 1890–1914" (Ph.D. dissertation, University of North Carolina, 1971), pp. 121–160 and esp. 121, 127–128, 132; and George E. Pozzetta, "The Mulberry District of New York City: The Years Before World War One," in Robert F. Harney and J. Vincenza Scarpaci, eds., *Little Italies in North America* (Toronto, 1981), pp. 7–40. See also Simon, *Public Opinion*; and Simon and Alexander, *Ambivalent Welcome*.

67. Higham, *Strangers in the Land*, p. 72; Pozzetta, "The Italians of New York City," p. 152.

68. Italian involvement in the labor movement is discussed at length in Chapter 8. For the attitude of northern Italians toward southerners, see Pozzetta, "The Italians of New York City," pp. 127–128.

69. Pozzetta, "The Italians of New York City," pp. 194, 199, 209, 217 ff.

70. Higham, *Strangers in the Land*, p. 187.

71. Simon, *Public Opinion*, pp. 211–223.

72. Simon, *Public Opinion*, pp. 13–14; Higham, *Strangers in the Land*, pp. 301–303. The 150,000 limit was finally put into effect in 1929.

73. U.S. Department of Commerce, Bureau of the Census, *Historical Statistics of the United States: Colonial Times to 1970* (Washington, D.C., 1975), pp. 105–106. Calculations of the number of Italians and Germans were done by the author.

Part II. The Adjustment of the Italians in Buenos Aires and New York City

1. See Introduction.

Chapter 4. Fare l'America

1. The Italians who went to Argentina as well as those who went to the United States referred to their respective destinations as America. The term *fare l'America* therefore means making it in the New World.

2. Herbert S. Klein, in "The Integration of Italian Immigrants into the United States and Argentina: A Comparative Analysis," *American Historical Review* 88, 2 (April 1983), pp. 306–339, offers an insightful and suggestive comparative analysis of Italian economic strategies and economic integration in the two countries that is relevant to Buenos Aires and New York City.

3. Argentina, *Censo 1895*, 2, pp. 47–50, and 3, pp. 272–273; Argentina, *Censo 1914*, 4, pp. 201–212.

4. Thomas Kessner, *The Golden Door: Italian and Jewish Immigrant Mobility in New York City, 1880–1915* (New York, 1977), p. 67.

5. Carlos F. Díaz Alejandro, *Essays on the Economic History of the Argentine Republic* (New Haven, 1970), p. 22; and Roberto Cortés Conde, *El progreso argentino, 1880–1914* (Buenos Aires, 1979), pp. 204–209. For an incisive analysis of the labor market in the preceding period, see Hilda Sábato and Luis Alberto Romero, *Los trabajadores de Buenos Aires: La experience del mercado, 1850–1880* (Buenos Aires, 1992).

6. Melvyn Dubofsky, *When Workers Organize: New York City in the Progressive Era* (Amherst, Mass., 1968), pp. 7–10; and Edwin Fenton, *Immigrants and Unions— A Case Study: Italians and American Labor, 1870–1920* (New York, 1975), pp. 378–379.

7. Dubofsky, *When Workers Organize*, pp. 1–5; Fenton, *Immigrants and Unions*, pp. 342–356.

8. James R. Scobie, "Buenos Aires as a Commercial- Bureaucratic City, 1880–1910: Characteristics of a City's Orientation," *American Historical Review*, 77, 4 (October 1972), pp. 1035–1073; Robert E. Shipley, "On the Outside Looking In: A Social History of the *Porteño* Worker during the 'Golden Age' of Argentine Development, 1914–1930" (Ph.D. dissertation, Rutgers University, 1977), p. 40.

9. Shipley, "On the Outside," pp. 52–56.

10. For New York, see Fenton, "Immigrants and Unions"; George E. Pozzetta, "The Italians of New York City, 1890–1914" (Ph.D. dissertation, University of North Carolina, 1971), pp. 320–329; John Koren, "The Padrone System and the Padrone Banks," U.S. Department of Labor, *Bulletin*, 9 (March 1897), pp. 113–129; and Louise C. Odencrantz, *Italian Women in Industry: A Study of Conditions in New*

York City (New York, 1919). For Buenos Aires, see Shipley, "On the Outside," pp. 66–69.

11. Koren, "The Padrone System," pp. 120–123; Wayne Moquin and Charles Van Doren, eds., *A Documentary History of the Italian Americans* (New York, 1974), pp. 99–110; and Pozzetta, "The Italians of New York City," pp. 320–329.

12. Odencrantz, *Italian Women*, pp. 272, 315.

13. Shipley, "On the Outside," p. 67.

14. Samuel L. Baily, "The Village Outward Approach to the Study of Social Networks: A Case Study of the Agnonesi Diaspora Abroad, 1885–1989," *Studi Emigrazione*, 29, 105 (March 1992), pp. 43–68, esp. pp. 55–56; and Romolo Gandolfo, "Notas sobre la elite de una comunidad emigrada en cadena: El caso de los Agnoneses," in Fernando J. Devoto and Gianfausto Rosoli, eds., *L'Italia nella società Argentina* (Rome, 1988), pp. 160–177.

15. Shipley, "On the Outside," pp. 67–69, 73.

16. Fernando J. Devoto, "Las cadenas migratorias italianas: Algunas reflexiones a la luz del caso argentino," *Studi Emigrazione*, 24, 87 (October 1987), pp. 355–373, esp. pp. 368–370. For a discussion of the relative permanence of the two Italian populations, see Chapter 2 of this book.

17. Kessner, *The Golden Door*, p. 52; U.S. Bureau of the Census, *Special Reports: Occupations at the Twelfth Census* (Washington, D.C., 1904), pp. 634–640. See also Klein, "The Integration of Italian Immigrants," pp. 313–317.

18. U.S. Bureau of the Census, *Special Reports: Occupations*, pp. 634–640. See also Robert F. Foerster, *The Italian Emigration of Our Times* (New York, 1919), pp. 342–354.

19. Fenton, *Immigrants and Unions*, pp. 342ff; and John J. D'Alesandre, "Occupational Trends of Italians in New York City," *Bulletin*, No. 8 (Casa Italiana Education Bureau, New York, 1935), pp. 160–169. See also Kessner, *The Golden Door*, pp. 52–59.

20. Miriam J. Cohen, *Workshop to Office: Two Generations of Italian Women in New York City, 1900–1950* (Ithaca, N.Y., 1992), pp. 39–59; Odencrantz, *Italian Women*, pp. 31–53; and Mary Van Kleeck, *Artificial Flower Makers* (New York, 1913). See also Kessner, *The Golden Door*, pp. 71–75.

21. Buenos Aires, *Censo 1887*, 2, pp. 35–36, 306, 379.

22. Estimates based on data in Buenos Aires, *Censo 1910*, 1, pp. 132, 135, 150, 155.

23. Kessner, *The Golden Door*, p. 52; Fenton, *Immigrants and Unions*, pp. 252 ff.; and my Buenos Aires six-district sample (see Appendix, section 3, and Table 45). Gutman's data on 4,169 Italian males in Greenwich Village in 1905 differ to some extent from Kessner's figures. See Herbert G. Gutman, *The Black Family in Slavery and Freedom, 1750–1925* (New York, 1976), p. 529. I have used Kessner's figures because they are based on a broader sample of Italians (Lower Manhattan, Harlem, and Brooklyn, and women as well as men).

24. For the United States, see Paul H. Douglas, *Real Wages in the United States, 1890–1926* (New York, 1966); Clarence D. Long, *Wages and Earnings in the United States, 1860–1890* (Princeton, N.J., 1960), pp. 109–118; Albert Rees, *Real Wages in Manufacturing, 1890–1914* (Princeton, N.J., 1961), pp. 120–117; and Dubofsky, *When*

Workers Organize, pp. 11–14. For Buenos Aires, see Cortés Conde, *El progreso argentino, 1880–1914,* pp. 211–240; Shipley, "On the Outside," pp. 123–200; and John Williams, *Argentine International Trade Under Inconvertible Paper Money* (Cambridge, Mass., 1920), pp. 189–196. For a comparison of the two countries, see Klein, "The Integration of Italian Immigrants."

25. Shergold, in his outstanding comparative study of the standard of living in Pittsburgh, Pennsylvania, and Birmingham, England, warns against the "statistical illusion" created by aggregate data on real wages. See Peter Shergold, *Working-Class Life: The "American Standard" in Comparative Perspective, 1899–1913* (Pittsburgh, 1982), p. 228.

26. U.S. Bureau of Labor Statistics, *Bulletin,* #131 (August 15, 1913), p. 50. *Bulletin,* #404 (March 1926), pp. 37–40, presents the data from 1907–1925.

27. U.S. Immigration Commission, *Reports,* 26, p. 225.

28. Argentina, Departamento Nacional del Trabajo, *Boletín,* #5 (June 30, 1908), pp. 245–251.

29. Shipley, "On the Outside," pp. 57–59, 132–137.

30. Dubofsky, *When Workers Organize,* p. 13.

31. U.S. Bureau of Labor Statistics, *Bulletin,* #172 (April 1915), p. 8.

32. U.S. Bureau of Labor Statistics, *Bulletin,* #146 (April 28, 1914), p. 18.

33. Díaz Alejandro, *Essays,* p. 27.

34. Shipley, "On the Outside," pp. 69–77. See also Aldo Ferrer, *The Argentine Economy* (Berkeley, 1967), p. 116.

35. Cortés Conde, *El progreso argentino,* p. 197.

36. See Table 35 and U.S. Immigration Commission, *Reports,* 26, pp. 201–204, 231–232.

37. See Table 37 and Shipley, "On the Outside," pp. 48–57.

38. For New York, see Robert C. Chapin, *The Standard of Living among Workingmen's Families in New York City* (New York, 1909); Louise B. More, *Wage Earners' Budgets* (New York, 1907, reprinted 1971); Odencrantz, *Italian Women,* pp. 161–216; State of New York, *Fourth Report of the Factory Investigating Commission* (Albany, N.Y., 1915), 4, pp. 1625–1668, 1785–1812; and U.S. Immigration Commission, *Reports,* 26, pp. 215–234. For Buenos Aires, see Cortés Conde, *El progreso argentino,* pp. 217–239, and Shipley, "On the Outside," pp. 173–200.

39. Chapin, *Standard of Living,* pp. 245–250; State of New York, *Fourth Report of the Factory Investigating Commission,* 4, pp. 1608–1609, 1619–1620, 1668.

40. U.S. Immigration Commission, *Reports,* 26, p. 226.

41. The only other work that provides these kinds of figures is More, *Wage Earners' Budgets,* p. 108. More studied only fifteen Italian families and found that 53 percent had balanced budgets, 20 percent had a surplus, and 27 percent had a deficit.

42. Chapin, *Standard of Living,* p. 240.

43. Chapin, *Standard of Living,* pp. 245–250.

44. The two most important of these surveys for our purposes were published in Departamento Nacional del Trabajo, *Boletín,* 30 (April 1915), pp. 130–135; and 33 (January 1916), pp. 203–211.

45. Baer shows that although rent fluctuated as a percentage of the budget, unskilled workers on the average spent approximately twice as much of their budget

on housing as did skilled workers. See James A. Baer, "Tenant Contention and the 1907 Rent Strike in Buenos Aires" (Ph.D. dissertation, Rutgers University, 1989), p. 37.

46. Shipley, "On the Outside," pp. 173–200.

47. Departamento Nacional del Trabajo, Boletín, 21 (November 30, 1912), pp. 305, 308.

48. Departamento Nacional del Trabajo, Boletín, 21, pp. 305–306, 308.

49. Klein has postulated the existence of the short-term strategy for Italians in the United States, but is less clear about the long-term strategy for Italians in Argentina. My focus just on the major urban centers of New York City and Buenos Aires has enabled me to develop the distinctions between the two strategies more clearly. See Klein, "The Integration of Italian Immigrants," pp. 306–346 and esp. p. 319.

50. Stephen Thernstrom, *The Other Bostonians: Poverty and Progress in the American Metropolis, 1880–1970* (Cambridge, Mass., 1973). See also Kessner, *The Golden Door*, p. 195, note 12.

51. Kessner, *The Golden Door*, pp. 52, 179–180.

52. Kessner, *The Golden Door*, pp. 114, 11–119.

53. Dubofsky, *Industrialism*, p. 13.

54. Argentina, *Censo 1895*, 2, pp. 47–50; 3, pp. 272–273; and Argentina, *Censo 1914*, 4, pp. 201–212.

55. Gustavo Beyhaut et al., "Los inmigrantes en el sistema ocupacional argentino," in Torcuato S. Di Tella et al., *Argentina, sociedad de masas* (Buenos Aires, 1966), pp. 85–123, esp. pp. 119–122; Foerster, *The Italian Emigration*, pp. 254–259; and Klein, "The Integration of Italian Immigrants," p. 321.

56. Figures calculated on the basis of the data cited in the previous note.

57. Buenos Aires, *Censo 1887*, 2, pp. 306, 379; and Buenos Aires, *Censo 1909*, 1, pp. 132, 135, 150, 155. Shipley notes the difficulty of determining occupational mobility, but nevertheless concludes that it was exceptional rather than the norm. His focus, however, is on the post-1914 period, during which such mobility declined compared to the preceding decades. See Shipley, "On the Outside," pp. 201–228. See also the classic earlier work of Gino Germani, *Estructura social de la Argentina: Análisis estadístico* (Buenos Aires, 1955), pp. 218–225.

58. The figures on Italian ownership of property of all types indicate the same trends as the data on home ownership. They are less reliable, however, because they include ownership of property anywhere in the world—and are less useful because the Census of 1887 does not include comparable data. See Buenos Aires, *Censo 1904*, pp. xcvi–xcvii, 89; Buenos Aires, *Censo 1909*, pp. lv–lvi, 101.

59. See Chapter 8 for the supporting data on the mutual aid societies.

60. Luigi de Rosa points out the importance of banks in Argentina—the Banco de Italia y Rio de la Plata (1872), the Nuevo Banco Italiano (1887), the Banco di Roma y Rio de la Plata (1889)—as a way for immigrants to send money back to Italy. See Luigi de Rosa, *Emigranti, capitali, e banche (1896–1906)* (Naples, 1980), pp. 217–232; and Luigi de Rosa, "Emigrantes Italianos, bancos y remesas; El caso argentino," in Fernando J. Devoto and Gianfausto Rosoli, eds., *La inmigración italiana en la Argentina* (Buenos Aires, 1985), pp. 241–270.

Chapter 5. Residence Patterns and Residential Mobility

1. This chapter is a substantially revised and expanded version of "Patrones de residencia de los Italianos en Buenos Aires y Nueva York: 1880–1914," *Estudios Migratorios Latinoamericanos*, 1 (December 1985), pp. 8–47.

2. Robert Park and Herbert Miller indicate areas and blocks where the Cinesi and several other village groups resided in New York, but they do not provide the addresses where individuals in these groups actually lived. See Robert E. Park and Herbert A. Miller, *Old World Traits Transplanted* (New York, 1921), pp. 146–158.

3. On the possibilities and problems of using nominal sources to study international migration, see *Estudios Migratorios Latinoamericanos*, 32 and 33 (August and December 1996). These issues are devoted completely to the subject.

4. For the complete data by census district, see Samuel L. Baily, "Las sociedades de ayuda mutua y el desarrollo de una comunidad italiana en Buenos Aires, 1858–1918," *Desarrollo Económico*, 21, 84 (January-March 1982), p. 502, table 8.

5. In 1898, New York City—which until that time had comprised only Manhattan and part of the Bronx—incorporated its neighboring counties to assume its current form: Manhattan, Brooklyn (King's County), Queens (Queens County), Richmond (Staten Island), and the Bronx. Thus, the pre- and post-1900 figures used in this chapter refer to different geographical boundaries of the city.

6. I have included in the text only a few representative examples of provincial clustering to illustrate the general pattern.

7. Buenos Aires, *Censo 1904*, pp. xxxi, 84; and Nora Pagano and Mario Oporto, "La conducta endogámica de los grupos inmigrantes: Pautas matrimoniales de los Italianos en el barrio de La Boca en 1895," in Fernando J. Devoto and Gianfausto Rosoli, eds., *L'Italia nella società Argentina* (Rome, 1988), pp. 90–101.

8. Antonio J. Bucich, *La Boca del Riachuelo en la historia* (Buenos Aires, 1971); Fernando J. Devoto, "The Origins of an Italian Neighborhood in Buenos Aires in the Mid 19th Century," *Journal of European Economic History*, 18, 1 (Spring 1989), pp. 37–64; and Ruben Granara and Lorenzo Ferro, long-time Boca residents, interviews with Samuel L. Baily (Buenos Aires, 10/28/1979 and 10/31/1979).

9. Samuel L. Baily, "Chain Migration of Italians to Argentina: Case Studies of the Agnonesi and the Sirolesi," *Studi Emigrazione*, 19, 65 (March 1982), pp. 83–88.

10. In addition to migration networks, the length of residence, the size of the migration from a village, and the settlement patterns in these villages were all important determinants of clusters in Buenos Aires and New York City. The greater the length of residence and the larger the number of immigrants from a specific village, the more likely the immigrants were to disperse and to form multiple clusters.

11. As I did with Buenos Aires, I have chosen a few representative examples to show the patterns of village and provincial clustering. There is little doubt that most Italian immigrants lived in village clusters, but exactly what percentage of the total Italian population did so is difficult to determine.

12. These estimates are based on Table 10 and other data presented in Chapter 2.

13. Thomas Kessner, *The Golden Door: Italian and Jewish Immigrant Mobility in New York City, 1880–1915* (New York, 1977), pp. 142–143, 153.

14. It is important to emphasize that my sample is confined to Manhattan and

does not include data on the other four boroughs of New York City. Thus it is possible that I have underestimated such outward movement. Yet the published census data include all Italians in New York City, and they clearly indicate that movement out of Manhattan to the other four boroughs of the city was, with the exception of Brooklyn, limited until after World War I.

15. Edward E. Pratt, *Industrial Causes of Congestion of Population in New York* (New York, 1911), esp. Table V and VI following p. 241. See also Donna Gabaccia, *From Sicily to Elizabeth Street: Housing and Social Change among Italian Immigrants, 1880– 1930* (Albany, N.Y., 1984), pp. 83–85, 98–99; and Kessner, *The Golden Door*, p. 150.

16. James R. Scobie, *Buenos Aires: Plaza to Suburb, 1870–1910* (New York, 1974), pp. 196–197; and Charles S. Sargent, *The Spatial Evolution of Greater Buenos Aires, Argentina, 1870–1930* (Tempe, Ariz., 1974), pp. 51–55, 153. Other useful works include Robert F. Foerster, "The Italian Factor in the Race Stock of Argentina," *Quarterly Publications of the American Statistical Association*, 16 (1919), pp. 347–360; Guy Bourde, *Urbanisation et immigration en Amerique Latine, Buenos Aires XIX et XX siecles* (Paris, 1974); Francis Korn, ed., *Los Italianos en la Argentina* (Buenos Aires, 1983); Leandro Gutierrez, "Condiciones de la vida material de los sectores populares en Buenos Aires: 1880–1914," *Revista de Indias* (January-June 1981), pp. 167– 202; and Eugenia Scarzanella, *Italiani d'Argentina, Storie di contadini, industriali e missionari italiani in Argentina, 1850–1912* (Venice, 1983).

17. James A. Baer, "Tenant Contention and the 1907 Rent Strike in Buenos Aires" (Ph.D. dissertation, Rutgers University, 1989), pp. 20–41, 59–83; Scobie, *Buenos Aires*, pp. 146 ff.; Sargent, *Greater Buenos Aires*, pp. 29 ff.; Kessner, *The Golden Door*, pp. 132 ff.; and City of New York, Tenement House Department, *First Report* (New York, 1903).

18. Sargent, *Greater Buenos Aires*, p. 78; Scobie, *Buenos Aires*, 182–191.

19. Sargent, *Greater Buenos Aires*, p. 82; Kessner, *The Golden Door*, p. 52.

20. Charles W. Cheape, *Moving the Masses: Urban Public Transportation in New York, Boston and Philadelphia, 1880–1912* (Cambridge, Mass., 1980), pp. 20–101; and David C. Hammack, *Power and Society: Greater New York at the Turn of the Century* (New York, 1987), pp. 230–258.

21. Sargent, *Greater Buenos Aires*, p. 69; Scobie, *Buenos Aires*, pp. 160–178.

22. Alfredo Canuti, interview with Samuel L. Baily (Numana, 5/12/1980); Lorenzo Ferro, interview with Samuel L. Baily (Buenos Aires, 10/31/1979); Park and Miller, *Old World Traits*, pp. 146–158.

Chapter 6. Family, Household, and Neighborhood

1. Peter Laslett, one of the pioneers in European family history, equates the family with the household. Kertzer, Bell, and Gabaccia—all of whom focus on the Italian family—distinguish between the family and the household. See Peter Laslett, "Introduction: The History of the Family," in Peter Laslett, ed., *Household and Family in Past Time* (Cambridge, 1972), esp. pp. 23–32; Peter Laslett, "Family and Household as Work Group and Kin Group: Areas of Traditional Europe Compared," in Richard Wall, Jean Robin, and Peter Laslett, eds., *Family Forms in Historic Europe* (Cambridge, 1983), pp. 513–563; David I. Kertzer, "Household History and Sociological Theory," *Annual Review of Sociology*, 17 (1991), pp. 158–159;

Rudolph M. Bell, *Fate and Honor: Family and Village, Demographic and Cultural Change in Rural Italy since 1800* (Chicago, 1979), pp. 72–77, 108–111; Donna Gabaccia, "Sicilians in Space: Environmental Change and Family Geography," *Journal of Social History*, 16, 2 (Winter 1982), pp. 53–66, esp. p. 54; Donna Gabaccia, "Kinship, Culture, and Migration: A Sicilian Example," *Journal of American Ethnic History* (Spring 1984), pp. 39–53, esp. p. 41; and Donna Gabaccia, *From Sicily to Elizabeth Street: Housing and Social Change among Italian Immigrants, 1880–1930* (Albany, N.Y., 1984), pp. 4–5.

2. For an excellent overview of these changes in interpretations and definitions see Kertzer, "Household History," pp. 155–179. See also Bell, *Fate and Honor*, pp. 72–77, 108–111; Glen H. Elder Jr., "History and the Family: The Discovery of Complexity," *Journal of Marriage and the Family*, 43 (August 1981), pp. 489–519; Gabaccia, "Sicilians in Space"; Gabaccia, "Kinship, Culture, and Migration"; Tamara K. Hareven, "The History of the Family and the Complexity of Social Change," *American Historical Review*, 96, 1 (February 1991), pp. 95–124; and Lawrence Stone, "Family History in the 1980s," *Journal of Interdisciplinary History*, 12, 1 (Summer 1981), pp. 51–87. In addition, see the seminal collection of recent scholarship by historians and anthropologists of the Italian family brought together in David I. Kertzer and Richard P. Saller, eds., *The Family in Italy from Antiquity to the Present* (New Haven, 1991), esp. the introductory essay, "Historical and Anthropological Perspectives on Italian Family Life."

3. These ideas originated in the earlier work of Laslett and Banfield. See Laslett, *Household and Family*; and Edward C. Banfield, *The Moral Basis of a Backward Society* (New York, 1958).

4. See Kertzer and Saller, *The Family in Italy*, pp. 1–19.

5. Kertzer and Saller, *The Family in Italy*, pp. 4–5.

6. Marzio Barbagli, "Three Household Formation Systems in Eighteenth- and Nineteenth-Century Italy," in Kertzer and Saller, *The Family in Italy*, pp. 250–270.

7. William A. Douglass, "The Joint-Family Household in Eighteenth-Century Southern Italian History," in Kertzer and Saller, *The Family in Italy*, pp. 287–303.

8. This and the following paragraph are based on Pino Arlacchi, *Mafia, Peasants, and Great Estates: Society in Traditional Calabria* (New York, 1983), pp. 23–35, 99–105, 186–191; Bell, *Fate and Honor*, pp. 67–112 and esp. 72–77; Gabaccia, "Kinship, Culture, and Migration," pp. 39–43; Sarah F. Harbison, "Family Structure and Family Strategy in Migration Decision Making," in Gordon F. De Jong and Robert W. Gardner, eds., *Migration Decision Making, Multidisciplinary Approaches to Microlevel Studies in Developed and Developing Countries* (New York, 1981), pp. 238–245; Virginia Yans-McLaughlin, "A Flexible Tradition: Southern Italian Immigrants Confront a New Work Experience," *Journal of Social History*, 7, 4 (1974), pp. 434–437; and Virginia Yans-McLaughlin, *Family and Community: Italian Immigrants in Buffalo, 1880–1930* (Urbana, Ill., 1982), pp. 83–85.

9. There are no figures available for the 1900 to 1914 period. The closest figures are those of 1939, which show 30 percent of the workforce in the Center, 20 percent in the North, 18 percent in the South, and 2 percent in Sicily. See Arlacchi, *Mafia*, p. 26.

10. Gabaccia, "Sicilians in Space," pp. 53–57; Gabaccia, "Kinship, Culture, and Migration," pp. 39–40; Gabaccia, *From Sicily to Elizabeth Street*, pp. xv–xxi; Donna

Gabaccia, "Italian Immigrant Women in Comparative Perspective," *Altreitalie*, 9 (January-June 1993), pp. 163–175; Yans-McLaughlin, "A Flexible Tradition"; Yans-McLaughlin, *Family and Community;* Virginia Yans- McLaughlin, "Comment on Donna Gabaccia Paper," *Altreitalie*, 9 (January-June 1993), pp. 180–183. See also Judith Smith, *Family Connections: A History of Italian and Jewish Immigrant Lives in Providence, Rhode Island, 1900–1940* (Albany, N.Y., 1985).

11. Massey and others who are able to use interviews and surveys have documented these points. Their work is suggestive for those of us working on historical migrations, which preclude the use of such sources. See Douglas S. Massey et al., *Return to Aztlan: The Social Process of International Migration from Western Mexico* (Berkeley, 1987), pp. 139–147, 172–173, 197–205.

12. For the specific data that support each of these points, see Tables 12, 13, 9, 10, 29, and 30.

13. My sample of two blocks on Elizabeth Street in 1900 shows that 73 percent of the adult Italians were married, 23 percent single, and 4 percent widowed. The data come from the manuscript federal census of 1900 and include all 246 Italian-headed households (1,235 individuals) on Elizabeth Street between Broome and Spring Streets in lower Manhattan.

14. These figures were developed from my six-district sample of the 1895 Argentine census. The percentage of married Italians living with spouses was as follows: District 3, 78 percent; District 5, 82 percent; District 15, 88 percent.

15. Ninety-four percent lived with their spouse. Baily, Elizabeth Street sample (1900); and Gutman, Greenwich Village sample (1905).

16. A lot of work has been done on marriage in Buenos Aires and other cities and towns in Argentina. For citations to this material see Samuel L. Baily, "Marriage Patterns and Immigrant Assimilation in Buenos Aires, 1882–1923," *Hispanic American Historical Review*, 60, 1 (February 1980), pp. 32–48; Eduardo Miguez et al., "Hasta que la Argentina nos una: Reconsiderando las pautas matrimonialies de los inmigrantes, el crisol de razas y el pluralismo cultural," *Hispanic American Historical Review*, 71, 4 (1991), pp. 781–808; and Carina Silberstein, "Inmigración y selección matrimonial: El caso de los Italianos en Rosario (1870–1910), *Estudios Migratorios Latinoamericanos*, 6, 18 (1991), pp. 161–190.

17. The figures on endogamous marriages among the Italians in Buenos Aires were even higher if we take into account "hidden endogamy." "Hidden endogamy" refers to marriage between an Italian male and a second-generation Italian female, or to marriage between two Argentines both of whose parents were Italians. For example, Foerster points out, "The conclusion seems appropriate that in Italo-Argentine marriages the bride is the native daughter of an Italian." See Robert F. Foerster, "The Italian Factor in the Race Stock of Argentina," *Quarterly Publications of the American Statistical Association*, 16 (1919), pp. 347–360, esp. p. 357. For further discussion of this issue see Baily, "Marriage Patterns"; Miguez et al., "Hasta que la Argentina nos una"; and Nora Pagano and Mario Oporto, "La conducta endogámica de los grupos inmigrantes: Pautas matrimoniales de los Italianos en el barrio de La Boca en 1895," in Fernando J. Devoto and Gianfausto Rosoli, eds., *L'Italia nella società Argentina* (Rome, 1988), pp. 90–101.

18. I present the New York data in text description because they do not lend themselves to tabular format. See Ira Rosenwaike, *Population History of New York*

City (Syracuse, N.Y., 1972), p. 118; and Niles Carpenter, *Immigrants and Their Children* (New York, 1969), pp. 234-235. Miriam Cohen notes that the endogamy rate among Italian men in New York City between 1908 and 1912 was 99 percent. See Miriam J. Cohen, *Workshop to Office: Two Generations of Italian Women in New York City, 1900–1950* (Ithaca, N.Y., 1992), p. 93, note 14.

19. It is clear that Italian women were having a disproportionately large percentage of the babies in Buenos Aires. This high birth rate is in part explained by the fact that during the mass migration years a disproportionately large percentage of the women who traveled were in the child-bearing age category. For our purposes what is important is the absolute number of children born to Italian mothers, not the rates of fecundity.

20. There are no data on the number of second-generation Italians in Buenos Aires; the government and the census takers defined them as Argentines. On the basis of a careful study of Italian and Argentine marriage data, however, it is clear to me that this number was substantial. See Baily, "Marriage Patterns."

21. Rosenwaike, *Population History of New York City*, p. 203. Miriam Cohen presents additional data to document the relatively high number of births among Italian women in New York in *Workshop to Office*, pp. 89–90. See also John W. Briggs's insightful article, "Fertility and Cultural Change among Families in Italy and America," *American Historical Review*, 91, 5 (December 1986), pp. 1129–1145. As with the Italian women in Buenos Aires, what is important to us is the absolute number of births to Italian women in New York rather than their rates of fecundity.

22. Scholars who have studied the subject disagree on the exact nature and extent of the changes in the family brought about during the migration process. Among the more important contributions to this debate over the last two decades have been *Journal of Social History* 7, 4 (1974), pp. 429–452, with Yans- McLaughlin's seminal article, "A Flexible Tradition,", and comments on that article by Alice Kessler-Harris and Charles Tilly; Cohen, *Workshop to Office*; Gabaccia, "Kinship, Culture, and Migration"; Smith, *Family Connections*; Micaela di Leonardi, *The Varieties of Ethnic Experiences* (Ithaca, N.Y., 1984); Elizabeth Ewen, *Immigrant Women in the Land of Dollars: Life and Culture on the Lower East Side, 1890–1925* (New York, 1985); and *Altreitalie*, 9 (January-June 1993), pp. 163–183, with Gabaccia's article "Italian Immigrant Women in Comparative Perspective" and Yans-McLaughlin's comments on that article.

23. John Modell and Tamara Hareven, "Urbanization and the Malleable Household: An Examination of Boarding and Lodging in American Families," *Journal of Marriage and the Family*, 35 (1973), pp. 467–479. Many authors document the existence of the malleable household in different places. See, for example, Yans-McLaughlin, *Family and Community*; Smith, *Family Connections*; Gabaccia, *From Sicily to Elizabeth Street*, and esp. "Sicilians in Space."

24. Gabaccia, "Sicilians in Space," pp. 54, 57–58.

25. The problem, as mentioned earlier, is that the Argentine manuscript census of 1895 did not specify the relationship of family members to each other, and the census takers infrequently and inconsistently indicated where new families and households began and old ones ended.

26. Maria Cristina Cacopardo and José Luis Moreno, *La familia italiana y meridional en la emigración a la Argentina* (Naples, 1994), pp. 11–15, 62–65.

27. My analysis of this sample compared to samples of Italians in six other districts of Buenos Aires indicates that the District 15 Italian households were of a somewhat higher occupational status than the others but similar in other respects. The percentage of extended families therefore was higher in this district than among all Italian families in Buenos Aires. Thus I have reduced the District 15 percentage of extended households by 15 percent to 17 percent and increased the number of nuclear households by the same amount. For the supporting data of this argument, see the Appendix.

28. I am not suggesting that a quarter of the Italian households in Buenos Aires included servants as was the case in the District 15 sample. But the District 15 figures alert us to the fact that some Italian households throughout the city did. Some of these households used servants to take care of boarders.

29. Arlacchi, *Mafia*, pp. 28–30; Ewen, *Immigrant Women*, pp. 14–16, 31–7, 101–104; Louise C. Odencrantz, *Italian Women in Industry: A Study of Conditions in New York City* (New York, 1919), pp. 15–21; Smith, *Family Connections*, p. 23.

30. See Chapter 4.

31. Odencrantz documents the importance of Italian women working outside the household for wages in New York City in 1912–1913. Her focus is on single women, but she also shows that 24 percent of the mothers in her 544 families worked outside the home. Odencrantz, *Italian Women*, pp. 16, 21. See also Ewen, *Immigrant Women*, pp. 24–27; and Robert E. Shipley, "On the Outside Looking In: A Social History of the *Porteno* Worker during the 'Golden Age' of Argentine Development, 1914–1930" (Ph.D. dissertation, Rutgers University, 1977). On the importance of women's roles in the contemporary immigrant family, see the insightful article of sociologist Silvia Pedraza, "Women and Migration: The Social Consequences of Gender," *Annual Review of Sociology*, 17 (1991), pp. 303–325 and esp. pp. 313–321.

32. Ewen, *Immigrant Women*, pp. 63–65, 100–102.

33. Some of the thinking that has most influenced my understanding of neighborhood can be found in Caroline B. Brettell, "Is the Ethnic Community Inevitable? A Comparison of the Settlement Patterns of Portuguese Immigrants in Toronto and Paris," *Journal of Ethnic Studies*, 9, 3 (Fall 1981), pp. 1–17; Kathleen Neils Conzen, "Immigrants, Immigrant Neighborhoods, and Ethnic Identity: Historical Issues," *Journal of American History*, 66, 3 (December 1979), pp. 605–615; Gabaccia, "Sicilians in Space"; Gabaccia, *From Sicily to Elizabeth Street*, esp. chapters 1, 2, and 5; Robert F. Harney, "Ethnicity and Neighborhoods," in Robert F. Harney, ed., *Gathering Place: Peoples and Neighbourhoods of Toronto* (Toronto, 1985), pp. 1–24; Robert F. Harney and J. Vicenza Scarpaci, "Introduction" in Robert F. Harney and J. Vincenza Scarpaci, eds., *Little Italies in North America* (Toronto, 1981), pp. 1–6; James R. Scobie, *Buenos Aires: Plaza to Suburb, 1870–1910* (New York, 1974), pp. 201–207; and Rudolph J. Vecoli, "The Formation of Chicago's 'Little Italies,'" *Journal of American Ethnic History* (Spring 1983), pp. 5–20.

34. Scobie, *Buenos Aires*, p. 201.

35. Scobie, *Buenos Aires*, pp. 201–207; Ewen, *Immigrant Women*, esp. pp. 59–74 and 165–184.

36. Gabaccia, "Sicilians in Space," and *From Sicily to Elizabeth Street*, pp. 1–34, 65–85.

37. Scobie, *Buenos Aires*, p. 207.

38. Kathy L. Peiss, *Cheap Amusements: Working Women and Leisure in Turn-of-the-Century New York* (Philadelphia, 1986).

39. See Maps 3 and 6. See also, Pozzetta, "The Mulberry District."

40. See Table 26 and City of New York, Tenement House Department, *First Report* (New York, 1903).

41. The twelve individuals from Sciacca indicated on the map are ones I was able to identify from my sample of the naturalization records. They are indicative of the many others who lived in the area who were not naturalized, and therefore not listed in the naturalization records, or who were naturalized in years other than the ones I sampled.

42. For example, the mutual aid society Agrigento was located at 83 Elizabeth Street, an area of settlement for immigrants from this province of Sicily, and the mutual aid society Salerno at 387 Broome Street in the center of a similar provincial concentration. See Map 8.

43. Robert A. Orsi, *The Madonna of 115th Street: Faith and Community in Italian Harlem, 1880–1950* (New Haven and London, 1985). See pp. 14–49 for a succinct account of the history of Italian Harlem.

44. For the location of village- and province-of-origin- based groups, see Map 9.

45. Orsi, *The Madonna of 115th Street*, pp. 33–34, 45–46. The quotation is from p. 45.

46. Orsi, *The Madonna of 115th Street*, pp. 45, 51–56.

47. As was the case with the immigrants from Sciacca in the Mulberry District, the fourteen immigrants from Potenza indicated on the map are but a few of the many from the town who lived in the area.

48. There were 126 people per acre in forty blocks of District 5 of Buenos Aires in 1895 compared to 508 in the fifteen blocks of the Mulberry District and 337 for the nine blocks in East Harlem. Argentina, *Censo 1895*, 3, p. 3.

49. For a more detailed discussion of the Barrio del Carmen see Samuel L. Baily, "Chain Migration of Italians to Argentina: Case Studies of the Agnonesi and the Sirolesi," *Studi Emigrazione*, 19, 65 (March 1982); and Romolo Gandolfo, "Notas sobre la elite de una comunidad emigrada en cadena: El caso de los Agnoneses," in Fernando J. Devoto and Gianfausto Rosoli, eds., *L'Italia nella società Argentina* (Rome, 1988), pp. 160–177.

50. The addresses of the Agnonesi indicated on the map come from the records I have sampled of the mutual aid society Colonia Italiana. Because many Agnonesi were not members of the Colonia Italiana or joined it in years that I did not sample, the numbers indicated on the map are only a small part of the total Agnonese population in the area.

51. There is much excellent material on the history of the Boca. See, for example, Antonio J. Bucich, "La Boca como centro inmigratorio hasta promediar del siglo XIX," *Cuatro Congreso Internacional de Historia de America*, vol. 4 (Buenos Aires, 1966), pp. 41–51; Fernando J. Devoto, "The Origins of an Italian Neighborhood in Buenos Aires in the Mid 19th Century," *Journal of European Economic History*, 18, 1 (Spring 1989), pp. 37–64; Armando Dighero, *Historia de la Asociación Ligure de Socorros Mutuos en su centenario* (Buenos Aires, 1985); Pagano and Oporto, "La conducta endogámica"; Nelida Redondo, "La Boca: Evolución de un barrio étnico," *Es-*

tudios Migratorios Latinoamericanos, 3, 9 (August 1988), pp. 269–280; and *La Ribera*, June 2, 1984, Special issue: *Centenario bomberos voluntarios de la Boca*.

52. Ninety-four percent of all Boca Italians in the 1855 census were Ligurians, and 84 percent of the Boca Italians who joined the Unione e Benevolenza between 1858 and 1862 were Ligurians. See Devoto, "Origins of an Italian Neighborhood," pp. 46–48; Baily sample of mutual aid society members.

53. By 1904, the Boca was still 33 percent Italian born and a similar percentage was second-generation Italian. The percentage of Ligurians was smaller than in the mid-1850s, but Ligurians still were in many positions of leadership and exercised considerable influence in the community into the twentieth century. See Buenos Aires, *Censo 1904*, pp. xxxi, 84; Devoto, "The Origins of an Italian Neighborhood"; and Pagano and Oporto, "La conducta endogámica," pp. 90–101.

54. Lorenzo Ferro, age seventy-two, interview with Samuel L. Baily (taped), the Boca, 10/3/1979.

55. I have been able to identify the specific addresses of these individuals from the mutual aid society records, but there were many more individuals living in the Boca from each of these towns of origin who were not members of mutual aid societies or who joined them in years I did not sample.

56. Ferro, interview.

57. We have more information than is generally provided by the census of 1895 because in this case the census taker used a separate book to record the information on each of the sixteen two-story buildings in the 1400 block of Almirante Brown. Unfortunately this census taker did not indicate from where in Italy the many Italians came.

Chapter 7. Formal Institutions before the Mass Migration Era

1. It is important to keep in mind that, as Brettell demonstrates in her work, the development of a formal ethnic community is not inevitable. Instead, she argues, we must view community formation as a strategy appropriate in some situations and not in others. Caroline B. Brettell, "Is the Ethnic Community Inevitable? A Comparison of the Settlement Patterns of Portuguese Immigrants in Toronto and Paris," *Journal of Ethnic Studies*, 9, 3 (Fall 1981), pp. 1–17.

2. Raymond Breton argues in his pioneering 1964 article on immigrant communities in Montreal that the "institutional completeness" of the immigrant community is a major determinant of which community or communities an immigrant will participate in, and that an institutionally complete immigrant community will "have the effect of keeping the social relations of the immigrants within its boundaries." The idea of institutional completeness is very useful, but our focus here includes what the respective groups of institutions can do to help the immigrants adjust. See Raymond Breton, "Institutional Completeness of Ethnic Communities and the Personal Relations of Immigrants," *American Journal of Sociology*, 70, 2 (September 1964), pp. 193–205.

3. Jorge F. Sergi, *Historia de los Italianos en la Argentina* (Buenos Aires, 1940).

4. The original building was completed and opened in 1872. A larger building was later constructed on Calle Gascon and opened in 1901. Since then a number of additions have been built and the hospital remains in operation today. For the his-

tory of the early years of the hospital, see Società Italiana di Beneficenza, *La storia dell'Ospedale Italiano* (Buenos Aires, 1923).

5. The history of the Italian mutual aid societies during this period can be found in Samuel L. Baily, "Las sociedades de ayuda mutua y el desarrollo de una comunidad italiana en Buenos Aires, 1858–1918," *Desarrollo Económico*, 21, 84 (January-March, 1982); Ema Cibotti, "Mutualismo y política en un estudio de caso: La sociedad 'Unione e Benevolenza' en Buenos Aires entre 1858 y 1865," in Fernando J. Devoto and Gianfausto Rosoli, eds., *L'Italia nella società Argentina* (Rome, 1988), pp. 241–265; Fernando J. Devoto, "Participación y conflictos en las sociedades italianas de socorros mutuos," in Fernando J. Devoto and Gianfausto Rosoli, eds., *La inmigración italiana en la Argentina* (Buenos Aires, 1985), pp. 141–164; Fernando J. Devoto, "La primera elite política italiana de Buenos Aires (1852–1880), *Studi Emigrazione* 26, 94 (1989), pp. 168–193; and Emilio Zuccarini, *I lavori degli Italiani nell República Argentina* (Buenos Aires, 1910). Much of my analysis is based on the rich collection of mutual aid society documents (membership records, reports of the executive committees and general assemblies, and financial statements) housed in the archives of the Unione e Benevolenza (see Appendix).

6. These conflicts are set forth in detail in Cibotti, "Mutualismo y política," pp. 253–257.

7. The detailed history of this conflict can be found in Cibotti, "Mutualismo y política," pp. 258–263, and in Hilda Sábato and Ema Cibotti, "Hacer política en Buenos Aires: Los Italianos en la escena política porteña, 1860–1880," *Boletín del Instituto de Historia Argentina y Americana "Dr. E. Ravignani,"* Tercera Serie 2 (1st quarter of 1990), pp. 20–23.

8. Devoto, "La primera elite," p. 183.

9. Cibotti, "Mutualism y política," and Sábato and Cibotti, "Hacer política en Buenos Aires."

10. For a discussion of the political system, see Chapter 3.

11. *L'Operaio Italiano*, 2/4/1879, 4/27/1879, and 11/13/1879; Sábato and Cibotti, "Hacer política en Buenos Aires," pp. 32–34.

12. Niccolo Cuneo, *Storia dell'emigrazione italiana in Argentina 1810–1870* (Milan, 1940), pp. 92 ff., 140–166, 208–229, 253–262; Tulio Halperin-Donghi, *Proyecto y construcción de una nación: Argentina, 1846–1880* (Caracas, 1982), esp. the extensive introduction; and Tulio Halperin-Donghi, "Comments," *American Historical Review*, 88, 2 (April 1983), pp. 338–342.

13. *L'Operaio Italiano*, 1/26/1879, 4/17/1879.

14. For the history of the Italian-language newspapers in Argentina, see Samuel L. Baily, "The Role of Two Newspapers and the Assimilation of Italians in Buenos Aires and São Paulo, 1893–1913," *International Migration Review*, 12, 3 (1978), pp. 321–340; La Patria degli Italiani, *Gli Italiani nell'Argentina* (Buenos Aires, 1928); and Ema Cibotti, "Periodismo político y política periodística: La construcción pública de una opinión italiana en el Buenos Aires finisecular," *Entrepasados, Revista de Historia*, 4, 7 (1994), pp. 7–23.

15. Sábato and Cibotti, "Hacer política en Buenos Aires," p. 22.

16. In 1887, the circulation figures of the major dailies in Buenos Aires were as follows: *La Prensa* 18,000; *La Nación* 18,000; *El Diario* 12,500; *La Patria Italiana* 11,000; and *L'Operaio Italiano* 6,000. See Buenos Aires, *Censo 1887*, 2, pp. 545–546.

17. Banco de Italia y Rio de la Plata, *100 años al servicio del pais, 1872–1972* (Buenos Aires, 1972); La Patria degli Italiani, *Gli Italiani nell'Argentina*.

18. Baily, "Las sociedades de ayuda mutua," pp. 508–510; Cibotti, "Mutualismo y política," p. 253; Fernando J. Devoto and Alejandro Fernandez, "Asociacionismo, liderazgo y participacion en dos grupos étnicos en areas urbanas de la Argentina finisecular: Un enfoque comparado," in Fernando J. Devoto and Gianfausto Rosoli, eds., *L'Italia nella società Argentina* (Rome, 1988), pp. 190–208, esp. pp. 204–208.

19. Almost all top leaders of the mutual aid societies, and especially of the largest and wealthiest ones, were businessmen or professionals. Only rarely did a skilled worker penetrate their ranks. See Baily, "Las sociedades de ayuda mutua," p. 509.

20. Very little has been written on the Italian community of New York during the pre–mass migration period. Most of the information that does exist can be found in newspapers such as *L'Eco d'Italia* and, beginning in 1879, *Il Progresso Italo-Americano*, and in George E. Pozzetta, "The Mulberry District of New York City: The Years before World War One," in Robert F. Harney and J. Vincenza Scarpaci, eds., *Little Italies in North America* (Toronto, 1981), pp. 7–40; George E. Pozzetta, "The Italians of New York City, 1890–1914" (Ph.D. dissertation, University of North Carolina, 1971); Robert F. Foerster, *The Italian Emigration of Our Times* (New York, 1919); and George J. Manson, "The 'Foreign Element' in New York City. 5. The Italians," *Harper's Weekly* (October 18, 1890), supplement, pp. 817–820.

21. Humbert S. Nelli, *Italians in Chicago, 1880–1930: A Study in Ethnic Mobility* (New York, 1970), pp. 158–159; Robert Park, *The Immigrant Press and Its Control* (New York, 1922), pp. 297, 304, 317–319, 342–344; Pozzetta, "The Italians of New York City," pp. 237–239; and Manson, "The 'Foreign Element' in New York City," p. 820.

22. The precise content obviously changed daily. I have based this and the following paragraph on a detailed analysis of the paper for July, August, and September 1886.

23. *Il Progresso*, 9/8/1884, 7/7/1886.

24. *Il Progresso*, 7/7/1886.

25. *Il Progresso*, 7/7/1886, 7/15/1886.

26. Pozzetta, "The Italians of New York City," pp. 231–234.

27. *Il Progresso*, 7/7/1886, 7/16/1886, 7/23/1886, 8/27/1886, 7/20/1890, 1/29/1891. See also Pozzetta, "The Italians of New York City," pp. 326–327.

28. I have not been able to locate, if indeed they exist, the kind of data for New York mutual aid societies that I was fortunate to find for Buenos Aires. The membership and financial records and the reports of executive committee and assembly meetings of at least some of these societies must have existed at one time, but I have not been able to find out what happened to them. The best existing sources of information on the societies are the Italian-language newspapers. This information is generally limited to notices of meetings, accounts of the celebration of Italian holidays, and certain community projects. It does not give us much insight into the internal workings of these organizations or the composition of their leadership and membership.

29. Edwin Fenton, *Immigrants and Unions—A Case Study: Italians and American Labor, 1870–1920* (New York, 1975); "L'elemento italiano rappresentato nelle asso-

ciazione di New York, Brooklyn, Hoboken, e Newark, 1884," Archive of the Center for Migration Studies, New York. The net worth of a number of these societies can be found in Commissariato Generale dell'Emigrazione, *Bollettino dell'Emigrazione*, 24 (1908), pp. iii–x, 1–9, 116–119.

30. Evidence on the ties of mutual aid societies with job placement and the padrone system during this period is limited. One contemporary noted such ties among Philadelphia's Italians and, by implication at least, the existence of the same thing in New York. See John Koren, "The Padrone System and the Padrone Banks," U.S. Department of Labor, *Bulletin*, 9 (March 1897), pp. 113–129, esp. p. 123.

31. Consul Riva's efforts to establish the Italian Home are documented in his dispatches and letters. See, for example, Ministero degli Affari Esteri, Archivio Storico, Rappresentanze Diplomatiche Italiane negli Stati Uniti (1861–1901), busta 62, fasciocolo 18.

32. Antonio Mangano, "The Italian Colonies of New York City" (M.A. thesis, Columbia University, 1903), reprinted in *Italians in the City: Health and Related Social Needs* (New York, 1975).

33. Robert A. Orsi, *The Madonna of 115th Street: Faith and Community in Italian Harlem, 1880–1950* (New Haven and London, 1985), pp. 50–54; Pozzetta, "The Italians of New York City," pp. 267–304; and Silvano M. Tomasi, *Piety and Power: The Role of the Italian Parishes in the New York Metropolitan Area, 1880–1930* (New York, 1975), pp. 61–116.

34. Orsi, *The Madonna of 115th Street*, pp. xiv–xviii, 55–64; Pozzetta, "The Italians of New York City," pp. 267–272; and Rudolph J. Vecoli, "Prelates and Peasants: Italian Immigrants and the Catholic Church," *Journal of Social History*, 2, 3 (1969), pp. 246–247.

35. Tomasi, *Piety and Power*, pp. 248–251; Edward C. Stabili, "The St. Raphael Society for the Protection of Italian Immigrants, 1887–1923" (Ph.D. dissertation, Notre Dame University, 1977); Vecoli, "Prelates and Peasants," p. 253.

36. Pozzetta, "The Italians of New York City," pp. 275–276.

37. *Il Progresso*, 8/16/1886 and 9/3/1886; Fenton, *Immigrants and Unions*, pp. 158–161; Rudolph J. Vecoli, "The Italian Immigrants in the United States Labor Movement from 1880 to 1929," in B. Bezza, ed., *Gli Italiani fuori d'Italia: Gli emigrati italiani nei movimenti operai del paesi d'adozione 1880–1940* (Milan, 1983), p. 266; and Rudolph J. Vecoli, "Etnica, internazionalismo e protezionismo operaio: Gli immigrati italiani e I movimenti operai negli USA, 1880–1950," in V. Blengino, E. Franzina, and Adolfo Pepe, eds., *La riscoperta delle Americhe: Lavoratori e sindacato nell'emigrazione italiana in America Latina 1870–1970* (Milan, 1995), pp. 507–525.

Chapter 8. Formal Institutions during the Mass Migration Era

1. Samuel L. Baily, "Sarmiento and Immigration: Changing Views on the Role of the Immigrant in the Development of Argentina?" in Joseph T. Criscenti, ed., *Sarmiento and His Argentina* (Boulder, Colo., 1992), pp. 131–142.

2. *L'Operaio Italiano*, 1/11/1881, 1/12/1881, 1/15/1881, 1/20/1881; and L. Favero, "Las escuelas de las sociedades italianas en Argentina (1860–1914)," in Fernando J. Devoto and Gianfausto Rosoli, eds., *La inmigración italiana en la Argentina* (Buenos Aires, 1985), pp. 165–207.

3. Domingo F. Sarmiento, *Obras completas* (Buenos Aires, 1948–1956), 53 vols., 36, *Condición del extranjero en América*, p. 66.

4. My estimates are based on figures in Favero, "Las escuelas de las sociedades italianas," pp. 203–205; Buenos Aires, *Censo 1887*, 1, p. 34; Argentina, *Censo 1895*; and Hobart Spalding, "Education in Argentina, 1890–1914: The Limits of Oligarchical Reform," *Journal of Interdisciplinary History*, 3 (Summer 1972), pp. 31–61.

5. See previous note.

6. This pattern was established during the previous period, as is discussed in Chapter 7.

7. Samuel L. Baily, "The Role of Two Newspapers and the Assimilation of the Italians in Buenos Aires and São Paulo, 1893–1913," *International Migration Review*, 12, 3 (Fall 1978), pp. 321–340.

8. In 1889, Cittadini, the dynamic founder and director of *La Patria*, went back to Italy for several years, and the paper came under the control of others. He returned to Italian-language journalism in Buenos Aires in the early 1890s, but did not resume the directorship of *La Patria* until 1902. Cittadini then published the paper for a decade, and in 1912, after more than forty years in Argentina, returned permanently to Italy. *La Patria* continued publication until 1931.

9. For circulation figures on which these estimates are based, see *La Patria*, 1/14/1899, 4/5/1903, 5/21/1904, 6/19/1904, and 1/7/1910; Buenos Aires, *Censo 1904*, p. 209; Argentina, *Censo 1914*, 9, p. 276.

10. Humbert S. Nelli, *Italians in Chicago, 1880–1930: A Study in Ethnic Mobility* (New York, 1970), pp. 158, 169, 269, note 7.

11. *La Patria*, 11/25/1898, 10/17/1900, 1/28/1907, 12/7/1910.

12. *La Patria*, 3/20/1901, 9/12/1902, 1/27/1906, 2/26/1907. The Italian government did not increase funding for the schools. The mutual aid societies, forced to choose between continuing their traditional social and economic benefits and supporting the schools, chose to reduce the number of schools.

13. *La Patria*, 9/4/1902, 9/12/1902; La Patria degli Italiani, *Gli Italiani nell'Argentina* (Buenos Aires, 1928).

14. Luigi Favero, "Los Scalabrinianos y los emigrantes italianos en Sudamerica," *Estudios Migratorios Latinoamericanos*, 4, 12 (August 1989), pp. 231–255.

15. Fernando J. Devoto, "Participación y conflictos en las sociedades italianas de socorros mutuos," in Fernando J. Devoto and Gianfausto Rosoli, eds., *La inmigración italiana en la Argentina* (Buenos Aires, 1985), pp. 144–145; Favero, "Las escuelas de las sociedades italianas," p. 205; and Gianfausto Rosoli, "Las organizaciones católicas y la inmigración italiana en la Argentina," in Fernando J. Devoto and Gianfausto Rosoli, eds., *La inmigración italiana en la Argentina* (Buenos Aires, 1985), pp. 214–216.

16. Favero, "Los Scalabrinianos," pp. 249–250. The distinction between religion and the church is also made by Orsi in his study of the Italians of Harlem. See Robert A. Orsi, *The Madonna of 115th Street: Faith and Community in Italian Harlem, 1880–1950* (New Haven and London, 1985).

17. Natalio R. Botana, *El orden conservador: La política argentina entre 1880 y 1916* (Buenos Aires, 1977).

18. In 1904, Buenos Aires had 950,891 inhabitants, of whom only 8 percent were eligible to vote in elections. Less than half that number actually voted in the election of March 6, 1904. See Buenos Aires, *Censo 1904*, pp. xcvii–xcviii.

19. Gino Germani, *Política y sociedad en una época de transición: De la sociedad tradicional a la sociedad de masas* (Buenos Aires, 1962), p. 203.

20. This story is related in Romolo Gandolfo, "Notas sobre la elite de una comunidad emigrada en cadena: El caso de los Agnoneses," in Fernando J. Devoto and Gianfausto Rosoli, eds., *L'Italia nella società Argentina* (Rome, 1988), pp. 160–177. For another example of a failed effort of Italians to participate in politics see Romolo Gandolfo, "Inmigrantes y política en Argentina: La revolución de 1890 y la campana en favor de la naturalización automática de residentes extranjeros," *Estudios Migratorios Latinoamericanos*, 6, 17 (April 1991), pp. 23–54. See Chapter 6 for a more detailed account of the Agnonese community in the Barrio del Carmen.

21. Membership records of the Colonia Italiana. In a similar although not identical situation, Basilio Cittadini ran for the Municipal Council in November 1897 and lost. See *L'Operaio Italiano*, 11/15/1897, 11/16/1897, 11/26/1897, 11/29/1897, 11/30/1897.

22. Banco de Italia y Rio de la Plata, *100 años al servicio del pais, 1872–1972* (Buenos Aires, 1972), pp. 28–30; and Dionisio Petriella and Sara Sosa Miatello, *Diccionario biográfico italo- argentino* (Buenos Aires, 1976).

23. *La Patria*, 4/3/1912.

24. The figures are estimates based on data in Buenos Aires, *Censo 1904*, pp. 212–235; Argentina, Departamento Nacional del Trabajo, *Boletín*, #4–12 (1908–1909); Diego Abad de Santillán, *La FORA* (Buenos Aires, 1933); Martin S. Casaretto, *Historia del movimiento obrero argentino* (Buenos Aires, 1946); Sebastian Marotta, *Movimiento sindical argentino* (Buenos Aires, 1961), 3 vols.; and Jacinto Oddone, *Gremialismo proletario argentino* (Buenos Aires, 1949). See also Samuel L. Baily, "The Italians and Organized Labor in the United States and Argentina, 1880–1910," *International Migration Review*, 1, 3 (Summer 1967), pp. 55–66; and Samuel L. Baily, "The Italians and the Development of Organized Labor in Argentina, Brazil, and the United States, 1880–1914," *Journal of Social History*, 3, 2 (Winter 1969–1970), pp. 123–134.

25. The history of the labor movement can be found in the accounts of some of the key participants cited in the previous note. In addition, see Samuel L. Baily, *Labor, Nationalism, and Politics in Argentina* (New Brunswick, N.J., 1967); Charles Bergquist, *Labor in Latin America: Comparative Essays on Chile, Argentina, Venezuela, and Columbia* (Stanford, 1986), pp. 101–137; Roberto Falcón, *Los origines del movimiento obrero (1857–1899)* (Buenos Aires, 1984); Hobart Spalding, *La clase trabajadora argentina: Documentos para su historia, 1890–1912* (Buenos Aires, 1970).

26. Diego Abad de Santillán, *El movimiento anarquista en la Argentina: Desde sus comienzos hasta 1910* (Buenos Aires, 1930); Osvaldo Bayer, "L'influenza dell'immigrazione italiana nel movimento anarchico argentino," in B. Bezza, ed., *Gli Italiani fuori d'Italia: Gli emigrati italiani nei movmenti operai dei paesi d'adozione, 1880–1940* (Milan, 1983), pp. 531–549; Iaacov Oved, *El anarchismo en el movimiento obrero en Argentina* (Mexico, 1978); and Richard A. Yoast, "The Development of Argentine

Anarchism: A Socio-Ideological Analysis" (Ph.D. dissertation, University of Wisconsin, 1975).

27. These are estimates based on the works cited in note 24. About 25 percent of the workers in small industry and manual arts were organized, but an additional 25 percent—perhaps unwilling or unable to pay union dues and thus to be counted as members—nevertheless supported the FORA and the UGT during the important general strikes. After 1906, there was a decline in membership of the FORA and the UGT and an increase in the number of autonomous unions.

28. See sources cited in note 24, this chapter. On wages and hours, see Chapter 4.

29. Buenos Aires, *Censo 1904*, pp. 212–235.

30. On government repression, see Chapter 3.

31. Donna Gabaccia and Fraser Ottanelli talk about these competing loyalties in terms of diaspora and proletariat nationalism. See their stimulating paper "Diaspora or International Proletariat? Italian Labor Migration and the Making of Multi-Ethnic States, 1815–1939," delivered at the 18th International Congress of the International Commission of Historical Sciences, Montreal, Canada (August–September 1995), forthcoming in *Diasporas*. See also Gabaccia's review essays, "Diaspora I" and "Diaspora II," forthcoming in the *Journal of Modern Italian Studies*.

32. Romolo Gandolfo, "Las sociedades italianas de socorros mutuos de Buenos Aires: Cuestiones de etnicidad y de clase dentro de una comunidad de inmigrantes (1880–1920)," in Fernando J. Devoto and Eduardo J. Miguez, eds., *Asociacionismo, trabajo e identidad étnica: Los Italianos en América Latina en una perspectiva comparada* (Buenos Aires, 1992), pp. 311–332.

33. Maria Ines Barbero and Susana Felder, "El rol de los Italiano en el nacimiento y desarrollo de las asociaciones empresarias en la Argentina (1880–1930)," in Fernando J. Devoto and Gianfausto Rosoli, eds., *L'Italia nella società Argentina* (Rome, 1988), pp. 146, 152–153; and Eugene G. Sharkey, "Union Industrial Argentina: 1887–1920" (Ph.D. dissertation, Rutgers University, 1978).

34. Fenton claims that there were 200 mutual aid societies in New York City in 1902. Mangano estimates that there were 150 in 1904. And Pozzetta believes that there were perhaps as many as 2,000 to 3,000 in 1910. See Edwin Fenton, *Immigrants and Unions—A Case Study: Italians and American Labor, 1870–1920* (New York, 1975), p. 50; Antonio Mangano, "The Italian Colonies of New York City" (M.A. thesis, Columbia University, 1903), reprinted in *Italians in the City: Health and Related Social Needs* (New York, 1975), p. 48; George E. Pozzetta, "The Italians of New York City, 1890–1914" (Ph.D. dissertation, University of North Carolina, 1971), p. 243.

35. "Le società italiane all'estero nel 1908," *Bollettino dell'Emigrazione*, 24 (1908), pp. 116–119; "Le Società italiane negli Stati Uniti dell'America del Nord," *Bollettino dell'Emigrazione*, 4 (1912), pp. 20, 31–36, 49. See also *Bollettino del Ministero degli Affari Esteri*, 124 (April 1898), pp. 1–8; and 369 (December 1908), pp. 1–154.

36. The average size of 175 seems reasonable since only a dozen or so societies had as many as 500 members and most had less than 150. Furthermore, most of the more than 300 societies not recorded in the 1908 survey were probably missed because they were small and recently established. See *Il Progresso Italo- Americano*, 11/5/1907, 11/6/1907, 11/9/1907, 11/11/1907, 11/13/1907, 11/14/1907; and *New*

York Times, 5/31/1896, 3/8/1903. *Bollettino del Ministero degli Affari Esteri,* 124 (April 1898) says that there were 224 societies with 17,086 members and worth 902,000 lire in that year. These figures are much closer to the estimates set forth in the text.

37. *Il Progresso Italo-Americano,* 9/20–21/1886, 9/20–21/1894, 9/20–22/1907; *New York Times,* 5/31/1896, 3/8/1903; Antonio Mangano, "The Associated Life of the Italians in New York City," *Charities,* 12 (1904), pp. 476–482 (reprinted in Lydio F. Tomasi, ed., *The Italian in America: The Progressive View, 1891–1914* (New York, 1972), pp. 106–112; Pozzetta, "The Italians of New York City," pp. 243–247; and Victor R. Greene, *American Immigrant Leaders, 1800–1910: Marginality and Identity* (Baltimore, 1987), p. 127.

38. Robert Park, *The Immigrant Press and Its Control* (New York, 1922), p. 92; Pozzetta, "The Italians of New York City," pp. 234–243.

39. For examples, see *Il Progresso,* 1/29/1891, 9/6/1894, 9/13/1907.

40. *Il Progresso,* 9/9–13/1894, 9/16/1894, 9/20/1894, 9/22/1894, 9/25–26/1894, 10/3–4/1894, 10/28/1894.

41. *Il Progresso,* 11/3–5/1907.

42. Pozzetta, "The Italians of New York City," pp. 330–334.

43. Edward C. Stabili, "The St. Raphael Society for the Protection of Italian Immigrants, 1887–1923" (Ph.D. dissertation, Notre Dame University, 1977), pp. 113–133, esp. p. 133.

44. Mangano, "The Associated Life of the Italians," pp. 108–109; and Luigi Villari, *Gli Stati Uniti d'America e l'emigrazione italiana* (New York, 1975), pp. 298–303.

45. Pozzetta, "The Italians of New York City," pp. 257–258.

46. *Il Progresso,* 9/20–21/1907; Mangano, "The Associated Life of the Italians," pp. 109–110; Pozzetta, "The Italians of New York City," pp. 265–266.

47. Silvano Tomasi, *Piety and Power* (New York, 1975), pp. 177–185.

48. Tomasi, *Piety,* pp. 98–102, 146. See also Mary Elizabeth Brown, *From Italian Village to Greenwich Village: Our Lady of Pompei 1892–1992* (New York, 1992).

49. Tomasi, *Piety,* p. 99.

50. Pozzetta, "The Italians of New York City," pp. 267–279; Rudolph J. Vecoli, "Prelates and Peasants: Italian Immigrants and the Catholic Church," *Journal of Social History,* 2, 3 (1969), pp. 246–247, esp. pp. 229, 246. Tomasi's figures indicate that in 1903 there was one Italian priest for every 2,660 Italian members and that by 1918 the number had increased to one priest for every 4,286 members. See Tomasi, *Piety,* pp. 101–102.

51. Paul McBride, "The Italian-Americans and the Catholic Church: Old and New Perspectives, a Review Essay," *Italian Americana,* 1, 2 (Spring 1975), pp. 275. See also, Mangano, "The Italian Colonies," pp. 36–40.

52. Orsi, *The Madonna of 115th Street,* pp. xv–xviii.

53. Pozzetta, "The Italians of New York City," p. 274; McBride, "The Italian-Americans," p. 277.

54. Pozzetta, "The Italians of New York City," pp. 375–6.

55. Giovanni E. Schiavo, *Italian-American History,* vol. 1 (New York, 1947), pp. 540–542.

56. *Il Progresso Italo-Americano,* 9/16/1894.

57. Schiavo, *Italian-American History*, p. 142; Salvatore J. LaGumina, "American Political Process and Italian Participation in New York State," in S. M. Tomasi, *Perspectives in Italian Immigration and Ethnicity* (New York, 1977), pp. 85–87.

58. David C. Hammack, *Power and Society: Greater New York at the Turn of the Century* (New York, 1987), provides a detailed analysis of New York City politics during the period. For the transformation of Tammany Hall, see pp. 158–172.

59. Pozzetta, "The Italians of New York City," p. 388. The Italian ambassador to Washington wrote to the Italian foreign minister in Italy in 1904 pointing out that the Germans, Scandinavians, and Jews were taken into account because they were in politics. He lamented the fact that "our co-nationals are not systematically registered in either of the two parties," and asked for help in getting more Italians involved in politics. See Ministero degli Affari Esteri, Serie Política (1891–1916), pacco 360, posizione 74.

60. LaGumina, "American Political Process," pp. 85–87; Pozzetta, "The Italians of New York City," pp. 384–385; and Hammack, *Power and Society*, p. 129. Tammany Hall was not unchallenged in its efforts to gain Italian votes. In 1909, the Citizens' Union established an Italian naturalization bureau and hoped in this way to bypass Tammany Hall. See *New York Times*, 7/24/1909.

61. Robert F. Foerster, *The Italian Emigration of Our Times* (New York, 1919), p. 399. See also Alberto Pecorini, "Italian Progress in the United States," in W. Moguin and C. Van Doren, eds., *A Documentary History of the Italian Americans* (New York, 1974), p. 94. Pecorini's estimate of Italian voters in 1909 was only three thousand. See *New York Times*, 7/24/1909.

62. Donald Tricarico, *The Italians of Greenwich Village: The Social Structure and Transformation of an Ethnic Community* (New York, 1984), pp. 56–62; Caroline F. Ware, *Greenwich Village 1920–1930* (New York, 1977), pp. 267–291. ("The Italians became adapted to it [the local political system] more than to any other institution in the locality, [which] made it central to the life of the community" p. 268.)

63. Fenton, *Immigrants and Unions*, pp. 257, 571–579.

64. Rudolph J. Vecoli, "The Italian Immigrants in the United States Labor Movement from 1880 to 1929," in B. Bezza, ed., *Gli Italiani fuori d'Italia: Gli emigrati italiani nei movimenti operai del paesi d'adozione 1880–1940* (Milan, 1983)," pp. 264–266.

65. John Koren, "The Padrone System and the Padrone Banks," U.S. Department of Labor, *Bulletin*, 9 (March 1897), pp. 113–129; Fenton, *Immigrants and Unions*, pp. 71–135; Marie Lipari, "The Padrone System," in Francesco Cordasco and Eugene Bucchioni, eds., *The Italians: Social Backgrounds of an American Group* (Clifton, N.J., 1974), pp. 373–383.

66. Among them were Errico Malatesta and Pietro Gori, who had lived in Argentina, as well as the anarchists Francesco Saverio Merlino and Giuseppe Ciancabilla, the socialists Matteo Passa, Dino Rondani, and Giacinto M. Serrati, and the anarcho-syndicalist Carlo Tresca. Vecoli, "The Italian Immigrants in the United States Labor Movement," pp. 271–273.

67. Vecoli, "The Italian Immigrants in the United States Labor Movement," pp. 279–280. The effort to organize the garment workers well illustrates the difficulties of incorporating the Italians into the labor movement and what was necessary to organize them successfully. This story can be found in Melvyn Dubofsky, *When Workers Organize: New York City in the Progressive Era* (Amherst, Mass., 1968),

pp. 40–106; Fenton, *Immigrants and Unions*, pp. 458–529; Steven Fraser, *Labor Will Rule: Sidney Hillman and the Rise of American Labor* (New York, 1991), esp. pp. 86 ff. and 107 ff.; Colomba M. Furio, "The Cultural Background of the Italian Immigrant Woman and Its Impact on Her Unionization in the New York Garment Industry, 1880–1919," in George E. Pozzetta, ed., *Pane e Lavoro: The Italian American Working Class* (Toronto, 1980), pp. 81–98; Pozzetta, "The Italians of New York City," pp. 353–359; and Vecoli, "The Italian Immigrants in the United States Labor Movement," pp. 293–297.

Chapter 9. Constructing a Continuum

1. Some of the sources I have used for San Francisco are Dino Cinel, *From Italy to San Francisco: The Immigrant Experience* (Stanford, 1982); Micaela Di Leonardi, *The Varieties of Ethnic Experience* (Ithaca, N.Y., 1984); Sebastian Fichera, "Entrepreneurial Behavior in an Immigrant Colony: The Economic Experience of San Francisco's Italian-Americans, 1850–1940," *Studi Emigrazione*, 32, 118 (1995), pp. 321–345; Robert F. Foerster, *The Italian Emigration of Our Times* (New York, 1919); Deanna Paoli Gumina, *The Italians of San Francisco, 1850–1930* (New York, 1978); "Gli Italiani in California," *Bollettino del Ministero degli Affari Esteri*, 284 (February 1904), pp. 3–103; Rose Doris Scherini, *The Italian American Community of San Francisco: A Descriptive Study* (New York, 1980).

2. Fichera, "Entrepreneurial Behavior," p. 327.

3. Mormino and Pozzetta found an equivalent situation with the Italians in Ybor City, Florida. There blacks were the underclass. See Gary R. Mormino and George E. Pozzetta, *The Immigrant World of Ybor City: Italians and Their Latin Neighbors in Tampa, 1885–1985* (Urbana, Ill., 1987).

4. For San Francisco, see Table 43. For New York, see Chapter 8.

5. Among the major sources I have used on São Paulo are Zuleika M. F. Alvim and José Sachetta Ramos, "Italianos en São Paulo: Dimensiones de la italianidad en el estado de São Paulo en 1920," *Estudios Migratorios Latinoamericanos*, 29 (April 1995), pp. 113–128; Franco Cenni, *Italianos no Brasil* (São Paulo, 1958); Estado de São Paulo, Comissão Central de Estadística, *Relatorio 1887* (São Paulo, 1888), pp. 9–23; Estado de São Paulo, Repartição de Estatística e Archivo, *Relatorio 1894* (São Paulo, 1894), pp. 64–119; Estado de São Paulo, *Annuario estatística 1944* (São Paulo, 1948); Fanfulla, *Il Brasile e Gli Italiani* (Florence, 1906); Foerster, *The Italian Emigration*, pp. 315–319; Michael M. Hall, "Approaches to Immigration History," in Richard Graham and Peter H. Smith, eds., *New Approaches to Latin American History* (Austin, Tex., 1974), pp. 175–193; Thomas H. Holloway, "Creating the Reserve Army? The Immigration Program of São Paulo, 1886–1930," *International Migration Review*, 12, 2 (Summer 1978), pp. 187–209; Tania Regina de Luca, "Inmigración, mutualismo e identidad: São Paulo (1890–1935)," *Estudios Migratorios Latinoamericanos*, 29 (April 1995), pp. 191–208; Luigi De Rosa, "L'emigrazione italiana in Brasile: Un bilancio," in Gianfausto Rosoli, ed., *Emigrazioni europee e popolo brasiliano* (Rome, 1987), pp. 153–167; José Arthur Rios, "Aspectos políticos da assimilacão do Italiano no Brasil (1)," *Sociologia* (São Paulo), 20, 3 (August 1958), pp. 295–339; Angelo Trento, "Emigrazione italiana e movimento operaio a São Paulo, 1890–1920," in Gianfausto Rosoli, ed., *Emigrazioni europee e popolo brasiliano* (Rome, 1987), pp. 229–256; Hen-

rique Doria de Vasconcellos, "Imigração italiana," *Boletim do Departamento de Imigração e Colonização* (São Paulo), 7 (1952), pp. 97–105; Antonio Franceschini, *L'emigrazione italiano nell'America del Sud* (Rome, 1908), pp. 447–510, 513–519, 530.

6. For example, see Fanfulla, *Brasile*, p. 812.

7. Fanfulla, *Brasile*, p. 841. For Buenos Aires and New York data, see Chapter 4 of this book.

8. Vasconcellos, "Imigração italiana," p. 104. See also Hall, "Approaches to Immigration History," p. 183.

9. Among the most important sources I have used on Toronto are August Bridle, "The Drama of the 'Ward,'" *Canadian Magazine*, 34, 1 (November 1909), pp. 3–8; Robert F. Harney, "Chiaroscuro: Italians in Toronto, 1885–1915," *Polyphony*, 6, 1 (Spring–Summer 1984), pp. 44–49; Franca Iacovetta, *Such Hard Working People: Italian Immigrants in Postwar Toronto* (Montreal, 1992); Franc Sturino, "Italian Immigration to Canada and the Farm Labour System through the 1920s," *Studi Emigrazione*, 22, 77 (March 1985), pp. 81–96; Franc Sturino, "Contours of Postwar Italian Immigration to Toronto," *Polyphony*, 6, 1 (Spring–Summer 1984), pp. 127–130; Toronto, Bureau of Municipal Research, *What Is "the Ward" Going to Do with Toronto?* (Toronto, 1918); John E. Zucchi, *Italians in Toronto: Development of a National Identity, 1875–1935* (Montreal, 1988); John E. Zucchi, "Italian Hometown Settlements and the Development of an Italian Community in Toronto, 1875–1935," in Robert F. Harney, ed., *Gathering Place: Peoples and Neighbourhoods of Toronto* (Toronto, 1985), pp. 121–146.

10. In some respects it would make more sense to compare the Italians in post–World War II Toronto with the other four cases, but because I am holding time constant I decided not to do this. For a good analysis of this later period, see Iacovetta, *Such Hard Working People*.

11. Zucchi, *Italians in Toronto*, pp. 43–45.

Bibliography

This is a list of the primary sources consulted for this book. Secondary sources are fully cited in the Notes the first time they appear in each chapter.

Manuscripts

Argentina

Colonia Italiana. Libri d'inscrizione dei soci, 1890, 1900, 1910.
República Argentina. Tercer censo nacional (1895). Manuscript schedules for Buenos Aires.
Società Ligure. Registro dei soci, 1899–1914.
Società Volturno. Libri d'inscrizione dei soci, 1893, 1903, 1913.
Unión de la Boca. Registros de los socios, 1885–1910.
Unione e Benevolenza. Libri d'inscrizione dei soci, 1858–1862, 1888, 1901.
Unione e Benevolenza. Elenco dei soci, 1895–1902.

Italy

Agnone, Comune di. Antonio Arduino. "Schemi particolari di demografia (dal 1532 al 1977) del Comune di Agnone nel Molise."
Agnone, Comune di. Registri degli atti di matrimonio, 1876, 1886, 1896, 1906.
Agnone, Comune di. Registri dei passaporti per l'estero, 1885–1900.
Agnone, Comune di. Foglio di famiglia, 1901.
Agnone, Comune di. Registro delle domande di nulla osta per ottenere passaporti per l'estero, 1901–1904.
Agnone, Comune di. Registro dei passaporti dal 1 gennaio 1907 al 10 maggio 1912.
Agnone, Comune di. Passaporti rilasciati dal 10 maggio 1912 al 9 dicembre 1923.
Agnone, Comune di. Registro dei passaporti per l'estero dal 1923 a 1953.
Italy. Ministero degli Affari Estari. Serie Política (1891–1916).
Italy. Ministero degli Affari Estari. Affari Politici (1919–1930).

Valdengo, Comune di. Registri degli atti di matrimonio, 1876–1916.
Valdengo, Comune di. Registri del passaporti, 1876–1916.
Valdengo, Comune di. Censo di 1901 manuscript schedules.

United States

Federal Census of 1901. Manuscript schedules for Elizabeth Street.
Federal District Court. Southern District of New York. Naturalization records, 1906–1921.
"L'Elemento italiano rappresentato nelle associazione di New York, Brooklyn, Hoboken, e Newark, 1884," Archive of the Center for Migration Studies, Staten Island, New York.

Government Publications

Argentina

Argentina, República. Departamento Nacional del Trabajo. *Boletín* (1907–1918).
Argentina, República. Dirección de Inmigración. *Resumen estadístico del movimiento migratorio en la República Argentina, 1875–1924*. Buenos Aires, 1925.
Argentina, República. Ministerio de Agricultura. Dirección General de Inmigración. *Memorias* (1897–1915).
Argentina, República. Ministerio del Interior. Comisión General de Inmigración. *Informes y memorias* (1869–1881).
Argentina, República. Ministerio de Relaciones Exteriores. Departamento General de Inmigración. *Memorias* (1882–1896).
Argentina, República. *Segundo censo de la República Argentina, mayo 10 de 1895*. Buenos Aires, 1898. 3 vols.
Argentina, República. *Tercer censo nacional. Levantado el 1º de junio de 1914*. Buenos Aires, 1916–1919. 10 vols.
Buenos Aires, Ciudad de. *Censo general de la población, edificación, comercio e industrias de 1887*. Buenos Aires, 1889. 2 vols.
Buenos Aires, Ciudad de. *Censo general de población, edificación, comercio e industrias de 1904*. Buenos Aires, 1906.
Buenos Aires, Ciudad de. *Censo general de población, edificación, comercio e industrias de 1909*. Buenos Aires, 1910. 3 vols.
Buenos Aires. Dirección General de Estadística. *Anuario estadístico de la Ciudad de Buenos Aires, 1882–1923*. Buenos Aires, 1892–1925. 25 vols.

Italy

Italy. Commissariato Generale dell'Emigrazione. *Bollettino dell'emigrazione*. Rome, 1902–1915.
Italy. Commissariato Generale dell'Emigrazione. *Annuario statistico della emigrazione italiana dal 1876 al 1925*. Rome, 1926.
Italy. Istituto Centrale di Statistica. *Cadasto agrario 1929*. Rome, 1935.

Italy. Istituto Centrale di Statistica. *Sommario di statistiche storiche italiane, 1861–1955.* Rome, 1958.
Italy. Istituto Centrale di Statistica. *Popolazione residente e presente dei comuni. Censimenti dal 1861 al 1971.* Rome, 1977.
Italy. Ministero degli Affari Esteri. *Bollettino* (1888–1915).

North America

Koren, John. "The Padrone System and the Padrone Banks." U.S. Department of Labor. *Bulletin,* 9 (March 1897), pp. 113–129.
New York, City of. Tenement House Department. *First Report.* New York, 1903.
New York, State of. *Fourth Report of the Factory Investigation Commission.* Albany, N.Y., 1915.
Schulteis, Herman J. *Report on European Immigration to the United States of America and the Causes Which Incite the Same: With Recommendations for the Further Restriction of Undesirable Immigration and the Establishment of a National Quarantine.* Washington, D.C., 1893.
Toronto. Bureau of Municipal Research. *What Is "the Ward" Going to Do with Toronto?* Toronto, 1918.
U.S. Department of Commerce. Bureau of Labor Statistics. *Bulletin* (1910–1926).
U.S. Department of Commerce. Bureau of the Census. *Special Reports: Occupations at the Twelfth Census.* Washington, D.C., 1904.
U.S. Department of Commerce. Bureau of the Census. *Thirteenth Census of the United States Taken in the Year 1910.* Washington, D.C., 1913.
U.S. Department of Commerce. Bureau of the Census. *Fourteenth Census of the United States Taken in the Year 1920.* Washington, D.C., 1922.
U.S. Department of Commerce. Bureau of the Census. *Fifteenth Census of the United States Taken in the Year 1930.* Washington, D.C., 1933.
U.S. Department of Commerce. Bureau of the Census. *Historical Statistics of the United States: Colonial Times to 1957.* Washington, D.C., 1960.
U.S. Department of Commerce. Bureau of the Census. *Historical Statistics of the United States: Colonial Times to 1970.* Washington, D.C., 1975.
U.S. Department of Commerce and Labor. Bureau of Statistics. *Statistical Abstract of the United States, 1911.* Washington, D.C., 1912.
U.S. Department of Interior. Census Office. *Twelfth Census of the United States Taken in the Year 1900.* Washington, D.C., 1901.
U.S. Department of Interior. Census Office. *Vital Statistics of New York and Brooklyn, 1885–1900.* Washington, D.C., 1901.
U.S. Senate. *Reports* of the Immigration Commission (Dillingham Commission). Washington, D.C., 1911. 41 vols.

Brazil

São Paulo, Estado de. Repartição de Estatística e Archivo. *Relatório do anno.* São Paulo, 1893–1915.
São Paulo, Estado de. *Annuario estatística 1944.* São Paulo, 1948.

Vasconcellos, Henrique Doria de. "Imigração italiana." *Boletim do Departamento de Imigração e Colonização* 7 (1952), pp. 97–105.

Newspapers

L'Aquilonia (Agnone), 1884–1889.
L'Eco del Sannio (Agnone), 1894–1914.
Fanfulla (São Paulo), 1893–1914.
L'Operaio Italiano (Buenos Aires), 1878–1898.
La Patria degli Italiani (Buenos Aires), 1898–1914.
Il Progresso Italo-Americano (New York), 1884–1914.
La Ribera. Suplemento Especial Centenario Bomberos Voluntarios de La Boca. Buenos Aires, June 2, 1984.

Index

9 780801 488825